Writing Copy For Dummies®

Guaranteed Ways to Make Your Copy Successful

- ✔ Emphasize an important benefit.
- ✔ Create a compelling offer.
- ✔ Think from the point of view of your customers.
- ✔ Write the way your customers talk.
- ✔ Build your copy with specifics.
- ✔ Maintain your focus on one key idea.
- ✔ Repeat the most important information multiple times.

Questions You Should Always Ask Before You Write

- ✔ What are the goals of this particular project?
- ✔ How does this project fit within the larger marketing strategy?
- ✔ What's in this for the customer?
- ✔ What are my customers' hopes?
- ✔ What do my customers fear?
- ✔ What do I want customers to do after reading my copy?
- ✔ Why would someone choose my product over competing products?
- ✔ What are the product's most important benefits and features?
- ✔ How does the customer buy or order this product?
- ✔ Why wouldn't someone buy this product?
- ✔ How will I/we measure or evaluate the success of this writing project?

How to Find Inspiration, Fast

- ✔ Try the product or service yourself.
- ✔ Talk to salespeople and customer service reps.
- ✔ Read customer letters and testimonials.
- ✔ Reread the product information sheets (the internal documentation that describes the product's qualities).
- ✔ Review your competitors' marketing material and find weaknesses you can exploit.

For Dummies: Bestselling Book Series for Beginners

Writing Copy For Dummies®

Cheat Sheet

How to Work More Creatively

- Imagine yourself in the customer's shoes.
- Invent both "carrots" (the benefits of buying your product) and "sticks" (the penalties for *not* buying your product).
- Write as if you were talking to someone you like and respect.
- Think of analogies. Finish this sentence: Your product is like . . .
- Flip ideas on their heads. For example, if your product builds strong bones, talk about the consequences of having weak bones.
- Absorb as much information about your product as you can and then stop what you're doing and go for a walk. You'll be amazed what occurs to you when you return — refreshed — to your desk.

Things That Customers Always Want to Read About

- Things that satisfy their desires.
- Things that help them overcome their fears.
- New information about things that satisfy desires or conquer fears.
- Reduced prices.
- Special deals.
- Free stuff.
- Things that are easier, cheaper, and/or more convenient.
- Things that make them feel good about themselves.

The Three Building Blocks of Copy

- Headlines present offers, benefits, news, or special features.
- Body copy presents facts, proof, and evidence to support your claims, promises, or story.
- Calls to action motivate response by promising (or repromising) a benefit in exchange for taking an action.

For Dummies: Bestselling Book Series for Beginners

Writing Copy
FOR
DUMMIES®

Writing Copy FOR DUMMIES®

by Jonathan Kranz

WILEY

Wiley Publishing, Inc.

About the Author

Jonathan Kranz is an award-winning copywriter and principal of Kranz Communications (`www.kranzcom.com`), a marketing communications firm serving consumer and business-to-business clients in high-tech, healthcare, banking, insurance, education, financial services, and other industries. His client list includes 3Com, American Express, Aon Insurance, Blue Cross Blue Shield, Boston University School of Medicine, Candela, Dell, Home Service Store, IBM, iparty.com, Lesley University, Liberty Mutual, Matchmaker.com, NCR, Publishers Clearing House, Reader's Digest, Reed Elsevier, Spaulding & Slye Colliers, Surebridge, Terra Lycos, Time Warner, and USTrust, among many others.

In addition, Jonathan is a published author of short fiction (*Missouri Review* and *Green Mountains Review*, among others) and has been a repeated guest essayist on National Public Radio's *All Things Considered*. He has taught writing courses at Harvard University Extension School, Emerson College, and Northeastern University.

Jonathan lives in Melrose, Massachusetts, with his wife, Eileen; two daughters, Rebecca and Anastasia; and a vast collection of LP records.

Dedication

To Eileen: *O mondo, pieno di pazzi innamorati!*

Author's Acknowledgments

I'm deeply grateful to Natasha Graf, the acquisitions editor who retrieved my book proposal from the slush pile and encouraged the book's publication. I also very much appreciate the hard work, brilliant insights, and enduring patience of Georgette Beatty, the project editor who helped me carve a finished book from a rough draft. In addition, I want to thank Tina Sims, the senior copy editor, and Roberta Rosenberg, the technical editor, for their sharp eyes, sage wisdom, and precise guidance. Natasha, Georgette, Tina, and Roberta, thank you!

Thank you, Eric Wholley, Sally Moren, and Paula Pinheiro, three wonderful colleagues and marketing experts who gave me answers and advice that got me through some tough spots in this book.

Finally, I want to thank three people who helped me get started in my copywriting career: Glen Wish, artist, friend, entrepreneur, and inventor of the WishDog, who gave me my first copywriting assignments; Jane Winsor, copywriter extraordinaire, who has been a frequent source of encouragement and inspiration; and Evan Stone, the best creative director I've had the privilege of working with and an all-around terrific human being.

Publisher's Acknowledgments

We're proud of this book; please send us your comments through our Dummies online registration form located at www.dummies.com/register/.

Some of the people who helped bring this book to market include the following:

Acquisitions, Editorial, and Media Development

Project Editor: Georgette Beatty

Acquisitions Editor: Natasha Graf

Senior Copy Editor: Tina Sims

Technical Editor: Roberta Rosenberg

Editorial Manager: Jennifer Ehrlich

Editorial Assistants: Courtney Allen, Melissa S. Bennett

Cartoons: Rich Tennant, www.the5thwave.com

Composition

Project Coordinator: Maridee Ennis

Layout and Graphics: Jonelle Burns, Andrea Dahl, Lauren Goddard, Denny Hager, Joyce Haughey, Stephanie D. Jumper, Michael Kruzil Heather Ryan

Proofreaders: John Greenough, Brian H. Walls, TECHBOOKS Production Services

Indexer: TECHBOOKS Production Services

Special Help
Josh Dials, Sherri Pfouts, Elizabeth Rea, Chad R. Sievers, Trisha Strietelmeier

---

Publishing and Editorial for Consumer Dummies

Diane Graves Steele, Vice President and Publisher, Consumer Dummies

Joyce Pepple, Acquisitions Director, Consumer Dummies

Kristin A. Cocks, Product Development Director, Consumer Dummies

Michael Spring, Vice President and Publisher, Travel

Brice Gosnell, Associate Publisher, Travel

Kelly Regan, Editorial Director, Travel

Publishing for Technology Dummies

Andy Cummings, Vice President and Publisher, Dummies Technology/General User

Composition Services

Gerry Fahey, Vice President of Production Services

Debbie Stailey, Director of Composition Services

Contents at a Glance

Table of Contents

Introduction

• •

You're about to get an inside look at one of the cheapest yet most powerful ways to motivate customer action: effective copywriting. In the thousands of marketing messages you're exposed to every day, you're surrounded by copy — the language of anonymous writers encouraging you to look, buy, shop, or respond. Yet, like the air, it's so pervasive that you rarely think about it — what it is or how it works.

While it serves the interests of the large, expensive advertising agencies to make you believe that copywriting is a mysterious process that only a worthy few can accomplish, the truth is, anyone with motivation, common sense, and a willingness to think clearly can write good copy. This book gives you everything you need to know to get the job done.

About This Book

The subject of this book is copy*writing*, the craft of writing advertisements and other marketing-related materials, not copy*righting*, the rules and regulations pertaining to intellectual property rights. I can help you with the former; for the latter, you're at the mercy of a lawyer.

Most other books on copywriting assume that the reader wants to be a copywriter; that assumption doesn't apply here. I wrote this book for people who *don't* want to write, but who *need* to write or review copy as part of their job or business responsibilities. Although those interested in the profession will find help in these pages (and even career tips in Chapter 19), *Writing Copy For Dummies* is primarily for entrepreneurs, professionals, businesspeople, office workers, and managers who need a fast, fun, and easy-to-understand guide that takes you through every step of a successful copywriting project.

This book is explicitly designed so that you *don't* have to read it cover-to-cover (I won't object if you do, though!). Instead, you can skim the Table of Contents and go directly to those sections that apply to your immediate needs. That means if you're assigned to write a press release that was due yesterday, you can go right to the press release chapter (Chapter 12, by the way) and find everything you need right there, period.

Whether you sell products or services, are targeting consumers or other businesses, or are writing advertising or publicity pieces, this book gives you practical, time-tested methods for putting the power of the written word to work for you. Because, amazing as it may seem, you can turn the fundamental writing skills you learned in elementary school into one of your most effective tools for making sales, attracting new customers, building revenues (or raising funds), and increasing profits. The secrets, and not-so-secrets, lie ahead.

Conventions Used in This Book

To help you navigate through this book, I use the following conventions:

- ✔ *Italic* is used for emphasis and to highlight new words or terms that are defined. A lot of copywriting examples are also set in italic.
- ✔ **Boldfaced** text is used to indicate keywords in bulleted lists and the action part of numbered steps.
- ✔ Monofont is used for Web addresses.

For simplicity's sake, I also stretched a few words to extend their meaning. Often when I refer to your "business," for example, I really mean any institution that you work for, including nonprofit or not-for-profit organizations such as schools, charities, or hospitals. Likewise, both "customers" and "prospects" refer to any persons you serve or would like to serve.

What You're Not to Read

If you're standing in a store right now weighing your decision to purchase this book, you may find it odd to stumble on a section about what *not* to read. Heck, as a writer, I sure find it strange to tell readers that they can skip some (or any) of my golden prose.

In any case, you can skip anything marked with the Technical Stuff icon and not suffer any harm. It's interesting stuff, to be sure, but nothing you can't live without. Likewise, you can save anything you see in the sidebars (the shaded boxes throughout the book) for a rainy day when you have more time on your hands.

Foolish Assumptions

Given the source (myself), most of my assumptions tend to be foolish. Of these, only a few need concern you:

- You have at least a fair command of the English language and its basic rules of grammar and punctuation.

- You're interested in copywriting because you have some sort of business objective in mind (for example, sales, profits, or new customer acquisition), or, if your objectives are currently nebulous, you have the desire and ability to form business objectives and pursue them.

- You're responsible for writing copy for your business or organization, but you're intimidated by the copywriting process and would like guidance on how to create and fulfill great ideas.

How This Book Is Organized

Writing Copy For Dummies is organized into six parts, with each part serving as a cluster of like-minded chapters focused on a particular topic. And as you see in the Table of Contents, each chapter is itself further subdivided into subsections that make it easy to identify the issues that interest you.

Part I: Understanding Copywriting Basics

In Part I, I cover the ideas, issues, and challenges common to *all* copywriting projects, regardless of format or marketing purpose. Chapter 1, for instance, defines the territory: what copywriting is, who uses it, and how to select tactics for your needs. In Chapter 2, I dive into the fundamentals of copy itself, such as writing captivating headlines and compelling body copy. Chapter 3 is something special, covering a topic rarely addressed in books on copywriting: how to collect information *before* you write and then turn your research into a springboard for generating brilliant ideas.

Part II: Direct Response Writing That Makes the Sale

While good writing inspires respect, great writing provokes action. That's what Part II is all about: copywriting that, in itself, serves as the virtual salesperson that collects, leads, closes sales, acquires new customers, and expands current business relationships.

Chapter 4 gives you an overall perspective of direct response writing and its key topics, such as selecting lists, forming offers, and testing results. In Chapter 5, I tackle the Grand Old Man of direct response writing: the letter. Chapter 6 shows you how to write brochures that put your products and services in your customers' laps. In Chapter 7, you find a comprehensive review of the remaining direct mail elements, such as reply devices and lift notes. Chapter 8 reveals the power of alternative mailing formats, such as self-mailers, postcards, and catalogs. Finally, Chapter 9 helps you apply the time-tested techniques of direct mail to the more modern innovations embraced in e-mail.

Part III: Building Awareness of Your Business

In Part III, I explore those writing techniques that make your products and services unforgettable and irresistible. Chapter 10 provides an introduction to branding on the cheap. In Chapter 11, you get everything you need to know to write memorable advertisements. Chapter 12 gives you the inside scoop on media exposure, including a blow-by-blow guide to writing the press release. In Chapter 13, I present a secret weapon ignored by other copywriting books and overlooked by most of your competitors: writing articles for and about your business.

Part IV: Managing the Sales Support System

Even when copy doesn't have the starring role in your marketing strategy, it can go a long way to support your objectives. In Part IV, I show you how to write copy that helps strengthen your relationships with customers. Chapter 14 talks about the Web and offers a number of inside tips for writing Web site content that attracts and holds visitors. In Chapter 15, you discover fast, easy ways to write and manage *collateral,* the miscellaneous materials that support the sale. Chapter 16 addresses the special writing challenges you'll meet when your customer is not a consumer, but another business.

Part V: Looking at Special Copywriting Situations

This book needed a place to talk about important copywriting topics that just didn't fit neatly anywhere else: This is the place. Chapter 17 discusses the delicate art of raising money (and gathering support) for nonprofit enterprises such as charities and political causes. When bad things happen to good copy, you find consolation — and practical fix-it advice — in Chapter 18. In Chapter 19, I take a detour from my mission to help nonwriters by addressing the career options of writers who want to turn pro.

Part VI: The Part of Tens

When you get stuck, turn to Part VI to get unclogged. Here, I put together three chapters of short-and-snappy tips, hints, and suggestions for getting started, solving problems, and finding inspiration.

Icons Used in This Book

One of the many smart things these *For Dummies* books do is use clever little visual clues — called *icons* — to help you identify different kinds of stuff. Here's what they mean:

Look for the bull's-eye for handy hints that make your work faster, easier, cheaper, or more successful.

Pay attention to this icon! It identifies the real, hard-core stuff that's absolutely essential in copywriting.

I don't want you to step on any land mines. That's why I use this icon to identify trouble spots and common problems — *before* they blow up on you.

This is the stuff you can safely ignore. Skip it if you're in a hurry; read it if you'd like more in-depth information.

You know how to get to Carnegie Hall, right? Practice! Same with copywriting. The "Try It" icon points out fun, hands-on activities that help you get a better grip on the techniques discussed in this book.

Where to Go from Here

If you're under the gun to finish a specific job — and fast — use the Table of Contents or the Index to find your project and go right to it. Remember, all *For Dummies* chapters are designed to stand alone: You get complete how-to information in each project's relevant chapter.

If you're in a hurry but have a few minutes to spare, I encourage you to start with Chapter 2 to get a firm grip on important basic issues, such as benefits, offers, and using a customer-centric perspective.

For those of you who actually have time to *plan* your marketing tactics in accordance with an actual honest-to-goodness strategy, take a look at those chapters that can help you select formats to match objectives, such as Chapter 4 on direct response, Chapter 10 on branding, Chapter 12 for public relations information, and Chapter 16 on business-to-business marketing.

When you find yourself at an impasse and don't know how to move forward, turn to Chapter 3 for help on uncovering information and ideas, Chapter 18 for problem-solving suggestions, and any of the Part of Tens chapters for immediate inspiration.

Part I
Understanding Copywriting Basics

The 5th Wave   By Rich Tennant

"We're starting to get responses from the mailer we sent out last week."

In this part . . .

Copywriting is the crossroads where business and language meet. Choose the right path, and you'll see a steady improvement in sales, growth, and profits. If you take your writing in the wrong direction, however, you'll find yourself in the dark place with brimstone and pitchforks.

This part leads you in the right direction. In these three chapters, I show you the general copywriting terrain, map out your options, and give you the basic tools for researching, forming, and writing messages that resonate with the most important people in your business: your customers.

Chapter 1

Writing Copy: Capturing Hearts, Minds, and Money

*P*icture me at the summer barbecue, my bare pale legs reflecting blazing beams of sunlight, my loud Hawaiian shirt howling with color. As I pass cold beers and overcooked hot dogs to my neighbors, someone I haven't met before may politely initiate conversation by asking me what I do for a living.

"Copywriting" typically draws blank looks, so I try to explain. "Marketing material," I say. "You know: Direct mail. Collateral. Public relations." Still the blank look. Finally, I just make things simple: "I write ads."

"Oh," they'll say. "Got it." For 99 percent of the population, copywriting is about writing advertising. That's only partly true. As you discover in this book, copywriting covers an enormous range of communications, from Web pages to white papers. Whatever the form, almost all copy shares two common characteristics: The author remains anonymous (there's no "by" anybody to be seen), and the language attempts to persuade you to do or believe something — usually in regard to the surrender of your cash.

In this chapter, I give you the five-cent tour of the copywriting world (sans beers and hot dogs). I show you what it is, who uses it, and how to select the options just right for your needs. So stop staring at my legs and read on.

What Copywriting Is (and Isn't)

Copywriting includes all the written communications used to sell, market, and promote products and services to prospects and customers. As a category, it's bigger than "advertising writing" because it also includes things such as brochures or Web sites. But it's smaller than "business writing" because it doesn't include nonmarketing communications such as interoffice memos.

That said, let me introduce two important ideas about copywriting repeated throughout this book: going beyond information and inspiring action.

Transcending information

Many copywriting projects begin with the reasonable desire to inform prospects and customers about your business and/or one of its products and services. But if all you want to do is tell your prospects about something, you're aiming too low — and you're not getting full value from your writing.

Telling is for journalists, teachers, and stool pigeons. Copywriting is about conducting business, not distributing information. Your job isn't to tell, but to sell — to spike your communications with messages that persuade, motivate, and build desire. In Chapters 2 and 3, I lead you into the three crucial elements that distinguish selling from telling:

- ✔ **A ruthless fixation on benefits:** These are the things your product does for the customer. By appealing to your prospects' self interests, benefits provide motivation — a reason to buy, act, or respond. See Chapter 2 to find out more about this essential characteristic of good copy.

- ✔ **A desire to make offers:** Selling is all about let's-make-a-deal. The deal you present — do this to get that — is called an *offer*. In Chapter 2, I give you the inside scoop on linguistic deal making.

- ✔ **A commitment to the customer's point of view:** Swallow your ego: If you want to create genuine rapport with your customers, you have to embrace and communicate from their point of view. In Chapter 3, I make several suggestions that draw you closer to your customers, such as collecting testimonials from happy customers.

Generating action

Information is often like a guest who overstays his welcome: just lying around, doing nothing, occupying space. You want more from your copy, however. Effective business requires action — from you, for starters, and then (you hope) from your customers.

Here's a way of doing business that immediately places you light-years ahead of your competition: Think of every piece of copy you write, whether it's a letter or an ad, not as a static project but as an agent of action. Instead of generating information, commit your resources — your time, money, and talent — to writing that *does things:* makes sales, builds leads, stimulates interest, draws customers, and so on.

When you approach a new writing project, always ask yourself two questions:

✔ **What does this do for my business?** Not all copy can (or should) close a sale, but all of it should serve a clear purpose that moves your business one step closer to your goals. If you can't define the purpose, that's an excellent warning sign that the potential project either is misconceived (the wrong match of project to purpose) or may be a waste of money.

✔ **What do I want the prospect to do after reading this?** Often, the answer is as simple as "Buy my product." But in many cases, the pathway to the sale is more complex and may involve numerous steps and way stations before the deal is done. In any event, be sure that your copy facilitates that next step by including all the information a customer needs to make that step and by being as persuasive as possible to encourage movement in your direction.

For basic information on creating a call to action, check out Chapter 2.

Recognizing Copy's Different Uses

When you think of all the things that can be sold and the services that can be provided, the range of potential copy content seems staggering. Look more deeply, however, and you'll see that most copy fulfills one (or a combination) of three primary uses. In descending order of immediacy, these are making sales, attracting customers, and building relationships.

Making sales

You can't get more immediate than this: Prospect reads copy; prospect buys product. Without any additional support (other than someone, perhaps, to take the order), your words make the sale.

The writing formats that can make direct sales include the following:

✔ **Direct mail:** With skill, you can turn ordinary mail into a powerful tool for targeting prospects with your offers and persuading them to buy. See Chapters 5 through 8, which cover direct response letters, direct response brochures, other elements in the direct response package (like reply devices), and stand-alone items like self-mailers, postcards, and catalogs.

✔ **Direct e-mail:** With e-mail, you can perform many of the functions of direct mail electronically. To find out how, see Chapter 9.

✔ **Advertisements with a direct response option:** Many of the advertisements you see simply want you to remember a brand. But those that offer a phone number and a deal — "Order now and get all twelve knives for four easy payments of $9.99!" — are making direct sales. Get more information about print, Web, and radio advertising in Chapter 11.

✔ **Web sites with ordering capabilities:** If your site can manage orders online, include copy that can make the sale on the spot. See Chapter 14.

Attracting customers

If you move one step further away in terms of immediacy and directness, you can use your copy as a lure to attract customers to destinations, such as retail stores or Web sites, where the final sale is made. Instead of selling, your copy helps build a foundation for a sale that may be completed at a later time and in a different "place." Formats for attracting customers include

✔ **Print and broadcast advertising:** Instead of making an immediate sale, you can create a memorable impression on the prospect that may influence future behavior. By trumpeting benefits, unique features, or especially attractive sensual characteristics, you can move your product into its own special spot in the prospect's mind. Check out Chapter 11.

✔ **Electronic promotions:** E-mail can do more than make direct sales. You can use e-mail (including e-newsletters) and Web sites to build brand (the image and attitude of your business) and direct traffic to your stores. By touting new info, helpful tips, and/or special promotions, you can continually motivate prospects and customers to visit and revisit your sites or stores. See Chapter 9 on e-mail and Chapter 14 on Web sites.

Building relationships

Furthest away from the immediate sale are those copy assignments that help you establish a rapport with potential customers. This objective is important when your product is complex, expensive, and/or requires the approval of multiple decision makers before the sale can be made.

When you're running a long-distance race to build relationships that may eventually lead to business, you want to establish credibility for your organization while educating your prospects. These methods can help:

- ✔ **Press releases:** If you can turn some aspect (or aspects) of your business into something newsworthy to a publication's readers (or a broadcaster's audience), the media may do the talking for you. To attract their interest, use the *press release*, a short and simple announcement that feeds news to the media, as described in Chapter 12.

- ✔ **Articles:** Nothing says authority like being an author. Whether you get your story published in a traditional print publication or an electronic e-newsletter, an article can help you (and by extension, your organization) be seen as the expert in your area of business. In Chapter 13, I show you how to turn news, human-interest stories, case studies, and how-to tips into effective ways to attract and hold the attention of your audience.

- ✔ **Collateral:** One way of maintaining your relationships with potential customers is with a regular diet of meaningful communications, packed with knowledge that your audience values. That's where collateral — a catchall category of information that includes brochures, pamphlets, sales sheets, and more — comes in. Find out more in Chapter 15.

Looking at People Who Produce Copy

Sure, professionals such as myself, who make a living by writing copy, write a lot of marketing materials. But as a class, the number of professional writers is much smaller than the number of people who *use* or *produce* copy for their business purposes. (I assume most of my readers are in the latter category.)

You don't have to be a professional writer to create excellent, professional-level copy. With the help of this book, you can either write the quality copy you need or be in a better position to evaluate copy written on your behalf.

Although the whole business of copywriting is associated with ink-stained wretches (or merlot-sipping hipsters), the real world of copy is populated with users who have a variety of objectives in mind. Chances are, you may see yourself in one (or more) of the following categories.

Owning a business

Perhaps you own a business, such as a flower or auto-body repair shop (or a combination of the two, which may prove interesting). Or you're an independent professional, such as an accountant or orthodontist. Chances are, you don't have the budget to turn to an agency for your marketing work. With the help of this book, however, you can either write your own copy or know what to look for should you choose to buy help.

Although all the information in this book is useful to you, you may find the following budget-minded topics especially helpful:

- ✔ **Quick and dirty direct mail:** With just a little time, a personal computer, and a laser printer, independent professionals have a particularly effective (and cheap) direct response option at their disposal. When you can identify your prospects by name and address, this simple direct mail process can get your message into their hands — and attract business to your door. (Check out Chapter 7 for more information.)

- ✔ **Postcards:** These mailing pieces are an inexpensive way of sending your message to prospects and current customers. If you have a special offer or event to promote, a simple postcard with concentrated copy can be an exceptionally cost-effective way to communicate. (See Chapter 8.)

- ✔ **Press releases:** A press release (see Chapter 12) is a simple announcement to the media that can give businesses a chance to garner favorable press exposure. By turning your expertise, experience, or new product offerings into news that matters to a publication's readers, you can attract media interest and build credibility with potential customers.

Managing a business, organization, or department

Instead of flying solo, you fly with a team of individuals with various responsibilities. Often, though not always, the scale of the marketing ambition (and its marketing budget) is comparable to the scale of the business. When your job involves making decisions regarding the appropriate allocation of resources (where you should spend your money), you should pay particular attention to the following areas:

- ✔ **Direct response:** Chapter 4 gives you an overview of direct response, a means of encouraging immediate action from your targeted prospects. You find suggestions for developing prospect contact lists and identifying appropriate communications formats that can help you go beyond writing one project to developing an ongoing, working system.

- ✔ **Branding:** In Chapter 10, I show you how you can associate your business with a bundle of favorable ideas, emotions, and associations. By separating you from the competition, the resulting identity, your brand, forms a solid foundation for all of your marketing efforts.

- ✔ **Sales to a business:** Chapter 16 provides special insights and strategic suggestions for those companies that target other businesses as their customers. You discover how to leverage the special desires and fears of businesspeople, and how to target your messaging to the specific needs of different titles or roles within the same organization. In addition, I give you tips for promoting events, seminars, and Webinars, popular marketing tools frequently used to help make business-to-business sales.

Raising money and getting support

Running side by side with those who use marketing to sell products and services are those who apply similar marketing skills for nonprofit or not-for-profit efforts: charities, political and social causes, some forms of education and healthcare, and so on. I have a special chapter just for you.

Chapter 17 helps you subsidize your organization's efforts with a practical guide for writing the classic fundraising letter. An appeal to the heart, the best fundraising letters use stories, personal perspectives, and precise descriptions of your organization in action to move the reader to give money. In addition, the chapter provides insights and strategic advice for writing political flyers and informational pamphlets or brochures that can build support for your organization, cause, political candidate, or institution of learning.

Helping, healing, or inspiring people

Within both profit and not-for-profit organizations, your promotional efforts aren't always mercenary (asking for money). Instead, you sometimes want to educate, inform, assist, heal, or inspire. (The most obvious example is healthcare providers who need to create materials to help patients understand diagnoses, treatments, and/or medications.) Chapter 17 includes information on writing political, healthcare, and education-related copy. In addition, the following topics are helpful:

- ✔ **Collateral:** Chapter 15 can help you write brochures, pamphlets, and other supporting materials loaded with practical information (and sometimes even encouragement) appropriate for a variety of audiences, including medical patients.

- ✔ **Newsletters:** If you want to create a vehicle for ongoing communications with the people you serve, newsletters (in Chapter 13) can help. By providing news, success stories, updates on new services, and more, you build a tighter bond with your audience and reinforce the organization's stature as an effective resource or problem solver.

Selecting the Right Tool: When and Why to Use What

From the tiny little tag line at the bottom of a print ad to the massive headline posted across an interstate billboard, marketing copy can show up in just about any shape, size, or form. Yet regardless of scale or format, almost all marketing copy falls into one of four major categories (which, not-so-coincidentally, correspond roughly to parts of this book): direct response, branding, public relations, and sales support.

Landing the sale with direct response

You go to the mailbox and find a letter that says you're preapproved for a credit card; all you have to do is return the enclosed form to apply. Whether you're motivated to reply, you've been hit with a form of direct response marketing: You got an offer you could fulfill right on the spot, without going to a store or talking to a salesperson.

Whatever its form — mail, e-mail, Web site, print ad, or radio ad — all direct response communications request a response ("call this number" or "return this card," among others) that, in turn, satisfies some promise made to the prospect. Many direct response communications are precisely targeted to specific names at specific addresses or phone numbers.

Direct response can be an exceptionally powerful way to market your business in the following situations:

- ✓ **You can conduct your business with minimal personal interaction.** If you can provide your product or service without the intervention of a store or a complex sales call, direct response may be the way to go. It's been a proven winner for subscriptions, collectibles, tools, apparel, crafts, toys, food supplements, and thousands of other things that can be easily delivered by mail or package services.

- ✓ **You're capable of identifying your targets.** To go to prospects directly, you have to know where they are. For mail and e-mail, you work with addresses and phone numbers of people who may be likely prospects. For radio, you need to identify time/program slots that attract your target audience. You don't want to buy time during a hip-hop program aimed at teenagers to sell vitamins for arthritis sufferers.

- ✓ **You want to generate leads for future sales.** Few people buy a car by mail. Fewer still commit their company to a multimillion-dollar purchase on the strength of a phone call. But direct response tactics can *initiate* the sales process by gathering leads — collecting a pool of responses to which you may direct further sales efforts. (See Chapter 16 for more.)

Several chapters in this book give you what you need to write successful direct response copy. Start with Chapter 4, an introduction to direct response, and then turn to those chapters that speak to the tactics that interest you.

Building businesses with branding

Many of the advertisements you remember (and, in the case of broadcast commercials, the associated jingles you can't get out of your head, try as you may) don't make direct sales. Instead, they hope to create a memorable impression — a brand — that influences your shopping behavior. The actual sale is deferred until you arrive at a store or other point of purchase: If the branding successfully resonates with you, you'll select that particular product among its competitors.

Brand marketing may be for you if the following traits apply to your business:

- ✔ **Your sale is indirect.** Consumers can't buy your cereal, toothpaste, or car wax directly from you but have to go to a store (owned by someone else) to get it. Branding helps put your product at the top of consumers' minds when that momentous occasion occurs. If you own a store, brand advertising can also direct customers to your retail location for ice cream, furniture, yoga lessons, or whatever you're selling.

- ✔ **You face many similar competitors.** The most dreaded word in marketing is *commodity:* a product, like crude oil, whose only distinction among competing sellers is price. Branding combats "commoditization" by creating a constellation of images, feelings, ideas, or even values that are unique to your branded product. It sets your product apart from its competitors, and it allows you to escape the race-to-the-bottom that comes when the only advantage you can offer is a cheaper price.

Chapter 10 surveys the branding landscape and copywriting's role within it. Chapter 11 gives you the basics for applying brand tactics to advertising.

Grabbing attention with public relations

Just as sales can be direct or indirect, so too with marketing messages. Instead of directly pitching your message, you can indirectly communicate through events that establish your virtues and values and through media coverage — in papers, magazines, journals, and more — that tell your story for you.

Public relations can be an important part of your marketing mix if the following situations apply to you:

- ✔ **Your product is complex or unusual or requires an educated prospect.** One of my clients helps banks apply interest-rate risk-management techniques to lower costs and boost profits. This topic isn't easy to explain in an ad or a letter, so my client produces newsletters and places articles in banking publications to explain what it does. Media coverage can be an excellent and inexpensive way to educate prospects before you close in on the sale.

✔ **You want to establish credibility and/or authority.** Everyone understands that a paid advertisement is biased (of course) to the one who places it. But actual articles in esteemed publications lend an aura of objective credibility to your story. They can be a terrific way to establish your organization's authority and expertise, or its commitment to values that are important to your prospects.

You can find an introduction to public relations and hands-on advice on how to make it work for you in Chapter 12. Chapter 13 goes even deeper, with step-by-step instructions for creating your own articles and publications.

Sustaining your efforts with sales support

Imagine a casting call for a major Hollywood movie: Among the beautiful and glamorous stars who capture all the attention are numerous subordinate players, such as character actors and extras, who fill out the rest of the cast. They may not be sexy, but the movie can't be made without them.

In marketing, the supporting cast is made of various miscellaneous materials including Web sites, brochures, sales sheets, pamphlets, and so on. They all support your sales efforts, and you may want to create them if

✔ **You need to fill in the gaps during the sales process.** A long time can elapse between the initial lead and the final sale. Collateral materials can sustain your message in the interim.

✔ **Your customers can't complete the purchase without more info.** Sometimes, your customers just need more facts before they can buy. When you're considering a software purchase, for example, you need to know whether it will work with your current hardware configuration and operating system. Supporting materials supply that information.

✔ **Your sales team insists upon it.** Salespeople hate to go on a call empty-handed, and they like to leave something behind. Your supporting material gives them props that can help them with their pitches.

For more on writing sales support stuff, turn to Chapter 15, where you can find a fat load of information with the skinny on brochures, white papers, and more. For Web sites, which can be designed to take orders, provide information, or deliver customer service, see Chapter 14. And to help you with the special sales and marketing requirements that arise when your customers are other businesses rather than consumers, see Chapter 16 for an overview of business-to-business copy strategies and tactics.

Chapter 2

Marching Ahead with Copywriting Fundamentals

*T*here's a famous anecdote, attributed to various politicians, that illustrates the difference between being well spoken and being a good speaker. Of the first politician in the story, audiences responded to his speeches by saying, "My, isn't he a good speaker?" Of the second politician, people responded by saying, "Let's march!" Although the first speech drew praise, the second actually accomplished the speaker's purpose: persuasion leading to action.

That's also the difference between good writing and good copywriting. You may admire a piece of writing for its rhythm, apt use of metaphor, and graceful application of language, but if it doesn't contribute to your business objectives — whether they're sales, more leads, or greater awareness of your products and services — it's not truly good copywriting. Good copywriting makes connections with your intended audiences (your customers or potential customers) that ultimately result in improved business performance.

Fortunately, you don't need to be a great writer to write great copy. Although having a sense of style and an ear for poetry is helpful, you can write quite profitably without them. But you can't write persuasive, customer-motivating copy without a firm grip on the proven principles that turn idle prospects into active customers. In this chapter, I introduce the fundamentals common to almost all successful copywriting assignments: promising benefits; making offers; telling stories; and using headlines, subheads, and body copy. As this book proceeds, you discover variations on these themes appropriate to specific challenges or projects. But by mastering these basics as soon as possible, you create a foundation for success. Let's march!

Writing Copy 101: The Building Blocks

Whether you're writing print ads or Web pages, brochures or e-mails, letters or postcards, you work with three basic elements: a headline that sets the bait, body copy that hooks 'em, and a call to action that reels 'em in.

Taking the lead: Headlines

In newspapers and magazines, the headline tells readers what the subsequent article is about, providing just enough information so that they can decide whether they want to read on. Marketing headlines provide information, too, but they also go an important step further: They make a promise, overt or implied, that appeals to your prospects' self-interests.

Avoid the temptation to write cute or clever headlines for their own sakes, under the mistaken belief that they attract readers' attention. Chances are, your message will suffer the same fate as the class clown who does anything to draw attention to himself: It'll be ignored.

Cute and clever *may* be acceptable, but only if your headline appeals to the one thing readers care about — *their self interest.* Every good copywriter needs to be familiar with the three time-tested, market-proven, cash-register-ringing ways to appeal to reader interests: Promise a benefit, make an offer, and deliver relevant news.

Promising a benefit

If you've ever interviewed for a sales or marketing job, you may have been hit with one of the classic stupid-interview-trick challenges: "Sell me this pencil." You may have been tempted to do something rather violent and obscene with that pencil, but to get the job, you had to demonstrate your understanding of features and benefits salesmanship.

Well, I'm not going to ask you to sell me a pencil (heck, I'm just grateful you bought this book), but I do want you to understand what features and benefits are and the absolutely crucial difference between them.

✔ **Features** are qualities or things that an item or service has, such as anti-lock disc brakes or a water-repelling exterior shell. Features are static characteristics, and they're almost always nouns or adjectives. The pencil, for example, has the following features:

- It's *yellow.*

- It's a *hexagon.*

- It has an *eraser.*

 Benefits are what the product or service does for the owner or user. They are, therefore, much more important than features because they include a what's-in-it-for-me motivation. They're active qualities and are almost always verbs, adverbs, or verbal phrases. They *save* people time and money, *protect* them from foul weather, *alert* them to danger, *make* them look younger and sexier, and so on. You can say that the pencil gives you the following benefits:

- Its bold color makes it *easy to find* on a cluttered desktop.

- Its ridged shape *prevents it from rolling* off your desk.

- Its built-in eraser helps you *correct mistakes* in a flash.

You may notice that in the preceding example, the pencil's benefits are intimately related to its features. In fact, I took each feature and uncovered its value — what the pencil does for people that makes it worth buying. Hold onto your hat (without, somehow, dropping this book) because I'm going to let you in on the single, most important secret to good copywriting: Transform features into benefits!

It may seem like marketing magic, but transforming features into benefits is easy. For any given feature, ask, "What does this do for my customer?" The answer is the benefit. For example, consider the call-waiting feature on your phone. What does it do for you? It alerts you to incoming calls, even when you're on the line with someone else. The benefit: You never miss a phone call. Simple, right? Yet it's amazing how many would-be marketers fail to take this fundamental step.

Transforming features into benefits

You can perform a little magic of your own by applying the question "What does this do for my customers?" to your product or service's features. For example, think about the energy-saving features built into many notebook computers: What does that do for the customer? It extends battery life, allowing users to get more work done between recharges — that's the benefit.

Now you can practice your newfound transformational skills. For the following features, apply the "what's-it-do?" question to uncover the feature's benefit, its value to the customer:

 The removable lining to a leather jacket

 The surge protector on an AC power strip

 A resealable potato chip bag

 A TV remote with extra-large buttons

 A word processing program with an auto-save option

After you identify benefits, the next step is working them into your headlines. Try this simple formula: A verb plus a desirable quality or thing that a customer might want equals a benefit headline. The stronger the desirability of that "thing," the stronger the benefit. Take a look at this example:

Turn your kitchen trash into garden-enriching super-fertilizer.

Here, the leading verbal construction, "Turn . . . into" leads the headline into the promise of an attractive new thing: "garden-enriching super-fertilizer."

You can improve on this strategy by adding a reinforcing feature to the principal benefit:

Enjoy younger, smoother skin in just 30 days.

The word "enjoy" is the active verb that sets the headline into motion, while "younger, smoother skin" is the desirable thing; "in just 30 days" is an additional feature that implies speed, another important benefit.

Sometimes a benefit is not something you desire, but something you want to defeat or overcome, such as debt, bad breath, or high credit card interest rates. For example:

Cut your healthcare insurance costs in half!

The promise in this headline is the reduction of pain — in this case, an expense trimmed by 50 percent.

Later in this chapter, I show you how to write body copy that fulfills the promise of the headline. You can get a jump-start on your sales story, however, by including in your headline an important *proof point* — some material fact or compelling logic that adds credibility to your headline while giving the reader a smooth transition into the body copy. Here's how it works:

Eliminate offensive odors with StenchAway, the only kitchen cleanser with bacteria-eating enzymes.

"Eliminate" is the verb, and "offensive odors" is the negative outcome the headline promises to overcome. This headline not only introduces the name of the product but also offers a reason why the product is better than its competitors: It's the only one "with bacteria-eating enzymes."

You need not follow the "verb + desire" formula to the letter to write an effective benefits headline. To get the name of your product (or business) into the headline, make it the subject of the sentence, like so:

Chlorolux renews the green in your grass!

Making offers

An *offer* is the promise of an exchange. In return for responding to your message, sending a check, filling out a form, or visiting your store this week only, your readers get a subscription, a discount coupon, a two-for-one deal, or whatever offer you wish to make.

A discount, special sale, or special price can be a particularly strong offer. When you have a great offer, consider leading with it in the headline, especially when your product is otherwise similar to other products or has a familiar benefit that no longer attracts attention.

The offer headline is the simplest kind of headline to write: You simply state the offer, or you present the offer and add the name of your store or the location where the offer can be obtained. The offer is the star, so you don't want to dim its shine by adding lots of verbal clutter:

> *Save 25% on all women's shoes at Toe Town.*

You can add a deadline or time limit to create greater urgency. Human beings tend to be expert procrastinators; by creating urgency, you encourage action (before your message is otherwise entirely forgotten):

> *Order one collectible coin kit by May 31, and get the second set for half the price.*

One of the most powerful marketing appeals is *exclusivity,* the sense (or illusion) that an offer is being made only to a select, special, or elite few, which just happens to include you! "You," in fact, is a great word to use in an exclusive appeal, because it speaks to the most important people in your readers' universe: them. Words such as "only," "special," and even "exclusive" may prove handy as well. The important thing about this offer is to expressly identify the audience and make them aware that the deal is indeed "exclusive."

> *For Yachtsman Today subscribers only: FREE 30-day trial of new PointX GPS system.*

Providing news

People value new information about issues and things that interest them. You can turn this curiosity to your advantage by constructing your headline from a tidbit of provocative information. Your goal is to break through reader apathy with new information and then link that new information to something readers value — something that makes them richer, healthier, safer, stronger, sexier, and so on. For example:

> *Latest NASA solar panels now available for energy-conscious homeowners.*

TRY IT

Multiplying your headline powers by three

Writer's block? Bah, humbug! You have at least three proven formulas for turning a piece of information into a compelling headline: benefits, offers, and news.

Suppose that you want to run an ad in the local paper for a car wash that has just added a rust inhibitor to its cleaning solutions. To promote the new feature, you're offering a $2 discount in April, reducing the price from $10 to $8. In a flash, you can multiply your headline power by three.

1. First, you can turn the feature — the rust inhibitor — into a benefit for your headline:

   Remove rust and extend the life of your car with Norustatal 9, only at Sugar Daddy's Car Wash!

2. Second, you can emphasize the discount offer:

   This April only: Get a deluxe car wash — and remove winter salt and rust — at Sugar Daddy's Car Wash for just $8!

3. Third, you can use the rust inhibitor as alluring news:

   New rust-fighting formula extends life of your car. Now at Sugar Daddy's Car Wash, no extra charge.

Now try your hand and write three different headlines (benefit, offer, news) for the following:

✔ A new Internet-based service that allows customers to use their network connection to make long-distance calls, with an average savings of 35 percent to 55 percent on charges.

✔ A flea collar that uses nontoxic, botanical essences to kill ticks and fleas; available at Pete's Pets — buy two, get the third free.

✔ A health club that offers advanced Pilates training — proven to help prevent osteoporosis — to all ages; sign up for one year at full price, get second year at half price.

In this instance, the "news" about the solar panels is reinforced with the credibility of NASA and linked directly to a specific audience — "energy-conscious homeowners."

TIP

You can create suspense by turning a "news" headline into a question that challenges what the readers already know. If the substance of the question is important enough to prospects, they'll read the body copy to satisfy their curiosity or allay their anxiety. One of the longest-running and most effective ads of all time led with this headline: "Do you make these mistakes in English?" The headline may seem tame now, but when the ad was launched in the 1920s, it touched on a profound anxiety among Americans, many of whom were first-generation immigrants from non-English-speaking countries trying to find upward mobility in the newly emerging world of white-collar work.

To write an effective "question" headline, be sure to promise a reward of meaningful news by hinting at the importance of your information and by implying that readers will find answers in subsequent copy — *if* they read on. For example:

Are you prepared for the 3 most important changes in this year's tax regulations?

This question suggests that if you don't know what the changes are, you're unprepared. In the copy that follows, you'd not only deliver (briefly) the news about the three changes, but you'd also link that information back to your service — in this example, a tax-preparation firm.

Fulfilling the promise: The body

After you capture your readers' attention with the headline, the *body,* or the bulk of the copy that follows, pursues the sale by fulfilling the promise stated or implied in the headline. (You build the body with *copy points*, facts, evidence, and/or ideas that support the case or story you've already introduced.) You don't need to scratch your head wondering what to do next. Just follow your headline's lead.

If you led with a *benefit,* your body copy must articulate the value of the benefit to the customer by clearly explaining what it does for the reader. For example:

Headline: *Chlorolux renews the green in your grass!*

Beginning of the body copy: *You weed, you fertilize, you adjust your pH — and your reward? A field of brown. It's time for Chlorolux, the lab-tested non-toxic lawn treatment that turns blah brown lawns into luscious fields of green.*

If you lead with an *offer,* explain the value or worth of your offer — what makes it desirable and special:

Headline: *Save 25% on all women's shoes at Toe Town.*

Beginning of the body copy: *Now through June 30, all women's shoes are 25% off at every Toe Town! Mino Blahchicks . . . Emilio Pedicrushers . . . La Stubbas . . . all the most famous and desirable women's shoes from Italy, France, Spain, and more . . . on sale now.*

If you lead with *news,* explain what the news means to customers by demonstrating the potential impact of your information on their lives:

Headline: *Are you prepared for the 3 most important changes in this year's tax regulations?*

Beginning of the body copy: *This year's tax regulations are more complicated than ever. But if you know the three most important changes, you may save yourself one big headache — and a lot of money. The first big change? Married couples can now file with exceptions for. . . .*

Following the lead is just the beginning. Whether you choose to lead with a benefit, offer, or news, you want to develop your copy within a logical shape — beginning, middle, and end — and be sure to include important subordinate information that builds credibility.

Shaping a story

In his *Poetics,* Aristotle declared that all dramas must have a beginning, middle, and end. Like, duh, right? For this he's esteemed a great philosopher? Indeed, for although it seems obvious, his simple observation leads to important conclusions, not just for dramatists, but for us humble copywriters, too. Aristotle's observation means that a good story isn't just a string of sentences, but it has discrete sections that serve different purposes; it also implies that a story is dynamic rather than static, continually changing as it moves along.

The body of a piece of copywriting is a story with discrete sections that serve different purposes as the body progresses. The three major sections are

✔ **The beginning:** You start by stating a problem or challenge to be solved, or an opportunity or desirable thing to be obtained. By doing so, you kick-start your story (your body copy) with a purpose. Your job? To identify the pain to be overcome or the pleasure to be embraced.

- A pain beginning: *Day after day, a silent enemy is destroying your car, inch by inch. Unless you take action. . . .*

- A pleasure beginning: *Just one month from today, your mirror can show you a lovelier, more youthful-looking you. . . .*

✔ **The middle:** In the middle, you introduce the "hero" — the product or service you offer that overcomes the challenge or obtains the benefit. This is the longest part of the body copy, and it shoulders the heaviest burdens (most notably, building credibility — see the next section). For now, however, the key task is to bring your hero (product or service) on stage, which could look like either of these scenarios:

- **Hero conquering pain:** You can write about your product as a means of overcoming a problem, removing an obstacle, or eliminating a pain, like this: *Now you can remove rust — and prevent its future growth — just by washing your car at Sugar Daddy's!*

- **Hero capturing the prize:** Present your product as the necessary ingredient — the hero — that helps the reader obtain something desirable, like this: *Simply massage the lilac-scented Blushwish Cream on your face twice a day, morning and night. You'll immediately feel a gentle, rejuvenating tingle, and within weeks, you'll enjoy smoother skin . . . fewer wrinkles . . . and a more radiant glow to your skin.*

✔ **The end:** The last step is to introduce the customer into the story. By taking the action you request — going to the store, dialing a number, visiting a Web site, returning a response device, and so on — the customer concludes the story and enjoys the happy ending: an escape from pain or an acquisition of pleasure. (I cover endings in detail in "Inspiring action: The close" later in this chapter.) In the end, you emphasize the action the reader must take (a store to visit, a number to call) to complete the story. Endings often look like these examples:

- **No more pain:** *Come to Sugar Daddy's Car Wash and put rust in its place — off your car!*

- **Satisfying desire:** *Call 1-800-NEW-SKIN today to order your first one-month supply of Blushwish at our special introductory price of. . . .*

Building credibility with evidence

If the first golden rule of copywriting is to emphasize benefits (what's in it for the customers), then the second most important rule is to build your case with *evidence,* specific factual material that can include the following:

✔ **Particular features of your product or service:** These include what your product or service does, how it's built, how it works, what it's made of, and so on. Perhaps you want to emphasize the genuine 24K gold of a fitting, the rack-and-pinion steering of a car, the Egyptian cotton in a fabric, or the portobello mushrooms in a sauce.

✔ **Sensual characteristics:** For items that are valued for what they are (such as food, jewelry, music, and clothes) rather than what they do, sensual characteristics appeal to the senses that whet our appetites for the product. Sensual characteristics can be the scent of a cherry blossom; the succulence of tender, young lamb; the whisper-soft touch of cashmere; the brilliant colors in a painting; and so on.

✔ **Quality of designers, engineers, artisans, or makers:** The special experience and expertise of the people behind a product or service add enormous credibility. You want breads prepared by bakers trained in France, cars designed by engineers with championship racing experience, marble floors crafted by Italian masons, investment advice from experts with 15-year track records of favorable performance, and so on.

✔ **Research results and statistical evidence:** Prospects love hard numbers that demonstrate superiority, preferably those measured by independent third-party sources. Your pitch is much more convincing when your bond returns are 23 percent higher than your competitors' returns, your kitchen food processor has a 30 percent greater food capacity, your microprocessor is 64 percent faster, your storm parka is 42 percent warmer, and so on.

✔ **Customer endorsements:** Your customer's opinions are always more credible than your own. When you can, use them. (See Chapter 3.)

When you write for a large organization, you don't write in a vacuum. In other words, the messages you craft for a specific piece are usually governed by branding, positioning, and mission statements formed long before your project was assigned. In addition to communicating the points particular to your task, you're expected to maintain the organization's larger messaging, be it "leadership," "innovation," "commitment to customer service," and so on. (For more on branding, see Chapter 10.) The danger, however, is that these larger, global messages may be too vague and abstract, or even overly self-flattering, to sustain credibility. Just saying that you're a leader, for example, doesn't make you one. High-minded claims often come across as empty-headed boasts.

As a writer, your job is to link every abstract theme or corporate vision to something concrete that manifests that claim. If you're obligated to position your company as a leader, you want to present material that embodies leadership. Maybe you sell more widgets in a greater variety to more people than any other company does. Or maybe your company set the standard for overnight delivery that your competitors follow. If your company is positioned as the innovator, don't shout that you're an innovator. Instead, show the reader the innovations — perhaps a new steam valve or a faster way to get passengers on board their flights.

Inspiring action: The close

Your final job as a copywriter is the most important yet the least complex of your tasks: to tell people what to do and how to do it. In a call to action, you want to provide all the necessary nuts-and-bolts information, plus add a few points to overcome the last remaining objections the prospect may have to responding (ordering or buying, for example).

Telling people what to do

Okay, you've made a promise and backed it with evidence. Now tell the customer how to fulfill your offer or how to buy or order what you're selling. Keep the following points in mind:

- **Restate the offer:** In a short ad, this may be unnecessary. But in longer copy, restating the offer is important. Be sure to briefly include what you're selling and any special terms — a discount, additional features, a time limit — that may accompany it.

- **Give the location:** Where can customers buy your product? If it's through general category stores, such as supermarkets or hardware stores, you may want to tell them what aisle they can find it in, if it's not immediately obvious:

    Look for Bingo's Instant Bagels in the freezer section of your store.

> If you're selling a specific store, identify its location using familiar landmarks:
>
> *Located on Rt. 5 in Bentham, next to the post office.*

✔ **Present the ordering options:** If your offer is obtained by ordering it instead of through a store, be sure to provide accurate, explicit information for each option. Typical options include ordering via a toll-free phone number, completing a form on a Web site, or returning a postage-paid card or form that must be completed and returned in a postage-paid envelope.

Overcoming customer inertia

Getting people to listen to you is hard; getting them to take action is even harder. Just as in physics, it takes a great deal of energy to overcome inertia in marketing. In other words, motivating a prospect to take action or to make a purchasing decision contrary to what he's accustomed to is never easy. Strong offers and compelling benefits are your best levers for moving customers. But you can increase your strength and gain a better chance of inspiring action by creating urgency and a sense of safety.

Urgency

It's one thing when I tell my kids to get ready for school; it's another when the bus is at the door. An imposed limitation, such as a deadline or limited offer, can be a great spur to action for many people. In your marketing materials, use limitations to defeat people's natural inclination to procrastinate. Instead of just making an offer, create a deadline, specific date, or other restriction, that sets a defined limit on your offer and demands action now. It's easy to do, as you see in these examples:

> *Act now! Our sale ends February 28!*
>
> *Save $40 on your first Dresden Doll when you order by November 15.*
>
> *We're giving away door prizes to the first 100 customers.*

Safety

The last hurdle before the sale (or other desired response) is the most emotionally loaded: fear. People are often afraid that your product won't work as promised, that they'll lose money, or that they'll look foolish if they buy from you. You overcome fear by removing risk. Here are the two easiest ways to eliminate risk:

✔ **Guaranteeing satisfaction:** Squirrels are smarter than they look: If you want to trap them, you better use a cage with spring-loaded doors open at either end; otherwise, squirrels just won't enter. Purchasing psychology works in a similar fashion in that people generally don't like making decisions that box them in. This is why offering a no-questions-asked, money-back guarantee is so effective. People like knowing they have a way out, though very few of them actually take advantage of the guarantee, even if they aren't "completely satisfied." The increase in sales that comes with a guarantee almost always vastly exceeds the cost of a few returns. In fact, many states require a 30-day return policy, so promising one doesn't add a new expense to your campaign.

✔ **Assuring safety in numbers:** People may admire rebels, loners, and rugged individualists in the movies, but in real life, few like to blaze new trails by themselves. They much prefer the well-worn, well-known, well-traveled path. Though common sense tells people that popular consensus is no guarantee of wisdom, they still find assurance in numbers. When sales figures are available to you, see whether you can incorporate them into your copy. For example:

The most popular power-washer in America!

You can also combine a safety-in-numbers message with a special offer that makes prospects feel that they have an "in" on a better deal. Supplement your "the multitudes have already done this" message with an offer that's even stronger than the one the multitudes have already responded to:

Millions have purchased the Jiminy Power-Washer for $39.95. Now, through this exclusive mail offer, you can get the Jiminy for only$29.95 — a $10.00 savings!

Adding the Finishing Touches to Your Foundation

Although headlines and body copy are the most common and frequently used elements of marketing writing, you're not limited to them alone. To help you communicate your message and highlight important points, you have a set of additional tools at your disposal, including subheads, captions, and callouts.

Deploying the power of subheads

Subheads are simply mini-headlines that are distinguished from ordinary body copy by being printed in a larger font or in a special type treatment, such as bold, underlining, or italics. They help you do two important things:

✔ **Break up long text:** Few things intimidate a reader like a forced march through many long paragraphs of unbroken text. Students or employees may have no choice but to hunker down and plow ahead. But potential customers have the power to reject marketing materials they don't like.

If reading your copy seems like a chore, guess what? Instant disposition to the circular file. Subheads break the text into more digestible, bite-sized pieces. By making the material easier to read, you also make it more likely to be read.

✔ **Emphasize important points:** Your most important point, be it an offer or the biggest benefit, is often incorporated in the headline. But you also have subordinate points, including additional benefits, special features, and/or special deals, that merit the extra attention a subhead provides.

Together, your headline and subheads should tell a complete sales story: benefit, offer, and other key points. That way, even people who skim your copy without reading the entire text get the gist of your message.

Writing subheads is much like writing headlines, except that you can think of subheads as working together in sets to help your copy flow. Here are a few examples of ways to approach subhead groups:

✔ **Leading with imperative verbs:** Because they're the action words of language, verbs have a particular significance for marketers. Using imperative verbs (verbs that make commands) is an especially vigorous way to lead your subhead clusters:

- *Double your profits in just six months.*

- *Get free collateral support for your customers.*

- *Order now to take advantage of our introductory discount.*

✔ **Writing "news" style subheads:** For a less aggressive, more informational approach, write your subheads as if they're previews to the important information to come in the succeeding paragraphs. As with "news" headlines, these subheads combine a tidbit of new information with a hint about how this news affects customers:

- *Starsat pulls in more stations for less money.*

- *Digital options let you control your viewing schedule.*

- *First 6 months free when you subscribe today.*

✔ **Working with verbals:** Consistency is a virtue that can help tie your subheads together for a more coherent read. As an alternative to leading with active verbs, you can lead your subheads with gerunds (verbs that serve as nouns) and/or participles (verbs that act as adjectives). There are no hard and fast rules about which is better, but in general, active verbs lend a more assertive tone to your copy, while verbals suggest a lighter approach. Verbal subheads may look like these:

- *Simplifying your purchase orders has never been easier.*

- *Backed with the best data security controls in the business.*

- *Ordering now gives you the 10% discount rate.*

Writing captions the right way

Captions are the brief bits of copy that accompany illustrations such as photographs, drawings, charts, graphs, and so on. They're pretty simple and only require you to do the following:

- ✔ **Identify the illustration:** You'd probably know that you need to tell the reader what the illustration is even if I hadn't mentioned it to you. If the illustration is a photo of one of your products, tell the reader which model it is. If it's a chart of comparative performance, explain exactly what's being compared and what conclusions can be drawn from it. The rule of thumb: No reader should ever have to struggle to understand the content of your illustration.

- ✔ **Link the illustration to the body copy:** This is the part that's often neglected. Don't create visual orphans, illustrations that don't seem to have any connection to the rest of the text. In addition to telling the reader what the illustration is, link it back to your story. If you have a photo of a person using a product, tell the reader how it illustrates an activity described in the body copy:

    The BizBuzz Table Saw's micro-adjustable fence makes cutting complex angles a breeze.

    If you're using a pie chart to illustrate a point discussed in the body, say so:

    Figure 3: In head-to-head studies, research shows that 32% of all basset hounds prefer Howlies rabbit-flavored biscuits.

Surprising your reader with bursts, callouts, and sidebars

The guiding principle to captions is integration: incorporating the illustrations into the body of the text. In this section, our tools do just the opposite: You use bursts, callouts, and sidebars when you want your information to stand apart from the rest of the copy, either because you don't want to interrupt the flow of your main story or because you have special information that's so important you want to draw extra attention to it.

Being bold with bursts

Bursts are short blasts of copy distinguished by some kind of graphic treatment, such as being set in a brightly colored oval, that attracts attention. Bursts are almost always used to announce offers or special features:

✔ **Offer bursts:** You see these all the time in print ads, on catalog covers, and even on envelopes. To write one, pretend that you're shouting with a bullhorn in a crowded marketplace — be quick and shameless. It may read like this:

- *50% off while supplies last!*

- *Buy one, get one FREE!*

- *Hurry! Sale ends March 7!*

✔ **Special-feature bursts:** Instead of promoting a sale or discount, some bursts announce an especially desirable feature or benefit. Again, make them short and sweet:

- *FREE shipping on all $25-and-up orders!*

- *Comes with genuine leather trim!*

- *Instant mulching saves time!*

Capturing attention with callouts

Callouts are brief selections of copy, often just two or three sentences, distinguished from the rest of the text by altered type treatment (made larger, set in italics, set in a different font, and so on) and segregated within a box or by bold lines on the top and bottom. Marketers have lifted the callout from journalists who often use them within articles to highlight important quotes or significant statements.

Like journalists, copywriters use callouts to draw attention to important information that can either be a repetition of something drawn from the body copy or something entirely new. They're usually less aggressive than the burst. If the burst is like a carnival barker's shout, the callout is more like a stage whisper or aside. Some of the most popular uses of the callout include

✔ **Customer quotes:** Callouts can be a perfect way of introducing favorable customer comments into a piece without having to weave them into the body copy itself. (For more on customer testimonials, see Chapter 3.) Callouts often looks like this:

"With the Simmons Group, our company was able to reduce our employee churn rate by 72% in just 90 days." Joe Blow, Happy Burger Enterprises

✔ **Compelling information:** When you're writing a particularly long piece, such as a big brochure or an executive white paper, you often want to repeat crucial information in a way that prevents it from getting lost in the rest of the text. The callout is an attractive way of making key ideas stand out. For example:

The Simmons Group has streamlined human resource operations in more than two hundred Fortune 500 companies nationwide, saving an estimated $3.5 billion in hiring, retention, and benefits-management expenses.

✔ **Important reminders:** Callouts can be a second chance to remind readers of impending time limits or special opportunities:

Remember, orders placed by 3:00 pm EST will be shipped the same day.

Sizing up sidebars

The longest of the alternative text options, *sidebars* are columns or boxes of copy set apart by a special graphics treatment. With plenty of room for paragraphs of copy, they allow you to present longer material that wouldn't otherwise work within the body copy. Popular uses of sidebars include the following:

✔ **Lists of features:** Instead of clogging a paragraph with a string of features separated by commas and/or semicolons, list them in a sidebar. (Many graphic designers use "bullets" to distinguish each element in a list.) They're easier to see and read, and you don't interrupt the flow of your main copy.

✔ **Miniature case studies:** Case studies are real-life examples of your product or service in action. (For more information on writing them, see Chapter 13.) Long studies make fine articles, but short ones of three or four paragraphs can be excellent sidebars.

✔ **Incidental information:** Sidebars are good places to communicate information that supports your sales message but doesn't merit inclusion within the body because it's not directly tied to your lead offer, benefit, news item, or story. Incidental info can be things like a summary of research results, a discussion of alternative uses for your products, or nitty-gritty ordering and shipping information.

Editing Your Work: The Grammar You Need to Know

Good news: Copywriting doesn't necessarily demand the strictest observance to formal English grammar. Because your objective is to build an empathetic rapport with your readers, you want to write the way they speak. Depending on the circumstances and your intended audience, using slang, sentence fragments, contractions, colloquialisms, and so on is perfectly acceptable. Yet you still want to maintain credibility, so not everything goes. Allow me to help you walk that fine line between informality and incomprehensibility.

For an exhaustive, yet easy-to-understand review of grammar, try *English Grammar For Dummies* by Geraldine Woods (Wiley). (Any grammarian who loves Jane Austen and New York City is all right by me.)

What your English teacher was wrong about

You've hunkered down to write, and man, the juices are flowing. One good idea just follows another. But just as you start to really smoke, a little demon appears on your shoulder: a tiny woman wearing a shapeless gray dress, with wire-rimmed glasses on her nose and a yardstick in her hand. It's your old English teacher! She's come back to haunt you, to challenge your grammar. Suddenly, inspiration has packed its bags without leaving a forwarding address. Your writing had ground to a halt.

Fortunately, many times you can ignore that little dowdy demon on your shoulder. These are just a few of the times when you can tell her to buzz off.

Using sentence fragments

According to the rules, "real" sentences must have complete subject-verb-object constructions; anything less is a "fragment" that must be rejected. Nonsense. As long as your fragments clearly communicate complete thoughts, they can be a perfectly acceptable part of your rhetorical tool chest for most assignments. When they're used thoughtfully, short fragments create pauses that bracket your ideas for greater emphasis. When they're used arbitrarily, they create confusion and disturb the rhythm of your writing.

> ✔ **Good use of fragments:**
>
> *Your renewed subscription to EZ Rider Reader gives you the low-down on what's up in custom bodies. The hippest highways and byways. Tips and secrets for boss details. And inside visits to the baddest shops and studios around. Why miss out? Renew today.*
>
> ✔ **Weak use of fragments:**
>
> *You know it's time. To renew your subscription. Order today. And get all the dope on what's happening in your neck of the woods. And in the 'hoods. Across the country.*

Ending sentences with prepositions

There are still some goose-stepping grammarians who insist that you can't end sentences with prepositions. They don't know what they're talking about. When it comes to this issue, they don't have a leg to stand on. Otherwise, I'd have to say, "They don't know the issues about which they are talking," or "They don't have a leg upon which to stand." This is just nonsense up with I will not put!

Yes, ending sentences with prepositions is perfectly acceptable, as long as your intended meaning is clear and the preposition isn't redundant. For example, you might ask, "Where are you going?" but not, "Where are you going to?"

Starting sentences with "and" or "but"

Some people say you can never begin a sentence with the conjunctions "and" or "but." But I say they're wrong. And plenty of grammar authorities support my case. Sometimes leading with "and" or "but" is the most effective way to make an effective transition. (Yet you don't want to overdo it.)

Using a thesaurus

I don't believe in burning books, but I'll make an exception for the thesaurus, a reference book of synonyms (words with the same or very similar meanings). The bane of readers everywhere, the thesaurus encourages writers to apply gratuitously overblown rhetoric (like this) instead of plain language (like that). You're better off using your thesaurus as a doorstop than a writing aid. With rare exceptions, short, simple words are best. Be a straight talker, not a pompous interlocutor ("windbag").

Using contractions and slang

Who says you can't use contractions? You didn't hear it from me. And dude, slang can be okay, too — as long as you're using the right slang with the right audience. When in Rome, speak as the Romans do. Use rad slang with the surf set, and use standard English with the business crowd. A word of caution, however: If you can't speak an insider's lingo with spot-on accuracy, don't even try. Just use simple, conversational English.

What your English teacher was right about

Oddly enough, English teachers aren't always wrong. Really. In fact, some of what they taught you (or tried to teach you) can help you be a more effective copywriter.

Using active versus passive language

In the active voice, the subject takes action. In "Caesar conquered Gall," the subject, "Caesar," is the agent of the action, "conquered." But if I were to write in the passive voice, "Gall was conquered by Caesar," the agent of the action now becomes buried in the predicate.

As a grammatical issue, the passive voice isn't necessarily wrong. But in most cases it's weaker, less emphatic writing. When you aim to encourage action, the passive voice undermines your impact. You want to make your products and services the agents of beneficial action in your prospects' lives. Think, "This product (subject) makes (verb) this happen (object)," not "This consequence was caused by this product."

Applying correct spelling and punctuation

You can get away with sentence fragments and slang, but incorrect spelling and punctuation undermine your credibility, making your company look stupid and eroding confidence in your professionalism.

Don't proofread your own work. Yes, of course you should go over everything you write and make corrections before submitting your writing. In fact, reading your work out loud is a terrific way to uncover some typos, grammatical errors, and perhaps some misjudgments in rhythm and tone. But the writer's review should never be the final check before printing and publication. Writers are too close to their own work, and they'll either replicate their errors in the editing process or "read" into their review what they thought they wrote, instead of what's actually on the page. If you can, have a professional proofreader review your work. At the very least, have someone with excellent English language skills review it.

Distrusting your word processor's spelling and grammar checkers

Don't trust spelling and grammar checkers. Just don't. Spelling checkers can't interpret the context of your word choices, so they can't, for example, distinguish among the correct uses of "there," "they're," or "their," or "it's" and "its." And the grammar checkers are notoriously incapable of interpreting complex sentences, often returning grossly incorrect advice. Turn the grammar checker off, and use the spelling checker only as a preliminary review to catch obvious errors. Then get a proofreader.

Reading literature (and lots of it)

In addition to implementing the basic points regarding benefits, offers, and a customer-centered focus, strong copywriters manipulate rhythm to control emphasis and deploy fresh imagery to attract and retain interest. These finer points of style, while useful, are difficult to teach because they emerge from the murky depths of taste, judgment, and imagination.

But if style can't be taught, it can certainly be cultivated. That's why I suggest that you read the same books most of your English teachers encouraged you (I hope) to discover: the poetry of Shakespeare, the novels of Jane Austen, the stories of Hemingway — that whole vast and wondrous feast of literature we, as English language speakers, have the privilege of enjoying as our own. No, you won't suddenly become a Keats or Coleridge, but you don't need to. Read for the sheer pleasure of it and over time — as if by osmosis — you'll secretly absorb a lesson or two. Your ear will become more sensitive to the music of language, and your writing will reflect a greater grasp of tone, rhythm, imagery, and figurative speech. And yes, your copy will become more powerful.

Chapter 3

Looking for Ideas: Finding Inspiration through Investigation

- -

In This Chapter

▶ Asking the right questions about products and services

▶ Figuring out important information about customers

▶ Doing research with the help of different groups

▶ Getting great ideas for your copy

- -

*P*ssst. Come here. Closer. That's it. I'm going to let you in on the Big Secret about copywriting. It isn't magic words that bedazzle prospects. Or a sure-thing formula for casting sales spells. It's more straightforward, yet even more wondrous than either of those things.

Here it is: More than 90 percent of the real copywriting work is done *before you write a single word.*

What is this real work? It's understanding the product or service you're selling. What it is and what it does — especially what it does for customers. How it's different from other products or services like it. Why it's special or desirable. Real work is looking for the qualities of your product or service that attract interest and promote action.

Real copywriting work is also understanding your customers. Who they are and what they want. Their fears and hopes. How they buy and why they walk away. What motivates them into action. It's looking for the emotions hidden under the masks of apathy and boredom.

Understand the fundamental who, what, why, and how, and you'll have a well-spring of *market insight* from which to draw your ideas and copy.

But beware the flip side of this coin! Proceed without understanding, without genuine insight into what you're selling and whom you're selling it to, and you will fail. You may come up with something cute or clever. Or even something that pleases your boss or your client. But without fundamental insight into your customers' psyche and your product's allure, you can't do what's most important: create compelling messages that attract customers to your product or service.

Gaining Insights about Products and Services through Questioning

I'm not knocking intuition or creativity; I'm just debunking the romantic idea that great ideas arise in our minds, full-blown, without any exterior input to nurture them. I want you to seek knowledge because it feeds intuition.

Consider Sherlock Holmes. In Sir Arthur Conan Doyle's stories, does he ever just storm upon a crime scene and impose a theory? The detectives with fast answers — the ones who are quick to say, "It's obviously" this or that — are always the foolish foils to Holmes's genius. What does Holmes do instead? Probes. Investigates. Asks questions. Pursues obscure details, often to the frustration of his less clever companion, Watson. From his odd pool of clues, such as tobacco ashes, animal hairs, and astronomical observations, comes understanding. Holmes gathers his facts and lets his intuition work while he plays the violin or smokes his meerschaum pipe. The end result? Brilliance.

Be like Sherlock Holmes. Begin with investigation and end with brilliance.

Collecting fundamental information

Start with the basics. What's for sale? Sometimes it's obvious: a car or a carpet-cleaning service. But in many situations — such as catalogs, for example — you need to be precise about the features and qualities of your products and services. Does your product come in different sizes? Different colors? Does it have options? How big is it?

What does your product or service do? Especially, what does it do for your customers or clients? These are *benefits,* the single most important attributes of any product and service. Does your product or service make life easier and more comfortable? Does it make the owner healthier, sexier, younger-looking, richer, or more attractive? Can it make chores easier and less burdensome? Does it add status or prestige to the owner? Can it make a business more effective, more cost-efficient, or more profitable? Can it grow revenue and market share? (For more on features and benefits, see Chapter 2.)

The time spent collecting all this information will be well rewarded: Your knowledge provides the necessary pool of facts, ideas, and insights that will help you craft your sales pitch to customers. If you're lucky, your company, organization, or client will give you internal data sheets that list the important features and benefits of the products and services you must write about. If you're not as lucky, you may have to twist a few arms, either by asking for this material yourself (from managers and colleagues) or by scheduling interviews with people, such as product development managers, who have this information locked between their ears. A list of some of the most common information that copywriters need follows:

✔ **General products**

- Dimensions

- Colors

- Accessories (batteries, for example)

- Uses/applications

- Shipping and handling information

- Product number (for ordering)

- Price

- Quantity pricing (if applicable)

- Ordering/purchasing information (including phone numbers, Web site addresses, and/or locations, and so on)

✔ **Apparel**

- Sizes

- Colors

- Textile/material

- Price

- Special instructions (for example, dry clean only)

✔ **Food**

- Flavors

- Ingredients

- Nutritional information

- Recipes

- Potential allergy issues

✔ **Collectibles**

- Dimensions

- Material (Is it ceramic? Bisque porcelain? Pewter?)

- Information about the artist(s) or artisan(s)
- Edition size (Is it a limited edition? How many are there? Is each item individually numbered?)
- Does it come with a certificate of authenticity?
- Information about how the product was made

✔ **Business-to-business services**

- What does it do?
- Who is it for?
- Is it backed/supported by a name familiar to the industry?
- Are there available articles about the service? Have the principals published anything about the service?
- Are demos available of the service?

Pursuing the power questions

Good copywriters write well. Great copywriters ask a lot of questions. Why? Audiences are bombarded with messages. To get through the noise, you must hone precise messages that drive your points home, fast. And to write those arrow-sharp messages, you have to slough off the trivia and dig up the gold — the attributes of your products and services that push your customers past indifference and into desire. Asking questions is your way of digging.

Asking the Passover question

Every Passover, Jews all over the world gather for a special meal called the Seder, at which the youngest participant asks, "Why is this night different from all other nights?"

The answer, of course, is that it's the night that commemorates the flight of the ancient Hebrews from slavery into freedom. Although you rarely, if ever, have to write about anything nearly as weighty, you should always ask the Passover question: Why is our product or service different? How is it different from the competition's similar products or services? These differences are precisely the issues worth emphasizing in your copy.

Sometimes you're lucky and you find something special: a desirable benefit that your product or service, and only your product or service, can deliver — at least in its category or industry. If so, you may have what's called a *unique selling proposition,* or USP, on your hands. Maybe your USP is guaranteed overnight delivery or a promise that kids' academic performance will improve by at least one whole letter grade. When you have a USP, flaunt it. It's often the foundation for great headlines, envelope teasers, brochure covers, and more. (For more on USPs, see Chapter 10.)

Wondering what's important

Not all information is created equal. Some bits of knowledge are much more valuable than others. The less important information may require mentioning, but the most important stuff deserves to be trumpeted, loud and clear. As you proceed, the hot stuff can form the core of your pitch and is often the focus of your headlines and opening sentences: It delivers the *why* — why prospects should be interested in what you have to say. The lesser material needs to be stated, but it should take a lower priority within your copy. How do you sort out the hot, important stuff that motivates customers from the tepid, bare-bones information that's necessary, but uninspiring? Here's an easy scale, in ascending scales from bathwater to steamy, for a quick comparison of the relative value of product or service information that you may obtain from data sheets or responsible personnel:

✔ **Tepid:** Basic features, such as standard accessories or color options, that are simply expected and arouse no special interest in consumers.

✔ **Warm:** Fundamental benefits, such as "saves money" or "promotes hair growth," that are genuinely useful but are also common among your competitors.

✔ **HOT!:** Unique benefits, backed with a guarantee that can't be found anywhere else. If yours is the only lawn mower under $200 with a free bagger, say so. If yours is the only dry-cleaning service in the neighborhood with door-to-door service, shout it out.

Understanding Whom You're Talking To

The one thing more important than understanding what you're selling is understanding *whom* you're selling to. People are not interchangeable. Pitching prime rib to animal activists, for example, probably isn't a good idea. But you do want to find parents with newborns if you're running a diaper service.

Sure, most of the time the marketing matchmaking game is more complicated than that. But just use common sense. When you understand what your prospects *want* — what motivates them to buy or take action — you stand a far greater chance for success. And understanding what people want requires a clear understanding of who they are and how they live.

Just how important is it to know and understand your audience? Ask the professionals who sell by mail. You know what they say is the number one determining factor for success? The list — the actual names and contact information required to reach prospective customers. Having accurate data, like the correct mailing address, for example, is one key to a good list. But selecting the *right* list is every bit as important. Whether lists are made up of magazine subscribers, homeowners, industry executives, or local doctors, it's absolutely crucial that direct marketers select lists that include the people most likely to be interested in what they have to sell. Picking the best lists requires a clear understanding of marketers' target markets. If they don't know their audience, no amount of copy finesse — no matter how brilliant — can save a marketing campaign. (For more on lists, see Chapter 4.)

There are some things you should always consider about your prospects. Whether you draw your understanding from direct experience with your own customers or through research (see the section "Researching on the Prowl, on the Cheap, and Often on the Mark"), these characteristics include

- ✔ **Age:** People's needs change as they move from childhood into adulthood, and through adulthood into old age. Young people just starting their careers have very different ambitions from older people planning to retire. The young father may be a hot prospect for life insurance, while the older retiree probably isn't.

- ✔ **Family:** Do your prospects have important family obligations to fulfill? Do they have children? If so, how old are they? The concerns of pre-schooler parents are not the same as parents putting kids through college.

- ✔ **Generation:** I know, I know. We've all had it up to here with talk about baby boomers, Generation X, Generation Y, and so on. Yet you still want to have a rough idea of your market's generational perspective. The calls to frugality and self-sacrifice that may appeal to Depression-era babies are unlikely to find a sympathetic ear with baby boomers more interested in self-fulfillment.

- ✔ **Interests:** Do your prospects like to cook, smoke Cuban cigars, or read romance novels? Understanding their interests helps you get inside their heads. And if you choose to offer a *premium* — a free gift (refrigerator magnet, T-shirt, bumper sticker, and so on) — you have a better idea of what they find attractive.

- ✔ **Values:** Are your consumers champions of Yankee self-sufficiency or active supporters of social justice? Are they motivated by religious faith, political ideology, career ambitions, or family values — or all or none of the above? As you discover in later chapters, successful writers speak in the language of their audience. Understanding their values goes a long way to finding that common ground.

- ✔ **Class/income category:** In many parts of the world, people are generally not comfortable identifying themselves or others as members of specific classes. But whether people openly acknowledge class distinctions, the material evidence of their existence can be seen every day. Think *New York Daily News* versus the *New York Times*. Softball league versus golf country club. Budweiser versus Sierra Nevada Pale Ale. WWF versus PBS. You may need to tread lightly, but understand where you tread.

- ✔ **Occupation/profession/employment:** On the consumer level, you're investigating another angle within lifestyles. In business-to-business communications, however, job titles and responsibilities become crucial. An expensive enterprise-wide accounting system, for example, has to be pitched simultaneously to different people at different levels within the company. These people are bound to have different desires. The IT person wants to know whether your system is compatible with technology the company already has; accounting people want to know whether your system manages and manipulates the appropriate data; and the CEO wants to be assured of a return on the company's investment. Understand what the different agendas are and be prepared to speak to each of them. (For more on B2B copywriting, see Chapter 16.)

Just as product or service information has varying degrees of value, so too with customer insights. Consider this scale of the relative importance of different types of customer information:

- **Tepid:** Understanding interests, such as golfing or gardening. This gives you some clue as to the subject matter you can speak to that's likely to be read.

- **Warm:** Understanding fundamental values, such as patriotism or artistic self-fulfillment. With this kind of insight, you begin to understand what kind of tone you should use or the kinds of angles you can emphasize.

- **HOT!:** Although all the customer info you acquire can give you clues to prospect desires, pay special attention to interests and values: These are the virtual gateways to the heart. For example, give some consideration to understanding powerful underlying fears and desires, such as the fear of aging or the desire for increased self-esteem. These are the hot buttons you want to push, right away, by linking your product or service to problems it helps overcome or pleasures it helps customers obtain.

Marketing research professionals call this accumulated body of audience information demographics and psychographics. *Demographics* refers to general population statistics, such as where people live, their income, age, family size, and so on. *Psychographics* includes the what-makes-people-tick information that's less easy to measure but is often even more important to understand: interests, values, beliefs, fears, hopes, and so on.

When you're speaking to people as a group, you're playing with fire. If you proceed with care and good judgment, you can stoke the hot points that'll warm up your audience. But cross the line into stereotypes and you're going to get burned. Suppose, for example, that you're writing a brochure for a retirement community. With an eye toward the needs of your audience, you may emphasize the community's security, convenience, and easy access to healthcare providers. So far, so good. All of these issues address genuine concerns common to many members of your target audience. But if you were to highlight bingo, shuffleboard, or lazy days in rocking chairs, you'd stray into the dangerous terrain of *stereotypes,* common clichés that have little bearing on reality. In this case, the stereotype would be both offensive and inaccurate. Today's retirees are typically healthy and vigorous, and they expect stimulating living options that respect their intellects and individuality. Your goal is to speak *to* your audience, not *down* at them.

Researching on the Prowl, on the Cheap, and Often on the Mark

A vast subsection of the marketing industry is dedicated to research. Through surveys, interviews, focus groups, and other devices, researchers slice and dice prospect attitudes and customer behaviors into statistical models that (hopefully) provide strategic direction for product development and/or marketing communications. Unfortunately, much of this work is very expensive and beyond the reach of many businesses. Fortunately, you may not need expensive, formal research in order to glean the insights you need to understand, reach, and motivate your customers.

Sometimes, the best source of info is right under your nose (figuratively speaking): the customers or salespeople you work with or near every day. They have things to tell you — *if* you're willing to listen. My amazement at the amount of quality information that can be obtained simply by asking is only exceeded by my astonishment that so many marketers rarely ask!

Talking to customers

Your best source of information about customers comes from the customers themselves and the people who work most closely with them. In addition to gleaning often-priceless information, you cultivate the goodwill that comes when you show respect for a person's knowledge, experience, and opinions.

So why do people buy your product or service? The answer may not be as obvious as you think. Maybe you think they come to your jewelry store for the great selection, when in fact yours is the only local store open until 7 p.m., giving people a chance to buy last-minute gifts after work. Whatever it is that attracts customers, don't assume — ask.

You can ask in person; by e-mail; and over the phone (if that's the way customers ordinarily do business with you — don't call them; ask questions when they call you). While you're completing an order or providing service, take a few moments to collect your customers' opinions. Chances are, they'll be flattered that you thought enough of them to ask. The most important question you can ask is *why* people buy your product or service. But you should also find out customers' opinions concerning the following topics:

- What do they like about their purchase?
- What don't they like?
- Do they have any complaints?
- Are there certain benefits and/or features that are especially important?

✔ How/when/why do they use the product? (The answer may not be that obvious. The people at Arm & Hammer found new life for their baking soda when they realized customers used it more frequently as a way to kill odors, not bake bread.)

✔ What improvements would they make?

✔ Are there ways to make the product/service easier to buy and easier to use?

✔ Would they buy again? Why or why not?

✔ Have they recommended the product/service to a friend or colleague? Why or why not?

Don't take the responses you get at face value, especially if they appear too favorable. Many people were raised with the if-you-can't-say-anything-nice-don't-say-anything-at-all philosophy and are reluctant to express a negative opinion, particularly to someone who represents the product or service.

Instead, play psychologist. Listen for hesitancies or sudden shifts in volume or tone. If your conversation is in person, look for breaks in eye contact or movements in the arms or legs. If the customer says, "Sure, I'm satisfied," but looks away and then holds his arms across his chest, chances are there's more to his story. Ask whether he's completely satisfied, or perhaps whether he's less than satisfied with something. Probe gently and you may find a different story — one that's closer to the truth.

Speaking to salespeople

Many times you simply don't have access to customers. Maybe they're far away. Or perhaps issues of confidentiality (as in healthcare) make it impossible for you to make direct contact.

In that case, you have to do the next best thing and talk to the people who regularly talk to customers. One of the best places to start is with salespeople. Don't give them forms to fill out. Speak to them in person (perhaps over a cup of coffee and a Danish — your treat, of course) or, if absolutely necessary, over the phone. Tell them your agenda upfront: You're looking for insights that can help you write more effective marketing materials. (Don't be surprised if their jaws drop in stunned amazement; too few marketers take the time to ask salespeople anything. You may find yourself with a friend for life.) Ask salespeople the following questions:

✔ What closed the sale?

✔ What benefits/features are most attractive?

✔ What makes prospects sweat?

✔ What do prospects hope for?

✔ What are the biggest sticking points and the major obstacles to purchasing?

✔ What do prospects/customers say about the competition?

✔ What features or improvements are customers asking for?

✔ If customers are "converts" from a previous competitor's product or service, why did they switch?

✔ When they don't buy, why not?

Meeting with service representatives

It always pays to talk to people in the front lines of customer contact. In service industries, these are, naturally, people who serve: waiters, doctors, teachers, accountants, car washers, and so on. On the product side, they can include repair people, help-desk operators, installers, customer service line operators, and others. See whether you can have some face time with service representatives; if not, perhaps you can arrange (with their supervisor's support and cooperation) a time when you can call and ask questions.

Although they may not have as much contact with prospects as salespeople do, service representatives (and providers) often have in-depth experience with customers. Pull up a chair and a cup of coffee and *listen*. Ask them the following questions:

✔ Does the product/service live up to customer expectations?

✔ What causes the most complaints?

✔ What creates the most satisfaction?

✔ Are there common themes in the complaints or the stories of satisfaction?

✔ What do customers like/dislike about the product/service?

✔ What changes have customers asked for?

When you talk to people at service desks or hotlines, just keep in mind that, by definition, they mostly hear complaints, not praise. Few people phone a company to rave about its service. Listen carefully, but remember that they often see only one side of the picture.

On the other hand, some companies actually do receive thank-you notes and letters of appreciation from customers for their product or service. Always ask if the customers have given permission to use their words in marketing or promotional materials, because their statements can come in handy. If the company regularly receives compliments, there may be an opportunity to systematically collect testimonials (with permissions) and, in the case of complex service businesses, to write case studies to support other marketing materials, such as Web sites. (See "Collecting testimonials from customers," later in this chapter, for more. For case studies, see Chapter 13.)

Coming Up with Brilliant Ideas

Ernest Hemingway once called the blank page "the white bull." Although writing is rarely as hazardous as bullfighting, it can seem as intimidating, especially when you feel short on ideas.

Allow me to be your picador. I can't fill the page for you, but I can help you master the bull.

Walking in your customers' shoes

Have you ever participated in a structured relaxation exercise? The kind in which a leader, with a soothing, steady voice, encourages you to take off your shoes and close your eyes while she creates an aural tableau of cool streams, flower-scented breezes, and a dappled forest floor of sun and shade? Ahhh. . . .

If you have, then you've experienced the power of the sensual imagination. By using your mind to activate your senses, you constructed an imaginary environment that created a context for relaxation. It doesn't matter that the landscape you imagine isn't real. To the degree that your imagination is engaged, the exercise is effective.

Instead of using this exercise to relax (you have work to do, after all), you can use it to help you see your product or service through your customers' eyes. One of the most powerful exercises you can do is take a walk in your customers' shoes — to imagine yourself as that person at the crossroads of making a purchasing decision. Be vigorously concrete and put all your senses into play. In your imagination, see the mall, smell the fast food, hear the background music or chatter. Make a physical world for your imaginary customers. Then add the emotional context and try to feel what your customers may feel: Are they harried? Stressed? Is this purchase one that brings excitement, such as buying a car, or one that brings anxiety, such as buying insurance? Imagine what it would be like to purchase your product, including all the obstacles or hassles that may be in the way. Imagine what your customers want, feel, fear, or hope for.

Sounds silly, perhaps? Many marketers would agree with you. Obviously they've never really put themselves in their customers' shoes. Because, for instance, if a hospital's marketers had "taken the walk," they would've realized that the last thing a worried patient wants to see when visiting a hospital

Web site for the first time is a message from the president. Sports entrepreneurs would've understood that football fans genuinely love the sport and won't accept gratuitous violence and half-naked cheerleaders as a substitute for exceptional athleticism. And maybe some otherwise well-intended business-to-business marketers would've known that executives are really busy and aren't interested in reading yet another white paper, unless it's germane to projects they're working on right now.

But you will be different. You'll understand what it feels like to flip through your catalog. You'll know that when customers see earrings they like, they want to know if the posts are stainless steel, because they're allergic to silver. And you'll know to include that information in your copy. You'll understand customers' frustration when they have a computer problem and aren't able to explain the problem in the technical language of the so-called support expert. And you'll know to write your copy in layman's language.

See and feel from your customers' point of view and then incorporate that understanding into your message and into your copy.

Why not become a customer yourself? (Unless, of course, you run a one-person business, which would prove difficult.) Call the toll-free number, visit the showroom, check out the Web site, or place an order. Experience the entire process yourself. With this fresh perspective, you just may discover a deeper understanding of the customer's point of view and of your business.

Collecting testimonials from customers

You don't always have to imagine your customers' points of view; often, they tell you themselves. When they complain or find fault, they give your business or organization an opportunity to improve. When they offer praise, they not only lift morale, but they also give you material you can use in your copy, *if* you have permission to do so.

Testimonials, or endorsements, can give your copy the credibility that comes with authentic customer experience. To the power of testimonials, you need to perform a few simple tasks:

- ✔ **Ask for them:** Yes, it can be that simple. When you know a customer is pleased, ask for his endorsement. In larger organizations, implement a policy in which customer service people make the request.

- ✔ **Get permissions:** In order to use an endorsement in marketing materials, you must have written permission first. Create a form (with the help of your lawyer or legal team, if necessary) for your customers to sign that authorizes you to use their endorsements and their names.

> ✔ **Keep them handy:** Gather permissions, quotes, and friendly letters, and put them all in one handy place — a file cabinet or a computer folder where a copywriter can get to them. You want them easily accessible when inspiration strikes, or when it doesn't and you want a gentle push.

Thinking in analogies

A friend of mine is the marketing director of a large printing company that can handle every aspect of a direct mailing campaign, from list management (getting names and addresses) to fulfillment (completing the orders). His dilemma: How could he turn his company's far-reaching capabilities into a simple, cogent message? How could he communicate the value of what his company does without falling into a quagmire of complex technical jargon?

His answer was to use an *analogy* (a comparison of similar things). In essence, an analogy says one thing "is like" another. By saying to the reader that a complex, unfamiliar thing is like a simple, familiar thing, you make the first thing much easier to understand.

In thinking about an analogy, my friend decided that his company is like one-stop shopping. However, that was a familiar idea that had already been exhausted by his competitors. Then he thought about the benefit of using his company — that it makes his customers' lives easier. He realized that using his company is like removing one more task off a busy person's to-do list. That analogy became the foundation of his campaign. The headline on his postcard read, "Want a shorter to-do list, Jonathan?" (He used digital printing to personalize the name on each card — very smart.) On the back, the card explained that the company had all the services and expertise the prospect needed for a successful string of focused marketing messages.

You can use the power of "is like" to find ideas that you can place at the heart of your marketing messages. Tell your readers how an important feature, benefit, or quality is like something they value, and then expand upon the analogy in your copy. Your objective is to compare your product (which may not be very familiar to your prospects) in a favorable way to an object or phenomenon that prospects are likely to know and understand. When the comparison is apt, the analogy lifts your business from the unknown into the safer, more comfortable territory of the known and appreciated. For example:

> ✔ Your delivery and errand service is like having a personal assistant. In this copy, speak to the convenience and ease of having a helping hand. You needn't put "is like" in the copy, either. The headline could say this:
>
> *Wanda's Wanderers — Personal Assistants for Busy Professionals Like You.*

> ✔ Your collapsible, adjustable wrench is like having a pocket tool kit. In this copy, speak to the value of carrying a portable "tool kit" in a pocket, purse, or glove compartment. Your copy may include this line:
>
> *It's a portable tool kit that fits in your pocket!*

Flipping an idea on its head

Try as you may, it happens: You just can't think of anything new or fresh to say about your product, business, or organization. When that happens, try this trick: Do a 180 degree turn and look at your offer from a perspective opposite the one you're accustomed to.

For example, instead of talking about the benefit of using your product or service, talk about the danger of *not* using it, with copy that explores the negative consequences of not making the response you request. Take a teeth-whitening product, for example:

✔ **Straight approach:** Show a model with perfect, white teeth and talk about how your product does the same for your customers.

✔ **Flipped approach:** Show a sad person without a smile, with copy that talks about how awful it is to be self-conscious about yellow teeth:

   Afraid to flash your not-so-ivories? It's time for DentaBrights. . . .

Or instead of talking about a fear your product overcomes, talk about the pleasure of successfully overcoming the fear. Your copy would extol the virtues (such as safety, confidence, convenience, among many other possibilities) that come when customers buy your product or service. Here's how that approach may work with disability insurance:

✔ **Straight approach:** Talk about the hazards of injury and loss of income:

   One broken bone could leave you just plain broke.

✔ **Flipped approach:** Talk about the comfort of knowing you're covered:

   My insurance has me covered, so I can concentrate on recovery.

Part II

Direct Response
Writing That
Makes the Sale

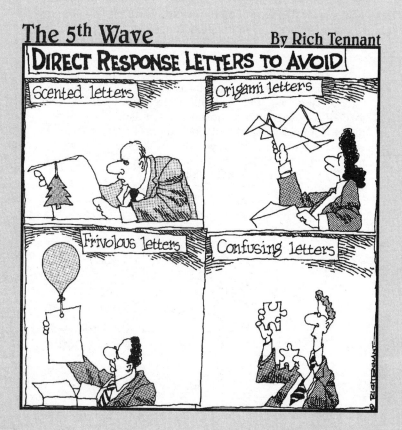

The 5th Wave   By Rich Tennant

DIRECT RESPONSE LETTERS TO AVOID

Scented letters

Origami letters

Frivolous letters

Confusing letters

In this part . . .

They say actions speak louder than words. But do "they" know that speaking the right words can lead to action? That's what this part of the book is all about: going directly to your prospects to motivate action — an order, a sale, a response.

Here, you discover ways to turn ordinary letters, brochures, postcards, e-mails, and more into some of your most productive, and cost-effective, sales representatives. No other form of copywriting is as powerful — or as exciting — as direct response writing! And after you master the essentials of direct response writing, you'll be well on your way to improving your skills in all other areas of copywriting, from brand advertising to public relations.

Chapter 4

Working with the Power of Direct Response

. . . .

In This Chapter

▶ Understanding the main characteristics of direct response

▶ Examining different direct response choices

▶ Applying the key ingredients to direct response copy

▶ Testing your work to find out what's effective

. . . .

*W*hy tell when you can sell? That's the essential premise of direct response marketing. As opposed to other forms of marketing communications that create brand identities or simply convey information, direct response writing carries a greater burden: It has to inspire action, bona fide responses from prospects. Whether your message is embedded in a letter, an e-mail, a radio spot, or another medium, all direct response marketing methods make an immediate appeal that asks prospects to *do something* to *get something*.

That's a lot of responsibility, but it's also an exciting opportunity. With direct response methods, your words become virtual salespeople, generating the sales that increase revenues and profits. No other kind of marketing writing operates under as much pressure — and not one is as rewarding, either.

I want to introduce you to direct response as soon as possible for one reason: When you learn to use language to land a sale, every other marketing writing project you tackle will be easier, more effective, and more productive. You'll have a foundation of real marketing street smarts and a talent honed by a deeper understanding of what moves prospects out of apathy and into action.

The great ad man David Ogilvy called direct response his "secret weapon" for success. Now you can uncover the secrets and use this weapon yourself.

Ready, Aim, Sell: The Important Traits of Direct Response

Three characteristics distinguish direct response advertising from its more familiar cousin, brand or awareness advertising (covered in Chapter 10). Although the latter strives to create favorable impressions the advertiser hopes you remember — a brand identity — all direct response advertising makes appeals to specially targeted audiences, is crafted to inspire action or a response, and can be precisely measured to determine its effectiveness.

Targeting your audience

Instead of making communications that impress a message on as many eyeballs as possible, direct response marketers do everything they can to limit their efforts (and direct their marketing dollars) to the prospects most likely to be interested in their offers.

In mediums that deliver the same messages to many people simultaneously, such as newspaper ads or radio spots, direct marketers lose precise control over who receives their messages. Although they can't target individuals, marketers can target groups by selecting media that reach the kind of market they want. They may place an ad for an estate planning workshop in *Modern Maturity,* for example, or an offer for an electronic games network on an alternative-format radio station. Marketers can collect audience information — including age, income, sex, interests, and other variables — from the publishers or broadcasters selling advertising space or time.

With mail and e-mail marketing, however, marketers can target individuals — real, live, distinct persons rather than aggregate groups. The group of individuals targeted in a direct mail campaign, with their relevant contact information (the complete address), is called the *list.* Short of sending a salesperson to Joe Blow's door, you can't get more direct in your aim than by sending him a message with his name on it.

The list, or audience, is the single most important element of a targeted direct response campaign. In descending order of impact, these are the factors that have the greatest influence on response (meaning people taking action after receiving your message): list, offer, format, copy.

Creating the list

The list consists of the people your messages go to. These lists are compiled from sources such as subscription information, warranty card returns, and voluntary contributions of contact information on Web site registration forms. Often, the raw name-and-address data is supplemented with lifestyle and interest information to create more definable lists, such as "Rhode Island residents with country club memberships and three or more cars."

Keep in mind that lists have the greatest impact on success. A weak message to the right audience has a far greater chance of success than a beautifully designed, brilliantly written message to the wrong people. If you have limited resources and must make tough decisions on where and how to spend your marketing dollars in a direct response campaign, concentrate on the list.

Lists need not be complicated. And their value is so great that building one is worth the extra effort. For many small businesses or independent professionals, the most effective list is one made of current customers who have given you permission to communicate to them. The secret to building a list is to offer customers something meaningful — to them — in exchange for their contact information. Here are a few proven winners:

- ✔ **Newsletters:** A newsletter is nothing more than a compilation of information that your audience values and is distributed on a regular basis. (See Chapter 9 for information on e-newsletters and Chapter 13 for the scoop on print newsletters.) An accountant, for example, may want to create a newsletter of business tips that encourages his customers to take action — that is, use his services — all year rather than just around tax time. Successful newsletter topics include cars, pets, wine, dolls, hobbies, crafts, books, floral arranging, finances, and health. The essential point is to speak to those customer enthusiasms and interests that are directly related to, and reflect favorably upon, your business.

- ✔ **Clubs:** Mortgages and rents run 24/7, even if your business runs the usual business hours. If you have retail space, you may want to think about opening during off-hours for special interest groups or clubs related to your business, such as book discussion groups for bookstores, weight-loss clubs for health-food stores, or how-to workshops for hardware stores. These clubs help you build loyalty and create opportunities for increasing sales. And the addresses you collect to send out announcements for upcoming meetings can become a list you can use for sending out additional marketing materials.

- ✔ **Coupons, discounts, and special offers:** The simplest approach is to collect names and addresses on the promise of exclusive access to coupons, discounts, sales, and special offers. Again, you're building bonds with your best, repeat customers.

Larger businesses with greater reach need more complex lists; for these, turn to professional list brokers, whose sole responsibility is to help clients identify, buy, and manage the most optimal lists possible for their needs.

Making the offer

The second most important variable in generating response is the offer, a promise that when your prospect takes action — calls a phone number, makes an order online, or talks to your sales staff —she gets something of value, such as free shipping, an early-bird discount, or a free whatnot. The offer is the reason why a prospect should respond: The stronger the reason, the greater the likelihood of a response.

Inviting prospects to contact you for more information is not an offer; it's an abdication of responsibility. If you're not prepared to make an offer, don't use direct response to market your business. (For ideas on creative ways to come up with offers for direct mail, see Chapter 7.)

As a copywriter within a larger organization, you may not have any say about the offer; it's usually just handed to you with the understanding that you have to do the best you can with it. When the offer is strong, such as a substantial discount, your job is easy: You proclaim the discount. But when the offer is soft or weak, such as an offer for a *white paper* (an executive "report" on a given topic or issue), you may have to dig deep to uncover the benefit of the offer and then sell the benefit. If I had to offer a report on Internet security, for example, instead of merely asking prospects to call for a security report, I might entice them with a question, "Do you know how to block the 5 most dangerous Internet viruses in the world?" Then I'd assure them that they can get the answer — by accepting the offer and taking action today.

Selecting the format

The third most important variable is the format — the physical shape, nature, or quality of your message. In direct mail, the format may be as simple as a postcard or as elaborate as a boxed gift (a dimensional with a premium, which you can read more about in Chapter 7). In print advertising, the primary format issue is size; in broadcast advertising, it's length of time. Format issues are a numbers game. It's about the amount of money you're willing to spend and the careful balancing of expense versus returns; you must justify the format's expense by the increase in response, revenue, or profits. (For more about direct mail format options, see Chapters 5 and 6 for letters and brochures; Chapter 7 on additional direct response package elements; and Chapter 8 for stand-alone items, including postcards and self-mailers.)

When you're writing for your own business, you can select your own format options based on strategy, budget, and expectations. When you work for a larger organization, you may not be the one making these decisions. Instead, you simply need to understand what you're working with so you can tailor your copy to the format.

Writing the copy

The words themselves are at the bottom of the response-impact list. Take heart — I'm not saying copy isn't important. On the contrary, because copy is the easiest variable to manipulate, it represents the least expensive means available for improving your marketing. Lists, offers, and formats can be expensive. But if you can double your response rate (or even improve it by as little as 10 percent) through copy alone, you have an extraordinarily cheap way of making your business stronger.

This entire book is dedicated, of course, to helping ordinary people use their good sense to write extraordinary copy; you find suggestions for improving your word power in every chapter. But even the top two variables in this section — list and offer — give you important clues for writing better copy.

- ✔ **Focus on the *who*:** Because your audience is of such paramount importance, it makes sense to write the way the audience speaks. Whether you're writing for banker or bikers, you should talk their talk.

- ✔ **Hone your offers:** Spend time making the offer as prominent and persuasive as possible by focusing on its benefit to the customer. (To learn about benefits, see Chapter 2.)

Inspiring action

The second distinctive characteristic of direct response marketing is that it provides a means for making the sale in the here and now. Through toll-free numbers, interactive Web sites, and postage-paid reply devices, prospects are encouraged to take action and buy now.

This buy-it-now quality is the most distinctive quality of direct response. Every aspect of a direct campaign — from list selection to creating offers, from choosing formats and design to writing copy — is intended to do one thing: increase response. (Or, in some cases, the goal is to increase the quality of the response by generating a larger order size or attracting a more qualified prospect for long-term business value.) Brand or awareness advertisers attempt to create a set of ideas or emotions (a *brand identity*) they hope you remember when you're ready to walk into a store and buy. But direct response advertisers don't give two hoots and a handshake about what someone may remember: They want to motivate action, now.

In subsequent chapters, I show you how specific copy elements help you create the smoothest and least interrupted path to the final sale as possible. For now, just keep in mind that direct response isn't about ideas — it's about action.

Measuring effectiveness

You may be familiar with an old joke about awareness advertising (you know, like the ads you see on TV for toilet paper or antacids) that has been attributed to a half-dozen different business leaders: "I know that 50 percent of my advertising doesn't work; I just don't know which 50 percent!" That's because directly attributing the sale of a roll of toilet paper or a bottle of antacids to any one ad or commercial is impossible. Something the company said or did *may* have helped spur the sale, but despite the best efforts of market researchers and MBAs, no one knows for sure.

Direct response advertising is different from awareness advertising. You can know what works and what doesn't. Direct's second characteristic (its drive toward action) is responsible for its third: Its effectiveness is measurable — not kinda, sorta measurable, but scientifically, objectively, and absolutely measurable, down to the last dime.

Suppose you send out a thousand letters with postage-paid reply cards and get 20 cards back requesting your widget. Simple math says you got a 2 percent response rate. Now add up the sum of the total sales and subtract the total cost of your mailing (list fees, creative charges, production costs, postage, and so on). The difference is the money made — or lost, if the campaign costs exceeded revenues. You can even divide the total cost of the program by the number of sales made and arrive at your program's cost per sale.

As you probably have figured out by now, you can get even more sophisticated and run the numbers inside, outside, and upside down to give you even more information about costs, value, revenues, and profits. But in the end, one point remains constant: Action is measurable, and these measures give your business or organization meaningful information on which to base future business decisions.

Check out "Is It Working? Testing Direct Response Writing" later in this chapter for the scoop on how to actually test your copy.

Scanning the Methods: A Brief Survey of Direct Response Options

Following is a summary of some of the most common forms of direct response tools, with references to the chapters where you find extensive advice and help.

Examining direct mail

The granddaddy of all direct marketing is direct mail, the stuff that arrives in your mailbox from people you don't know, selling stuff you didn't ask for. This kind of unsolicited mail is also known as *junk mail,* and according to the mass media, you're all supposed to hate it. But consider these facts:

- **Direct mail works.** It's an incredibly powerful, measurable, and relatively inexpensive way of generating sales or business leads. The reason you receive so much of this mail is because it's effective.

✔ **It isn't "junk" if it matches your interests.** Yes, I can live without the umpteenth credit card solicitation that I'm sure is waiting for me today. But I actually appreciate the mail related to my hobbies and interests. I didn't ask for the catalog of books on homemade stills (and iron furnaces and backyard PVC cannons), but I sure enjoy getting it. (And no, Mr. Gummint Revnyoo Agent, I don't have a still in my basement. Honest.)

✔ **Bitter words are often fermented from sour grapes:** Next time you see an antimail piece on television or read one in your paper, consider this: Those pieces are courtesy of competitors who understand that every marketing dollar spent on direct mail is a dollar denied their station or newspaper. Worse, there's more than a whiff of hypocrisy in these diatribes: Many of the same media outlets that whine about direct mail and direct response advertising use these very same techniques to sell subscriptions, ad space or time, and other related products or services.

✔ **It subsidizes the regular mail:** You may think that first-class mail is too expensive as it is, but would you prefer to pay a dollar or more for the same stamp? You'd have to — if the post office didn't have direct mail to deliver.

Dollar for dollar, direct mail represents an outstanding marketing option for many organizations, but especially for small to mid-sized businesses that require the maximum return for their marketing budgets. One of the most productive tools for generating sales or leads (for follow-up by salespeople) is the classic direct mail package that includes the following pieces:

✔ **An outer envelope with a "teaser":** See Chapter 7 for information on writing teasers that get envelopes opened.

✔ **A letter:** The most important part of the package, the letter is an opportunity to tell a one-on-one story to your prospect. Chapter 5 shows you how.

✔ **A brochure:** The brochure supports your letter by virtually placing the product or service in the prospects' hands with vivid, concrete details. I walk you through, step by step, in Chapter 6.

✔ **A reply device:** You discover the most effective ways of writing reply devices — the things customers return to accept your offers — in Chapter 7.

And as many direct response ads often say, "But wait, there's more!" In addition to the classic package I've described, you may want to consider postcards or self-mailers (featured in Chapter 8), big "gift" packages called dimensionals (Chapter 7), or the addition of other elements to your packages, such as lift notes and teasers (see Chapter 7).

Considering print advertising

Most ads in newspapers and magazines are brand or awareness ads intended to grab a piece of your memory or draw you to a retail store. Direct response ads, by contrast, make an offer that you're asked to reply to immediately, usually by phone, but now often via the Web as well. You can find more about writing ads in Chapter 11, but for now, I want to draw your attention to two things that usually distinguish the direct ad from its branding cousin:

- ✔ **They're chock-full of benefits and features:** Direct ads sometimes look unsophisticated because they're usually short on snazzy graphics. But they tend to be loaded with benefits and features, lovingly detailed in paragraphs of copy. I call it the cornucopia effect: an overwhelming impression of abundance that can be obtained for oh so little.

- ✔ **They're long on copy:** Ad copy is supposed to be short and sweet, right? Not necessarily. In fact, direct ads tend to be long in order to accommodate all the benefits and features that drive response. If you think these direct guys are just doing it all wrong, remember this: When you see a direct response ad (one that requests immediate action) more than once, you know its results have been measured, and you should suspect that the ad has been tested against alternative copy options. That long copy is there because *it works.*

Direct response print ads don't have the one-to-one targeting power of direct mail addressed to specific recipients. But in exchange for the loss of precision, you gain breadth. In one stroke, you hit a larger audience. The key is to identify the most effective periodicals for ads — the ones most likely to be read by people who are most likely to become your customers. (See Chapter 11 for more information about ad placement.)

Broadcasting your message

Even the airwaves carry direct response marketing. On radio, these are the ads that ask you to call now for the best prices on car insurance. On television, these are the ads you're most likely to make fun of — you know, for knife sets that cut tin cans and watermelons, 6-week "miracle" exercise equipment, and 12-in-1 kitchen gadgets. They all promise amazing products at a ridiculously low price and then promise even more products for an even better price . . . *if you call now!*

Direct response television requires production budgets and in-bound telemarketing capabilities (people to answer the phone and take the orders) that are beyond the scope of this book. But you can find suggestions for radio advertising in Chapter 11. When you don't have lists of names and addresses you can use for direct mail, and you have an offer you can clearly and passionately articulate within 30 seconds, direct response radio may be a cost-effective option for generating business. (Be sure that you run your spots on stations — and at time slots — that reach your desired audience.)

Using Web sites and e-mail

Web sites and e-mail have added new wrinkles to old direct response formulas. While interactivity may be overhyped as a virtue, you can't deny the advantages of electronic media:

- ✔ **Speed and value:** As opposed to ordinary mail, e-mail can be distributed in a flash — and without postage, either. Web sites aren't quite as inexpensive as entrepreneurs had hoped, but from the customer's perspective, nothing rivals the Internet for fast and far-reaching comparison shopping.

- ✔ **Hyperlinks:** With the power of hyperlinks, prospects can virtually tailor communications to their own needs. Hyperlinks let writers shift much of the messaging burden out of e-mails (which can focus on hard-hitting offers) and provide a convenient way of delivering in-depth info in a Web site without clogging the primary pages with excess information.

- ✔ **Data collection:** Direct marketers love data. With the right computer systems in place, marketers can capture all kinds of information from site visitors and e-mail readers, thus providing important insights on customer behavior.

You can find detailed information about writing e-mails in Chapter 9 and about Web sites in Chapter 14.

Cooking Up the Crucial Ingredients to Direct Response Writing

In subsequent chapters, I go into the exhaustive (yet not exhausting, I hope) details that help you craft successful, cash-accumulating, business-building mail, ads, e-mails, Web sites, and more.

But before I guide you into the recipes for each individual medium, I want to explore a few of the common copy ingredients for effective direct response marketing, regardless of medium.

Serving the offer fast and often

It seems so obvious and basic that you can't imagine anyone would fail to do this (especially large advertisers with multimillion-dollar budgets), but I have to say it upfront because writers frequently (and regretfully) neglect this point: Present your offer — the thing you're selling and the terms you're making — as soon as possible. After you say it once, say it again. And again.

In so many ways, good copywriting is like storytelling. You create drama by showing readers how, with the power of your product or service, they can "heroically" achieve their desires or conquer their fears. But in one very important way, direct response copy is not like a story because (and I want you to remember this, even if you have to tattoo it into your palm) you give away the end at the beginning. Even when you have a lot to say about your product, you bring the conclusion — your offer — into the story right away and then backfill additional persuasive material as you move along.

I tell you the particulars when I show you each medium and method in the chapters to come. But it's worth thinking about this concept correctly from the start. You can think of this one idea in two different yet complementary formulas.

The grabbing-the-brass-ring formula

This is the rough sketch of a copy strategy when you're making an offer for something desirable, such as beautiful jewelry, delicious mail-order mangoes, or a package vacation to the Bahamas:

1. **Show readers the vision.**

   Within the headline or opening copy, tell the reader about the benefit: looking good, eating well, or enjoying a wonderful vacation.

2. **Offer the "ring."**

   Either within the same headline or within the first few lines of copy, introduce your offer as the means for obtaining the desirable end: the jewelry that makes you look good, the tasty and healthy mangoes, or the relaxing everything-included vacation plan.

3. **Go on the quest.**

   Show the reader how and why your offer, in Step 2, fulfills the desire created in Step 1. And be sure to restate the offer along the way.

The overcoming-pain-and-fear formula

As the Buddha said (I'm paraphrasing), the flip side of desire is fear. This is the formula for benefits that help you overcome things you don't want, such as high taxes, ill health, and dirty clothes:

1. **Make readers hurt.**

   Describe the pain to be avoided: the taxes, disease, and dirt.

2. **Show readers the cure.**

   Introduce your offer — the tax counseling, vitamins, or laundry detergent — as the "cure" that helps the prospect overcome the pain.

3. **Prove it works.**

   In the rest of the copy, show the reader how and why your offer, in Step 2, overcomes the pain described in Step 1. And oh yeah, restate the offer a few times along the way. (Have I said that before? You bet — because I want you to remember it. And that's why I want you to repeat your offers.)

Setting out carrots and sticks

In a spy novel I once read but whose title I can't remember (perhaps the author should've restated it throughout the book), a malevolent spymaster tutors his protégé on the art of manipulation with the following advice: A moral man may be able to resist bribery, and a brave man may be able to endure pain, but it is a rare man who resists your will when there's an immediate reward for obeying it and an impending punishment for resisting.

Gosh, if the evil spymaster were to ever forgo international intrigue, he'd make an excellent direct marketer! Why? Because he understood the power of carrots and sticks. One of the most powerful ways to generate response is to set out reasons why responding to your offer brings wonderful benefits (the carrots) *and* why not responding sustains or even increases pain (the sticks).

Whenever you can, set up carrot-and-stick offers. Tell your readers all the good things that come by responding to your offer, and suggest the bad things that may occur (or remain the same) by not responding.

Writing carrots and sticks simply means articulating the favorable consequences of accepting your offer and the undesirable consequences of doing nothing. Here are a couple examples:

- ✔ **Weight-loss plan:** Your offer is a video, book, and workbook package that helps people lose weight permanently.

  - **Carrot:** Buy into the plan, lose weight, and keep it off.

  - **Stick:** Don't buy the plan and stay trapped in yo-yo dieting that doesn't work.

✔ **Market trends analysis reports:** You offer businesses a subscription to a service that monitors market trends across the country and in the business's specific service regions.

- **Carrot:** The reports help executives plan and execute market-sensitive business plans.

- **Stick:** You may not use this service, but your competitors do (or will) and they'll beat you to the punch.

Is It Working? Testing Direct Response Writing

In itself, measurability is a wonderful thing, but it leads to something even more wondrous: testing, the ability to manipulate various aspects of your direct response campaign to identify options that increase response, revenues, and/or profits.

The essence of marketing testing is exactly the same as it is in science: You compare two or more units (in our case, copy) in which everything remains the same except one thing: the variable you manipulate for your test. That way, you can be sure that your variable — whether it's a different list, offer, headline, or more — is truly the element responsible for the change in results.

I suggest a simple, three-step process to basic copy testing:

1. **Choose your variable.**

   In the next section, I show you some of the most popular elements you can test in copy. Whatever you choose, be sure to select just one thing at a time.

2. **Split your groups.**

   When you run a print ad in a newspaper or magazine, you can request an "A/B Test" that divides the final output into two groups: the control ad that serves as a baseline for measurement and a test run that's almost the same, except for the variable (a different headline, a different offer) that you choose. In mail, a similar principle applies, except that one list receives the control; the other, the test.

3. **Create a means of distinguishing the responses.**

   You may be wondering how you can determine whether the source of your response is from the control or from the test. Excellent question! You need to alter the response mechanism in some way that indicates the source. In e-mail campaigns, for example, you can alter the response hyperlink so that control and test responses go to separate inboxes or separate Web pages. In print ads and mail, you can use different phone numbers, or you can ask people to request different employees, say, Brian for the control group or Jill for the test (those aren't the employees' real names, of course). (Big organizations print something called *key codes* on their catalogs and mailings; now you know why the service rep asks for your key code when you place your order.) Whatever way you segregate your response, be sure that whoever's responsible for receiving them maintains a running count you can review and use.

Testing your concepts

Concepts are the ideas behind the words, such as a 50 percent sale or an emphasis on the delicious flavor of your strawberries. When you want to maximize your impact, you test those elements that have the greatest impact on response. In copy, those elements are the benefit and the offer.

The following elements are the most fruitful concepts to test, the ones that have the greatest effect on results. Your selection of what to test depends on what's available to you. If you have only one offer to make, for example, you would want to test a benefit against your offer. If your offer is weak, you may try testing various benefits against each other to determine which is most attractive. Here are the basic choices:

- ✔ **Offer versus offer:** What's more attractive — offering free shipping or a 15 percent discount on orders over $100? Note the subtle possibilities here: The over $100 offer may actually lower response yet increase profitability by encouraging higher sales per order. Testing is the way to find out. Because offers are second only to the list (the people your message goes to) in their impact on response, most copy testing should start with the offer itself. Here's an example of an offer test:

  Get 25% off your next order of Furniture Wizard.

  Or

  Get free shipping when you order Furniture Wizard today.

- ✔ **Benefit versus benefit:** Many products and services have multiple benefits; testing may be the best way of knowing which benefit has the greatest appeal and attracts the most results. For example, consider these two benefits for an upholstery repair kit, one of which emphasizes savings and simplicity; the other, an opportunity to find treasure:

  Now there's a fast and easy way to repair your precious furniture — for just the price of the spare change you can find under the cushions!

  Or

  Turn yard sale "trash" into living room treasure with the Furniture Wizard upholstery repair kit.

> ✔ **Benefit versus offer:** Not sure whether your offer or your most attractive benefit is more compelling? Test them against each other. The marketer for the repair kit may want to increase sales by testing an offer against one of the preceding benefits:
>
> *Save $10 off the retail price when you order the Furniture Wizard by phone, today!*

Choosing the best places to test

Simplicity is one key to good testing. In direct response copy, which can be as brief as a Web site banner ad or as long as a four-page (or more) letter, changing all the copy is both impractical and undesirable. For the test to be meaningful, you just want to change a small part of the copy, and the parts that are most productive to test are, naturally, those that have the greatest impact on response. These are the places where you should apply the previous suggestions for copy testing:

> ✔ **Headlines:** In print ads, self-mailers (stand-alone mail packages without envelopes), and Web sites, the headline is the copy most likely to be read; testing, therefore, should begin here. (For general information on headlines, see Chapter 2.)
>
> ✔ **Johnson Box and postscripts:** After the envelope is opened, the parts of your letter most frequently read by prospects are the Johnson Box (the headline above the greeting) and the postscript (the "PS"). Manipulating these elements gives you the most bang for your testing buck. (See Chapter 5 for more on these items.)
>
> ✔ **Outer envelope teasers:** The brief lines of copy on the envelope of a letter or direct mail package, known as the *teaser,* serve the same function as the e-mail subject line: They help all the Hamlets out there who get your mail and wonder, "To dump or not to dump? That is the question." The right teaser gets more mail opened and read, so teasers are often the first copy tested in many coordinated direct mail campaigns. (For more information on teasers, see Chapter 7.)
>
> ✔ **Subject lines:** The most important part of a direct response e-mail is the subject line that appears in the recipient's inbox: This is the copy that determines whether your e-mail is read or deleted. Subject-line tests can help you identify copy that leads to greater rates of opened e-mail. (For more information on subject lines, see Chapter 9.)

Chapter 5

Writing Direct Response Letters That Win Business

*W*hen it comes to your business — what it is, what it does, and what it offers — you're a fountain of information. You know shapes, sizes, characteristics, and the hows and wherefores. You may even have a firm grip on features and benefits, and you're filled with enthusiasm for the special qualities of your product, a vital something none of your prospects should live without.

But you can't turn prospects into customers until you give that information *form* and shape it into a message. To make the sale, create the lead, raise the money, or inspire a visit to your store, you have to take your blocks of information and build them into a persuasive case that always reaches the same conclusion: Buy this. Call today. Take action now.

That's what the sales letter is all about. It's your opportunity to transform the raw material of fact into an irresistible call to action. Sure, other forms of communication can make a case for your business (and I cover many of them in this book). But even in the era of electronic communications, the letter retains a special power. It has the ability to create a bond between you and your prospect that no other medium can match.

Read on, and you'll have the power to generate some action of your own.

I'm talking about direct response letters, not correspondence. *Direct response letters* stimulate action (a purchase, an appointment, a visit to a Web site, and so on) among prospects or customers. Correspondence includes all the individually crafted letters you may compose in the course of everyday business, such as requests for proposals, commendations of employees, or memos to business partners; you can find help on writing business correspondence in books on general business writing.

Looking at the Common Characteristics of Successful Letters

Every day, you're bombarded with letters from a variety of sources who have little in common: a credit card company, your dentist, the local oil-change shop, a cancer charity, maybe your mom. They offer different things, and their stories range from pleas to promises, but if they're successful, they share many of the same characteristics and common elements that have proven themselves over time.

If your letter incorporates these characteristics, you can be confident that you're on the right track, even if the execution is wobbly in the details. But if your letter is lacking in any of these areas, even if it's as smoothly polished as lyric poetry, beware — you're not applying the power available to you, and you'll lose customers and sales.

They're personal, immediate, and involving

You can't get more direct than this — as soon as the recipient opens the envelope, you create an illusion: This is my message to *you*. Sure, no one will mistake your mail for a letter from a long lost friend, but still, your letter basks in the glow of intimacy — it's just you and me, kid.

The letter is not the place to boast about how long your company has been in business or to trumpet your commitment to excellence. Instead, the strong letter creates empathy. Through both content (what you say) and tone (how you say it), you tell the reader, "I understand you and your needs." By demonstrating that understanding, you build confidence and credibility.

Here's how:

✔ **You can use "you."** Yes, despite what your English teacher told you, you can and by all means should use the second person — "you." When you write, pretend that you're speaking confidently to someone you know, like, and trust. You're never lecturing. You're engaging in a helpful conversation in which the other person's voice isn't heard but is anticipated and valued.

✔ **Tell the readers what's in it for them.** Speak to the significant benefits for readers. You're not important; the readers are. They want to know, "What's in it for me?" Of course, you have an agenda — that's why you're writing. But you can't connect to your readers unless you write to their self-interests, not your own. For example, you say, "Save $15 when you order now," not "I need your order so I can grow my business."

✔ **Speak in the reader's language.** This isn't a time to show off your vocabulary. Your style and your choice of words should match your reader's style. A letter to information technology professionals should speak in their technical lingo; a letter to baseball fans should have the slang and punch of a sports column. You're entering the reader's turf: When in Rome, do as the Romans do. Writing to bankers? Then be prepared to talk about basis points and yield curves.

✔ **Be a mirror.** Ultimately, the best letters (and in fact, all the best marketing materials) aren't really about you, your business, or even its products and services — they're about your customers. Your letter should be a mirror. When prospects read it, let them see themselves: their hopes and fears, their values and dreams, and their best idea of who they are or would like to be. A subscription pitch to parents, for example, might begin, "You know how important it is to read to your children. And nothing pleases you more than the light in their eyes when . . ."

They're stories that don't end . . . until the reader takes action

You know how fairy tales work: Once upon a time there was a village or forest or kingdom. It's a great place, except for an evil spell, a horrible dragon, or a prince who desperately needs a princess. Then one day the hero gets a magic ring, finds the mystic sword, or discovers a sleeping beauty. The hero applies his ring, sword, or lips to the task, and — *voilà!* — everyone lives happily ever after.

Successful letters follow the emotional logic of fairy tales. You begin by establishing a pain to be resolved or a desire to be fulfilled, which is just another way of saying, "Once upon a time . . ." Once upon a time you had hair loss, but now with Men's Miracle Hair Cream . . . Once upon a time your customer service was weak, but now comes StatsVault Customer Relations Solutions . . . Once upon a time you paid too much in credit card interest charges, but with the Everest Card. . . .

Like the fairy tale, your story has complications and fascinating details that suspend disbelief. And you introduce a magic intercession, except that in the place of the ring, sword, or beauty, you offer your hair cream, customer relationship management (CRM) software, or low-interest credit card.

But the persuasive letter differs from the fairy tale in two important ways: the reader is the hero of the story, and the story can't have a happy ending until the reader takes action. You lose your hair until you buy the hair cream. You lose track of your customers until you get the software. You lose too much money in interest until you're approved for the new card. In sum: You lose until you take action and win.

They make a powerful case, point by point

Here's the one broad, far-reaching generalization I stand behind: Broad, far-reaching generalizations generally stink. Why? Because you can't build credibility with puffery, boasting, self-flattery, and large, vague abstractions.

You *can* build credibility with facts and evidence, and the more specific the facts and evidence, the more believable they are. I call these specific facts or evidence *proof points* because they give the reader tangible, meaty proof to substantiate your promises or claims.

See for yourself. Which statement in each of the following examples is more compelling?

> *Men's Miracle Hair Cream is the best hair-growth product on the market today.*
> **or**
> *Independent laboratory tests show that Men's Miracle Hair Cream increases hair-growth by an average of 36% in just two weeks, beating the nearest competitor by more than 20 percentage points.*

> *StatsVault Customer Relations Solutions help you save money.*
> **or**
> *According to Pigeon Networks COO Melissa Coffee, "Since we deployed StatsVault six months ago, we've cut our customer churn rate in half and increased our per-customer revenues by 32%."*

The Everest Card is the low-interest card.
or
The Everest Card gives you a guaranteed fixed 8.5% APR, NO annual fees, and NO extra charges for cash advances.

So how can you get *your* point across to your prospects? You have three solid options:

- **Hard numbers:** Putting hard numbers on your statements lends an aura of objective scientific fact to your arguments. "Save $50" beats "Save money." In addition, the more precise the number — saying "51.7%" rather than "more than 50%" — the more credible your statistic. (For more information on hard numbers, see the section "Developing the middle of the letter," later in this chapter.)

- **Testimonials and anecdotes:** People believe people who are like themselves. In this case, that refers to other prospects who became customers. Direct quotes from your customers or anecdotes that illustrate real-world success go a long way toward establishing trust. (For more information on testimonials, see the section "Developing the middle of the letter," later in this chapter.)

- **Reasons why:** You want to distinguish your claims from those made by your competitors. Give your reader reasons why your product and service can really deliver on your promises. Perhaps the hair cream has a special ingredient, oxynol psuedominide, that was found in the follicles of especially hairy chimps and then proven to grow hair on humans. Perhaps your CRM software is backed with proprietary data integration coding that no other CRM software has. And maybe the Everest Card can maintain such a low rate of interest because it's offered exclusively to finance-savvy credit customers who have established a clean credit record for at least five years. Unique features, experience, research, and special strategies can be among the reasons why your offer deserves immediate attention.

They tell the reader exactly what to do

A good letter casts a spell — it heightens interest, stimulates desire, and, when the magic works properly, inspires action. After all that hard work, don't break the spell by forcing the prospect to stop and think about what he's supposed to do. A hesitant prospect is a lost customer.

Successful letters leave nothing to chance and tell the prospect exactly what to do in order to buy the product, get the premium, start the subscription, or end world hunger. Tell readers what they can expect when they take action, and tell them precisely what action to take. Here are some examples:

Check the "Yes, I want hair!" box on the enclosed card and return it to me, in the postage-paid envelope, by March 30 to receive your free sample of Men's Miracle Hair Cream.

Participate in the free Customer Relations online seminar by calling us toll-free at 1-800-123-4567 or registering online at www.statsvault.com.

Complete and return the enclosed application to apply for the Everest Card and reduce your credit card interest rate today.

Tinkering with the Nuts and Bolts of Your Letter

In addition to considering the story within your letter, you need to think about a few mechanical issues such as length, format, and overall look. Properly executed, your mechanical choices help make your material easier to read; proceed carelessly, however, and you may undermine your impact by discouraging prospects and losing their attention.

The long and short of it: Determining letter length

Few copywriting issues are as contentious, or as misunderstood, as the issue of length. Most of the time you're probably tempted to keep your letters short, reasoning that attention spans are also short, and you don't want to frustrate your readers and lose business.

If that's been your belief, then the following fact may surprise you: In test after test, longer copy almost always generates more response or more sales than short copy. How can that be? Consider the psychology. If you or your marketing colleagues have done the homework correctly, the people you're mailing to should be an audience that can be reasonably expected to have an interest in what you sell. For example, you might send a letter offering a golf magazine to a list of country club members. (For more information on preparing a direct mail list, see Chapter 7.) If you're wrong, your copy can never be short enough. But the people who *are* interested demand complete information — everything they need to make a decision that makes them feel good about themselves.

That's why many successful letters are as long as three or four pages. Ultimately, you must base the decision about length on a careful cost/benefit analysis: Shorter letters are cheaper to produce, but the expense of a longer letter is justified when it produces results that exceed the additional expense. (That's another reason why testing is so important. For more, see Chapter 4.)

Here are some general guidelines on letter length:

- ✔ **Consider going long** when the letter you're writing is directly asking for the sale, right then and there. In this case, your letter is a stand-in for a living salesperson and needs to make all the arguments and press all the emotional hot buttons that a salesperson makes on the way to closing a sale. For this reason, among others, subscription letters and fundraising appeals often run from two to four pages long.

- ✔ **Consider going short** when you're asking the prospect to take an intermediary step — such as visiting a Web site, requesting a sample, or calling for an appointment — instead of consummating a complete sale. Here, your goal is to move the prospect closer to a sale that will be completed elsewhere. For this reason, many letters intended to generate leads, such as invitations to seminars, are merely a page long.

Crafting an easy-to-read letter

Remember your high school or college textbooks, packed with columns of dense, long-winded prose? Just the sight of all that black text could make your heart sink. As a student, you had no choice but to plow on or fail. But as a customer, you can read only what you want to (and you won't be tested on the material!).

The same goes for your customers. If your letter looks intimidating — if the thought of getting through it is akin to climbing a mountain — stick a fork in yourself because you're done. Regardless of total length, you want your letter to look inviting and easy to read. Here's how:

- ✔ **Write short sentences and short paragraphs.** Try to keep your sentences nice and simple. And, with some exceptions, limit your paragraphs to just two or three sentences.

- ✔ **Leave lots of white space.** No crowding! Separate your paragraphs with a clean, clear line of empty space.

- ✔ **Use subheads and bullets.** Break up the letter with the occasional mini-headline, in bold print, that helps tell your story and interrupts the monotony of long strings of text. You can also use bulleted lists and indented paragraphs for graphic impact.

- ✔ **Bring attention to key phrases.** You can add special formatting, such as underlining, boldface, italics, larger font, or a different colored text, to help highlight the most important phrases or information. These styles boost the impact of your most important points and add visual drama to the overall letter — *if* you don't go overboard. Remember, they create impact through contrast. If you use special formatting too often, you diminish their effectiveness.

> ✔ **Use familiar typefaces.** In the old days, copywriters were encouraged to use Courier type (it looks as if it were pulled from a typewriter) to sustain the illusion of a personal letter. Today, the jig is up (we all know unsolicited mail when we see it), but it's still a good idea to use a familiar typeface, such as Times New Roman (it looks like the type in most newspapers). Times New Roman is easy on the eyes, and tests have demonstrated that many readers prefer it. And for Pete's sake, set the font size to at least 11 points or more — no one wants to squint to read your letter.

Writing Great Letters, Step by Step

Regardless of length or content, most marketing letters consist of the same familiar elements:

> ✔ **Headline:** This element, called the Johnson Box, establishes the most important message of the letter.
>
> ✔ **Body:** The bulk of the letter itself, the body develops your message/story.
>
> ✔ **Call to action:** Usually stated toward the end of the body, this element tells the reader what to do to get your offer.
>
> ✔ **Postscript (PS):** Located after the signature, the postscript often restates the offer, the call to action, or an important benefit.

If you've just turned to this chapter in a panic because you must write a sales letter first thing yesterday morning, concentrate your efforts on the Johnson Box and the PS. These elements are most likely to be read by even the most casual prospect and, therefore, are the elements most likely to affect response rates.

Otherwise, I'd advise you to pour a cup of coffee — the writer's best friend — and read the following pages carefully. The body of the letter, while read less often than the headline or the PS, is read by people who have a greater interest in your wares and are more likely to respond.

Creating a special headline called the Johnson Box

The Johnson Box is a headline that goes above the salutation ("Dear Friend") that formally begins the letter. Sometimes it is indeed graphically distinguished from the rest of the copy with a surrounding rectangle; more often, it simply draws attention to itself by being printed in bold, italics, or larger type. (See Figure 5-1 for an example of a Johnson Box in a sample letter.)

So if it's just a headline, why the heck is it called the Johnson Box? Like Frankenstein's monster, the device is named after its creator, the late Frank H. Johnson, a direct mail pioneer and the recipient of the first annual National Association of Direct Mail Writers award in 1966. He developed the technique to draw extra attention to key messages, and his idea proved so successful that it's become a standard practice.

The Johnson Box encapsulates the most important part of your message in a headline that may be a brief phrase — "On sale now!" — or as long as two or three sentences. Because I'm confident that people read the Johnson Box, even if they ignore the letter body, I tend to prefer a longish headline.

When it works well, the Johnson Box makes your main point and provokes further reading. Writing an effective Johnson Box is a big responsibility, but fortunately, you have a number of proven, time-tested options to help you. The best option for you is the one that leverages your strongest sales point, be it a compelling offer, a magnificent benefit, or an irresistible story.

Leading with your offer

The *offer* is the thing your prospects get when they take the action you request. If you have a strong offer, especially for a product or service that has already established its name, reputation, and desirability, you can come out swinging with the offer itself, as shown in the following examples:

> *Act now for a FREE 2-week supply of Men's Miracle Hair Cream. Here's how . . .*

> *Exclusive offer: Order one 12-oz. bottle of Men's Miracle Hair Cream, and get the second bottle, absolutely FREE!*

> *Save $25.95 when you order a six-month supply of Men's Miracle Hair Cream through this exclusive mail offer.*

Leading with the most important benefit

When your product is less familiar than other similar products and you need to persuade the reader of its value, try leading with a compelling benefit. Consider these examples:

> *You've spent a lot of money collecting customer data. Now there's a way to turn data into dollars.*

> *When it comes to customer behavior, knowledge is money. Get the customer insights you need for increased profitability. StatsVault Customer Relations Solutions shows you how.*

> *Give us a year, and StatsVault Customer Relations Solutions will give you a 25% increase in customer satisfaction, guaranteed.*

Leading with news

Suppose that you don't have a strong offer or that the benefit of your product is so obvious or familiar that it's no longer exciting. Try offering *news* — new information that has real value or meaning to your prospects. You can use literal news pulled from recent headlines (if it's relevant to your business), awards or recognitions, or simply unfamiliar information your audience may consider helpful. Here are some ideas of how to lead with news:

> *Interest rates are falling. Take advantage of record low rates with the Everest Credit Card at 8.5% APR.*

> *For the third year in a row, the Everest Credit Card has been ranked Number 1 in customer satisfaction. Shouldn't our card be your card?*

> *Warning: Many credit cards come with expensive hidden fees. Apply now for the low-interest card with NO additional fees — the Everest Credit Card.*

Leading with pain

The flip side of desire is fear, and fear — or the desire to be rid of pain — can be just as powerful a motivator as the promise of a benefit. Your goal is to position your product or service as the hero, the thing that frees prospects from pain or fear — if they accept your offer and take action.

Appealing to people's fear or pain is not a tactic for the faint of heart, as it carries the risk of associating your business with something negative or undesirable. If you proceed with the pain approach, be sure that your letter quickly offers the promise of relief that comes with your product, as shown in the following examples:

> *Does lost or thinning hair make you look older than you really are? Discover the secret to a fuller, more youthful looking head of hair.*

> *As you read this letter, your competitors are using consumer data to steal your customers. Are you prepared to fight back?*

> *If you're not carrying the Everest Credit Card, you're probably paying too much money in interest, month after month, year after year.*

Leading with a combination of hooks

In the first example under "pain," the opening question stimulates fear (Does lost or thinning hair make you look older than you really are?), while the following sentence promises a benefit — Discover the secret to a fuller, more youthful looking head of hair. By combining the techniques, you can double the impact of the Johnson Box.

Creating your own Johnson Box

Grab some scrap paper and try creating a Johnson Box! Based on the information here, write four different letter headlines, each with a different emphasis: offer, benefit, news, and a combination of any of those two.

Here's the background: Your company sells electric scooters for people with limited mobility and is launching a marketing campaign targeted to senior citizens. With extensive research as its guide, your company has manufactured a new scooter especially for seniors. It weighs less than its competitors, has ergonomic controls designed for easy manipulation by arthritic hands, and has a special seat with a patented AssistaLift technology to help people with weak or injured hips get on and off the scooter. The scooter, called the Mobilla, has recently received a design award from the American Society of Geriatric Occupational Therapists. By returning the enclosed card or calling the toll-free number, prospects can receive a free video demonstration of the scooter and a special discount card entitling them to 10 percent off the standard retail price.

I'm sure that you can come up with many successful headlines, each different from the last. Although you can approach this Johnson Box many different ways, I'd like to make a few suggestions:

✔ Keep in mind that a relevant prospect could be a senior who needs the scooter or a person who cares for that senior. Think about headlines that appeal to both.

✔ Your scooter may have many benefits and features. When choosing a benefit to emphasize, select the one you imagine would be most important to your targeted prospects: the senior with disabilities.

✔ Remember, the Johnson Box is usually the first part of the letter that gets read. Write your headline in a way that gives you and your reader an easy transition into the body of the letter and its story.

You can make any number of combinations. For starters, try joining a benefit with an offer:

> *Lower your interest rate with the Everest Credit Card. And earn 5,000 frequent flier miles when you return your application by January 30!*

Up for a challenge? Try mixing more than two approaches. Here's one that combines news, fear, an offer, and a benefit:

> *Long-distance customer satisfaction rates have declined 21% nationwide — and customers are switching carriers in record numbers. Call now for our free "Hold the Phone: Retaining Long-Distance Customers" white paper and see how you can stop attrition in its tracks.*

Building strong bodies, paragraph by paragraph

The *body* of the letter is all the stuff between the salutation and the close. It builds on the promise you made in the Johnson Box and creates an irresistible case for why you can fulfill that promise and why the reader should take action now.

Your first obligation is to get your reader from one sentence to the next, guiding them, by the sheer force of carefully crafted prose, from your initial claim to the call to action. You want your letter to flow easily from beginning to end.

Over time, many of the best and most experienced marketing hands have developed a number of formulas to help copywriters structure their letters. One of the most famous is AIDA, which stands for attention, interest, desire, and action. According to the AIDA formula, you begin your letter by attracting attention using benefits, offers, news, and so on. Then you build interest by expanding your case. With proof points as evidence, you arouse desire for your product. (See the section "They make a powerful case, point by point," earlier in this chapter, for more on proof points.) Finally, you make the call to action, the thing the reader does to get your product or service.

AIDA is a darned fine formula, and others are just as good. Frankly, I find it difficult to remember any formula, and I don't believe you need to memorize any of them. But I do believe that all good letters have the following "P" words, usually in the following order:

- **Pleasure and pain:** A good letter creates anticipation for the satisfaction of a desire (pleasure) or the relief from pain. This is your lure for attracting the reader's interest toward your product.

- **Promise:** Whether it's an offer or a benefit, your letter always implies a promise to the reader: When you buy this service or respond to this letter, you'll get something of value in return. It could be youth, clearer skin, longer life, greater social status, or simply an appealing discount, but whatever it is, it makes the customers' lives better than they had been before they responded to your letter.

- **Proof:** No one will simply take your word for anything. You make your case by proving it, by submitting evidence, testimonials, statistics, facts, and reasons why you can fulfill the promise you've made. (See "Developing the middle of the letter," later in this chapter, for more on statistics and testimonials.)

- **Purchase:** The ka-ching moment. Through the influence of your persuasive power (and a little bit of luck), the prospect will follow your call to action and become that most esteemed of correspondents: a customer.

Greetings! Writing the salutation

With few exceptions, your greeting is going to be "Dear" something. The significant issue is whether you can personalize the greeting.

- ✔ **Personalized greetings** incorporate the actual name of the prospect into the salutation: "Dear Mary Jones." Although the personalized greeting is preferred (it usually results in higher response rates), it requires special capabilities: the integration of list data — the names — into the text of the letters, and a printing process that can print these variable-text documents. (For more information on list data, see Chapter 7.)

- ✔ **Generalized greetings** simply place a generic referent after the "Dear," as in the familiar "Dear Friend," allowing you to mass-produce the same letter to all readers. Ideally, you want to use a greeting that's broad enough to include all your prospects yet has a specificity that matches your letter content: "Dear Tennis Enthusiast," "Dear Taxpayer," "Dear Concerned Citizen," or "Dear Jazz Fan."

Beginning your letter: The opening paragraphs

Getting started is always the most difficult part. But you can make your job much easier by focusing your attention on just three things the opening paragraphs of your letter should do, which I explain in the following sections.

Siding with the reader

Begin with a sentence or two that shows that you know what it's like to be in your readers' shoes. Instead of talking at your reader, you build a rapport that establishes empathy and credibility. These sentences often start with second-person introductions such as "As you know" or "Like you, many people . . ."

The empathetic opener is especially effective when the sale involves a degree of intimacy, such as health care, personal care products, or sensitive financial issues. By creating an opener that's the verbal equivalent of putting your arm around the prospect's shoulder, you can remove the obstacles of shame, embarrassment, or just general discomfort. Here's an example:

> *Like many men in their twenties, I started losing my hair. Not a lot at first, but more and more each day. And, truth is, with every hair I lost, I lost some of my self-confidence, too.*

> *Then a friend told me about Men's Miracle Hair Cream, and my life began to change. If you're losing your hair, I want to pass the good news to you, too.*

The empathetic approach also works for the opposite kind of subject: products and services that aren't personal at all but involve specific expertise, such as in engineering, high-tech, medical device, or business-to-business services. Here, the goal is to demonstrate your understanding of complex material and its impact on your prospect. Look at this example:

When you dig for data, do you uncover the gold you've hoped (and paid) for? Or do you find frustration — the inability to connect the data you know you have with the marketing matrixes you need for success?

Frankly, it's time you got the payback you deserve from your data. StatsVault Customer Relations Solutions can bridge the gap between raw data and actionable information.

Note that in addition to being empathetic, the preceding examples introduce benefits (a changed life, actionable information) and establish the momentum of a story: They present a problem (hair loss, poor data access) and then give the reader a solution (the hair cream, StatsVault).

When you have topical news, the empathetic opener is a convenient way to exploit it. And it's easy, too, as this example demonstrates:

You may have heard about declining interest rates in the news. Now you can take advantage of today's markets with the only credit card that begins low and stays low — the Everest Credit Card.

At just 8.5% APR, the Everest Card is one of the lowest interest-rate cards available. And it's guaranteed to remain at the rock-bottom 8.5% rate for as long as you make your monthly payments.

Picking up from the headline

You've already written the Johnson Box, so why not let it do more work for you? You can pick up the thread of the story where the headline left off.

Suppose that this is your headline:

Millions of men have REGAINED a full head of thick, youthful hair. Now you can too — at half the price.

Then your letter could begin:

There's no reason you should accept hair loss. Millions of men just like you have already discovered the secret to restoring their hair to its youthful vigor: Men's Miracle Hair Cream.

Now you can enjoy the same successful results, but with an even better deal. Through this exclusive mail offer, you can get the same Men's Miracle Hair Cream that sells nationwide at $49.59 — for only $24.99!

Connecting to the rest of your story

The third thing a good letter opening does is build a bridge to the heart of the story, such as your key benefit or special offer. You do this by setting up a problem to be solved, a pain to be overcome, or a desire to fulfill. Here's an example:

Today, marketing dollars are scarce. You're expected to generate maximum results with minimal budgets.

A tough task, no doubt. But the treasure you seek could be in the data you already have — if you have the power to unlock it. The key? StatsVault Customer Relations Solutions.

The preceding example has an empathetic quality, and you could easily write a headline to lead into it. Perhaps, "Your mission: Get more results with smaller marketing investments. StatsVault shows you how." In other words, each of the examples actually has all three virtues: empathy, continuity with the headline, and an easy transition to the rest of the letter. That's your objective, and if you can combine all three into your opening, you can be confident that you're off to a great start!

Developing the middle of the letter

Good news. Even though the middle is the longest part of the letter, it's the easiest to write. After you set up your lead in the Johnson Box and the opening, all you have to do is develop it. Your job? Expand on the whys and hows of your story.

And I have even more good news. You have many ways to develop your story, and they're all effective. Your choice of options becomes a matter of the information available to you, the nature of the product or service you're selling, and the predilections of your readers.

- ✔ **Present evidence.** Research, surveys, tests — any of these may be a source of statistical evidence to support your case. Consider presenting information such as how much money people can save or earn, how much weight they can expect to lose, how much time they can save, or how much bigger, faster, and smarter your offer is compared to your competitors' offers. Such evidence can all help you build your case. If you can easily incorporate the source of the data within the letter, do so: "According to a recent report from Outen A. Limb Associates . . ." But try not to use footnotes: Small print intimidates prospects and may send them running.

- ✔ **Quote customers.** Do you have permission to quote happy customers who've said terrific things about your business? If so, let them speak on your behalf. Testimonials in which speakers express initial skepticism (much like what's in the mind of the reader) but then are satisfied beyond their wildest expectations are, of course, especially helpful. (See Chapter 3 for more on collecting customer testimonials.)

- ✔ **Reveal subordinate benefits.** Got more good benefits? Whip them out. Call it the "but wait, there's more" formula. After you use the big, most important benefit as your lead, you can usually find other benefits that, while less significant, can still support the sale. In addition to increasing the amount of hair, maybe the hair cream prevents dandruff, adds body, and brings color to dull or gray hair.

✔ **Identify important features.** The important word here is "important." Less important features are things that are incidental to the product or service, such as the shape of the hair cream bottle or the color of the Everest Card. The important features are those that help explain how or why your product can fulfill the benefits you promise. These include special ingredients, such as the oxynol psuedominide proven to make hair grow. Other important features may be your business's unique expertise, the portability and durability of your product, the security of your software, and so on.

✔ **Describe how it works.** Before your prospects will put money in your coffers, you need to put pictures in their heads — pictures of how your product will work for them. These explanations may be unnecessary for things that are already well understood, such as credit cards, but for products that are new or poorly understood or that inspire skepticism (such as hair growth), a brief explanation of how they work can go a long way. Make it easy — try to present your "demonstration" in a handful of short, easy-to-understand steps, generally no more than three or four.

Closing the deal: Asking for the response

The letter ends when you ask the reader to do something to get something — the call to action. It can be as simple as this:

> *Call 1-800-123-4567 to reserve your seat at the next "Mining Profits from Data Mining" seminar.*

Or your call to action can be more elaborate:

> *Take the next step to turn data into profits. Come to the next "Mining Profits from Data Mining" seminar coming to your area on May 12. Participation is free, but seats are limited. Call 1-800-123-4567 today, or register online at www.statsvault.com, to reserve your seat.*

Whether brief or elaborate, the call to action always tells readers what to do to get what you offer. You can do a few things, however, to make your call to action more enticing:

✔ **Create urgency.** Inertia isn't just a physical phenomenon; it's a key to customer psychology. Without applied exterior force, prospects just don't move. One of most successful ways to apply psychological force is to create urgency by establishing a time limit. (This is the reason for all those "for a limited time only" warnings you see on TV all the time — even though the same ad has been running for years.) People hate the idea of losing something, even if it's something they don't yet have. So set a time limit for your offer and create the threat of loss — if they don't act now.

✔ **Make a guarantee.** Few things kill sales more quickly than uncertainty, fear of disappointment, or fear of wasting money. Whenever possible, offer a money-back guarantee. It's the simplest way to overcome a prospect's fears, and the costs incurred by the few returns you'll get will be more than overcome by the resulting increase in sales.

✔ **Provide multiple response options.** In the old days, responding to your offer was simple. Prospects responded by returning the enclosed postage-paid card or envelope. Then came toll-free telephone numbers. Now they also can reply through Web sites and e-mail.

Frequent testing suggests that different folks like different strokes and that offering several options tends to increase response. Just keep in mind that you want to make responding easy, not complicated. So if you request a check or a credit card number with the response, be sure to include a postage-paid envelope to either hold the check or protect the privacy of the card number.

Time limits, guarantees, and response options have to be in place before you promise them to your readers. Make sure that you or your colleagues are fully prepared to accept time limits, honor guarantees, and handle inquiries from multiple response paths before you commit yourself (and your organization) in print.

✔ **Finish strongly in the last paragraph.** You may call this the "re" paragraph, because most of the time it's an opportunity to *re*state the big benefit and to *re*mind prospects how important it is to *re*spond to your offer. Consider this example:

You owe it to yourself to get the best interest rate possible on your credit card. Complete and return the enclosed form today to apply for the Everest Credit Card and join the savvy consumers who know how to enjoy the high life without the high rates.

PS: Writing the postscript

After the Johnson Box, the postscript, or PS, is the second most frequently read element of the letter. It goes just below the closing ("Sincerely," signature, name, and title), and because prospects may read it without any reference to the body of the letter, it should contain — you guessed it — the benefit and the offer.

You may be growing weary of all this talk about "benefit and offer." I tell you to place one or both in the Johnson Box, in the opening paragraphs, in the middle, in the end, and then again in the PS. Isn't this repetitive? You bet! In marketing, repetition is a virtue, not a vice. People shouldn't ever have to hunt for the benefit and the offer, because you will serve it to them, not once, but many times — perhaps with a slightly different emphasis and wording each time, yet always retaining the same meaning and message.

If anything, the good postscript heightens the urgency of the offer when it restates your message, as in this example:

> *PS: A new head of hair can be the beginning of a new life — and a new you! But you have to take the first step. Call 1-800-123-4567 before midnight, April 30, to save 50% on your first six-month supply of Men's Miracle Hair Cream.*

Despite the virtues of the PS, at times you may choose not to use one. Sometimes you'll want to write a "blind" letter, a piece of mail designed to look like genuine personal or business correspondence rather than a form letter. To make this camouflage work, you strip out all the elements that look like marketing mail: no Johnson Box, no subheads between paragraphs, and, if your letter is intended to pass as business correspondence, no PS. (See Chapter 7 for more information on camouflage.)

Putting the Pieces Together: A Sample Letter Shows You How

A painting may be made of paint, canvas, and brush strokes and formed with an eye for color, space, and gesture, but understanding the elements alone can't give you complete insight into the finished piece. The whole is greater than the sum of the parts. In fact, the way all the pieces work together is what defines a great work of art.

Now, there's a big gap between great art and my letters, but the principle is similar: You can't get the whole picture until you *see* the whole picture. With that in mind, I offer you a whole letter (see Figure 5-1). It's not a template, nor is it necessarily a model, but it does demonstrate just one of the thousands of ways a letter can put all the pieces together for maximum impact.

I want to walk you through a few points about this letter to give you a clearer idea of how it works — and how the pieces I examine in detail earlier apply within the context of a complete letter.

Keep in mind that True and Total Fitness doesn't exist; I made it up just for this chapter. I imagined the letter as part of a complete package with a brochure and a response card, and I chose to write a long letter because I'm asking for the money upfront (and I want you to see a letter that includes as many techniques as possible). (See Chapters 6 and 7 for more information on brochures and reply devices.)

Is your current diet and exercise plan killing you?
As a physician, it's my professional duty to urge you to STOP.
There's a safer, healthier way to be fit—True and Total Fitness.
It's designed personally for you, forever.
And it's GUARANTEED...

Dear [PROSPECT]:

Despite the best intentions, your current fitness program could be killing you. And I'm not just talking about the way you feel after another exhausting workout—or another day of near-starvation dieting. It's a disturbing medical fact.

FACT: More than **67%** of all dieters who successfully lose weight **will gain more than they lose** within one to three years after the initial loss.
FACT: This year, **45%** of all adults will lose time from work because of an **exercise-related injury.**
FACT: Most diet and exercise plans lead to an **increase in stress** by as much as **32%.**

These are the troubling medical truths revealed within the recent Journal of Physical Health report, "Stress, Injury, and Bad Habits: The Deadly Secrets Behind Diets and Exercise."

The authors—all physicians and medical researchers at America's leading teaching hospitals—came to their conclusions after spending a decade studying the most popular diet and exercise techniques in America today. I know, because I'm one of those physicians.

The truth is, you need a *personalized* **plan for success.**

My colleagues and I sifted through a mountain of data, tests, surveys, and lab results. (You can see the complete report on my Web site, *www.trueandtotalfitness.com*.)

In the end, we found the same problems with every so-called "miracle" diet and exercise plan. Lack of coordination between diet and exercise. Failure to track and measure results. No professional oversight of activity. And worst of all, a "one-size-fits-all" mentality that placed all participants in the same plan, regardless of size, weight, or medical fitness.

In short, we found a recipe for failure. Then we discovered a formula for success: **coordinated planning plus personal attention equals total fitness.**

We call it True and Total Fitness. You'll call it a lifetime of better health.

My colleagues and I put together a simple but thorough plan that puts all the pieces together, safely and effectively. Not just for immediate results, but for a lifetime of better health. Here's how **True and Total Fitness** works:

- We perform a **complete evaluation** of your current health status, including diet, weight, cardio-health, muscle strength, stress levels, and more.
- We give you a **personalized fitness plan** that coordinates diet, exercise, and stress-reducing activities all together.
- We **monitor your progress** to help you meet your goals—and avoid potential hazards.

The **True and Total Fitness** plan is not about drugs, fad diets, or expensive exercise equipment. It's about good science—and people who care enough to pay attention to you.

Since 2001, more than 2.5 million people have lost more than 375 million pounds and gained new levels of energy they never thought possible!

(Over, please)

Figure 5-1:
This sample letter demonstrates all the elements in action.

The **True and Total Fitness** plan is also tried and true. There are currently 2,537,643 (and counting!) participants. Each one has lost, on average, approximately 15 pounds. They've also improved their cardiovascular health...improved muscle tone...reduced stress...and reduced the occurrence of injury and disease.

Don't take our word for it. In the brochure that comes with this letter, you'll read true stories from satisfied **True and Total Fitness** members. In sum, our members experience:

- An average weight loss of **15 pound in just 4 months!**
- Lower **blood pressure** by 36-42%!
- An average **32% reduction** in cholesterol and triglyceride levels!
- An increase in muscle-to-fat ratio of approximately **24%!**
- Plus a marked reduction in stress and colds, and an **increase of energy and vitality!**

Take the first step today—your success is guaranteed!

When you become a **True and Total Fitness** member, you get:

1) A complete fitness assessment **reviewed by an accredited physician.**
2) **A customized, personal fitness plan**, written just for you, with simple step-by-step suggestions for diet, exercise, and stress reduction.
3) A password-protected **personalized Web site** for constant communications with your own professionally-trained Fitness Manager.
4) Exclusive access to discounted meals, vitamins, and supplements—just for **True and Total Fitness** members.

Best of all, your success is guaranteed. Try **True and Total Fitness** for 30 days. If you don't experience a significant improvement in your health, or if you are in any way unsatisfied with your program, <u>we'll return all your money to you, no questions asked</u>. (But the fitness plan is yours to keep—our gift to you!)

Call to action — **Act now and save 50% on your initial participation fee.**

More than 2.5 million happy, healthy participants have signed on to **True and Total Fitness** for an initial sign-up fee of $200 plus a monthly $12 subscription charge. But through this exclusive mail-only offer, **you can join for only $100**, plus the monthly charge! Simply call (123) 456-7890, or visit us online at www.trueandtotalfitness.com, or return the postage-paid True and Total Fitness Form.

Please, don't kill yourself with diets and exercise plans that are doomed to fail. Take charge of your health with a personal, customized plan that's just right for you. Act now—take advantage of our special half-off membership offer and join True and Total Fitness today!

Sincerely,

Dr. Everett M. Walcomb, MD

Dr. Everett M. Walcomb, MD
Medical Director, True and Total Fitness

Postscript — PS — Coordinated, customized planning plus personal attention is your formula for fitness success! Take advantage of our exclusive membership offer and save $100 when you join True and Total Fitness today!

Note the following parts of the letter in Figure 5-1:

- ✔ **A Johnson Box with a surprise:** Okay, so this is a long headline, but in addition to including a benefit ("safer, healthier way to be fit"), introducing a guarantee, and even naming the product, it springs a surprise in order to capture attention: A physician is telling the reader to *stop* dieting and exercising!

- ✔ **An opening that expands the headline and establishes credibility:** I'm taking a risk by not going immediately for the offer. Instead I use a slow-burn approach that expands on the premise of the Johnson Box — "your current fitness program could be killing you" — and establishes authority by referencing the writer's credentials as a doctor and a published researcher. My strategy? Empathize with the prospects' dissatisfaction with their current diet and exercise plan (it is exhausting and leaves you starving) and establish True and Total Fitness as something truly and totally better.

- ✔ **A personalized approach:** The benefits of a good fitness plan are familiar to all of us. But to distinguish my promise from the hundreds of similar promises that prospects have heard before, I have to give True and Total Fitness a fresh angle, a special "reason why" that separates it from the pack. I use a subhead to declare this distinguishing quality: "The truth is, you need a *personalized* plan for success."

  Most people like to think of themselves as special. Offering something customized or personalized can be a powerful lure to people who are focused on the most important persons in the world: themselves.

- ✔ **Loads of proof points, offered in a variety of ways:** The fundamental premise is that True and Total Fitness is the better fitness plan because it's personalized. The middle of the letter has to prove it. Note that I use a number of techniques that I discuss earlier in this chapter: statistical evidence ("This year, 45% of all adults will lose time from work"), a demonstration of how it works ("complete evaluation," "personalized fitness plan," "monitor your progress"), a bulleted list of benefits, and a numbered list of features.

- ✔ **An end with an unbeatable offer:** Remember, to get action, you have to overcome inertia. So, in addition to offering a guarantee, I throw in a limited-time-only (urgency!) half-price offer — savings of $100!

- ✔ **One more time:** The PS restates the premise in a new way — "Coordinated, customized planning plus personal attention is your formula for fitness success!" — and then brings it all home with yet another statement of the offer.

Chapter 6

Creating Direct Response Brochures That Sizzle and Sell

. . . .

. . . .

*W*hen I was a kid, there was still such a thing as the door-to-door sales-man. He, hardly ever a she, traveled with an extraordinary tool that gave him almost magic sales power: the sample case.

Why was it magic? Because it put the product not just in front of the customer's eyes but in her hands. Take a dust brush, for example. A skillful salesman not only allowed the customer to handle the brush but also encouraged her to try it. The customer could feel the way it fit into her hand and test the strength of its bristles. She could smell its newness and enjoy the way it swept up a nasty spill of coffee grounds with minimal fuss.

This tangibility was so important and so effective that good salesmen knew that if they could just get the prospect to try the product, they were three-quarters of the way to closing the sale.

Things change. The rise of two-income households wiped out the market for door-to-door sales. But the need for tangibility, for bringing the look and feel — and sometimes even the smell and sound — of a product in direct contact with the customer, hasn't changed.

Your product or service has to be physically, materially real to prospects before they'll buy. Because you can't present your wares before them in fact, you must present them virtually, by your power to stimulate their senses and imagination with words and pictures. Your tool? The brochure.

If you take this observation to heart and understand that the great brochure is never merely descriptive but is the virtual equivalent of the salesperson's case, then you, too, will draw your prospect much closer to the sale.

Putting Brochures to Work

Too many brochures are like bad employees — they're expensive, they don't do much, and then when you really need them, you can't find them anyway! Why are so many brochures so bad? For starters, they're often limited to description and the conveying of information. And that's not enough to motivate a prospect.

You can, and should, expect more from your brochures and make them work. Instead of providing information, they should provoke action. Instead of describing, they should be selling (pushing benefits). They have a role, in fact, that complements the letter. (For more information on direct response letters, see Chapter 5.)

This chapter focuses on brochures that sell specific products or services and are usually created as part of a mailing to prospects, with an accompanying letter. Other kinds of brochures, usually called "corporate capabilities" brochures, describe an entire company or organization and are used as handouts at trade events or "leave-behinds" at sales calls. I discuss these brochures in Chapter 15.

Recognizing how brochures are similar to letters

Direct response letters and direct response brochures often share the same cozy space within an envelope and, in many ways, share similar techniques and objectives. (For information on writing letters, see Chapter 5.) Here are some of the ways that letters and brochures are similar:

- **They're focused on benefits.** Like the letter, a brochure doesn't confine itself to telling the reader what the product is but explains what it does for the reader.

- **They include a call to action.** Letters and brochures often travel together. But because you have no way of knowing for sure which will be read, both items have to include all the information necessary for getting the response or making the sale.

- **They speak the prospect's language.** You keep your corporate jargon at bay (with a whip and a chair if necessary), and to win prospects to your point of view, you write the way your customers talk.

Understanding how brochures differ from letters

Viva la difference: For all the similarities between brochures and letters, brochures offer special opportunities that just can't be accomplished through a letter alone. These differences set brochures apart:

✔ **Brochures are graphic.** They can include photographs, illustrations, drawings, charts, graphs, and other visual elements to help you tell your story. For the writer, this graphic quality is both an opportunity and an obligation; it's an opportunity to visually reinforce your message, but it's also an obligation to write copy that works with and supports the graphic material. (For more information, see the section "Getting graphic: Working with design," later in this chapter.)

✔ **Brochures are modular.** Brochures are folded in a variety of ways that divide them into separate sections called *panels*. Although it's possible, and even common, to design some sections across multiple panels, all brochures have a cover and back panel, plus room inside. Many brochures include perforated panels that can serve as response cards or coupons. (For more information, see the section "Examining popular brochure formats," later in this chapter.)

The modularity of the brochure requires an entirely different way of thinking than the letter. Visually, letters simply run top to bottom, encouraging a narrative approach of beginning, middle, and end. But brochure panels interrupt the flow and let you think of discrete sections, with each part or panel assigned to a different task: One panel can be dedicated to the benefit story, another to a product's feature options, and a third to the call to action and the reply card. You can choose from many successful ways to structure a brochure, but you always have to account for panel layout when you think about your copy structure.

✔ **Brochures are samples cases, not fairy tales.** Letters and brochures operate under different metaphors. The letter creates drama — the fairy tale — by establishing a desire or fear and giving the hero (the prospect) a chance to secure a happy ending by taking action. (For more, see Chapter 5.) The brochure is less narrative, and its purpose — like the samples case — is to be the virtual equivalent of placing the product in the prospects' hands. You're stimulating the imagination. By the time readers finish your brochure, you want them to have a clear picture of what owning or using your product or service is like.

✔ **Brochures are less limited by tradition.** Letters draw power through their similarity to personal correspondence — the more "real" they seem, the more credible and trustworthy they become. Brochures, on the contrary, have no heritage other than marketing and advertising and may actually become more attractive with novelty. Being new and different can have its payoffs (it can attract the attention of jaded, seen-it-all consumers), but you're limited by expense — novel layouts often cost much more to design, print, and mail.

Planning Your Brochure's Layout, Panel by Panel

When planning a letter, you think about length — the number of pages — but the format is pretty much predetermined and rarely varies from Johnson Box, salutation, body, closing, and postscript. (For more information on the format of a letter, see Chapter 5.)

Brochures are another story. They come in a bewildering number of dimensions (width by height), folding patterns, and number of panels or pages. As a writer, you may find the format handed to you, without input on your part, or you may be asked to make suggestions. Either way, the brochure's modular nature makes it impossible for you to write the copy before you understand what the format will be.

Unless your brochure follows a pamphlet format (a number of pages stapled into an enclosing cover), your copy flows onto panels. Let me explain my terminology. If you take a sheet of ordinary 8½-x-11-inch paper, lay it horizontally before you, and then fold it in the middle, you have one fold. As long as you hold the paper open to its full horizontal width, you see two sides: One is the exterior side, front and back; and the other is the interior, side by side. Although you have one piece of paper, the fold has now created four *panels:* the exterior cover, the exterior back, and, counting from left to right when you flip the paper over, interior panel 1 on the left and interior panel 2 on the right.

Now I'm going to belabor the point with a slightly more complex example. Take another sheet of 8½-x-11-inch paper and lay it horizontally again, but this time, make two folds, dividing the paper into thirds. You bring the right-hand side over toward the left so that the right third of the paper covers the middle third. Then you draw the remaining left third over the other two, making a compact, narrow brochure that fits just perfectly in a #10 business envelope. Give yourself a round of applause — you've just created the classic six-panel brochure, also known as the "slim jim."

Examining popular brochure formats

Theoretically, you can design brochures in an almost infinite number of ways. But to contain costs, paper standards and the dimensions of readily available envelopes constrain the formats. Sure, you can create custom formats for greater impact, but you'll pay a considerable premium for the privilege. Most of the time, you'll probably opt for one of these standard formats:

✔ **The six-panel slim jim:** Precisely because it can be constructed from a standard paper size and fit into an ordinary envelope, the slim jim is perhaps the most popular direct mail brochure format — you've seen it zillions of times. (See it again in Figure 6-1.) Now I'm going to ask you to take a closer look.

On the inside, the slim jim has three interior panels. But look what happens to the other side: You get a front cover, a back cover, and then one remaining panel that the prospect doesn't see until she opens the front panel. This underlying panel (which, when the slim jim is completely folded, obscures the second and third interior panels) is often called the *flap panel* or the *payoff panel.*

Pay close attention to this payoff panel. Because it's revealed only when the prospect lifts the cover, it gives the slim jim the ability to deliver the written equivalent of the combination punch. It's like a two-person comedy routine: The cover headline becomes the setup (a provocative question or an incomplete thought), and the headline on the flap panel becomes the payoff, a thought that answers or completes the setup on the cover. I go into more detail about writing headlines and payoffs in "Going to the top with headlines," later in this chapter, but now I want you to get in the habit of thinking about the impact of format on copy.

✔ **The accordion:** Designed to fit into the ordinary #10 envelope, the accordion features eight to twelve panels that unfold like, well, an accordion. Given the volume of space available for copy, the accordion is a popular design for information-rich communications, such as conference promotions and wholesale product lines.

✔ **The jumbo:** Take that same 8½-x-11-inch sheet of paper, but lay it vertically and fold it top to bottom — that's the jumbo, and it measures 5½ x 8½ inches. The jumbo has only four panels, but with a larger cover area, it allows you more room to deliver a graphic with greater impact. It can work as a vertical format with the fold on the left so that it opens like a book, or as a horizontal that folds at the top so it opens like an invitation. Either way, you have the option of treating the interior panels as discrete design elements or as one big page, like a poster.

✔ **The invitation:** One step smaller than the jumbo, the invitation has four panels, measures 5 x 7 inches, and always opens bottom to top. The concept is simple: Because it looks like an invitation, it increases the likelihood of being opened. And indeed, in most cases, it is used for invitations — to seminars, exhibitor booths, conferences, professional events, and the like.

✔ **The 8½ x 11:** This one is usually a 17-x-11-inch sheet of paper folded once to give you four very large panels. You can also create six-panel versions of this beast, folded from a 25½-x-11-inch sheet. You mail these in large 9-x-12-inch envelopes in the hope that sheer size alone will attract enough curiosity to get recipients to open them. The six-panel version folds like a slim jim — so far, no one's petitioned to call it the "wide clyde" or the "fat matt."

Getting graphic: Working with design

As a copywriter, you don't have complete responsibility for the brochure message. Whether you work with a designer or assume the role yourself, remember that the visual impact of the brochure is every bit as important as the words themselves.

Searching for a designer, sight unseen, can be a scary process. Here's how to make it easy: Look at your colleagues' materials, and when you see something that interests you, ask for the designer's name and number. But don't just shop on design alone; ask about price and, more importantly, the quality of the working relationship. You want to work with a diplomatic partner, not a precious prima donna. If you decide to design the piece yourself (which I don't recommend unless you're really confident you're capable of doing professional-level work), be sure to use a computer program that creates files compatible with your printer's systems. If you're not sure, ask your printer for advice.

All marketing materials communicate twice: first, in a rapid, split-second blur that conveys the overall "feel" of the material, and, second, through the material's literal content.

Your prospects get the second message only if they take the time to read your work — at this stage, copy may be slightly more important than design. But graphic design has the upper hand in the first stage, when prospects instantaneously and, almost subconsciously, absorb the look of your material.

In that first split second, they assess its value. Does this thing look professional or amateur, credible or untrustworthy? Does it look real and honest, or phony and disreputable? Think of a first introduction to a potential business partner: If that person shows up at a meeting in a stained Hawaiian shirt and tattered Bermuda shorts, you form an opinion of his value before the first words come from his mouth. Likewise, no matter how skilled your writing may be, if the production looks cheap, sloppy, or careless, you lose the sale before you begin. Conversely, if you use high-quality paper, clean design, and skillfully applied graphics, you communicate professionalism before anyone reads the first word.

Creating a good first impression may be the most important job of graphic design. But you and your designer should cooperate thoughtfully for other reasons:

- ✔ **Joint impact:** Integrating your headline with a graphic image exponentially increases the impact of your message. Combining an image of a wrecked car with a headline about the need for collision coverage, for example, makes a car insurance message much more memorable. (For more information on how to make the most effective match of words to photographs or illustrations, see Chapter 11.)

✔ **Visual information:** Charts and graphs can sometimes be more effective than words in communicating some information, such as trends, statistics, and numerical comparisons. You want to work with your designer to assign the appropriate information to text or graphics.

✔ **Captions:** Captions that explain the image and link it to the rest of the brochure copy should accompany images that illustrate the product or how it's used. (For more on writing captions, see Chapter 2.)

✔ **Layout issues:** You must treat the space available for words and pictures like valuable real estate. The writer and designer must work together to decide what goes where and to figure out the relative amount of space available for imagery and text.

The design of your brochure can vary in complexity from a simple type treatment (just words, no pictures) on plain paper to four-color photography on high-gloss paper with fancy *die-cuts* (cut-out shapes or "windows"). But each degree of increasing sophistication comes with an increase in cost. Be sure that the ideas you brainstorm with your designer fit in your budget; when in doubt, check with your printer, preferably early in the design stage when you still have time and flexibility to make changes.

Going to the top with headlines

Although most copy projects — such as letters, print ads, and sales sheets — pair one headline with one set of body copy, brochures may include one, two, three, or more headlines within its contents.

Think about it. The cover, of course, always has a headline. Then you may choose to write a major heading to encompass all the interior panels. And when you work with a six-panel format, you also have a flap or payoff panel that can carry a headline. The secret is harmony — getting all these headlines to work together.

Take a look at your headline options, starting from the simplest and moving to the most complex. (For a refresher on the general guidelines for writing headlines, see Chapter 2.)

Writing a headline for the cover only

Your cover headline can be as basic as the name of your product or service, or it can involve a number of distinct lines.

✔ **Name only:** Plain and simple, this headline is just the name of your product, such as "Kensington Landscaping Services." It's the easiest option, but without a benefit or the suggestion of a story, it's not particularly compelling.

✔ **Kicker plus name:** You can add drama by lifting a technique from your local newspaper. Sometimes journalists put a line of text above the headline to draw interest to the article and establish its context:

City faces largest budget deficit in decade:
Mayor O'Malley Proposes Layoffs, Cuts in Services

In a similar way, copywriters can use the kicker to introduce a benefit to the headline:

Introducing the easiest way to enjoy a lush, luxurious lawn:
Kensington Landscaping Services

✔ **Name plus tag line:** Think of this as the inverse of the kicker-plus-name headline; instead of putting the hook above the name, you're putting it underneath. The line under the company name is often a *tag*, a short phrase or sentence that defines the unique qualities of your product or service. (See Chapter 10 for more information about tag lines.)

Kensington Landscaping Services
Expert Care for Exceptional Lawns

✔ **Kicker, name, and tag:** You can put all three lines together to create a mini three-act drama:

For the distinguished property:
Kensington Landscaping Services
English Gardens for American Homes

Writing headlines on multiple panels

In the preceding examples, the cover carries a complete message. But you can provoke interest by deliberately fragmenting your message across multiple panels.

✔ **The one-two combination punch:** The headline on the cover serves as the lead, while the subsequent headline — either on the flap panel in a six-panel format or across the interior panels in a four-panel brochure — serves as the payoff or punch line.

- Here's a combination for an invitation that embeds the benefit on the cover while saving the name of the event for the interior:

  Cover: *You're invited to lift your leadership skills and take the next step in your career.*

  Interior headline: *Register today for the Learning to Lead seminar sponsored by Broderick Executive Coaching Group.*

- With a six-panel format, you put the payoff headline on the flap panel that prospects see when they open the brochure:

    Cover headline: *You have talent and experience, but can you offer* ***the one crucial quality*** *Fortune 500 companies demand from their executives?*

    Flap panel headline: *Leadership. Some are born with it. For everyone else, there's Broderick Executive Coaching Group.*

✔ **Three headlines together:** For maximum dramatic impact, you can break your story into three parts: cover, flap panel, and interior headline:

    Cover headline: *Dirt dreads it. Stains fear it. And every Klensomatic Carpet Cleaner comes with it.*

    Flap panel headline: *Steam heat!*

    Interior panels headline: *In test after test, Klensomatic steam heat carpet cleaners leave the competition in the cold!*

Producing solo, duo, and trio headlines

Your mission is to write three types of headline treatments — cover, cover plus payoff, and a triple combination — to give your client three different ways of approaching her brochure. The client, Mary Leaves, owns Round Table Books, a successful independent bookstore in a medium-sized city that caters to a mixed crowd of college students, urban singles, and intellectually curious professionals who appreciate the store's eclectic book selection.

Mary is launching a book club that offers author readings, coffee socials, discussion groups, and special discounts. In the previous year, she's collected names and addresses at the register; now she wants to mail a letter and brochure promoting the new club, Nights at the Round Table. (Please don't groan.)

You can use the name, kickers, tag lines, and payoff headlines. Feel free to invent benefits and features for the club, but keep the following thoughts in mind:

✔ Mary Leaves doesn't have much of a budget for this brochure. She's thinking of a six-panel format that fits in an ordinary #10 business envelope.

✔ Although she can't afford new photography, she does have a couple well-executed photographs of the store's interior and of happy (and reasonably attractive) customers.

✔ Mary is smart and demands flexibility. She wants the brochure to work with a letter in its first mailing, as a stand-alone piece she can give out at the register, and as a piece she can send on its own for future mailings.

Organizing Your Brochure's Interior Content

In general, brochure content includes three things:

- ✔ **The *what*:** A compelling summary of the thing being offered and its principal benefit.

- ✔ **Variations on *how* and *why*:** A concrete picture of how your product and service work, why they work, and the variety of options (if any) available to the customer.

- ✔ **Purchasing instructions:** A call to action that tells the customer how to get the offer. In fact, many brochures include a perforated tear-off panel that serves as a reply device. (For more on reply devices, see Chapter 7.)

That's the mile-high view. But as you get closer to your material, the picture gets a bit more complicated. At the down-to-earth level, the content of your brochure is determined by the nature of your business, your offer, and its unique set of benefits and features. Because the range of possibilities is so great, giving you a firm rule as to what content should go on what panel is impossible.

Driving the story with subheads

Though I can't give you a fixed rule about *where* to place information in your brochures, I can — in all confidence and integrity of conscience — give you the professional, inside secret to organizing your information: Use subheads to tell the story.

Subheads are like miniature headlines. Like headlines, they introduce ideas and are placed above blocks of text or body copy. But they tend to use fewer words than headlines, and they deploy a type size that's often bigger than the body type yet smaller than the headline type. (See Chapter 2 for in-depth information on how to write subheads.)

Subheads stand out from the rest of the text, which means that people can read them at a glance. When you're ready to write the interior copy, start with the subheads. Here's why:

- ✔ **People can read them by skimming.** Many prospects don't read all your copy but simply skim its contents. If nothing else, they at least see and read the subheads.

> ✔ **Subheads help you organize the contents.** Subheads make your life easier. You begin by putting all your major points into subheads. That done, you know that all the essentials are in place, and the remaining work is largely a matter of filling in the blanks.

How do you know whether you've done a good job? If a prospect can pick up all the key points about your story from the subheads alone — the offer, main benefit, most important features, and the call to action — then you've successfully organized the brochure with appropriate subheads. I lift my glass, er, coffee mug, to you!

Take a look at Figure 6-1 to see subheads at work.

In a way, you can read the subheads in the brochure in Figure 6-1 as answers to questions the prospect is likely to ask:

Q: So what's this Green's all about?

A: Go online, and let Green's get your groceries.

Q: Why would I want to do that?

A: When you have better things to do. Like living.

Q: C'mon, you can't be serious. What's the deal?

A: In a few minutes, you can do all your shopping for a week.

Q: How can I trust you to shop for me?

A: We cherry-pick the best.

Q: You promise?

A: Absolutely guaranteed.

Q: Okay, but why should I act now?

A: See for yourself and get your first delivery, FREE!

Q: Got anything else for me?

A: Special offers and coupons, too!

Q: I'm sold. How do I get started?

A: Get your Green's. Come to www.greens.com and we'll do the shopping for you.

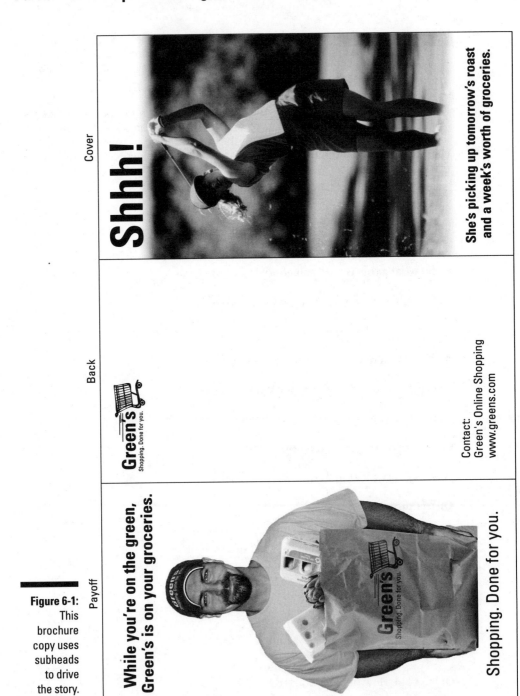

Figure 6-1:
This
brochure
copy uses
subheads
to drive
the story.

Interior Panel 1

Go online, and let Green's get your groceries.

When you have better things to do. Like living.

Grocery shopping. It's got to get done. But now, you don't have to do it. Green's will do it for you.

You get the same succulent meats...farmfresh produce...and huge selection of goods. All the quality you expect from Green's, delivered directly to your door. And it's fast, too. Place your order by 3:00 pm, and we'll be there the next morning.

In a few minutes, you can do all your shopping for a week.

It's this easy:

1. Go to www.greens.com and schedule a delivery time.
2. Pick out your groceries.
3. Pay with your ATM or credit card.
4. Lean back and relax—you're done!

Interior Panel 2

We cherry-pick the best.

At Green's, your order is filled by the strictest, most demanding shopper in the world, the Green's Picker. When you ask for fruit or vegetables, only the freshest, juiciest, blemish-free produce will do. Meats and fish? Our Pickers follow a 10 Point Checklist for age, color, texture, and firmness—only the best will reach your basket.

After the Pickers carefully pack your order, it's individually inspected before delivery by a Green's Quality Control Inspector who makes sure you get everything you asked for—and in peak condition.

Absolutely guaranteed.

It's the Green's Guarantee: You get what you asked for at the time you asked for it. If you disagree, if you're disappointed at any time in any way, you get your money back instantly, no questions asked.

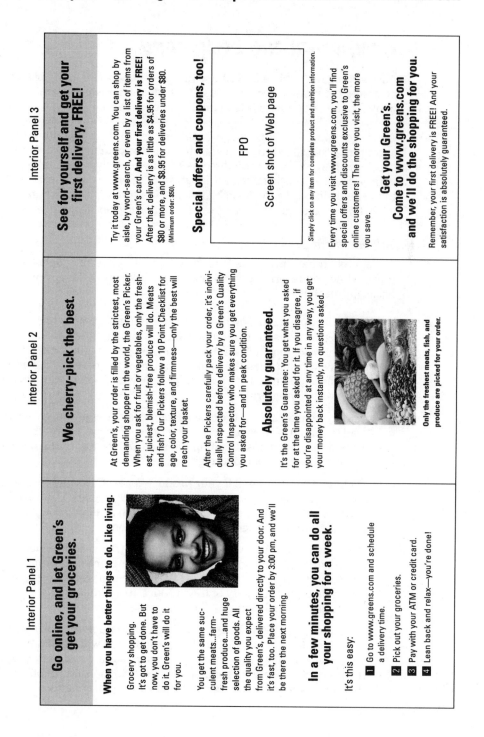

Only the freshest meats, fish, and produce are picked for your order.

Interior Panel 3

See for yourself and get your first delivery, FREE!

Try it today at www.greens.com. You can shop by aisle, by word-search, or even by a list of items from your Green's card. **And your first delivery is FREE!** After that, delivery is as little as $4.95 for orders of $80 or more, and $8.95 for deliveries under $80. (Minimum order: $50).

Special offers and coupons, too!

FPO

Screen shot of Web page

Simply click on any item for complete product and nutrition information.

Every time you visit www.greens.com, you'll find special offers and discounts exclusive to Green's online customers! The more you visit, the more you save.

Get your Green's. Come to www.greens.com and we'll do the shopping for you.

Remember, your first delivery is FREE! And your satisfaction is absolutely guaranteed.

Composing the body copy

After writing the subheads, you use the body copy to fill in the blanks and complete the picture. Each subhead tells the reader what to expect in the copy that follows; your job is to fulfill that obligation.

Like letter copy, brochure copy should be easy to read: Use simple sentences, short paragraphs, and the everyday language of your audience. In the brochure, however, you have the opportunity to draw a detailed portrait of your product or service offer. Although some issues — such as attentiveness to the audience and a focus on benefits — are true for all brochures, some important differences between products and services deserve your attention.

Talking about products

As concrete things, products lend themselves to physically detailed descriptions. When you're writing about the following types of items, consider a few basic approaches:

- **Tools:** If you're featuring tools or other things that aren't necessarily exciting in themselves but are desirable for what they do, describe the product in action. Tell the reader how the pneumatic socket gun is 50 percent faster than the manual tool, how the titanium molar extractor pulls impacted wisdom teeth, or how your fence-post digger drives holes with less effort.

- **Luxury items:** Revel in the sensual aspects of the product. Talk to the reader about the creamy, soft touch of genuine cashmere; the hand-crafted rosewood dashboard in the sedan's interior; or the ocean-fresh flavor of your shipped-overnight oysters.

- **Technical components:** If your product is geared toward machinists, engineers, surgeons, and other professionals, provide detailed specifications of relevant physical qualities, such as dimensions, weight, material, strength, speed, pressure, and so on.

- **Collectibles:** Teddy bears, figurines, model trains, sports memorabilia, and other such products attract a loyal, sometimes passionate, following, so write from the heart. With all the enthusiasm of a devoted fan, describe the authenticity of the product, its richness of detail, and its rarity and unusual virtues.

- **Toys and other items bought for fun, entertainment, and amusement:** Combine the sensuality of the luxury approach with the enthusiasm of collectibles writing. The tone of your copy should match the nature of the product — lively, informal, and yet rich in the kinds of physical detail that make the product present in the reader's imagination.

Talking about services

Unlike products, many services lack a physical "thingness" that lends itself to easy description, and by being abstract, some services may seem remote: Try picturing "personal financial assistance" or "incentive alignment processes" in your mind. Here are a few secrets for making esoteric services immediate, real, and important to the reader:

✔ **Write about what the service does for the reader:** Yup, it's our old friend "benefit" under another mask. Instead of focusing on the literal service — mowing lawns and trimming hedges — the landscaper can talk about saving time and creating a more beautiful environment. Instead of talking about numbers, accountants can focus on uncovering tax savings and ensuring fiscal accountability.

✔ **Establish the service provider's authority and credibility:** The integrity of a service is rooted in the people who provide it. To overcome prospect skepticism, assure the reader of the provider's credibility. For example, you can mention the number of years of experience, the books the service provider has written, special certificates and degrees, unique or unusual skills or areas of expertise, awards the provider has received, membership in relevant associations, or lists of recognizable clients. Your goal is not to boast but to demonstrate the service provider's ability to deliver on promises.

✔ **Demonstrate the working process:** Just as you can demonstrate how a product works, you can describe a service's working process. In the Green's brochure sample in Figure 6-1, I use a short, four-step process to show how easy it is to get groceries from Green's. But you can also use this demonstration to distinguish your service from its competitors. Kensington Landscape Services, for example, could begin its work process with a soil analysis and design plan, establishing it as an elite service that does much more than mow lawns or trim hedges.

Adding Supporting Elements to Your Brochure

In addition to including photographs, charts, and other illustrations, you can write supporting elements to build your case. You can incorporate the following elements into the main body of your copy, or you can ask the designer to set them apart as callouts or sidebars with a special graphic treatment that sets them apart from the text. (For more information on callouts and sidebars, see Chapter 2.)

✔ **Quotes and testimonials:** A favorable word from a happy customer goes a long way toward establishing your credibility. (See Chapters 3 and 12 for more information about collecting quotes and testimonials.)

✔ **Miniature case study:** You can combine the true-life quality of the testimonial with the demonstration by creating a brief case study: a short example of how a satisfied customer successfully used the product or service. (For more on case studies, check out Chapter 13.)

✔ **Hypothetical example:** Like a miniature case study, the hypothetical example presents your product in action — but it's an action that never really occurred. It's written almost exactly in the same way as the case study, except that you make it perfectly clear that your story is speculative: "For example, here's how our credit record database can help your growing business."

✔ **Lists of benefits or features:** To illustrate the value of your offer and break the monotony of long lines of text, you can create bulleted lists of benefits or features led by a subhead that introduces the list, such as these:

Every Kensington Landscaping contract gives you. . . .

Broderick Executive Coaching prepares you for these leadership challenges:

✔ **Alternative uses:** Occasionally, you have the good fortune to work with a product that can be used (and purchased) for reasons beyond its original intended purpose. (Remember when baking soda got a new life as a refrigerator deodorizer?) If your skin cream can also soothe insect bites, say so — you may pick up a few extra sales.

✔ **A quiz:** To engage the reader, create a brief quiz with five to ten questions to demonstrate the applicability of your offer to the prospect. Here are some examples:

Is it time to upgrade your lawn and garden? Take this one-minute quiz and see.

Do you have the leadership skills you need to advance your career? Answer these ten questions to find out.

Each question can then reinforce the stated premise of the quiz, as in these examples:

Would you like the look of your lawn to complement the beauty of your home?

Do your colleagues routinely seek your advice on important issues?

Make the quiz simple — all the questions should require a plain yes or no. And structure the questions so that the answers you want — the ones that qualify the prospect for your product or service — are either all "yes" answers or all "no" answers. That way, you can conclude with a call to action:

If you answered yes to three or more questions, you're ready to take the next step for a greener, more beautiful landscape. Call 1-800-123-4567 today for a free no-obligation landscape assessment.

Chapter 7

Completing the Direct Response Package

- -

In This Chapter

▶ Getting the envelope opened with teasers

▶ Improving response rates with reply devices and lift notes

▶ Giving gifts to lure high-level prospects

▶ Deploying "quick and dirty" direct mail you can do in a day

- -

Although letters and brochures form the core of most direct response mail packages, they rarely travel alone. At the very least, they're packed in an envelope that recipients must open before they can read them, and many times they're accompanied by elements such as reply devices (ordering forms) and supporting messages called *lift notes*. (If you'd like additional information, see Chapter 5 for details on letters and Chapter 6 for more on brochures.)

These additional package elements help you in two ways. First, *teasers* — the copy that appears on the outside of the envelope — and unusually sized "dimensional" mail are designed to spare your message from the circular file and get your package opened. Second, reply devices and lift notes reinforce your message and can help you increase response rates.

In this chapter, you find a number of tips on how you can use teasers, reply devices, lift notes, and dimensional mail to boost the effectiveness of your direct response mail. And as a special treat to all those who work alone or are understaffed, I show you how an ordinary PC and laser printer can put you on the fast track to direct mail that you can launch in as little time as one day!

Come-Hither Copy: Writing the Teaser

The teaser is copy written on the outside of the envelope with one goal in mind: to get the prospect to open the envelope. The teaser's job may be limited, but it sure is important. If the teaser isn't enticing enough to persuade the recipient to open the envelope, the rest of the package is wasted.

As the name suggests, the teaser teases: It provokes, stimulates, and raises curiosity — but it never satisfies. To be effective, the teaser has to elicit a desire without delivering the goods. To obtain satisfaction, the prospect must open the envelope and read on. There are many ways to write a teaser, but they all share this quality of desire and frustration (kind of like some relationships I've had).

Knowing when to use (and not to use) the teaser

An interesting teaser can encourage people to open an envelope. Yet the letters that people are most likely to read are the ones that come from someone they know — or look like they come from someone they may know. Putting a teaser on the envelope tips your hand; because no one puts teasers on personal correspondence, the teaser is a sure sign of unsolicited mail. Quite a dilemma, isn't it?

I can't give you an absolute rule for when to use or abandon the teaser, but I can tell you the factors to consider when making your decision.

Using the teaser when your mail looks unsolicited

Think about how your mail is going to look. If you use a window envelope so that the address on the letter can double as the mailing address (a way to save money on production costs), then your mail already looks unsolicited. Likewise, if you use a return address that includes your business name, if you apply metered postage (printed in ink) rather than stamps, or if the envelope isn't an ordinary size or color, then recipients already know that they're getting marketing mail.

When your prospects know that a sales pitch is coming, then your best bet is to give them a reason to hear it out. In this case, a teaser is a wise choice; it gives you an opportunity to convince prospects that yours is a piece of mail that deserves their time and attention.

Thirsty koalas, red kangaroos, and me

In the early days of my copywriting career, I was assigned to write a mailing insert for a nature video about the Australian outback. The producer, a publisher famed for its vivid photography of nature at its most outlandish, successfully created the equivalent of a steamy potboiler by concentrating on cunning predators, strange mating rituals, and elaborate schemes for disguise and survival.

As a good copywriter should, I watched the movie and made notes of the most provocative details. In the copy itself, I highlighted a number of these fascinating facts and told readers about the treats to come: When they watched the video, they would discover that koalas never drank water, but got all their H_2O from eucalyptus leaves. They would see why kangaroos rolled around in the red desert sand: to give themselves a natural sunscreen against the scorching heat.

Convinced I had done well by using compelling details, I submitted my copy, expecting applause. Instead, I got a stunning rebuke from the client: My copy was too satisfying! He explained that I selected the right details but went wrong by describing them too completely. "You gave it all away," he said. "Why should anyone buy the video?"

He suggested I rewrite the same facts in a way that left the reader in suspense. Instead of telling prospects how the koala got its water, I wrote, "Discover the amazing secret of the koala — the marsupial that survives without a sip of water!" For the kangaroos: "Red dirt keeps kangaroos alive in 110-degree heat — see how!"

The copy was approved, the video sold well, and I learned an important lesson: Tease, don't please. Provoke interest, but don't allow prospects satisfaction until they become customers.

Abandoning the teaser for a personal look

But suppose that you use a plain white envelope of an ordinary size, with a regular first-class stamp and a return address that either doesn't identify your business or is unlikely to raise alarm — from a doctor's office, for example. Your mail will look like personal correspondence — as long as you don't stick a teaser on it.

I recommend not using a teaser when you want a personal look for your letter and when, indeed, the content has a personal, or at least neighborly, aspect to it. Who might use a personal approach? Perhaps a physician establishing a new practice in a community, a neighbor running for a spot on the school board, or a swim instructor offering lessons at the local Y.

WARNING!

When you use the personal look as camouflage, you run the risk of miring yourself in an ethically murky gray area. Apply this general rule: If you can reasonably anticipate that readers won't be terribly disappointed when they open the envelope, then the personal look is probably okay. But if you can expect that many readers will feel conned or tricked, be careful. At the very least, identify yourself on the return address. (For more information, see "Considering matters of ethics," later in this chapter.)

Checking out options that open envelopes

So how do you provoke interest without providing satisfaction? If I tell you, I'm contradicting myself, but I'm going to tell you anyway. In fact, I give you several ways to write effective teasers.

Asking provocative questions

Every question demands an answer — which, of course, is withheld until the envelope is opened. The most successful questions play on our strongest emotions, fear and desire. Consider these examples:

> *Do you know the 5 red flags that can target your tax return for an IRS audit?*

> *Can you name the 3 fruit juices that help you lose weight and lower your cholesterol?*

Each of the above questions gain power by promising a clearly quantified payoff — 5 red flags or 3 fruit juices — that will concretely satisfy the reader's curiosity. But you can also write more open-ended questions to raise doubts that demand resolution:

> *Is your processing plant prepared for upcoming environmental regulations?*

> *Can you find the hidden treasure among the "junk" in your attic?*

Be sure that your questions always contain an implicit promise of important information inside the envelope. For example, the question "Would you like to make more money?" fails to tantalize the reader with anything new. But the question "Do you know how to make $1,000 a month with just a few hours of your spare time?" implies a way to make money the reader doesn't know yet — but could discover by reading the rest of the package.

Promising a reward

Who doesn't like a present? One of the best teases is to promise a reward for opening the envelope. Here are three easy rewards:

- ✔ **Discounts:** Giving a discount? You can lead with it on the envelope:

    Get 50% off your next order of checks. Details inside.

- ✔ **Premiums:** Some direct mail packages are like kids' cereal boxes — they promise a gift, or *premium*, inside:

    Inside: 100 personalized address labels, absolutely FREE!

- ✔ **Offers:** If your offer is especially strong, try using it in the teaser:

    Get a FREE growth light when you order just $25 or more in seeds. Here's how. . . .

Reminding people of your relationship

Face it: Most people greet unsolicited mail with considerable skepticism. One way to prevent an instant toss to the trash is to remind readers of your current relationship with them (assuming that this relationship exists — and this technique works only when it does). Consider two of the most popular ways of leveraging a relationship:

- **Appeal to exclusivity:** We (and I'm including myself here) like to think of ourselves as special, so an "exclusive" offer taps into our vanity. You can easily combine a relationship reminder with an appeal to exclusivity:

  For readers of Golf World ONLY: Premium access to St. Andrews! Details inside.

- **Combine with an offer:** Simply add an offer to the relationship reminder:

  Dodge Caravan owners save 50% off their next oil change — coupon inside!

Creating urgency

Posting a deadline can inhibit an easy dismissal of your offer. People may find that throwing a piece of mail away is harder if it's their last chance or if time is running out. To create urgency, add a deadline to any of the approaches I describe earlier:

Order your personalized cards by November 15 and get 50% more cards at no additional cost!

There's still time to participate in our next Franchises & Finances seminar — but you must reserve your FREE seat by February 28.

URGENT: Your Podiatry Association disability coverage expires in January — unless you renew by December 15.

Tying the teaser to the Johnson Box

In any mailing, the teaser is the first thing read. The letter headline — or Johnson Box — is usually the first part of the letter to be read. (For more information about Johnson Boxes, see Chapter 5.) The teaser and the Johnson Box, therefore, have a natural relationship to one another. Following are the two most common ways of tying the teaser and the Johnson Box together:

- **Restate the teaser message in the Johnson Box:** Often the simplest approach is best. When you have a strong offer, a compelling benefit, or a terrific story lead, you can use it twice. In this example, I just expand the message a little bit the second time around:

  Teaser: *Subscribe to Garden Magic for two years and get the third year FREE! See inside for more information.*

> Johnson: *Thousands of green thumbs have subscribed to Garden Magic for only $19.95 a year. Now you can get an even better deal: Subscribe today for two years and get the third year FREE!*
>
> ✔ **Make the Johnson Box a payoff to the teaser:** To create drama, you can write the teaser as a setup question or statement that is fulfilled in the letter headline. (For more about payoffs and headlines, see Chapter 6.) In the following example, I use a question teaser that's partially answered in the Johnson Box:
>
> Teaser: *At least 4 common foods have been known to kill — do you know what they are?*
>
> Johnson Box: *If you had read Dr. Brunswick's latest book, Eating for Life, you'd know that grapefruit juice and prescription pain medicines can form a lethal combination. Read the rest of this letter for 3 more killers — then order Eating for Life for only $29.95, a 25% savings off the bookstore price!*

Selecting the best teaser option

With so many options at your disposal, how do know what's best for your particular needs? It depends on your particulars: the nature of your product or service, the quality of the information you have at your disposal, and the strength (or lack thereof) of the offer you can make. Here's a handy guide:

✔ **Strong offer:** When you have an especially strong offer, consider the angle that promises a reward or the urgency approach (by adding a deadline to the offer).

✔ **Strong benefits:** If you suspect that the benefit of your product is more compelling than the offer you can make, try the provocative question approach or a tie-in with the Johnson Box that exploits your benefit with drama.

✔ **Strong relationship:** Do you have a loyal customer base that's passionate about your brand? Take advantage of your good fortune by using your name in your teaser to remind readers of your previously established relationship.

✔ **Strong news:** If your package is built around "news" (important new information of value to your prospects), consider a provocative question approach ("Did you know . . . ?"). If the news is strong enough, you can connect the teaser to a Johnson Box that provides additional story information.

Considering matters of ethics

Occasionally, I get junk mail disguised as something else: a check, an invoice, or an "official notice" marked FEDERAL as if it were from the U.S. government. At the most extreme, I've received subscription offers masked as "renewal

Having fun with your own teasers

When I'm assigned to write direct response mail, I often start with the teasers because they help me conceive the entire package . . . and because they're a lot of fun. See what you can come up with for the following situations:

✔ You're a real estate broker introducing your-self to potential home sellers with a letter and a handy pamphlet, "10 Tips for Selling Your Home."

✔ You're an antiques dealer inviting prospects to a free assessment party, kind of like *Antiques Roadshow,* at the local community center.

✔ You're a company that installs wireless net-works for small to medium-sized busi-nesses, and you're offering free network hubs for clients with 25 or more computers to connect.

✔ You're a hospital-affiliated social worker starting a support group for cancer patients and their families.

Here are a few things to think about:

✔ Do all of these situations merit teasers?

✔ Can you think of ways of embedding the benefit in the teaser?

✔ For each of these situations, what's the best way of getting the reader into the envelope — leading with the offer, a premium, or the promise of important information?

notices," as if someone in my household were already receiving a magazine that's now up for another year's subscription.

Every one of these mailings inspires a double pang of disgust: first, as a con-sumer who resents being conned and second, as a copywriter who hates the way these phony packages reflect on his profession.

Some people argue that these tricks get envelopes opened, which is the only standard that matters. But set aside my ethical qualms for a moment and think this through: If your letter or package serves as your introduction to prospects, how do you think they'll feel when they open the envelope and realize that they've been tricked? Will they think favorably of your business and its products and services? Or will they fling your letter away in anger? You know the answer.

Answer Me! Creating the Reply Device

The purpose of your direct response mail is, of course, to solicit a response. Depending on the nature of your business or your offer, you may want the prospect to respond by phone, e-mail, the Web, or regular mail, via a reply device you include in the package.

For a mailed response, the reply device usually comes in one of two forms:

✔ **The postage-paid business reply card (BRC):** About the size of a post-card, the postage-paid BRC includes your address and the necessary mailing indicia (postage) on one side and a brief form on the opposite side for the customer to complete. Like any other postcard, the postage-paid BRC doesn't offer privacy and isn't a good choice for soliciting credit card numbers or intimate information. It is good, however, for bill-me-later options, event registrations, free gift offers, and the like.

✔ **The BRC plus a business reply envelope (BRE):** When you ask for money, credit card numbers, or personal information, you include a postage-paid envelope, the BRE, with the reply card. The BRE is often a #9 envelope, which measures 3⅞ inches x 8⅞ inches (so that it can fit in the familiar #10 envelope, which is 4⅛ inches x 9½ inches), and is printed with an address and mailing indicia. Because the BRC no longer requires its own mailing information, you have more liberty with its structure. In many cases, the BRC can be a perforated tear-off from a brochure (or even specially designed letters) rather than an independent unit. For more information about business reply mail in general and specific guidelines for getting a mail permit for your office, visit the U.S. Postal Service online at www.usps.com.

Regardless of the physical structures of the reply device, the copy content is always similar and includes a name for the reply device, instructions, reply options, and space for the respondent to include contact information (if this hasn't already been preprinted on the device).

Naming the reply card

At some point in your letter and/or brochure, you ask the prospect to respond — the call to action — and if a reply card is among the response options, you have to refer to it by name. Yes, you can simply call it the *reply card* and be done with it. But in many instances, you want to maintain the tone or "feel" of your package, and it may be appropriate to give the reply card a name consistent with the rest of your message. If so, the headline to the reply card is often the name you invent for it. I recommend something short that includes the name of your product, the name of your business, and, if there's room, an implied benefit, such as "Wealth Builders Seminar RSVP." Here are a few additional examples:

Magnet Digest *Subscription Renewal Form*

Freedom Disability Insurance Application Request Form

Society of St. Martin Membership Application

RUSH: Lean-Body Vitamin Supplement Packs

Check out Figure 7-1 for an example of a reply card.

Front

Personal Planning Acceptance Form

Simply complete and return this *Personal Planning* Acceptance Form, or call 1-800-123-4567, to receive 12 issues of the finance bulletin that can reduce your debt burden, build your portfolio—and add luxury to your lifestyle!

☐ **YES! A year from now, I want to enjoy a stronger financial status—guaranteed.** Send me 12 monthly issues of the *Personal Planning Bulletin* so I can get on the inside track to greater wealth and security. My success is guaranteed: If I don't believe I'm richer and more financially secure a year from now, I get my entire subscription fee back!

☐ Maybe. Send me the first issue of the *Personal Planning Bulletin*. If I decide not to keep my subscription, this issue is mine to keep, absolutely free.

☐ No. I have all the money I want and I don't need easy, expert ways to reduce debt, lower my taxes, build my wealth, or plan for a stronger, more financially secure future.

Name:_____   Title:_____

Organization:_____   Home Phone: (___)_____

E-mail:_____   Work Phone: (___)_____

Address:_____   City:_____ State:___ Zip Code:_____

Back

Return Address _____

_____

_____

Mailing Indicia

Company
Street Address
Suite 123
City, State Zip Code

Figure 7-1: Reply card copy includes a name, instructions, and multiple reply options.

Embedding the benefit in the reply options

After all the heavy lifting involved in writing a letter or brochure (or both), you may be relieved to know that the reply card copy is usually short and sweet. It isn't, however, insignificant. For many prospects, the reply card is the only element of your direct mail package that they actually keep. That's why it's important that your reply card restates your most important messages.

Under the name at the top of the reply card, include a brief paragraph that summarizes your offer, primary benefit, and guarantee (if there is one) and provides ordering instructions that, once again, tell customers what to do and what they get for doing it. In Figure 7-1, for example, I embed the key benefits in the instructions: "reduce your debt burden, build your portfolio — and add luxury to your lifestyle!"

In addition to the messaging you include in the introductory paragraph, you should always restate the benefit within the reply options: the "yes," "maybe," and "no" that prospects may check in response to your offer.

Holy logical inconsistency, Batman! Why in the world would a prospect bother to reply just to say no? If that doesn't seem logical to you, you're right. But since when have human beings been logical? In test after test, reply devices with a "no" option have consistently outperformed devices without it. Why? No one knows for sure. But if it works, use it. And here's another good reason for including a "no" option: Doing so gives you an opportunity to explain the negative consequences of not accepting the offer.

Here's how to write the options:

- ✔ **Yes:** Because this is the option you *want* prospects to take, the "yes" option comes first. It's often made prominent by bigger or bold type, and it always tells prospects, once again, what they'll get and the benefit of getting it. In Figure 7-1, I include both the benefit — "stronger financial status" and "the inside track to greater wealth and security" — and a reminder of the guarantee.

- ✔ **Maybe:** In many cases, you may give prospects an intermediary offer that doesn't obligate them to give you money but allows you to keep the sale alive. In Figure 7-1, the "maybe" offer is a free copy of the magazine that prospects may keep without obligation, whether or not they choose to subscribe.

- ✔ **No:** The object of the "no" option is to make prospects uncomfortable. You want to make it clear that by rejecting the offer, prospects are losing something good and may be susceptible to some threat or pain. In Figure 7-1, prospects are told that by choosing "no," they're losing ways to reduce debt, lower taxes, build wealth, and plan for a better future.

Collecting contact information

The rest of the reply device is usually devoted to fields that collect the customer's contact information: name, address, phone number, e-mail, and so on. You may also ask for more sensitive information, such as credit card numbers. (For more on finding a designer, see Chapter 6.)

The most important thing you need to consider is the prospect's concern for privacy. You may want to add a disclaimer that reassures prospects that their information remains confidential and won't be shared or sold to third parties. If you do indeed intend to rent or share customer information, add a check box option that allows customers to participate (or not) in future mailings. It could look like this:

> *Many of our customers appreciate news, coupons, and other offers from us and other quality vendors we work with.*
>
> ❑ *Yes, please keep me informed with future offers and updates.*
>
> ❑ *Yes, stay in touch with me, but don't share my contact information with any other party.*
>
> ❑ *No, I don't want any further communications. Please keep my contact information confidential.*

Writing Lift Notes: Another Way to Tell Your Story

The *lift note,* a miniature letter or note that accompanies a larger letter, gets its name from its intended purpose — to "lift" or increase response. In theory, the lift note is an additional opportunity to sell by approaching the prospect from a fresh angle. The decision whether to use a lift note is entirely economic: If testing shows that the lift note increases revenue to a degree that exceeds the additional expense of producing it, the business uses lift notes. Lift notes are especially popular in subscription mailings and fundraising appeals. (For more information on testing your writing, check out Chapter 4.)

Graphically, the lift note is usually smaller than the letter and is often folded as if it were a personal message. In fact, that "personal" quality is frequently reinforced by using a scriptlike font similar to handwriting, or by using the Courier font to mimic a typewritten note. To distinguish the lift note from other elements in a direct mail package, it may be printed on a paper stock with a different color or texture.

In content, the lift note is similar to the letter and includes all the important letter elements: a one-to-one approach, richly described benefits, and a clear call to action with a compelling offer. (For more about letters, see Chapter 5.) But for the lift note to be effective, it needs to distinguish itself from the letter and the brochure by offering a new perspective. The following sections describe tactics that are among the most popular for writing lift notes.

Creating a personal message from the president

In this approach, an authority figure associated with the business — for example, the president, publisher, medical director, or chairperson of the charity committee — adds her *personal* perspective to the story in an effort to build a stronger bond with the prospect. As the writer, you assume the role of the authority figure and write from that person's would-be perspective. (Because the authority figure's name is printed on the note, be sure to get her approval before printing.) The lift note says, in essence, "I am like you, and because you're like me, you'll also find value in our offer."

In Figure 7-2, the president of Mutual of Kalamazoo uses his personal experience as the bridge between the product he's selling — Health Cash supplemental insurance — and the prospect. The distinctive elements are the casual, friendly tone ("Believe me, I wasn't thinking about Health Cash coverage then either, but boy, am I glad I had it!") and the use of precise details, such as the cost of the adjustable bed and Feeley's sleeping problem.

Reproducing a customer testimonial

You can bring the lift note one step closer to the reader by reproducing a *testimonial* — a first-person anecdote or story about the product or service — from a satisfied customer. In addition to having the direct and personal quality of a lift note from an authority figure, the customer testimonial gains credibility from its source: a customer who was once a prospect, just like the reader.

The testimonial lift note is limited by the resources available to you. You or your organization must have a process in place for collecting customer comments, quotes, and testimonials *in advance* of your specific project needs. (For more information on testimonials, see Chapter 3.) If you have relevant quotes available to you that are too short to fill an entire lift note, you can group several of them together under a headline that says, in effect, "Here's what our customers say about us."

Dear Mutual of Kalamazoo Customer:

Like you, I didn't give much thought to Health Cash supplemental insurance.

Until one day, last November, when I was cleaning out my gutters. My ladder slipped from under me and I fell 12 feet. Believe me, I wasn't thinking about Health Cash coverage then either, but boy, am I glad I had it!

I didn't suffer any serious injuries—thank goodness—but I did get a broken arm and two very bruised ribs that made sleeping difficult. While my health insurance covered most of the medical costs, it didn't cover the deductible for the emergency room visit, the cost of a new adjustable bed, or the expense of occupational therapy after my cast was removed.

My expenses ran into the thousands. Fortunately, my Health Cash supplemental insurance covered it all. Everything! And that meant that my expenses were one less thing for me to think about.

Please, if you don't have Health Cash supplemental insurance, now is your time to apply—the enrollment period ends February 15, and when you act now, you can lock-in this year's rates for the coming year.

Learn from me. I hope you'll never have a need for supplemental medical coverage. But life has a way of pulling surprises (and ladders!) out from under us. Think about Health Cash now, so you don't ever have to think about additional medical expenses later.

Sincerely,

Max Feeley

Max Feeley
President, Mutual of Kalamazoo

Figure 7-2:
A personal lift note from the president establishes a connection with a prospect.

Sweetening the offer

Instead of altering the perspective by seeing through the eyes of a new speaker (the authority figure or the customer), you can look at a new aspect of the offer itself. You have a number of options:

✔ **Add more to the offer:** Reward prospects for reading the lift note by giving them an additional discount or additional quantities at no additional cost by acting now. Sometimes marketers give prospects a "secret" code to add to the reply card to get this special, additional incentive. Here's an example:

At only $24.95, 500 SunPlus vitamins are a terrific deal. But we'll go one step more. Write "shine" in the Code Box on the enclosed SunPlus Order Form, and we'll send you an additional 250 vitamins absolutely FREE!

✔ **Reveal an additional benefit:** Keep the same offer, but use the lift note to demonstrate an additional benefit you hadn't previously discussed:

You know that Nonoxatall is the number one fuel injector cleaner favored by America's leading stock car drivers. But did you also know that Nonoxatall removes water from gas lines and extends engine life?

✔ **Focus on another feature:** Take the preceding idea, but instead of writing about another benefit, focus on a new feature:

Late breaking news: The latest Connectme personal communicator now includes a GPS chip that can relay your location to any cell phone!

✔ **Give away a premium:** Finally, you can sweeten the offer by adding a free gift to people who respond to your exclusive mail offer:

You may have seen the Counter-Top Cooker on TV. Or read about it in your favorite food magazine. But in an exclusive deal available ONLY through this mail offer, we'll give you a FREE set of four professional-grade Teflon spatulas when you order your Counter-Top Cooker by July 31!

Sending Presents: Big Dimensional Mail

At the opposite extreme from the little lift note are oversized packages, almost always accompanied with a gift, called *dimensional mail* or, sometimes, *lumpy mail*. Like other direct response packages discussed in this book, dimensional mail usually includes letters, brochures, and reply devices. But dimensional mail distinguishes itself by its size and shape and by the impact of the enclosed premium. Whether delivered in boxes, tubes, or large express-delivery envelopes, big mail makes a big impression.

Producing dimensional mail, however, is more than a matter of adjusting to a larger scale; it's a whole other strategy for communicating your message. Frankly, dimensional mail is expensive; when you add up the cost of the premium, the package design, and the postage, you arrive at a significant sum. To consider using dimensional mail, you should feel confident that its impact justifies its cost.

Knowing when to use dimensionals

In fact, the extra expense of dimensional mail is justified by one thing: access. As expensive as they may seem, dimensional packages can be the most cost-effective way of communicating to hard-to-reach prospects. Who are these people?

✔ **Executives and senior managers:** Many big-ticket items, such as comprehensive computer services and corporate-wide insurance policies, must have the approval of senior management or even C-level executives (chiefs of this and that). Unfortunately, these people are notoriously difficult to reach. In fact, one responsibility of their support staff is to screen out unsolicited mail, which includes mail from you. But few people throw out a box or tube without at least looking inside to see what it's about. And if a free gift is indeed inside, few subordinates risk their boss's wrath by opening the box themselves. Hence the power of dimensional mail: It almost always gets opened by the intended recipient.

✔ **Affluent consumers:** Willie Sutton, the infamous bank robber, once said that he robbed banks because "that's where the money is." Marketers also know where the money is, so many of them target rich people because they're, well, rich. To defend themselves against a barrage of marketing material, many wealthy consumers are selective about what they'll open and read. The dimensional package is a way to get past their initial defenses.

Given the expense, you can't afford to waste your time mailing dimensionals to the wrong people or to the wrong addresses. Typically, dimensionals are used when the universe of qualified prospects — the number of people who are capable of buying from you or who are authorized to purchase from you — is relatively small. Even then, professional direct marketers take pains to be sure that they have an accurate list of names and addresses, often initiating their campaigns by calling ahead to each prospect to confirm the accuracy of the contact data. (For more, see "Preparing your list of prospects," later in this chapter.)

Matching your copy to the enclosed gift

In most aspects, copy for the dimensional is no different from any other marketing mail; the rules for teasers, letters, brochures, and reply devices still apply. The new wrinkle is the gift that's enclosed in the big box you're sending. That gift or premium has to tie in with the story or the offer; as the copywriter, you're responsible for doing the tying.

Tying the premium to the story

You don't just want to send any gift. You want to deliver something that establishes a connection between your prospect and your business. One of the best ways to do this is to work with a premium that reflects or expands the story you tell in the other package elements, the letter, and the brochure.

A few years ago, I worked with a medical group that offered an unusual supplement to ordinary health insurance: "boutique" physical examinations exclusively for executives. These exams were much more thorough than the usual physical and were accompanied by first-class perks, such as cappuccinos and leather recliners in the waiting room. The key benefit had a bottom-line appeal: Premium health services keep your most expensive personnel alive and kicking. But the creative team gave the mailing a soft touch by enclosing a terrific book, Mitch Albom's *Tuesdays with Morrie,* the story of the author's friendship with a dying mentor. In one stroke, the premium communicated two important things: Good and talented people die, and my client is thoughtful. My letter and brochure, therefore, had to carry the twin themes of business accountability (don't lose your most precious assets) and a commitment to caring.

Tying the premium to the offer

Instead of relating the premium to the story, you can tie the premium to the offer. This is an especially attractive option when the premium in the box is a lure to an even bigger and better gift that comes later — if the prospect responds. For example, I had a client who sold multi-million-dollar customer relationship management (CRM) software. To jump-start the sale, he wanted to attract Fortune 500 executives to an all-day seminar promoting his product. The hook? Free driving lessons at a famous racetrack in Florida. We connected the premium to the offer (race car lessons) by shipping beautiful desktop models of the Dodge Viper sports car. My copy talked about both the virtues of the software and the value of the lessons. To make a stronger link to the offer, I used a number of racing metaphors, such as "pull away from the pack," to drive home the message.

Applying the power of size — on the cheap

Don't be discouraged by the cost of dimensional mail. You want to get past the gatekeepers but don't have the budget for a full-blown package plus premium? Consider using Priority Mail from your local post office. For less than $4, you get a heavy-duty oversized envelope with guaranteed two-day delivery of anything under a pound in weight. (Greater weight costs more.) For a little more money, go with a FedEx two-day envelope: In addition to being reasonably inexpensive, delivery is guaranteed and trackable. Stuff it with the usual letter and brochure or throw in an article reprint about your business. (For more on articles, see Chapter 13.) Sure, it's a heck of a lot more money than first-class postage, but you're buying an opportunity to get your message to people who are otherwise almost impossible to reach.

Quick and Dirty: Direct Mail in a Day

Direct response mail doesn't have to be expensive in order to be effective. In fact, if you have a personal computer, a laser printer, and standard word-processing software, you have everything you need to do your own quick and dirty direct mail.

What makes quick and dirty direct mail quick and dirty?

- ✔ **It's cheap:** You can use your own stationery or plain white paper and envelopes. You're going to create your own list of contacts, so you don't have to pay for a list broker. And chances are, you already own or have access to the tools you need to make it work.

- ✔ **It's fast:** When you have all the elements in place — your tools, stationery, data (contact information), and your copy — you can easily print and mail 200 or 300 letters in one day. Honest!

Quick and dirty mail isn't for everyone. If your branding requires some sophistication and your message demands graphics, you need to invest some more in your package. (For more information on branding, see Chapter 10.) But for many small businesses and sole proprietors with a clearly defined target market (for example, homeowners within five miles of your store, northeast IT managers in the food processing industry, or customers who have already freely given their address information to you), quick and dirty mail can be a wonderfully cheap way of communicating a personal marketing message. You just need to follow a few simple steps.

Making an offer people can't refuse

Give people a reason to respond — and whatever you do, don't waste your time by asking prospects to call for more information. "More information," is not an offer; it's a cop-out. You have a number of dirt-cheap options at your disposal:

- ✔ **Offer a discount:** Tell your prospects that when they bring this letter to you or call for a meeting, you'll give them a discount off the standard price.

- ✔ **Offer a premium:** When they come to your store or make an appointment, they'll get a free calendar, a baseball cap with your logo on it, or a free home energy analysis. The kind of premium you offer should match the nature of your business.

✔ **Offer ten free tips:** When you can't think of anything else, here's a classic approach that doesn't cost you a thing: Write up ten free tips that prospects can get when they respond to you. What do you write about? If you run a beauty salon, give away Hollywood's top ten secrets for more beautiful skin. If you're a stockbroker, try ten technology stocks to watch in the upcoming quarter. An auto repair shop? How about ten tricks for better gas mileage? Chances are, you know something of value that you can translate into a giveaway.

Preparing your list of prospects

The one essential for any direct mail is data, which in this case refers to a list of addresses and often names, too. The big-league, direct-response professionals use *house lists,* which are customer data maintained by the businesses themselves, or they turn to *list brokers,* people who rent lists of addresses culled from a variety of sources.

But this is quick and dirty mail, so you're not going to buy lists from anybody. Instead, you're going to do one of two things:

✔ **Work with your own house lists:** If you already have customer information (and permission to use it), great. If not, you can build a house list by literally asking your customers for their information, such as at the cash register or other appropriate points of contact. Despite legitimate concerns about privacy, people will give you their contact information — *if* you promise them something in return and promise to keep the information to yourself. To collect addresses, offer your customers a chance to participate in a book discussion group, get early announcements on new products, or receive exclusive coupons and discounts.

✔ **Hunt for information yourself:** Personally, I use the Web to seek out potential customers (marketing and advertising agencies) and collect their contact info. (This technique is an accepted ethical practice for targeting business prospects but is regarded as a dangerously intrusive practice for identifying consumers.) You can do the same, either online or with the humble phone book. When you're targeting businesses, you may be able to save time by not taking the extra steps required to obtain individual names. Instead, you can use the name of the organization followed by a title. For example, I use a generic "Attn: Creative Director" on my envelopes and "Dear Creative Director" in the letter salutation; no name is necessary.

Gathering your tools

You don't need much, but you do need a few things — most of which you already have!

✔ **Personal computer with word-processing software:** Specifically, word-processing software that has a mail merge feature. Fortunately, the most popular word-processing software programs, including Microsoft Word and Word Perfect, have this feature. Note that you create three different file types:

- **Data files:** You know that contact information I asked you to collect? This is where it goes. You follow the specific instructions of the software you're using, but in general, you create fields, such as "name," "title," "organization," "address," and so on, to accommodate the information you're collecting. Make sure that you create two separate fields of data, "address 1" and "address 2," for the street address to accommodate locations that require multiple lines, such as One Hammond Center, 22 Church St.

- **Form files:** This is the actual document, such as the envelope or the letter, into which your data will flow. But instead of typing in the address as you do with an ordinary letter, you place a code that tells the software where to insert specific data: the name, address, city, state, zip code, and so on. Again, follow your software's instructions.

- **Merge files:** When you finish collecting data and writing your form documents, you tell the software to merge the data and the form files to create a third file, the *merge file* that integrates the two into the actual envelopes and letters you print out.

✔ **Laser printer:** Laser printers are fast, produce print that doesn't run when wet, and are usually capable of printing envelopes in batches. And the end result is a professional-looking document — not a mess of dots and ink smears. (If you don't have a laser printer, you can bring your computer file to a print ship or full-service office supply store and ask them to run the printout for you.) Most laser printers are up to the task; just be sure the model you have (or are interested in buying) can easily print on batches of envelopes, as well as ordinary paper.

✔ **Stationery:** You need something to print on, either custom stationery preprinted with your letterhead on it or plain stationery — good old ordinary white paper you can buy at any office supply store or stationery shop. I recommend printing directly onto the envelopes rather than generating stickers; the printed address looks more like one-to-one correspondence.

WARNING!

As long as you're printing on envelopes, you may be tempted to create a teaser, too. Unless you have an absolutely brilliant reason to do so, I advise against it. With a personal address, an ordinary envelope, and a hand-applied stamp, your mail looks like personal correspondence: Why spoil the illusion with a teaser? You'll probably get more people to open your mail by not printing a teaser on the envelope.

✔ **Stamps:** Bless the United States Postal Service! When I first started my business, I had to lick stamps (or find some other way to moisten them); now you just peel them off a roll or sheet. Alternatives to stamps, such as metered mail and permit mail imprints, are available, but I'd forgo their use for the same reason I discourage using the teaser on your quick and dirty mail: They're a red flag that tells the recipient, "This isn't correspondence!"

✔ **Envelope sealer:** Stamps have progressed, but most envelopes still must be moistened to be sealed. Save your tongue for better things. Little sponge-topped squeeze tubes can do the trick, but the best thing I've found for the job is a liquid glue that comes in a roll-on-like application device; when you're faced with 200 envelopes to seal, this is the way to go. You can find these roll-on glues at office supply stores. (You can try self-adhesive envelopes as well, but test one first in your laser printer before committing to a box. Sometimes the intense heat of the printer gums these envelopes shut.)

✔ **Inserts:** Sure, you're writing a letter. But maybe you want to include something else as well. Because I'm talking quick and dirty, I'm not asking you to write and print a brochure to insert. I often enclose lists of clients and representative projects, photocopied back to back. Other inserts may include coupons, reprints of an article you've written (or an article written about you), ten free tips similar to the ones I discuss in the section "Making an offer people can't refuse," or flyers with more detailed information about your product or service. (Check out Chapter 13 for information on writing articles and Chapter 15 for details on flyers and other collateral.)

Assembling your mail

After you print your merge files (letters and envelopes), you simply assemble the pieces. I do my assembling in stages: With piles of envelopes and letters in easy reach, I do the stuffing first, then get my glue and do the sealing, and, finally, put the stamps on.

Putting letters into envelopes isn't rocket science (I use this as an opportunity to blast mid-'60s garage rock on my stereo), but watch for one important thing: Make sure that the addresses on the letter and envelope match before you seal your mail and send it on its way!

Chapter 8

Going It Alone: Self-Mailers, Postcards, Catalogs, and More

In This Chapter

▶ Working with self-mailers and postcards

▶ Creating compelling catalog copy

▶ Describing products for online auctions

*I*n marketing, there's no such thing as a one-size-fits-all solution. Sure, the classic direct response package, with its envelope, letter, brochure, and reply device, is a versatile and effective tool for many purposes — but not all of them.

Sometimes you want to communicate less formally, and don't want (or need) to create multiple elements for one mailing. Sometimes you want to lead with an item, like a postcard, that's conspicuously simple and to the point. Sometimes, frankly, you simply want to select an option that costs less money per product sold. In these and other cases I discuss, the classic package may not be right for your product or your purposes.

Fortunately, you have a number of alternatives for marketing with mail. In this chapter, I show you the most popular solo formats: direct-mail pieces that serve as self-standing, integrated units that don't have envelopes to open or extra pieces to pack together.

Read on to get insider points and a handle on the strengths and trade-offs of self-mailers, postcards, and catalogs. I also give you a few inside pointers for a new marketing medium you may want to consider: the online auction.

Creating the Self-Mailer

You want to use an attractive piece of mail without all the complexity of the classic package? Take a look at the self-mailer. The self-mailer combines some of the narrative qualities of the letter with the graphic capabilities of the brochure in a single unit that's mailed without an envelope. Typically, it's multipaneled like the brochure and held together with wafer seals that prevent it from unfolding in the mail. What would otherwise be the back panel in a brochure is used instead for the address, return address, and postage. In other words, it's an entirely self-sufficient mailing medium.

Knowing when to use (and not to use) the self-mailer

The self-mailer has two advantages over the traditional letter package:

- ✔ **It saves money:** By eliminating the letter and the envelope, the self-mailer can save money in production and postage costs. And you can include the reply device (see Chapter 7) as a perforated tear-off card, creating one seamless message printed on one sheet of paper.

- ✔ **It packs a graphic punch the reader can't escape:** Many envelopes just don't get opened — that's why teasers are used to provoke curiosity. (If you're curious about teasers, see Chapter 7.) But the self-mailer goes one step further by letting you put a powerful combination of headline and graphics on the cover itself, where the recipient can't help but see it.

Unfortunately, there's no such thing as a free lunch. Although the self-mailer is usually cheaper and can be punchier, it does have its limitations:

- ✔ **It's not as great a medium for stories:** Without the intimacy of a letter, the self-mailer isn't as good a medium for introducing a deep benefits story. That's why many direct marketers are reluctant to use self-mailers for one-step sales in which the prospect is asked to purchase on the spot; self-mailers simply don't have enough room to stimulate sufficient desire or overcome all the likely objections. For the same reasons, a self-mailer may not be the best way to introduce your business to prospects or to generate leads for your sales staff.

- ✔ **It lacks a sense of privacy:** The casual quality of the self-mailer makes it a dicey medium for tackling sensitive subjects such as health care, insurance, financial issues, and other issues many people take personally. The information is exposed for all to see — not hidden in an envelope.

Over time, the self-mailer has proven successful for several specific purposes:

- ✔ **Event promotions:** Seminars, conferences, speaking engagements, adult education courses, and professional association activities are among the events that self-mailers frequently promote. In this context, the self-mailer is like an invitation on steroids: Its flexibility of format and greater size give it plenty of space to sell the event, provide illustrative graphics, and even list course options or speaking schedules.

✔ **Additional offers to established customers:** When you've already built a relationship with a customer and no longer need to tell your story or sell the value of your organization, you can use the self-mailer to generate repeat business or offer new products and services. Personal computer manufacturers, niche record labels, and some specialty hobby products are examples of businesses where this tactic can work. Your goal is to build on previous success by offering additional products to customers who are already comfortable with you.

✔ **As one element in a multiwave campaign:** Just as educators appreciate repetition as a tool for learning, marketers repeat their messages to gain traction with prospects. Rather than make a one-shot pitch, many marketers approach their prospects with a series of related messages — a *campaign.* In direct response marketing, that means planning a number of mailings, or *waves.* To prevent the message from going stale, marketers often change formats along the way. By offering a different look (and one that's less expensive as well), the self-mailer can serve as an excellent follow-up to a more elaborate letter package preceding it. The self-mailer can offer a different look at a lower price.

Writing the self-mailer's front panel

The graphic front panel gives the self-mailer its most important distinction because it communicates your message instantly. Concentrate the lion's share of your time and talent, especially if you're in a hurry, on finding or developing a gripping visual and on writing an irresistible headline to work with it.

A successful front panel should do the following:

✔ **Provoke curiosity** that can't be satisfied until the prospect reads the rest of the self-mailer. (For more information on provocation, see Chapter 7.)

✔ **Integrate the graphic and the headline** into a coordinated message for maximum impact. (For more on using visuals, see Chapter 11.)

Stimulating interest at first sight

The front cover hooks readers and lures them inside. Your bait can be

✔ A desirable benefit

✔ A threat to be overcome

✔ A story that piques curiosity

In Chapter 2, you can find information on writing headlines in general. Here are a few examples that illustrate desire, threat, and story-telling in self-mailers:

- ✔ **The heart's desire:** Create a headline and graphic combination that speak to the prospect's desires or dreams. Remember, the "stuff" you're writing about may be golden in your prospects' eyes, so use the evocative language of romance – emphasize charm, beauty, and excitement, and let your writing sing:

    - For a dealer in collectible coins mailing to current customers, here's an idea that combines the desire for a rare, precious item with urgency:

        Cover image: A sparkling pile of brilliant gold coins.

        Headline: *Just in! 16th century Spanish doubloons from the Caribbean. (But hurry – interest is high and supply is limited!)*

    - For a gated community that has already mailed an impressive information kit to prospects, here's a follow-up piece that offers something fresh by introducing a new, very desirable benefit:

        Cover image: Photo montage of people enjoying golfing, cocktails, fishing, dancing, and so on.

        Headline: *For the residents of Towering Oaks, vacation begins at home, every day. . . .*

- ✔ **The worst fear:** You can flip desire on its head and present a threat that the recipient can resolve only by opening the self-mailer. Like the "heart's desire" tactic, this appeal is emotional. But this time, your language isn't romantic or dreamy, but clipped, serious, and maybe even somber. Consider these examples:

    - For consumer financial advisors specializing in retirement planning, here's an approach that combines empathy with fear:

        Cover image: An elderly woman sitting in an unattractive recreation room watching television.

        Headline: *What are your plans for retirement?*

    - People hate the idea of something being taken away from them, even if it's something that's never been truly theirs but has only existed as a possibility in their imaginations. For the gated community, here's a final piece in a multiwave campaign with a last-chance appeal:

        Cover image: An elegant home with a SOLD sign on the front lawn.

        Headline: *Time's running out. This is your last chance to secure a new home in the exclusive Towering Oaks community!*

✔ **The compelling story:** You can lead the prospect into the package by introducing a "story" the reader would like to complete. Your goal is to keep the reader in suspense; readers shouldn't find satisfaction until they read the rest of your copy. It could look like these examples:

- For the coin dealer, here's a story that appeals to the excitement of the product itself:

   Cover image: Illustration of swashbuckling pirates raiding a Spanish galleon.

   Headline: *400 years ago, they stole Spanish gold. Now you can share in their treasure. . . .*

- For the retirement planners, here's a story that implies a happy ending under difficult circumstances:

   Cover image: Photograph of a healthy, happy older couple enjoying coffee on a wooden sloop under sail.

   Headline: *Just 5 years ago, they were certain they couldn't afford to retire. Then they talked to SilverLife Retirement Planners.*

Connecting with a payoff

Because the self-mailer is constructed of folded panels, you can build your headline strategy around the idea of "payoff punch." You use the front cover as a set-up for a payoff headline that appears when the prospect opens the self-mailer.

The key to a payoff approach is to deliberately make your headline incomplete; think of the headline and the subsequent payoff line as a broken amulet that becomes whole only when the two are joined together. The easiest method is to write the headline as a question that is answered by the interior payoff. The other common technique is to write a partial headline, a sentence, phrase, or thought that isn't completed until the reader opens the mailer and reads the payoff. Here are few examples of the payoff in action:

✔ **An event mailer:**

   Cover image: Group shot of older people of mixed gender and mixed ethnicity, looking contentedly into the camera.

   Headline: *What do they know about retirement planning that you don't?*

   Interior payoff headline: *Smart adults plan ahead. Now you can too — when you register for the FREE SilverLife Retirement Seminar.*

✔ **A new offer to current customers:**

   Cover image: Photo of security guards about to open the back of an armored car.

Headline: *A coin collection so rare we have to limit our offer to the first 1,000 respondents only.*

Interior payoff headline: *The Spanish Galleon Specie Collection. Now available in just 1,000 stamped and numbered limited-edition sets!*

✔ **A conclusion to a multiwave campaign:**

Cover image: Photo of closed gate and gatehouse at entrance to an attractive residential development.

Headline: *Don't deny yourself access to Springfield's most exclusive community.*

Interior headline payoff: *You can still own a home in Towering Oaks — if you make your deposit by February 7.*

Crafting the self-mailer's interior copy

In style, tone, and content development, writing for the self-mailer should follow most of the guidelines established for letters and brochures. (See Chapters 5 and 6, respectively, for in-depth explanations.) Like those forms, your self-mailer should do the following:

✔ **Use subheads** to tell your story at a glance.

✔ **Integrate graphics and text** for persuasive impact.

✔ **Promise a desirable benefit** to the prospect and demonstrate how your product or service can fulfill that promise.

✔ **Speak in the tone and vocabulary** familiar to the reader, as if your copy were part of a conversation among friends or colleagues.

✔ **Establish an empathetic rapport** with the reader, putting your organization on the reader's side.

✔ **Look professional** in the reader's eyes. The self-mailer isn't a do-it-yourself project. Have an experienced copy shop print it.

✔ **Organize its message** panel by panel, just like a brochure.

Producing Postcards

Like self-mailers, postcards fly solo but are even simpler: They have only a front, typically with a graphic and a headline, and a back, usually with a message toward the left and space for the mailing indicia (addresses and postage) on the right. They can be as small as the familiar 3½-x-5½-inch card issued by the post office, or they may be oversized, for which you pay more postage. (Visit the United States Postal Service online at www.usps.com for details on dimensions and postage rates.)

Knowing when postcards are right (or wrong) for you

Postcards are perhaps the least expensive way to put your message in the mail. Like the self-mailer, they deliver a headline/graphics combination the recipient can't ignore. But you face a clowns-in-the-tiny-car dilemma — squeezing a lot of messaging into so small a space isn't easy. And in addition to being cheap, the postcard runs the risk of *looking* cheap, too. You should consider using postcards when the format's virtues — informality and cost-efficiency — match your objectives.

When postcards are a good choice

The simplicity of the postcard plays to your advantage if you're doing any of the following:

- ✔ **Selling a commodity:** Lots of businesses establish themselves not by virtue of *brand* (a unique set of characteristics or values associated with a particular name) but by simply offering common goods or services at a decent price from a convenient location. These include many of the businesses you find on Main Street, America: pizza parlors, nail salons, dry cleaners, car washes, mom-and-pop hardware stores, and so on. They're not out to establish national name recognition; they just want to lure you in with a good deal. When the ambition is modest and the product is simple, postcards can be a very effective form of marketing. (For more on branding, check out Chapter 10.)

- ✔ **Making a short-term promotion:** For the Main Street businesses mentioned previously, or even for larger chains, the postcard can be a good tool for short-term promotions that are easy to understand, such as holiday sales, two-for-one offers, clearances, and major discounts.

- ✔ **Sending a reminder or concluding a campaign:** After launching more elaborate marketing efforts through other media, you can use the postcard as a supporting effort to remind prospects of an offer or to make one last, inexpensive pitch to prospects who remain unmoved by previous communications.

- ✔ **Attracting prospects to your trade booth:** Many organizations that go to the time and expense of exhibiting at trade shows support their appearance — and increase their visibility — by sending a preliminary postcard to show attendees. This application may seem narrow to you, but it's the most frequent reason I'm assigned to write a postcard!

- ✔ **Drive traffic to your Web site:** As I discuss in greater detail in Chapter 14, building a Web site, in itself, doesn't attract visitors. A quick postcard is one way of drawing attention to your site and can be especially effective if the postcard trumpets something visitors can physically *do* there, such as make orders online, conduct research, or swap messages with people who share similar interests.

When postcards are a poor choice

Postcards suffer many of the limitations of self-mailers, but even more so. If you're trying any of the following things, don't be tempted to save money by mailing your message as a postcard:

- ✔ **Building new relationships:** With the exception of the Main Street businesses discussed previously, the postcard makes for a weak introduction to your business. It just doesn't have enough space to tell your story nor the visual heft to make a favorable impression.

- ✔ **Selling complex products or services:** Again, consider the amount of room you have. The postcard simply doesn't have enough space to discuss more complex products and services, such as asset allocation policies or health insurance options. When you need to educate your audience about your product or service, look to a format that gives you more room, like the direct response letter package.

- ✔ **Addressing issues of a personal or intimate nature:** Hey, postcards are exposed to the world. Want to talk about the agony of psoriasis? Put an envelope around it.

- ✔ **Creating an elegant impression:** Trust your intuition on this: You'll find it awfully difficult to sell high-end products, such as four-star restaurants, luxury automobiles, and leather-bound books, with an obviously low-cost mailing medium.

Putting together the postcard

I'm going to make the job of preparing your postcard easy because you need to make your postcards simple: Concentrate on the offer. In the arsenal of marketing artillery, the postcard is a rifle shot. Use it to sell a discount, a prize, free delivery — something that's instantly recognizable as a good deal. Face it: A postcard has just enough space to link a benefit to your offer and leaves little room for anything else.

Focus your energy on the headlines — the lines of copy that will be most prominent on the front and on the back. The front headline is an opportunity to work with a graphic image. (For more details, see "Stimulating interest at first sight," earlier in this chapter.) The headline on the back can restate the offer or serve as a payoff that fulfills an idea begun on the cover. (See "Connecting with a payoff," earlier in this chapter, for more information.)

Check out Figure 8-1 for an example of postcard copy.

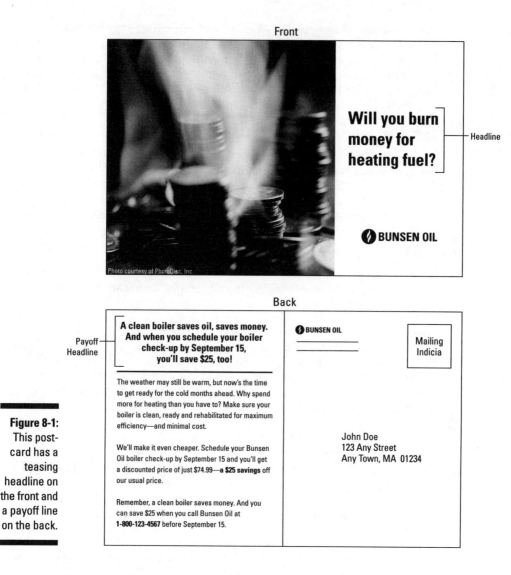

Figure 8-1:
This post-
card has a
teasing
headline on
the front and
a payoff line
on the back.

Creating the postcard headline

I recommend two simple approaches to the cover headline:

✔ **Shout out the offer:** Give the prospect a picture of your product or service and then use the headline to announce your deal. For example:

Cover image: Photo or illustration of lawn mowers.

Headline: *Spring's around the corner. Save $50 off the TrimMaster 5000 at Waldo's Downtown Hardware.*

✔ **Tease and then promise:** You can add emphasis to the benefit of the offer by using a cover headline that plays on desire or fear. In Figure 8-1, my cover headline speaks to the fear of losing money, an idea graphically illustrated with an image of burning money. The headline on the back connects the idea with the offer — "A clean boiler saves oil, saves money" — and then goes straight to the $25 discount offer.

Filling in the postcard body copy

It's cramped in here! You have room to do only two things: articulate the benefit (if necessary) and explain the offer.

In Figure 8-1, I had to give the reason why prospects should care about cleaning their boilers — it saves oil and money. But in many instances, no such explanation is necessary. For example, you either need a lawn mower or you don't.

In any event, you must make the offer clear. Make sure that the reader knows exactly where to go, what number to call, or what terms are necessary in order to get your offer.

Postcards that attract trade show attendees to your booth have another wrinkle: Chances are, prospects don't remember your booth location. Therefore, you want to encourage prospects to keep the postcard and bring it with them to your booth. How? Treat the postcard as if it were a coupon, but instead of a grocer's discount, attendees get a free gift or an opportunity to enter a drawing when they bring their cards to your booth.

Making the Sale with Catalog Descriptions

In most forms of direct response marketing, you, the copywriter, play a starring role. Your ideas often lead the creative development. But now, I'm afraid I have some painful news: When it comes to the creative work for catalogs, copy takes a back seat to graphics. You know it's true. What do you do when you pick up a catalog? You skim. You look at the pictures. You read the copy only after a picture has caught your eye.

The picture, usually a photograph but occasionally an illustration, leads the way by attracting the prospect's attention. Your job is to close the sale. And you close the sale by doing two things:

✔ **Emphasizing the most important benefit or attraction:** When the product *does something* for the prospect, such as remove grease faster or fix flat tires in an instant, you play up the benefit. When you sell products that are valued not for what they do but for what they are, such as apparel and jewelry, you focus on the most attractive features, perhaps the virgin wool in the genuine Scottish sweater or the exclusive cut of your laser-shaped diamonds. When your product has several potential benefits, and you must chose one to highlight, choose the one that has the greatest value to your prospects (to the best of your knowledge) or a benefit that isn't available with competing products.

✔ **Providing all the descriptive information the prospect needs:** You're requesting a purchase right then and there, so buyers have to know about sizes, shipping weights, special features, color options, number of pieces, age appropriateness (for children's toys, for example), and so on.

As if nailing the most important benefit *and* all the necessary description aren't enough, you're also required to sustain the tone of the catalog, whether it be the no-nonsense straight-talk of a technical catalog or the sentimental conversation of a stuffed animal book. You can deduce the appropriate tone from previous issues of the catalog, but if you're lucky, the marketing director has a formal document that describes the *brand identity* (what your catalog means to which people) and provides guidelines for tone and "voice." And oh, one more thing: You must accomplish all this in a minuscule amount of space, typically a headline plus two to four short sentences of body copy and maybe a caption if you're luscky.

Linking pictures to text with headlines

Every block of catalog copy begins with a headline, usually set above the text — like a print ad — or placed as the first line of text with a distinctive type treatment (larger font, bold print, and so on). The headline serves as a *link* between the picture and the descriptive block of body copy. After the graphic has attracted interest, the headline takes the sale one step further and leads the reader into the text. Because it's at a premium, your headline has to make this "link" as quickly as possible; it has to be short. You have a variety of choices:

✔ **Identify the item:** Simply state the name of the item. Although this tactic may not have a lot of sell appeal, it's a successful way to help customers quickly find what they're looking for in a no-nonsense catalog. Here are a few examples:

> *12V Portable Drill with Speed Chuck, Index*
>
> *Limited Edition "Gimme Hug!" Statuette Signed by Liz Charming*
>
> *Vinyl Appliance Covers*

✔ **State the benefit:** Tell readers what the item will do for them. If a product has a number of potential benefits, select the most attractive one and save the rest for the body copy. Look at these examples:

> *MoistureLock Crystals Water Your Plants While You're Away*

> *Keep Cool in Even the Hottest Weather*

> *Travel Slacks Defy Wrinkles*

✔ **Lead with an active verb:** More a style than a strategy, leading with an active verb adds energy and excitement to your headline — a virtue that's especially important when space is at a premium. In many, but not all, cases, the active verb technique is combined with a benefit.

> *Blast away engine grime in seconds!*

> *Light a fire (in his heart)!*

> *Seal leaks, save on plumbing $$$!*

✔ **Lead with a special offer:** Sometimes a cataloger wants to spice up a familiar or common item with a special: a discount, free gift, or free shipping. If so, you can add the offer to the headline:

> *50% off while supplies last!*

> *Get a FREE chew toy with each Auto-Feeder!*

> *Free shipping when you order 2 or more.*

Writing catalog copy with personality

Getting the voice of your catalog personality into your body copy is one of the most difficult challenges a copywriter faces. But it's also fun, because you get the chance to really show off your chops. Try this on for size: You're going to write about one product three times — for three catalogs with three different personalities!

Your product is a cookbook of Italian peasant recipes written by a famous television chef. Here are your catalogs:

✔ *Snidegrass and Fannochio,* an upscale catalog of expensive kitchen products

✔ *Handy Housewares,* a digest-sized catalog of home goods featuring items that make

housekeeping easier, faster, and more enjoyable (or at least less burdensome)

✔ *Current Publications,* a black-and-white catalog of book titles for public library librarians looking for books of interest to their patrons

Ask yourself these questions before you start writing:

✔ What tone is appropriate for each catalog audience? What is the catalog's voice?

✔ Should you describe the same features of the cookbook for each catalog, or should you highlight different things, depending on the interests of the catalog audience?

Depending on the catalog's policy, you may be required to conform to one headline rule with every product (such as "Every headline must include the product name" or "Lead every headline with a verb") or you may be able to mix and match, based on the particular needs of the product. When in doubt, ask the creative director responsible for producing the catalog.

Many catalogs create special graphic icons for important features such as free shipping, new products, or items exclusive to your particular catalog. These are often placed just before or after the headline. Find out what icons are available to you (ask the creative director) and how you're to indicate their placement in your copy.

Writing mountain body copy in molehill space

After prospects are lured by the graphics and hooked by your headlines, you reel 'em in with the body copy. In a handful of words, you must communicate the important benefits and features, provide all the necessary product specifications, and sustain the personality of the catalog. Fortunately, you have a couple tools to help you:

✔ **The merchandise information form (MIF):** This standardized form, filled in by either the manufacturer or the catalog's merchandiser (the person who selects products for the catalog), describes, in detail, the features, benefits, and characteristics of the merchandise itself. Pictures of the products or even the products themselves usually accompany the MIF. (No, you don't get to keep them!) Ideally, you get one complete form for each product you write about.

✔ **The personality of the catalog itself:** Most catalogs have (or at least aspire to) a distinct personality that sets them apart from their competitors. (The exception is the wholesale catalog, usually for businesses, that lists prosaic items with a minimum of sell description: Think machine parts, office supplies, farm equipment, and so on.) That personality is embedded in several things:

 • The selection of merchandise — say, practical versus luxurious, or serious versus entertaining

 • The graphic look of the catalog

 • The rhetorical tone or *voice* of the copy, whether it be snappy, snobby, down-to-earth, fun-loving, adventurous, decadent, or rational

Some catalogers go so far as to write a profile of their catalog, as if it were a real person with an age, gender, lifestyle, values, and ambitions! This profile helps the copywriter incorporate the catalog personality into the book. Ask the creative director if a profile is available to help you.

In essence, catalog body copy combines information about the specific item (usually from the MIF) with the personality of your entire catalog. Because space is limited, you must select the most important benefits and features; the personality emerges in the way you articulate them. Following are examples of copy blocks for various catalog personalities:

- ✔ **Luxurious, indulgent, and exclusive:**

  Cantonese Silk Scarves by Larchmont
  Available exclusively at Larchmont Designs, the Cantonese Silk Scarf is modeled on rare patterns originally brought to the states by intrepid Yankee traders. Today's scarves impress with the same brilliant hues, but are woven from a superior silk found only in the Canton provinces' most remote mountain villages. Available in the following patterns: Crane, Bamboo, Mountain Landscape. Choose violet, crimson, or emerald green. 12" x 48".

- ✔ **Serious and business-like:**

  12V Portable Drill with Speed Chuck, Index
  Contractor's grade, heavy-duty BlackHeart 12V portable drill with speed chuck, drill index, extra 12V power supply, AC recharger, and DuraLux water-and-shatter proof carrying case. Reversible. Adjustable speed settings for masonry, metal, and tile, as well as wood and fiberboard. Shipping weight: 15 lbs.

- ✔ **Fun and frivolous:**

  Keep Cool in Even the Hottest Weather
  So it's 98 degrees in the shade and people are pointing at you, the wacky person with the fan in your hat! What do you care? You're the one who's cool — literally! Our sporty baseball cap features a small but powerful fan that gives you a constant, cooling breeze. Comes in Cool White, Fan Tan, and Oh Baby Blue. Requires 2 AA batteries, not included.

In addition to selling with information and personality, consider these ideas:

- ✔ **Holidays:** Watch the *drop date* (when the catalog is scheduled to mail). If you're mailing during a major shopping holiday such as Christmas or Valentine's Day, and the holiday is relevant to your catalog, don't forget to incorporate a holiday theme ("a welcome gift for the holiday season") in your copy. (You'll know the drop date when you get all the product information.)

- ✔ **Cross-sells:** Some products naturally go together, such as shirts and ties. If one product in your catalog is a natural match for another in your book, say so:

  A perfect complement to our capris — see page 12!

✔ **Alternative uses:** If your item has an alternative use that isn't immediately obvious to your readers, tell them about it, and you may increase sales. Here's an example:

The SheerMagic scissors are also perfect for cutting meats, poultry, and even frozen foods in a flash! Buy two: one for the sewing room and one for the kitchen!

Bid on This: Writing Descriptions for Online Auctions

When you go to eBay or one of its competing Web-based auctioneers, what do you get? In essence, a catalog of the world's attic, filled with descriptions of just about anything from pocket change to luxury yachts. The variety of people who sell through online auctions is almost as broad:

✔ **Regular Joes and Janes:** Ordinary people who treat the auction like a yard sale: A way to make a little cash on the side.

✔ **Professional Joes and Janes:** Some people go a step further and make the auction business their full-time job. On weekends, they scour yard sales and flea markets for stuff they can post online during the week.

✔ **Retailers with special inventory:** Over time, some stores, such as used bookstores, collect items that may attract a greater price if they're offered within a marketplace larger than the one served by their retail location. These business owners may place their big-ticket items online to fetch the highest price possible.

Although the descriptive quality of auction copy is similar to catalog copy, the online auction turns the usual marketing game on its head. You don't seek out prospects; they seek you — *if* you have what they want. Armed with powerful online search tools, they go on the prowl for the things that interest them. If your description matches their desires, you may have a customer. Your goal is to write a description likely to attract the highest number of potential bidders. Here's how:

✔ **Put the most important words in the title:** The default option on the eBay search tool is to search for terms in the title only. Therefore, you must put the terms most likely to be searched in the title. In Figure 8-2, I give not only the full name of the item and its manufacturer — Leonard Flying Dutchman — but also include a descriptive term important to enthusiasts, "prewar," and a catch-all phrase for train hobbyists, "train set complete."

✔ **Be ruthlessly specific in your description:** You're asking people to make contractually binding bids on something they can't see in person. To build confidence in the value of your item, be as specific as possible in your description. Include dimensions, age (or date of manufacture), serial numbers, nature of construction (if applicable), and precise visual details.

✔ **Include alternate spellings and misspellings:** You may notice that in Figure 8-2, I spell "collectible" two ways. (I also include the alternative spelling, "collectable.") This is no oversight. Potential bidders may run a search for titles and descriptions with either spelling, and I want to capture both. You may even want to include common misspellings of terms that people may be likely to use in a search for your item.

✔ **Use the "Completed Items Only" feature:** Under its Advanced Search tab, eBay allows you to select "Completed Items Only" to see auction results over the previous 30 days for descriptions that include your search term. This tool can give you extraordinary insight into how items similar to yours have fared. Use it to get ideas for setting opening bids and reserves and for finding words most likely to attract the right prospects.

✔ **Show pictures:** Descriptions with pictures attract more attention than those without. If you have pictures, post them. You can find how-to instructions on the auction sites.

✔ **Tell the truth:** Obviously, I don't encourage you to lie. But I also don't want you to waste time with meaningless hyperbole such as "wow!" or "best in its class," or "don't pass on this one." And your descriptions should include not only details but also defects, if any — a warts-and-all approach. In my sample, I point out the minor scuffing on the locomotive. By being honest, I build credibility with potential bidders; they can trust that this isn't a too-good-to-be-true deal.

Title ———

Figure 8-2:
This
speculative   Description ———
auction
description
is loaded
with search
terms and
details.

Prewar Leonard Flying Dutchman train set complete

Rare collectible! Complete Leonard Trains "Flying Dutchman" "O-gauge" set, with all cars, original boxes, track, and AC controller. Dated 1937, modeled on famed streamlined Flying Dutchman passenger service between New York and Chicago in the Depression. Set includes 4-6-4 "Hawkwind" diesel locomotive, #3421-A, with trademark Leonard "Huff n' Puff" smoke and silver art-deco detailing on black, steel-plate body—excellent condition, no rust on wheels, some minor scuffing on right side (see photo). Comes with three Pullman cars, #2667, with collectable "Faux-wood" interior paneling. Original boxes, some mildew, no tears or structural damage. Original "AC Commander" power supply and controller. 16 pieces of track: eight curve, eight straight. Buyer pays $20 shipping and handling, UPS Standard. Money order or cashier's check only. Please e-mail questions before bidding.

Chapter 9

Blasting Away with E-Mail

· ·

In This Chapter

▶ Knowing when to use e-mail for marketing

▶ Overcoming the delete key with effective e-mail

▶ Developing e-newsletters that work for you

· ·

A h, e-mail. What could be more tempting to a marketer than a medium that's cheap, easy-to-use, and capable of reaching millions of people with a click of the mouse? But alas, is there any other medium that has become so reviled by so many people, so quickly?

Spammers are e-mail marketers who stuff millions of inboxes with unsolicited messages. Unfortunately, their abuse of e-mail has made legitimate e-mail marketing much more difficult. As if the challenge of writing a compelling message isn't enough, with e-mail, you have to make special efforts to prove that your message isn't spam.

This chapter helps you avoid the stigma of spam by giving you tips, suggestions, and guidelines for writing solid marketing e-mails that survive your reader's itchy Delete key trigger finger. I also show you an electronic publication medium, the *e-newsletter,* that you can use to sustain customer communications, increase orders, and build better business relationships.

Determining Whether E-Mail Is Right for You

Every morning, millions of bleary-eyed workers turn to their computers and, with one hand on the mouse and one finger on the Delete key, scroll through the muck in their e-mail inboxes, eliminating spam.

What classifies an e-mail message as *spam?* It's unwanted (and some would say, unwarranted) e-mail messaging delivered simultaneously and almost indiscriminately to hundreds of thousands of people. Sure, you could argue endlessly about what makes a message unwanted by some people and acceptable by others, but in reality, the situation is simpler: Nine times out of ten, messages from strangers are perceived as spam and quickly deleted.

The following sections explain what you need to think about when you're deciding whether e-mail is the most effective way to reach your prospects and customers.

Using e-mail to your advantage

So what's e-mail good for? It can be a superbly efficient and effective way of maintaining your relationships with current customers or with prospects you've already been introduced to. Here are some of the possibilities:

- ✔ **Announcing new offers to your customers:** Got a new product to tempt your customers with? E-mail is an inexpensive way to tell them about it. Put the offer upfront in the e-mail message, and then link them to your Web page where they can read more about it. (For more on creating Web sites for your business or organization, check out Chapter 14.)

- ✔ **Providing quick service to your customers:** E-mail's speed can't be beat for sending bulletins, notices, advice, or any other communications necessary for providing or maintaining customer service.

- ✔ **Pushing prospects further down the sales pipeline:** Complex, multistep sales often involve many points of contact with your prospects. Using e-mail can be an excellent way of keeping the fires burning with a hot prospect and keeping them in touch with all the right people.

- ✔ **Making follow-up contact in a campaign:** In a multiwave marketing campaign, e-mail can serve as an inexpensive follow-up to previous mailings. This is an especially popular technique for driving conference attendance; as the date of the event approaches, e-mail is a great way to encourage last-minute registrations.

The key word to remember is "relationship," and like any healthy relationship, the success of your e-mail marketing approach depends on mutual consent. So what's the secret to sending e-mails that get opened and read? Getting permission to send them, first. (See "Asking Permission to Send E-Mail" to learn how.)

Understanding when to avoid e-mail

Although e-mail users have a fair degree of tolerance for unsolicited snail mail, they have little patience for e-mail from strangers. They're afraid of viruses, worms, and other Internet bugs; they resent the intrusion into their personal inboxes; and because they have to pay for e-mail services, they don't like subsidizing e-mails they don't want. As a marketer, you're in for a bumpy ride if you use e-mail to contact new customers. Consider the following pitfalls:

✔ **Prospecting:** Initiating contact through a broad e-mail campaign can be exceptionally difficult. If you're trying to make that crucial first contact with people who have neither bought from you before nor had some previous contact with you — via a sales call, a telephone conversation, or some activity on your Web site — consider some other, less pesky form of introduction, such as direct response mail. (See Chapter 4.)

✔ **Generating leads:** Expensive or complicated sales often involve a multi-step process that begins with an effort to identify qualified or interested prospects. These *leads* are handed over to salespeople for subsequent contact. Lead-generation programs are often the first attempt to communicate with a prospective customer to eventually result in a sale — not an easy thing to do with e-mail. Remember, when recipients don't know you already, they'll probably delete your e-mail. If your lead-generation campaign is also a first contact, you should probably look to another medium first.

✔ **Using rented lists:** Just as you can buy or rent lists of names and addresses (and other data) for paper-based mail, you can buy lists of e-mail addresses. List brokers crow about how inexpensive these lists are — practically a penny per address or less! Such a deal! But you get what you pay for. What list brokers don't tell you is how poorly these rented e-mail lists perform. These lists may work well for the companies that initially compile the e-mail addresses. But the original companies have established some kind of relationship with the e-mail recipients; you haven't. Your odds for successful marketing aren't good if you start with a rented or purchased list.

Asking Permission to Send E-Mail

Professional e-mail marketers call the request for permission to send e-mail the "*opt-in.*" The goal of the opt-in is to build a *house list* (a list of prospect and/or customer names and contact information that belongs to your business) of prospects who have consented to receiving e-mail messages from you.

Although rented lists generate notoriously poor results, response rates to e-mails posted to the house list are often excellent. Double-digit response rates are not uncommon, and I've participated in campaigns that pulled response rates as high as 30 percent! (To find out why you should stay away from rented lists, check out the preceding section.)

Given the solid performance of house lists, building one is well worth your time and effort. Make the smart move and start building the list *as soon as possible*, before you even plan your first e-mail campaign. Building a list takes time, and if you postpone collecting permissions until you have a campaign in mind, you'll be frustrated with delays. But if you start now, you'll have a list ready and waiting for action when you need it.

Building a house list with opt-in requests

Building your house list is a fairly straightforward process. Assuming that your company has a means for collecting, storing, and organizing incoming e-mail addresses, you need to do two things: Create an opt-in request and place the opt-in request where prospects will see it.

Composing an opt-in request

Follow these four steps to create an opt-in request.

1. **Ask for the prospect's e-mail address.**

2. **Ask for permission to send e-mail to that address.**

3. **Tell the prospect exactly what kinds of messages you'll send to that address, such as special offers, event announcements, news bulletins, newsletters, and so on.**

4. **Assure the prospect that you won't share the e-mail address with anyone else.**

    Be honest and upfront if you have a business partner or subsidiary who will use the address as well.

The opt-in request is often framed as an offer — in exchange for the e-mail address, you'll send what-have-you — and looks something like this:

> *Would you like to receive our free e-mail newsletter, Heritage House Happenings? Simply type your address in the following box. Your privacy is important to us — please be assured that your e-mail address will not be sold or shared with any third party under any circumstances.*

If you plan to use the e-mail address to promote new products or offers, say so. Many people want to keep abreast of your latest-and-greatest, and asking permission can be as simple as this:

May we send you e-mails announcing our latest products and special offers? If so, check the "Yes" box below. Your e-mail address remains confidential and will not be shared with any third party.

Putting your opt-in request to work

After you've crafted the perfect opt-in request, where do you put it? Here are the most popular locations:

- ✔ **On your Web site:** People who have made the effort to seek you out on the Web may be very amenable to getting more information from you. All you have to do is ask. If your site requires a registration form, you can put the opt-in there. You may also want to place a For More Information link on many, if not all, of your pages that lead the prospect to your opt-in request. (For more on informative Web sites, check out Chapter 14.)

- ✔ **On your reply devices:** When you target your prospects with traditional mail, add an opt-in request to the reply device (the thing customers send back to you) itself. (See Chapter 7 for more on reply devices.) You're already paying for postage and production — why not get more value from your reply device? Let it help you build your house list.

- ✔ **On your order forms:** In catalogs or on the Web, place the opt-in request on the same form customers fill out when ordering your products. (For the scoop on catalogs, see Chapter 8.)

Creating the opt-out

The flip side of the opt-in is — you guessed it — the *opt-out*. On every e-mail you send, include an opportunity for the prospect to be removed from your e-mail list. This opt-out serves both as a corrective for people who may have been included in your list by mistake and as a continual reassurance of confidentiality and control for everyone else.

Most opt-outs consist of two things: a reminder of why the recipient is getting the e-mail and an opt-out link to a Web page that automatically removes the address and confirms that the removal has been made.

In an e-mail, the opt-out often looks like this:

You are getting this e-mail message from Brandon Associates because you requested updates from us. If you received this e-mail in error, or would no longer like to receive e-mail updates from Brandon Associates, <u>click here</u>.

Or you can make the opt-out simple and to the point:

To unsubscribe from our e-mails, <u>click here</u>.

What with all the opt-ins, opt-outs, database management issues, and potential legal liabilities, e-mail marketing can become overwhelming, especially for a small business. Fortunately, there are third-party vendors who will manage the technicalities for you (for a price, of course). Run a Web search for "e-mail marketing" to see your options.

Writing Your E-Mail Message (and Not Getting Deleted)

Before you write your e-mails, think of the battles they have ahead of them. Inboxes can be harsh environments, and your messages will probably arrive among a cluster of other messages, many of them outright spam. To survive the coming purge, your messages must be brief, clear, and to the point.

Creating subject lines that don't get dumped

The *subject line* is the first line of defense when it comes to saving the life of your e-mail message. This short line of text identifies your e-mail in the recipient's inbox. If your subject line fails to convince the recipient that your e-mail is worth reading (and is safe to open), your message is destined for dumping.

Devising effective subject lines

What are the keys to subject lines that get your e-mails opened? For starters, keep them short — no more than 60 characters (counting characters *and* spaces), and you're better off if you stay in the 35–50 range. And don't worry about writing complete sentences; fragments are entirely acceptable as long as your meaning is clear.

Not sure if your subject line is too long? Most word-processing software includes a word count feature that also counts characters. Highlight your subject line and then click on Word Count under the Tools menu.

Here are a few ideas that have proven successful for subject lines:

✔ **Personalize, if possible:** If you or your organization has the data management capability (a function of your in-house computing resources) of merging the recipient's name into the subject line, give it a shot. Many tests show a substantial increase in the e-mail open rate when the subject line is personalized. Here's what it can look like:

- *Three craft ideas for Mary Wakefield*

- *Bill Malden, you're due for an oil change*

✔ **Identify yourself:** When you have a strong (and favorable) relationship with your customers, you can build confidence in your e-mail by simply identifying yourself in the subject line, like this:

- *Recent acquisitions at LaFebvre's Antiques*

- *UBlastIt Software service upgrades*

✔ **Identify the content:** When in doubt, tell recipients what they can expect when they open the e-mail. Be clear and concise, like this:

- *Medical conference registration form*

- *Better ideas for home construction*

✔ **State a benefit:** Tell recipients what your offer will do for them. Entice them into wanting more information with phrases like this:

- *Improve your golf swing*

- *Get more from your database*

✔ **Trust your instincts:** Whatever approach you choose, let it sit for a while (overnight if possible, or after a coffee break), and then read it to yourself. Go with your gut. If your subject line sounds like something you wouldn't open yourself, rewrite it.

Avoiding "sales language"

People read e-mail subject lines the way they look through front door peep-holes: with anxiety and distrust. That's why it's important to avoid a hardball sales lead that confirms the recipient's worst suspicions. Strong sales language (such as "Free trial" or "Your best time to buy") that can work well in other contexts — in print ads or direct mail, for example — can bomb miserably in your recipients' inboxes.

In fact, many of the words, phrases, and techniques that I love in headlines should be scrupulously avoided in subject lines! These include language that either is commonly targeted by popular spam-filtering software or is known to arouse suspicion and mistrust among recipients. Some common offenders are

✔ **"You":** It breaks my heart to say it, but putting "you" in a subject line is almost always a sure tip-off that the e-mail is coming from a stranger. There are exceptions to this rule, but in general, think twice about using the second person in subject lines.

✔ **Exclamation points:** Just don't use them in subject lines! Especially a series of them!! It makes you sound like a used-car dealer in a late-night TV spot!!!

✔ **Let's-make-a-deal words:** Yes, you're going to make offers *inside* the e-mail, but to get the e-mail opened, your subject line should avoid most of the more familiar offer-language buzzwords, such as the following:

- Free

- Sale

- Only

- Limited-time

- Urgent

- Opportunity

- Information

- Deal

Messaging in a minute: The e-mail body

In the early days of e-mail, you may have seen e-mail as merely an electronic version of a letter or a memo. Like letters, e-mails could be personalized with salutations and concluded with a signature; like memos, they could be addressed to groups of people as a fast way of keeping everyone informed.

Fashioning a few subject lines

Writing good subject lines isn't a walk in the park — it usually takes me longer to write a decent subject line than it does to write the body of the e-mail itself! Truth is, there's no substitute for practice. For each of the hypothetical e-mails below, write two subject lines that use two of these four approaches: personalization, identifying yourself, identifying the content, or stating the benefit. (For more on these approaches, see the section "Devising effective subject lines" in this chapter.)

✔ You're sending an e-mail announcing the arrival of the latest bulletin from Stoneham Investments. This issue features articles on commercial real estate trends, three technology stock picks, and a guide to investing in commodities overseas.

✔ You're sending an e-mail inviting recipients to a fundraising event for a local cancer charity, Ribbons of Hope. The event is scheduled for May and will feature dancing, live big-band music, and a karaoke contest.

✔ You're sending an e-mail introducing five new textile patterns to customers of Quilters Be!, an online retailer of fabrics for quilters.

But today, most e-mail users can receive HTML (hypertext markup language) e-mail, an innovation with a wrinkle that changes everything: the *hyperlink*. Simply move your cursor over the link, click it, and — bingo — you're off to a new message (and almost a new world). The hyperlink has changed communications in three ways.

- **It redistributes information.** On paper, you have to communicate the complete story upfront. Hyperlinks make that kind of comprehensive communication unnecessary. You can write the e-mail as a summary or preview and then let the hyperlinks carry the reader to more in-depth information. Your new copywriting challenge? To motivate the reader to click on the links.

- **It changes expectations.** Now that almost everyone knows how to point and click, fewer people have the patience to sit and read — especially as they sort through the glut of mail in their inboxes. They want the gist, and they want it fast. If interested, people point-and-click through the appropriate hyperlinks to get further information. That means you have to make your e-mails brief.

- **It puts even more pressure on the offer.** With hyperlinks, prospects don't simply want a reason *to buy* — they demand a reason *to click* on your links. Giving a reason and motivating a prospect are just two ways of saying that you must make a strong offer. In effect, you must tell the prospect, "Follow this link, and you'll get a reward for your efforts."

In practice, these three principles become general guidelines for how you should use e-mail's electronic, interactive qualities to your advantage. Take a look at how these principles work in the sample e-mail in Figure 9-1.

In Figure 9-1, I start with a subject line combining identification, "at Baguette Films," with content, "New Wave DVDs." When prospects open the e-mail, they see the rest of the sample. The following sections cover how it works.

Reinforcing the relationship with letter conventions

The ordinary conventions of a letter, such as a salutation and a closing, reinforce the personal connection that's essential to a strong business relationship. (For more on letters, see Chapter 5.)

In Figure 9-1, I pretend that I don't have the power to personalize my greeting. Instead, I use a catchall that identifies the prospect's participation in my movie club: "Dear Baguette Films Member."

Using headlines and subheads to communicate at a glance

Remember, time is of the essence — so don't expect readers to give you much of theirs. You're certainly not obligated to use headlines and subheads, but they allow you to communicate the essentials quickly.

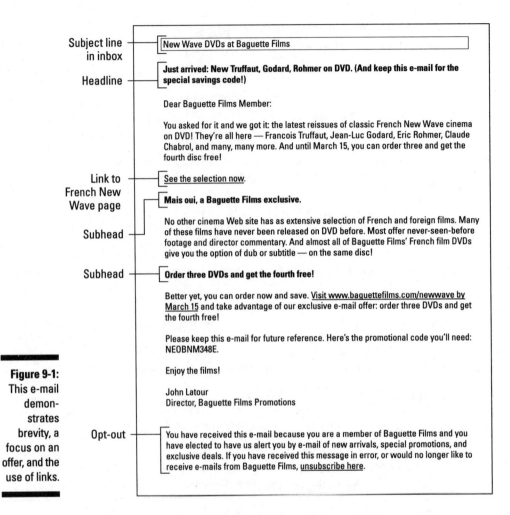

Subject line in inbox

> New Wave DVDs at Baguette Films

Headline

> **Just arrived: New Truffaut, Godard, Rohmer on DVD. (And keep this e-mail for the special savings code!)**
>
> Dear Baguette Films Member:
>
> You asked for it and we got it: the latest reissues of classic French New Wave cinema on DVD! They're all here — Francois Truffaut, Jean-Luc Godard, Eric Rohmer, Claude Chabrol, and many, many more. And until March 15, you can order three and get the fourth disc free!

Link to French New Wave page

> See the selection now.

Subhead

> **Mais oui, a Baguette Films exclusive.**
>
> No other cinema Web site has as extensive selection of French and foreign films. Many of these films have never been released on DVD before. Most offer never-seen-before footage and director commentary. And almost all of Baguette Films' French film DVDs give you the option of dub or subtitle — on the same disc!

Subhead

> **Order three DVDs and get the fourth free!**
>
> Better yet, you can order now and save. Visit www.baguettefilms.com/newwave by March 15 and take advantage of our exclusive e-mail offer: order three DVDs and get the fourth free!
>
> Please keep this e-mail for future reference. Here's the promotional code you'll need: NEOBNM348E.
>
> Enjoy the films!
>
> John Latour
> Director, Baguette Films Promotions

Opt-out

> You have received this e-mail because you are a member of Baguette Films and you have elected to have us alert you by e-mail of new arrivals, special promotions, and exclusive deals. If you have received this message in error, or would no longer like to receive e-mails from Baguette Films, unsubscribe here.

Figure 9-1:
This e-mail demonstrates brevity, a focus on an offer, and the use of links.

As opposed to the subject lines, all the familiar suggestions for headlines and subheads apply: Write "what's in it" for the prospect by focusing on compelling benefits, important features, relevant news, and/or outstanding offers. (For a refresher on writing headlines and subheads, see Chapter 2.) Here's how they work in Figure 9-1:

- ✔ **The opening headline** announces news, "Just arrived:" and gives the reader a reason to keep the e-mail, the "special savings code."

- ✔ **The first subhead** reinforces the theme and plays on an attractive feature, exclusivity: "Mais oui, a Baguette Films exclusive."

- ✔ **The second subhead** simply shouts the offer: "Order three DVDs and get the fourth free!"

Putting the offer link in multiple places

Even in a short e-mail, repetition is a virtue. People tend to devour e-mails in quick gulps, so it pays to restate your offer frequently; you don't know when or where your readers may "bite." Many marketers like to put the offer at both the top and bottom of the message, or even within a graphic *callout* (a design element that pops out at the reader) at the side. This is what I did:

- ✔ After stating the offer in the first paragraph, "you can order three and get the fourth disc free!", I put a link to the offer directly underneath it, "See the selection now."

- ✔ Near the end of the e-mail, I state the offer two more times — once in the last subhead and again in the paragraph just underneath it where I embedded the second link: "Visit www.baguettefilms.com/newwave by March 15. . . ."

Moving long copy to a Web page

With discipline, you can get the gist of your message — your offer, its value, and the terms for accepting the offer — in as few as 200 to 250 words (about a page's worth of copy). Honor your readers' short attention spans, and then use hyperlinks to carry readers to Web pages where the story is fleshed out.

In Figure 9-1, Baguette Films members are promised a variety of French New Wave DVDs. Instead of listing them all, I name a few famous directors and then use the "See the selection now" link to drive them to a complete list (and an opportunity to take action and buy the DVDs immediately).

Including feature/benefit copy

Even though space is at a premium, you still need to build your case with *features* (things the offer has or is) and *benefits* (things the offer does for your reader) in order to convince prospects of your offer's value. Because space is at a premium, plan to prune: Include only those features and benefits that, to your best understanding of the prospect, hold the greatest attraction. (See Chapter 3 for insights about understanding your customers.)

In Figure 9-1, I limit my feature/benefit story to one paragraph, beginning with "No other cinema Web site" and concluding with "Baguette Films' French film DVDs give you the option of dub or subtitle — on the same disc!"

Using descriptive links

Sometimes a link can be as simple as "Click here," but you may increase click-throughs by writing links that tell readers exactly what they'll find when they click. There's no rule that insists that hyperlinks must be confined to five or so words: Use as many as needed to let readers know exactly what they'll find at the other end of the link.

For BaguetteFilms, "See the selection now" tells prospects where to find the French New Wave DVDs.

Remembering the opt-out

Even when prospects opt-in to your e-mail program, the opt-out serves as a continual reassurance that they remain in control. The Baguette Films opt-out is the last paragraph in Figure 9-1.

Using E-Newsletters to Maintain Contact

E-newsletters (or electronic newsletters) have emerged as a popular format for frequent communications with customers or hot prospects. Like print-based newsletters, e-newsletters contain news, tips, and information of interest to an organization's target base. (For more about traditional print newsletters, see Chapter 13.) But e-newsletters have important distinctions that allow you to do the following:

- ✔ **Avoid printing or postage costs.** You can and should spend money for top-notch design, but saving money on printing and postage is one perk of moving to electronic publishing that your wallet will thank you for.

- ✔ **Collect data about reader behavior.** If you have the IT capabilities *and* will post most of the newsletter content on the Web (connected to your e-newsletter with links), you can track the click-throughs to measure the popularity of your material. The more sophisticated tracking technologies can even record the length of time readers spend on each article! With this kind of feedback, you'll know where to invest your time writing subsequent issues, be it to create tips, stories, case studies, new product descriptions, and so on.

- ✔ **Take a "here today, gone tomorrow" approach.** When you get a printed communication, the quality of the paper and the way your content is printed are part of the message. Yes, e-newsletters speak through graphic design, but that design no longer has the material heft of print. (For more on e-newsletters' design, see "Managing format and tone," later in this chapter.) E-newsletters are short-lived. On the downside, they communicate less commitment on your part than print newsletters; on the upside, they can be much more casual in tone, allowing you greater rapport with your readers.

Understanding the function of e-newsletters

With e-newsletters, you have two broad categories of potential readers: current customers and prospects with whom you've made substantial previous contact. Their needs (and your place in the mix) are different enough to merit some thought.

✔ **Current customers:** They've already bought something from you, but you still have plenty to sell — from additional products and services to maintenance of their existing orders. The desires of current customers take different shapes:

- **An emotional attachment to your brand:** Some products — such as motorcycles, collectible statuettes, luxury cars, or recorded music — really get people fired up. For those audiences who just can't get enough information about the objects of their devotion, an e-newsletter builds loyalty and serves as a terrific way to introduce related products and services.

- **A need for current, industry-specific information:** Many purchasers of complex business products, like enterprise resource planning software or benefits management services, yearn for accurate, up-to-date information about your product or about their industry. Your e-newsletter can meet their educational needs *and* reinforce your position as a wise advisor and trusted resource.

✔ **Prospects who have been previously contacted:** For those purchases, especially in a business environment, that are expensive or require approval from several people (or both), the sales cycle between contact and closing can take as much as a year or more. The initial lead becomes one part of a long process that may require numerous meetings, proposals, and other efforts. In this context, the e-newsletter can be an excellent way of keeping your prospect informed and maintaining the lines of communication.

Good e-newsletters represent a serious commitment of time and talent. If your product is simple or doesn't inspire a desire or need for in-depth information, the e-newsletter is probably a waste of your resources.

Developing content for e-newsletters

The content for e-newsletters can be similar to print newsletters. (See Chapter 13 for details on print newsletters and writing articles in general.) But the speed with which you can produce and distribute the e-newsletter gives it a whole new level of timeliness, allowing you to respond forcefully to current trends and late-breaking developments in your business or industry.

Many of the most successful e-newsletters build each issue around one lead article (frequently used as the basis for the subject line) and fill in the holes with shorter, subordinate material.

As a writer for your business, you walk a narrow tightrope: Your ultimate objective is to improve your business relationships and grow your revenues. But if you focus your e-newsletter on your business with content that simply trumpets your virtues without any regard for the needs and desires of your readers, you'll lose readers and your e-newsletter will fail.

Your goal as a copywriter is to create a platform of information and expertise that positions your organization as a helpful friend, a smart advisor, and a knowledgeable authority. Within that context, you can weave in references to your products and services. But when these references appear, they should always be at the service of the reader instead of being self-serving.

But if your organization fits the framework I outline in "Understanding the function of e-newsletters," earlier in this chapter, you should have no trouble developing content that reinforces the bonds you've built with customers, or would like to build with prospects.

Stepping out with lead articles

Your *lead article* is your e-newsletter's big story, both in content and in length. Here are a few ideas for material:

- **Latest industry news:** Write about a hot topic or breaking story involving your customer's industry or interests. For example:

    UBettaLot Acquires Lotza Lotteries in Stock Swap

    SparkleMatic Introduces New Line of Rhinestones for Crafters

- **Advice or analysis:** It can be a cruel, competitive, and confusing world out there. Dig deep into your organization's expertise and produce material that can help a busy businessperson or befuddled consumer; your efforts will be appreciated. For example:

    Controlling Workers Compensation Costs with Statistical Modeling

    Understanding the New Model Rocket Licensing Regulations

- **How-to:** Similar to the advice article, the how-to gives explicit information on solving problems, facing challenges, or just having fun. A how-to article is an outstanding way to encourage customers to try alternative uses for your products or services that they may not have considered before.

    Five Ways to Expand Your Market Reach Without Busting Your Budget

    Turn Your Spring Nursery Into a Winter Herb Garden

- **Case studies:** The next best thing to reading about yourself is reading about people like you. *Case studies,* brief reports about how someone used your product or service to solve a problem or improve her business or life, give you a chance to build real-life drama into your e-newsletter while demonstrating how your business works in action. For example:

    Pizza Express Saves Millions with Delivery-Tracker Software

    Lancaster Patterns Help Pamela Winchester Take Quilting Blue Ribbon

Filling in the gaps with additional material

Round out your e-newsletter with shorter pieces that accompany the lead article. Consider these options:

- **Customer features:** They keep you in business, so make your readers the stars. Create a regular feature that profiles one of your customers in each issue. In addition to flattering the people you write about, you're showing your customers and prospects how important they are to you. For profile subjects, ask your sales people to identify happy customers who would be willing to cooperate.

- **Product updates:** Tell your readers when they can expect to see your latest products or newest services. Similarly, you can write about new features appearing on your Web site, new regions or areas in which you're doing business, or important new clients.

- **Events, conferences, and seminars:** Let readers know about your organization's upcoming appearances at events, speaking engagements, association meetings, conferences, and other gatherings. Even if readers choose not to attend, announcing appearances reinforces your company's status as a significant presence in its field.

- **Reminders and general information:** Don't forget the nitty-gritty — reminders of how people can contact you, make orders, contact service support, and other mundane yet important info that deserves repeating.

- **Teasers and forwards requests:** You build anticipation for your next issue by telling readers what to expect in the previous issue. For instance:

  In next week's issue, "10 Tips for Streamlining Your Product Development Process."

  And if you'd like the recipient to share your newsletter with colleagues or friends, say so:

  Please forward this newsletter to other members of your organization.

Like any other e-mail communication, permission is crucial. Promote your e-newsletter by creating opt-in subscription opportunities on your Web site or within your e-mails. And don't forget to include an opt-out option (that would discontinue the subscription), with each issue. (See "Asking Permission to Send E-Mail," earlier in this chapter, for more information.)

Managing format and tone

When it comes time to assemble and produce your e-newsletter, you have to decide which format to use. The most common options are

- **Plain-text e-mail:** Unfortunately, some people can receive only plain-text e-mails because of the age of their computers or the nature of their Internet services. If your list of e-newsletter subscribers contains a substantial number of these people, you have two options. Bite the bullet and go with a plain-Jane, no-frills version of your newsletter within the e-mail, or send a plain e-mail with a Web site address that readers type into their browsers to reach an attractive e-newsletter on your Web site.

✔ **HTML e-mail:** HTML allows you to bring quality design into your e-newsletter. If you go the HTML route, you, the copywriter, are responsible for the words, while a designer skilled in HTML is responsible for the look and feel.

I recommend a hybrid approach that sends a brief HTML e-mail to your readers with headlines and short, two- to three-sentence summaries of the available content; for the complete articles, readers click on hyperlinks directing them to appropriate pages on your Web site. It's a best-of-both-worlds approach: You get the brevity you need for successful e-mail communications, while giving yourself all the space you need to produce excellent e-newsletter content.

Whatever you do, don't send your e-newsletter as an attachment! Some Internet service providers won't allow your attachment to pass. Even if the attachment gets through, it could come up against plenty of corporate firewalls that will intercept it. And even when these hurdles are cleared, many people refuse to open attachments for fear of accompanying viruses.

Finally, take a light-handed approach to the tone of your newsletter. The fleeting quality of e-newsletters lends itself to an informal, personal manner. You're not writing literature for the ages — you're creating a useful and entertaining resource that people can look forward to and learn from, even if they're busy. Use "you," speak friend to friend, and have fun.

Part III
Building Awareness of Your Business

The 5th Wave   By Rich Tennant

"How about this-'It's not just CRAP, it's Mel's CRAP'? Shoot! That's no good. I hate writing copy for this client."

In this part . . .

Build a better mousetrap and the world will automatically beat a path to your door? If you really think so, I hope you have an appetite for solitude — and the taste of mousetraps. Because unless you build the path and put up signs along the way, you'll find yourself with a lot of unsold inventory, waiting for a doorbell that never rings.

This part of the book is all about building a better path and telling the world all about it. I give you an introduction to branding and the scoop on writing articles. I also show you how to write more productive advertisements and how to use the media as a partner for your success by using press releases and press kits.

Chapter 10

Basic Branding 101

● ●

● ●

*B*randing has come a long way since cowboys thwarted cattle rustlers with a hot iron applied to a calf's behind. (Some folks may say, however, that branding has never gotten far from the bull.) Over time, in fact, some businesses have come to value their brand — as opposed to their manufacturing capabilities or financial savvy — as their single most important asset. After all, when you take away the "Coca-Cola" from Coca-Cola, all you have left is fizzy, flavored water. The value of a Coke is in all the things most people associate with the name — fun, tradition, America. That's branding in a bottle.

A *brand* is a set of images, attributes, feelings, and ideas people associate with your business and its name. Because the stakes can be so high, vast oceans of ink have been spilt on the black magic of branding. I intend to contribute only a modest stream — just enough information to be useful to a writer. Though few of you probably plan to create the next Ronald McDonald, all of you can benefit from an appreciation of brand basics. Even if you don't have the millions of dollars it takes to launch a major branding effort, you too can apply the fundamentals to make even a small business more competitive. If you're interested in finding out more about branding, check out *Marketing For Dummies,* 2nd Edition, by Alexander Hiam (Wiley).

I call my modest approach Barbershop Branding in honor of my local hair cutter, Eric, who has done an ingenious (and inexpensive) job of distinguishing himself from at least a half-dozen local competitors. Though many of his tactics don't involve writing, his thinking can be applied to copy. And I throw in guidance for writing branding-specific elements — positioning statements, copy platforms, tag lines, and mission statements — as well.

Creating a Sense of Unique Value with Branding

Branding is as much about what you're not as what you are. Remember the game of Duck, Duck, Goose? You brand yourself as a goose precisely because you don't want to be one of a dozen indistinguishable, completely forgettable ducks.

To be a duck is to be a commodity, like a gallon of gas or a slab of bacon. Without marketing, one commodity is like another. And when there's little to distinguish one commodity from another, guess what happens? Consumers simply reach for the lowest price or the most convenient location. Branding is the effort that marketers make to distinguish their product or service as something special — not a commodity — and is therefore worth paying an additional premium, or driving an extra mile, to get.

Don't confuse the brand with the *logo*, the graphic icon that's used to represent the brand. Although the logo is important, it should be created *after* all other aspects of the brand (positioning, market, personality, price points, and so on) have been determined. Unfortunately, some agencies claim to create brands for their clients, yet they merely design logos and letterheads. Don't allow their confusion (or deliberate misrepresentation) to mislead you: Branding is about who you are, not what your return address looks like.

Though many of the most famous brands are associated with large organizations, those of you with small or independent businesses shouldn't feel intimidated or discouraged. Good branding is more about smart thinking than big spending. With a little savvy, even a small business can establish a favorable identity — a brand — that can make it special in its customers' eyes.

As an introduction to branding, I want to introduce you to a small (but large-minded) businessman: my barber, Eric. When Eric graduated from barber school and began his search for a shop of his own, he had no illusions about the competition he'd face; in fact, he passed many of their shops every day. But within a few weeks, he found what he was looking for: a retiring barber with a Main Street location. Better yet, he saw something inside that may have turned away other prospective buyers: old-fashioned barber chairs, the ones with white-enameled steel frames and red leather upholstery.

He liked that old-fashioned look and decided to expand upon it. The old chairs reminded him of the barbershops of his father's day, and when he thought about it more deeply, he realized something: Barbershops weren't just places where men got their hair cut; they were refuges, places where men could chat and vent steam out of earshot of girlfriends and wives, mothers and mothers-in-law. And, Eric considered, men had fewer such refuges today.

The birth of branding

In the murky years of its origins about a hundred years ago, branding had as much to do with power as it had to do with marketing. You can think of the situation as a kind of food chain with consumers on one end and producers on the other. In the middle were the grocers who provided goods to consumers, and middlemen wholesalers who distributed products to grocers.

Consumers bought their goods from local stores where, instead of shopping among aisles of boldly displayed products, they approached the counter to request what they wanted: a pound of sugar, a sack of flour, a bar of soap. All of these products were entirely generic — commodities — that had no names to indicate their origin. The grocer bought his commodities wholesale from large, powerful middlemen called *jobbers* who distributed vast amounts of these commodities to smaller stores and extended credit to the grocers, too. At the beginning of the chain were the mills that produced the flour and sugar, and the factories that made the soap.

The producers at the beginning of the chain were not happy, because the jobbers held all the power. As long as a cracker was just a cracker, one indistinguishable from another, producers had no leverage; the jobbers set the price, and the producer could either accept it or lose the sale to a competitor willing to meet the jobber's terms. And as far as the grocers and consumers were concerned, as long as the prices were reasonable, they were content.

The only way out, producers realized, would be to create demand for a product they, and only they, could provide: Not just any cracker, but a Uneeda cracker, packaged in individual, sanitary boxes. Not just any salt, but Morton's salt, which has an anticaking additive that lets it flow, even when it rains. Not just any soap, but a bar of Ivory soap, whose purity contributes to its buoyancy.

Hence, branding: the creation of a unique "value" (real or illusory) that can be satisfied only by purchasing the branded product. Hence, too, the famous phrases "Ask for it by name" and "Accept no substitutes," promoted by brand advertisers who wanted consumers to demand their products at the store. When they did — and history, of course, tells us they did — grocers insisted on these brand products, too. The jobbers, in turn, were forced to meet the producers' terms or risk being eliminated from the equation when producers sold directly to retailers, which is what often occurred. For the complete story, read *Satisfaction Guaranteed: The Making of the American Mass Market*, a wonderful book by historian Susan Strasser (Random House).

Today, brand-name manufacturers and powerful retailers still duke it out for control of shelf space and price points. But brands themselves are now inseparable from consumers' ideas about shopping — and indeed, from the concept of personal identity. Coke or Pepsi, anybody?

Without even thinking about it as branding (he just thought it was good business sense — and he's right), he made the "old-fashioned male refuge" the theme for his shop. He put sports pictures on the walls and men's magazines ("lad mags," not porn) out on the chairs. All his barbers wear the traditional white cotton uniform jackets. And no haircut is complete without "arching," a final cleanup near the ears and the back of the neck finished with hot shaving cream and a straight razor. Finally, Eric decided that his shop wouldn't cut women's hair, period.

Eric started with three chairs, got a fourth, and just recently added a fifth. Business is booming, even in a town that has at least six other hair salons on Main Street alone. Why is he doing so well? It isn't price; his isn't the cheapest cut in town. Eric's shop thrives because he offers an experience men can't get anywhere else in town. That experience — a good men's cut in a relaxing place — is associated with Eric's barbershop. That's branding, and it's good business.

So what can you learn from Eric? I think there are four main points, which I cover in the following sections.

Differentiating yourself

In formal marketing speak, differentiating yourself from other businesses that do what your business does is called *positioning*. To position your business, you take your business category, such as party planning or fence construction, and add a twist (perhaps parties that feature live music, or fences in an arts-and-crafts style) that gives your business a unique "position" in your customers' minds. I show you how to position your business in "What makes you special? Writing the positioning statement," later in this chapter.

From day one, Eric positioned himself apart from the pack. Inspired by a barber chair and the memories it invoked, Eric chose to run a shop unlike any other in town: an old-fashioned barbershop that offers straightforward haircuts and shaves and doesn't offer shampoos or perms. He's willing to be different and to make that difference his mark or brand.

Shaping a special experience

A good brand is about more than words or images: It implies a special experience that can be obtained or enjoyed only by buying your product or service.

Although reading your copy isn't, of course, the same thing as experiencing the product or service you sell, good copy should reflect the nature of your business, what it's like to buy or use your product or service. That's why the promotional material for healthcare providers sounds empathetic and compassionate, why ads for amusement parks are breezy and fun, and why perfume ads are often sexy and mysterious.

Eric understood that he sells more than just a haircut — he offers an experience his customers can't find in other nearby barber shops, a relaxing environment of male camaraderie where men can shoot the breeze about sports, politics, and women (probably in that order).

As a writer, you want to control rhythm, tone, diction (word choice), and point of view to suggest the experience of doing business with you or your organization. Although many of these qualities may spring intuitively in your writing style, you can improve your copy by formally making your writing choices part of your brand identity. The official document for recording these choices is called the "copy platform," which I talk about in the section "Guiding force: Developing a copy platform," later in this chapter.

Living the brand, not just saying it

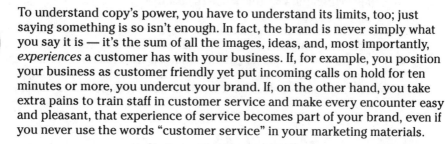

To understand copy's power, you have to understand its limits, too; just saying something is so isn't enough. In fact, the brand is never simply what you say it is — it's the sum of all the images, ideas, and, most importantly, *experiences* a customer has with your business. If, for example, you position your business as customer friendly yet put incoming calls on hold for ten minutes or more, you undercut your brand. If, on the other hand, you take extra pains to train staff in customer service and make every encounter easy and pleasant, that experience of service becomes part of your brand, even if you never use the words "customer service" in your marketing materials.

Before you commit a promise to writing, be sure your business can fulfill that promise in practice. If what you say about your business doesn't match what your business does, you won't fool your customers; you'll just be kidding yourself.

Eric lives and breathes his brand. When he opened for business, he didn't hang out a sign that said "Eric's Old-Fashioned Barbershop for Men" or run ads talking about his shop as a refuge. Instead, his business embodies the brand in all its details, from the chairs in the room to the pictures on the wall and, most importantly, to the quality of the haircut. Eric enforces a code he calls "The Rule of the Chair": After customers are seated, they "own" the chair and can have anything they wish — haircut, shave, or beard trim — no matter how long it takes and how many customers may be waiting.

Having the courage not to be all things to all people

You can't please everybody. In fact, trying to do so can be very bad business. By definition, to be distinct means setting limits on who you are and what you do. Unfortunately, many businesspeople lack the courage to stick to their distinction, fearing the loss of revenue that might occur if they were to some-how limit their business: The expert in truck repairs fears turning away car owners, or the liquor store owner doesn't emphasize wines for fear of losing beer customers. Year after year they trudge along (if they survive), squeaking by in the middle of a pack of similar competitors. They fail to realize that by emphasizing their distinction — and building a real brand — they can increase more business than they'll lose. Remember this golden rule: When you try to be all things to all people, you become nothing to everybody. In your copy, you should pursue you distinction fearlessly. By doing so, you attract the people who matter: Potential customers for *your* kind of business.

Eric definitely knew this rule. Early on, he made a crucial business decision that probably made his competitors shake their heads in derision: He decided not to cut women's hair. His detractors would object that by serving men only, Eric immediately eliminated 50 percent of his potential business universe from being customers. Was this a bad decision?

No, it was a shrewd decision. But it takes courage to make it because it seems contrary to common sense. If Eric cut women's hair, too, he would undermine his brand and become just another hair salon. By staying true to his vision, however, Eric created a distinction so attractive that its drawing power has more than compensated for the loss of women as potential customers.

Building a Brand Message from the Ground Up

In the big-picture perspective, everything you write is part of your brand. Your choice of products, offers, and benefits; the way you address your customers; and even the professionalism of your execution (or the lack thereof) speak to your brand.

But your job as a writer may sometimes require a special focus on branding. For example, some writing assignments have the express purpose of building a brand identity rather than landing a sale or inspiring a purchase. Among these types of writing, in fact, are two that consumers don't read — the positioning statement and the copy platform — both of which are intended as guidelines for your organization's marketing efforts. The remaining two — tag lines and mission statements — are among your organization's most explicit statements of identity and are things that consumers see.

What makes you special? Writing the positioning statement

Back in the early 1980s, some wise marketing types (such as Al Ries and Jack Trout) took a close look at many of the most successful brands, in categories from toothpaste to automobiles, and noticed that the biggest sellers all had something in common: Each occupied a special place in the consumer's mind, a place that became known as a *position.* Although many toothpastes had a minty flavor, a lone one was the "chloride toothpaste favored by dentists." They also noticed that after a brand staked a claim on a position, it was very difficult to displace; competitors would do better to claim top spot on a different position rather than share a position with a leader. In toothpaste, for example, all other brands that tried a "dentist-approved" position got slaughtered by the leader, while those that took a different approach, such as "the breath freshener for sexy singles," found success by occupying a different position.

Although marketing theories are as susceptible to fads as anything else (remember Total Quality Assurance, anyone?), positioning has taken root as one of the fundamentals of branding. Establishing your position, in fact, is now regarded as one of the crucial first steps toward formulating your brand; as a copywriter, you may be asked — as part of a long, jargon-loaded process known as a *branding exercise* — to create a positioning statement.

Even if you have the good fortune to work for yourself or within a small business, you should seriously consider writing a positioning statement. You have nothing to lose but a few hours of your time. Yet the rewards could be enormous: You get a deeper insight into your business and may gain a way to lift your business above its pack of competitors.

It may sound intimidating, but a *positioning statement* is nothing more that a combination of two defining characteristics: a special product or service quality and the special audience or market you're trying to reach. Take the Volvo, the Kia, and the Mercedes-Benz, for example. All three of them are cars, of course, but their positions are entirely different:

- ✔ **Volvo:** Its quality is safety, and its target audience tends to be safety-conscious consumers such as parents.

- ✔ **Kia:** This automaker positions itself on economy, with a focus on commuters and/or multicar households.

- ✔ **Mercedes-Benz:** The focus here is on luxury for status-conscious consumers.

To write a positioning statement, simply follow this formula by substituting your terms for the variables in the brackets:

[Name of product or service] is the [defining quality] [category] for [audience description] consumers.

Consider these examples based on the cars mentioned earlier:

- ✔ *Volvo* is the *safety-engineered car* for *safety-conscious* consumers.

- ✔ *Kia* is the *economy car* for *two- and three-car households.*

- ✔ *Mercedes-Benz* is the *luxury car* for *status-conscious* consumers.

You'll note that you've never seen these statements in any car ads. So what's the point? Focus! With the position on hand, marketers (and the copywriters working with them) know *what* to talk about and *who* to talk to. Kia doesn't waste time arguing about speed and performance — that's not its turf. Instead, it plays on its strength as a dependable and inexpensive second vehicle. Likewise, Mercedes-Benz doesn't bother to defend its high price; as far as this automaker is concerned (that is, in terms of the market it's positioned to target), if you have to ask about price, the Mercedes isn't for you.

If you're working on a new product or a new business, write the positioning statement before you do anything else. If the product or service is already well established, and you're writing within a large organization, ask if the company has a formal, approved positioning statement in place. The positioning statement is crucial: It helps you identify your message, the benefits and features you want to emphasize in your copy, and the nature of the audience you want to speak to.

Guiding force: Developing a copy platform

Television sitcom writers work with a thing called a "bible," a book of background information for their program and its characters. On one level, this bible is a practical tool for maintaining continuity: It makes sure that the writers don't say Joey graduated from Rutgers in one episode and then Harvard in the next episode. But it also serves as a source of inspiration and a wealth of information about motivation, attitude, emotions, and ambitions.

Likewise, marketing writers can work from a *copy platform,* an informal set of guidelines that ensure consistency of message and purpose across all marketing materials, whether they're ads, direct mail, Web sites, or brochures. Because the platform is intended for internal use only (yours or your organization's), there's no single standard for what it should look like. It can be as simple as a one-page list of bulleted points, or it can be a multipage document with many subsections.

The only meaningful standard is utility; the platform should be a helpful guideline to you and/or other writers in your company. In general, it should include everything a writer needs to know about an organization's general messaging — that is, everything except the specifics that pertain to a particular project, such as a new e-mail campaign — and establish any explicit rules (such as a Web site address that must always go with the logo, or a restriction against using contractions) a writer must obey. Most copy platforms include some, or all, of the following elements:

✔ **Positioning statement:** The positioning statement defines the special quality of your product and the special audience it's intended for. (See the previous section for the scoop.) Suppose you run a tutoring service for high school students called Everest Tutors. Your special, distinctive focus may be on improving achievement behaviors in underachieving students, so the position statement could be: *Everest Tutors is a one-on-one learning program that instills achievement skills, techniques, and behaviors in previously under-achieving high-school students.*

✔ **Key benefits:** This list should include the product or service's most important benefits that must be emphasized (often in headlines or within offers) and the supporting benefits that help round out the pitch. For Everest Tutors, the key benefit is improved academic performance, with elevated confidence as a significant supporting benefit.

✔ **Key features:** These features support your product's key benefits. They're the qualities that make the benefits possible and, when described in copy, make your promises believable. Everest Tutors' key features are its one-on-one approach, its skills-oriented lesson planning, and its application of behavioral psychology techniques that reinforce and reward achievement behaviors.

✔ **Product personality:** In its tone, rhythm, and diction, good copy should reflect the personality of your product or service. It can be caring and compassionate, technical and authoritative, professional and no-nonsense, fun and breezy, sexy and stylish, and so on. You can think of personality as the *way* your business fulfills its benefits and features, the attitudes, beliefs, and interpersonal qualities that it embraces in its everyday conduct. As a company that addresses a sensitive and important need — to improve a young person's academic prospects — Everest Tutors needs to be both compassionate and authoritative.

✔ **Audience characteristics:** Good copy speaks to the needs, concerns, values, and most importantly, the passions of its market, and it speaks the language (casual versus formal, humorous versus technical, and so on) of its audience. The tutoring business faces a complex stew of prospect emotions, ranging from parental concern, worry, and/or fear, to student shame, apathy, carelessness, and/or hope. In its communications, Everest Tutors has to assuage the more frightening feelings (like fear and shame) and build on the optimistic emotions (like pride and hope). For more on understanding your audience, check out Chapter 3.

✔ **Rules and regulations:** Finally, every brand has a set of do's and don'ts that must be followed to ensure consistency. In addition to the graphic standards for such things as colors, fonts, and logo treatment, all marketing material must conform to specified copy rules. As part of its effort to encourage a more mature outlook among the students it serves, Everest Tutors, for example, may make it a rule to never refer to its students as "teenagers" but always as "young adults."

Producing tag lines you can use repeatedly

A *tag line* is the written equivalent of a logo: It's a brief, catchy phrase that accompanies all of a company's marketing materials. If anything fulfills the cliché of the writer's wastebasket overflowing with crumpled paper and rejected ideas, it's writing a tag line. Why? It has to be written for the long run. Once agreed upon, the tag is used repeatedly for a very long time.

Tag lines are almost always condensed expressions of one of two things:

✔ **Position:** Your position defines what you do (or are) for what kind of people (or market). Although the formal positioning statement is used as an internal guideline, not as an external marketing message, it often serves as the foundation for the tag line. It tells you what's special about your product or business, and what audience it wishes to reach with its special qualities. Both pieces of information can make a priceless contribution to your tag line. For example:

  • **Coca-Cola:** Coke has run through a number of tag lines in its long history. One tag that stays in my mind is "It's the real thing™," a statement that positions Coke as the genuine drink for people who value authenticity. (At the same time, the tag line implies that Coke's competitors are fake and that the beverage is consumed, therefore, by phonies.)

  • **Nike:** Nike gathered a lot of attention (if not a big increase in sales) with its tag line "Just do it.®" In one direct imperative of three mono-syllabic words, Nike told the world that it makes a serious athletic shoe for active people who don't accept excuses for not being active.

✔ **Unique selling proposition (USP):** If your product or service can promise something wonderful that it alone can deliver, you may have what market-ing wonks call a "unique selling proposition." (No, this is not something said in a singles bar that provokes face slapping — there's nothing unique about that.) Because the USP combines a benefit with exclusivity — a claim your competitors can't make — the USP makes a powerful foundation for a tag line:

  • **Federal Express:** In its early incarnation, when super-fast delivery was something special, Federal Express touted its offer in a famous tag line: "When it absolutely, positively has to be there overnight®." The deliberate redundancy of "absolutely, positively," both four-syllable adverbs, reinforced the promise while adding a sly touch of self-deprecating humor.

  • **Morton Salt:** In 1911, Morton Salt became the first company to overcome the frustration of caking (damp, clogged salt) by adding magnesium carbonate to sodium chloride. But the company needed a way to communicate the benefit without indulging in a chemistry lesson. The resulting slogan is one of the wittiest, most memorable, and most successful tag lines ever: "When it rains it pours®." In five short words, Morton transformed what may be the ultimate commodity — salt — into one of the first great consumer brands.

To write a tagline, try this simple, three-step process:

1. Pick your positions and/or USPs.

Make a short list of possible position statements or unique selling propositions for the product or service you're selling. You may need to collaborate with your marketing department — or get input from your colleagues — to get your company's positions and USPs. These form the base for your work, for the tags you'll improvise, so limit yourself to no more than five. Here are two examples:

- **Position:** *Melody Matchmakers is the online dating service for music lovers.*

- **USP:** *Melody Matchmakers is the only dating service that matches people based on musical tastes.*

2. Play with your positions and/or USPs.

Now for each position or USP you (or you and your colleagues) selected, write at least five brief, catchy phrases that embody the meaning, spirit, or intent of your underlying position or USP. If there was ever a time to have creative fun, this is it. Puns, wordplay, rhymes, metaphors — they can all be part of your game. Remember, you're not carving words into stone; at this stage, feel free to let your imagination roam. At this point, you just want to generate ideas. Later, you can whittle them down to identify the tag that best fits your business, your message, and your target market. Here are two ideas for each of the tag approaches:

- **Position:**

  Make beautiful music together.

  Because the best love songs are duos.

- **USP:**

  Find someone in your key.

  Where dates are in tune.

3. Pray for cooperative collaboration.

Suppose that you write 5 witty variations on 5 positions and/or USPs for a total of 25 tag line options. Think you're done? Hah! Your work is just beginning. If you work for yourself, now's the time to critically assess your work: Which option most memorably represents your business's special purpose? But if you work within an organization, you submit your tag line to the rest of the marketing team (or whoever helps with marketing) and begin the rounds: Together (I hope), you and your team agree on the best tags — perhaps three to ten — and then you go back and write up to a dozen more tags that continue in that same direction. Brace yourself for the long haul: Expect to go through several rounds of discussion before you arrive at a solid tag line everyone agrees on (or at least grudgingly agree to).

Making mission statements — if you must

Call me crazy, but wasn't there a time when people knew what they were doing — or at least what they wanted? Businesses made money; hospitals healed the sick; churches saved souls. Then, in the 1990s, it seemed as if everyone lost his way; suddenly no one was capable of doing anything without having a "mission" first. Worse, they seemed intent on sharing this great vision — The Mission — in a "mission statement": a high-minded (and usually heavy-handed) declaration of purpose and values.

Mission statements are like maps in a foreign language. If you know where you're going, you don't need one. If you don't know where you're going, it won't help you. And don't be seduced into believing that they're useful tools for communicating anything meaningful to either your employees or your customers. When you visit a company's Web site, do you bother to read the mission statement? And if you do, do you believe it? Neither do your employees and customers.

But if you're absolutely forced to write one because . . . well, just because . . . here's what you do:

1. **Identify the organization's values.**

   These are all the things that typically follow the phrase "we're committed to." You're not allowed to admit that you're in business to turn a profit, so be sure you're committed to lofty ideals such as customer service, uncompromised quality, community enrichment, neighborhood empowerment, or shareholder value. If you'd like to eliminate world hunger or raise the dead, go ahead and throw that in, too. Believe me, the higher-ups will give you tons of values and commitments for you to sift through; the hardest part is getting them to agree on the ones that should be included in the mission statement.

2. **Mention a few ways you'll fulfill those values.**

   Frankly, many mission statements begin and end by declaring values. But if you want to add at least a little meat to the bones, mention a few ways your organization actually intends to live up to its commitments, perhaps by investing in research, building superior products, exploring new markets, or returning all customer inquiries in 24 hours or less.

   As far as tone and voice go, the universal standard is grim seriousness. After all, the organization is saying something "important." Fortunately, most mission statements are mercifully brief, and are usually limited to two or three paragraphs.

Chapter 11

Writing High-Powered Ads for Your Business

*T*he word *broadcast* has been so deeply associated with television and radio for so long that most individuals no longer recall the word's original context: agriculture. To *broadcast* is to sow seeds by casting them broadly over a field rather than placing them carefully within furrows or rows. Given the indiscriminate sweep of electromagnetic waves over a vast area, you can easily see how broadcasting became an appropriate metaphor for radio and television transmissions.

Broadcasting is also a terrific metaphor for advertising in general. Unlike direct marketing methods that carefully place the seed of a message in targeted media — like mail or e-mail — advertisements cast your message over a large area that you much less precisely target. You may have a general understanding of the kinds of readers, viewers, or listeners you're reaching, but you can never predict exactly who receives your message.

Your challenge is two-fold: to place your advertising where people amenable to your message are most likely to receive it, and to create ads that hold the attention of the people most likely to become your customers. Because this is a book specifically about writing and not advertising in general, I'm going to spend a little bit of time talking about placement and a lot of time talking about writing. (To find out more about advertising in general, check out *Advertising For Dummies* by Gary Dahl [Wiley].)

Inside this chapter, you can find an in-depth discussion of print advertising (newspapers and magazines, also known as *display advertising*), some information on similar advertising for the Web, and a brief discussion of do-it-yourself radio advertising. With effort and imagination, you too can master these forms of advertising — and cast your message far and wide.

The big-name, big-budget television advertising you see is so expensive that it's almost never an option for organizations without millions of dollars to invest in professional production and media placement. You may, however, want to consider the resources of your local stations and/or cable providers. They often have complete studios and creative resources at your disposal. Again, see Gary Dahl's *Advertising For Dummies* for more information.

Putting Your Message in Print

Print advertising, paid commercial messages run in newspapers, magazines, and other periodicals, is a viable option when you want to throw a wide net over a market you can define by interest, demographics (such as age or income), or geography (where consumers live, work, or shop).

Driving sales versus building a brand

Your must make your first important decision based on this question of purpose: What's your advertising objective? Most advertising falls into one of two categories: a direct effort to drive sales or an attempt to build a brand.

Ads designed to drive sales usually share a few common characteristics:

✔ **They're offer-centric:** Sales ads often highlight . . . sales! Or they feature discounts, special savings, two-for-one deals, and so on. You may see something like this:

20% to 50% off all men's wear at Gilligan's Aisles!

✔ **They talk about specific products and services:** Sales ads give you details about the features and benefits of the particular products or services they promote. For example:

Remove winter ice in seconds with FreezeGone!

✔ **They're time and/or location specific:** Many sales ads drive prospects to specific stores for specific events or times:

President's Day Dodge Blowout at Marty's Motors on the Miracle Mile!

Instead of selling the features and benefits of products and services, brand ads sell the brand: a set of images, ideas, and feelings consumers associate with a name or business. (For more on branding, turn to Chapter 10.)

Brand ads tend to share many of the same qualities:

- ✔ **They're conceptually based:** Brand ads often communicate an abstract quality, such as *elite* or *fun-loving*, rather than specific benefits or features. They also don't focus on locations, prices, and offers.

- ✔ **They address "identity":** Brand ads not only communicate something about their own brand identity (business characteristics), but also often want to tell you who *you* are. Consumers deeply associate many famous brands with certain identities: safety-conscious drivers, rebels, sophisticates, and so on.

Keep in mind that many successful businesses use both kinds of ads in a complementary marketing scheme. You see brand ads that establish the identity of an automobile as exciting, safe, or status-conscious, and then you see local ads for car dealers that promote sales, features, and price.

For the overwhelming majority of readers, I recommend that you focus on sales-driven advertising, not brand advertising. To be effective, brand advertising requires an extraordinary investment in research, creative development, and persistent media placement — and that means big bucks. Frankly, brand advertising is usually a game for high rollers and even the biggest and brightest players can suffer large losses. (Remember the "new" Coca-Cola?) If you're ready to enter brand advertising, you're ready to work with an agency. For the rest us, sales-driven advertising is the way to go — and that means developing ads that focus primarily on offers and benefits, not identities or emotional associations.

Knowing where to place your print ad

Placing an ad is like aiming a shotgun — you want to point your firepower where it can have the greatest impact. In advertising placement, you have two major considerations:

- ✔ **Geography:** For most small, main-street businesses, the issue is location. You want to place your ad in publications that cover the same ground as your customer base. If your business is limited to a local reach, such as a hair salon or a tax preparer, stick to the local paper. If your business has more of a regional reach (think car dealership or an upscale restaurant), you may want to consider a larger metro-area paper or a regional magazine.

- ✔ **Audience:** When your business doesn't depend on location (because you can do business on the Web or over the phone, or you have a specialty — say, Oriental rugs — that can attract people from a considerable distance), your ad should appear in publications that reach audiences similar to your customer base. If you sell luxury items, you want publications that have upscale subscribers; if you sell home medical supplies, perhaps focus on magazines geared toward older readers.

Print advertising isn't cheap. As you weigh your options, you need to balance cost against the reach of the publication, the number of readers it reaches, and the quality of the match between reader base and your desired prospects.

Generating "good enough" ideas for print ads

When you're ready to create your print ad, you may think you need a brilliant idea. An idea that bedazzles readers with its wit, charm, and cleverness. An idea that customers talk about for years to come. An idea, alas, that seems light-years away from the little thoughts that you scrawl on sheet after sheet of paper before crumpling them up and throwing them away in disgust.

Relax. You don't need to be brilliant — you just need to *sell*. In the pursuit of cleverness, too many ads collapse under the weight of cheesy puns, puzzling humor, and abstract concepts so far removed from any direct connection to a product or service that many people can't identify what a company is actually selling. (I'm thinking, for instance, of a lot of Super Bowl ads: The day after the game, Americans huddle around the water cooler and say, "That thing about the midget and the flame-thrower — was that an ad for potato chips, luxury sedans, or ED medication?") If you remember the basic principles of salesmanship — highlighting strong offers, compelling benefits, unique or special features — you'll find it easy to come up with *good enough* ideas that actually *work*. (For more ideas on searching for ideas, see Chapter 3.)

Begin your search for good enough ideas with these two thoughts in mind:

- ✔ **Remember your customer:** The most important part of your message is not what you want to say about your business, but what your customers need to hear. Don't waste precious ad space flattering yourself when you need to speak to customers' concerns, benefits, hopes, and fears.

- ✔ **Keep it simple:** A good ad has just one lead idea, be it an offer, a benefit, or a story. You can certainly include subordinate thoughts — your convenient hours or additional services — but don't let anything compete with your main idea: You'll create confusion and lose sales.

Because the copy you create is so closely tied to the type of ad you write for, I give you a quick rundown on the characteristics of several types of ads. This background can help you create copy that matches the mission and goal of your particular ad.

Making an urgent offer

Space is always at a premium. One of the most effective ways to take advantage of limited space is to lead with a strong offer, one that holds a lot of appeal to your customers, such as a deep discount. Better yet, you can go one step further and make your offer urgent by adding a time limit to encourage immediate action. On the plus side, offer ads present an unambiguous and easy-to-understand message for your customers with a clear appeal to action. On the other hand, offers cost money. Discounts cut into your margins and any "freebies" you provide usually come out of your pockets. The offer ad may be especially effective when

✔ Your business is already familiar to your readers.

✔ Your product or service is simple, common, and/or well understood.

✔ You face a number of competitors with similar goods or services.

✔ You want to drive traffic to the point of sale: your store, Web site, or phone number.

Good offers may look like this:

✔ For a pizza shop:

> *Anthony's March Madness: Get one FREE cheese pizza when you order two or more large pizzas to go!*

✔ For a hospital-sponsored blood-pressure screening:

> *Milk, sugar . . . good heart health. Come to Danny's Donuts on Tuesday mornings for a complimentary cup of coffee and a free blood pressure check from the staff at Mercy Hospital.*

Emphasizing an important benefit

Enough about you — tell me about . . . me. Or at least what benefits your product offers to me. Benefits articulate a clear reason *why* your product or service should matter to the prospect and add the crucial motivation necessary to turn tire-kickers into actual customers. In essence, you're saying, "This is what my product *does* for you – when you get up and buy." If you have a strong benefit to tout, and you don't want to lead with an offer, consider leading with a benefit, especially when

✔ Your business isn't well known or understood.

✔ You want to distinguish the value of your product or service from your competitors' products and services.

✔ You want to introduce a new product or service by demonstrating its importance.

In practice, your benefit lead may look like these examples:

✔ For a new real estate agency:

> *Get the best price for your home! Creon Real Estate uses the southwest's largest property database to determine your house's true value.*

✔ For a local dentist:

Just 30 days to a brighter, whiter smile. Dr. Sheila Molar is now taking appointments for the new Simu-Smile Ultra-Violet Whitening treatment plan. Four visits once a week will give you the smile you've always dreamed of.

Making the product the hero

Sometimes you're lucky; consumers find your product so desirable that all you have to do (almost) is announce its availability. This tactic works well when the demand for your product or service is already so strong you can almost taste it. (While I'm writing this chapter, a new big name donut shop is about to open in my neighborhood. There isn't a soul in town who isn't aware of its upcoming presence, and many are counting the days until its grand opening. The hot donut is the hero: All the company has to say is, "We're open!") But don't kid yourself: This approach only works when there's a genuine demand you can take advantage of. These occasions may occur when

✔ You sell luxury items, such as furs or fine art.

✔ You can *piggyback* on other publicity or advertising — very common with products or services that have been established in the prospects' minds through publicity or widespread brand advertising, such as automobiles or popular brand-name apparel.

✔ You sell a technically complex item to a knowledgeable market.

Your copy should focus on the "heroic" product by providing its name (or model number) and any memorable features that will make it instantly identify it for your audience. These ads may run something like this:

✔ For an oriental rugs dealer:

Just in from Kabul — hand-selected lot of rare Persian carpets.

✔ For a manufacturer of electronic testing devices:

New Z3000 DataPlus Oscilloscopes with extended frequency range and wave-form modeling capability.

Putting the customer in the ad

Just as you can make the product the hero, you can also give the customer a starring role — with real customers or with *stand-ins,* real people who simply represent the customer. (See Chapter 3 for information on working with cooperative customers.) Whether these ads are written in second person (you), third person (he, she, they), or first person (I, from the point of view of the customer pictured in the ad), they always tell a personal story, one that emphasizes the customer's feelings and attitudes. This customer-centric approach is ideal when the subject at hand, such as healthcare or financial recovery, demands empathy and sensitivity. To the degree that the personalization subordinates benefits or offers, however, it may weaken your primary sales message. Be sure you're comfortable with the trade off. You may want to consider the customer-centric ad when

- ✔ Your business demands a personal touch.

- ✔ You want to emphasize service or customer satisfaction.

- ✔ You want to overcome obstacles to the sale by using *safety-in-numbers* psychology — *other people use our product, so why not you?*

Here's what your ad may look like:

- ✔ For an insurance agency — a photo of a concerned adult with the following headline —

  My doctor saved my life, but my Waco Disability Plan saved my livelihood.

- ✔ For an asset manager — a photo of suited managerial types facing the camera —

  Thousands of benefits managers have entrusted billions in pension funds with Hanover Physt. Here's why . . .

Reporting the "news"

You can break through the communications clutter by offering *news*: significant information of interest to your targeted prospects. Delivering real news is both a great way of attracting attention and implying your expertise: It tells prospects that you're on top of current developments. When working with a news approach, use the news media as your model: Write in a straightforward style loaded with facts and free of puns or other "cute" touches. The news strategy is especially good when

- ✔ Your business is complex and ever-changing — like healthcare or financial services.

- ✔ Your industry or profession faces considerable skepticism that you must overcome.

- ✔ You want to add credibility and authority to your message.

Here are a few examples of news in action:

- ✔ For an HMO plan for seniors:

  Medicare-backed HMOs can help seniors save on pharmaceutical costs.

- ✔ For a direct-seller of vitamin and other health supplements:

  NIH report: Shark cartilage relieves arthritis symptoms by 32% to 73%!

Writing your print ad

I think of the ad as a two-part machine: The first part is a *hook* to attract a reader's attention, usually made of a headline alone or a headline with some sort of graphic imagery; the second part is the *line* that reels the reader in with body copy that completes the sales pitch.

In some advertising, such as classified ads, all you have to work with is a headline and a couple lines of copy. But most of the time you work with *graphics* — a photo or illustration that attracts the eye. Because the overwhelming majority of readers see the headline and image without taking the time to read the body copy, the initial graphic hook is extraordinarily important. If you're in a hurry, cooperate with the graphic designer (the person responsible for the art, layout, and "look" of the ad) and focus your efforts on creating as strong a headline/graphics combination as possible. If your hook is strong enough, your body copy may be as simple as a phone number, Web address, or street address.

Creating hooks with graphics and headlines

From black-and-white line drawings to four-color photographs, a designer has a variety of ways to illustrate your ad. Regardless of their sources, however, these images serve a number of different strategic purposes. In order to write copy that complements the design, take a look at how the major visual strategies can work with the headlines you create. In most situations, you and the designer agree on an image before you write, allowing you to integrate your copy with the art. The designer is usually responsible for finding the appropriate art; conflicting opinions about imagery (if any) are resolved by the powers above, be they creative directors, marketing managers, or the clients themselves. Ultimately, whoever foots the bill gets the final word. (For details on different ad approaches, check out "Generating 'good enough' ideas for print ads," earlier in this chapter.)

The beauty shot

One obvious, and often sufficient, approach is simply to use a professionally executed photograph or illustration of the product. This is an especially appropriate choice when the product's chief benefit is beauty or sensual appeal — such as jewelry, clothing, or fine furniture.

The beauty shot is a natural tie-in to the news approach in its simplest form — as an announcement — or to a product as hero approach or a simple offer. The copy should be brisk, enthusiastic, and brief (because you're counting on the image to carry the weight of your message). Here's how beauty shots can work:

✔ **News/announcement:** In this approach, write your headline to simply connect the image of the news. Keep your copy short and simple.

Image: Men's silk ties

Headline: *Ties from Wendell Lyon. At Sherman's on the Mall.*

✔ **Product-as-hero approach:** Now you can stretch out a little and apply some romance to your copy. Got a great metaphor, allusion, or popular saying that may be appropriate? This is the time to try it out.

Image: Stunning diamond necklace

Headline: *The Vinelli Diamond Flame. Matched only by the fire in her eyes.*

✔ **Offer:** Treat this like any other offer headline (see Chapter 2) but be sure you make a clear connection to the imagery.

Image: Assortment of handsomely arranged deli meat platters

Headline: *Super platters for the Super Bowl. Starting at just $15.95 at Johnny's, this week only.*

The action shot

When products perform a function or do something helpful for the consumer, you can show the product in action to illustrate the benefits it provides. Your job isn't to explain the image (the activity should be crystal clear — if it isn't, pick another picture) but to articulate the action's meaning or value to the prospect.

✔ **Benefit approach:** With a handful of crisp words, simply state the value of your product or service in action.

Image: Carpet steamer cutting a clean path through a dirty rug

Headline: *Restore your carpet to its original beauty in minutes!*

The stand-in

Instead of featuring your product or service, you can present images of people who serve as *stand-ins* for your prospects. Many insurers and health-care providers, for instance, use photographs of people — in various degrees of distress or relief, depending on the message — to create an empathetic connection with their prospects.

✔ **Customer-as-hero headline:** Images starring people are a natural for the customer-as-hero approach (see "Generating 'good enough' ideas for print ads" for details). In the headline, articulate *how* your product helps (or brings value or meaning) to the person in the image and by extension, your customers.

Image: Businesswoman clutching a stack of reports

Headline: *One call to Business Express yesterday is taking care of business today.*

The visual metaphor

Although you can illustrate some services, such as landscaping, with an action shot of people at work, you may find that many services, such as insurance actuarial analysis, are difficult if not impossible to capture on film. What to do? You can present an *as if* picture of something that's like your service — a visual metaphor for what the company does.

The visual metaphor often creates a brand identity for either a complex product or service or for a company that needs to create a distinctive position within a crowded field of competitors. Visual metaphors are far less common in sales-driven advertising.

- ✔ **Brand identity:** Put on your thinking cap and roll up your sleeves. Your challenge is to connect the visual metaphor to your brand message. In the following example, I link rock-climbing to career advancement.

  Image: A suited executive scaling a cliff

  Headline: *Broderick Executive Coaching Group: Moving up is easier when someone shows you the ropes.*

Original visual metaphors can be powerful ways to communicate your message. But many ideas, such as the sports metaphor, have become tiresome clichés — their use may not reflect favorably on your business. If you can't think of a fresh visual metaphor, use a different graphic approach.

Developing body copy

Just because far fewer people read the body copy than the headline doesn't mean the body is unimportant; on the contrary, you can be sure that those who take the time to read body copy are among the most motivated prospects. Your job is to turn interest into action by making your best case for a sale.

In the body, you expand or defend the initial claim or promise you've made in your headline, be it an offer, benefit, or item of news. Your copy need not "sparkle" (and should never draw attention to itself), but should always construct a solid sales pitch by using specifics — the facts about your product or service that support your case. In particular, good body copy briefly answers two crucial questions for your potential customers:

- ✔ **Why should she buy it?** Part of the answer is embedded in the strategic approach you took with your headline/graphics combination hook. If you lead with the offer, you answer *why?* by developing the offer. If a benefit takes the lead, you explore the value of the benefit. The body copy is always an extension of the promise you make with your hook.

- ✔ **How can she buy it?** Sometimes you get so carried away with your ideas that you forget the basics: When, where, and how consumers can purchase your product or service. After you hook your customers' desire, don't fail to tell them how to fulfill it.

Check out Figure 11-1 for an example of print ad copy.

Headline — Milan. Florence. Your living room.

Subhead — Averetti Fine Furniture adds an Italian accent to your home.

The dramatic angles of Tuscan design. The sensuous touch of Roman leather. The bold colors of Florentine silks and textiles.

Bring them home—from Averetti Fine Furniture. Averetti is the North Shore's leading importer of the finest Italian home furnishings. And unlike some furniture importers, what we present on the floor we carry in stock, guaranteed.

Take advantage of our weekend hours, noon to 7:00 pm, or our extended weekday hours, Tuesday through Friday, 8:00 am to 8:00 pm. We're right off Exit 24 on Rt. 5, opposite the cinema.

Averetti Fine Furniture
Italian, By Design
1-800-123-4567

Figure 11-1:
Copy for
a print ad
that builds
on the
appeal of a
luxury item.

In Figure 11-1, the advertisement takes the product-as-hero approach (check out "Generating 'good enough' ideas for print ads," earlier in this chapter) by displaying exquisite Italian furniture in elegant surroundings. The headline and subhead promise that Averetti Fine Furniture brings the glamour of Milan and Florence into the consumer's home.

Here's how the three paragraphs of body copy work:

- The body copy begins by building on the premise established in the hook — the promise of sophisticated elegance: "The dramatic angles of Tuscan design. The sensuous touch of Roman leather. The bold colors of Florentine silks and textiles."

- The second paragraph introduces the fulfillment: "Bring them home — from Averetti Fine Furniture." It also adds supporting points: Averetti is "the North Shore's leading importer" and "what we present on the floor we carry in stock, guaranteed."

- The third paragraph explains how to purchase by presenting the business hours and location, including a reference to a landmark: the cinema.

Advertising on the Web

Your Web site can be, in itself, a comprehensive marketing communications vehicle. (I discuss Web sites in detail in Chapter 14.) But as so many people discovered in the initial online rush, a Web site isn't like the baseball diamond in the film *Field of Dreams* — building it doesn't mean they will come. Unless you make concerted efforts to drive traffic to your site, establishing your Web site can be like setting up a lemonade stand in the middle of the woods — a lonely and losing proposition.

The goal of the Web ad is simple — get people to your site. In your print or mail media, you draw attention to your *URL* — the string of characters you type into your browser to get from site to site. In e-mail, you can include a hyperlink. On the Web itself, the most popular ways to drive traffic include search engine marketing, banner ads, and pop-up ads.

The search is over! Using search engine marketing

Your best hope for advertising on the Web rests with *search engine marketing*, a set of techniques and advertising purchases designed to give a Web site greater visibility at the Internet's most popular search sites and includes both the quality of your position within a given search and/or the sponsored advertisements that often accompany them. Search engine marketing has two huge advantages:

- ✔ **You catch the attention of motivated prospects:** On search engines, people . . . search. They search for medicines, advice, insurance, radio transmitters, and what have you. Unlike other Web advertising methods that impose themselves on people regardless of their interests, search engine marketing targets only those people who demonstrate an active interest in what you have to say or sell.

- ✔ **You catch people at the beginning of their search:** Every other medium — including mail, broadcasting, and print advertising — has something of a hit-or-miss quality; you can never be sure you hit people at the right time. But when you deploy search engine marketing, you make your move at an optimum moment — when customers are just beginning to explore their options.

When people visit search engines or *directories* (lists of relevant resources hand-picked by the site's operators rather than automatically placed by software protocols), they type words related to their interests, such as "used snow blowers" or "asthma control," in the appropriate field in the hopes of finding relevant Web sites they may visit. As a marketer on the opposite end of the search, you want visibility within the results your prospect sees. The goal of search engine marketing is to give your site as high a ranking as possible within the returned results when customers use keywords — such as "Italian furniture" or "Springfield oil change" — relevant to your site. You can do this in a number of ways:

✔ **Search engine optimization:** To get a high ranking, you *optimize* your site to obtain a high ranking for important keywords on the popular engines. Because different search sites use different techniques — say cataloging by experts versus using *spiders* to collect info — and they deliberately change their secret methods to discourage people from gaming the system, optimization is always a moving target. This is less a job for ordinary copywriters than it is for dedicated Web professionals who keep abreast of the latest search engine developments. For more, see *Search Engine Optimization For Dummies* by Peter Kent (Wiley).

✔ **Paid inclusion:** Yes, you can still submit your Web site to the major search engines for free. But to guarantee a listing in a more favorable position, you're also invited to pay for inclusion. This can be a very cost-effective approach to ensuring a good ranking for your site.

✔ **Keyword-based ad placements:** The last option is also the most intriguing. Under this ad placement plan, you submit a bid for what you're willing to pay per click-through for a small ad that appears whenever someone submits the keyword(s) you select. The higher your bid, the higher your ad appears among your competitors. You typically draw the money from an account you establish with the search site, so you can precisely control your ad spending to the dollar.

I like this kind of advertising because it gives you bulletlike precision for your money. In effect, you pay to show your ad to the segment of the overall Internet-user population that demonstrates active interest in something that may be relevant to your site and to your business.

From a copywriting point of view, writing the keyword-based ad is simple: Scrupulously follow the instructions of the search site itself! The sites have a vested interest in assuring visitors that keyword searches produce relevant results. As part of their campaign for credibility, they impose strict rules regarding what you can or can't say in the keyword-based ads. Although the specifics vary from site to site, the general rule is that your headline contains the relevant keyword or keywords, and that the subsequent copy, which is brief, contains factual information about your site with little or no marketing hype.

In practice, a keyword-based ad often looks something like this:

✔ For an electronics supplier who purchases the keywords *vacuum tubes*, the supplier might write the following crisp, no-nonsense copy:

Headline: Pre-tested **vacuum tubes**

Super-short body: For audio and guitar amps. Thousands new, new-old-stock, or used.

www.tubeland.com

Considering banners and pop-ups

Banner ads and pop-up ads enjoy the same status as spam: Consumers revile them with an intensity in proportion to their intrusiveness. Maybe that doesn't matter, because you want to win customers, not popularity contests. But a good deal of data suggests that the *click-through* rates (the number of times people use the embedded hyperlink to visit your site) of these ads aren't high enough to justify either the expense or the ill will they often generate. Dollar for dollar, these ads often fail to produce the pull you pay for.

If you're still curious about banners and pop-ups, read on.

- ✔ **Banner ads:** The closest equivalent in the online world to ordinary print advertising, the banner ad is a short, *static ad* (it stays in one location) you place on other Web sites. It can include fixed and/or animated graphics and may feature a cycle of two or three messages that rotate within the given space. Clicking on the ad leads the reader to your site.

  Space is at a premium on Web sites, so copy for banner ads almost always takes one of two approaches:

  - • **An offer** that gets straight to the point and looks something like this: *Get the best rate on your car insurance. Click here to compare and save.*

  - • **A teaser** that suggests something attractive without giving away the ultimate destination: *Where can you find thousands of new singles a day?*

- ✔ **Pop-up ads:** Imagine turning the page of your morning paper and having an advertisement leap into your face. On the Web, *pop-up* ads — little boxes of advertising that seem to appear out of nowhere — don't quite assault the reader, but they do demand your attention by blocking out something you're trying to read. In copy, they tend to be longer than banner ads, but they also favor offers and teasers as lures. More timely promotions, such as movie ads, often take a news approach: *Coming to theaters February 18: Teen Slash Fest LXII.*

Tuning In: Advertising on the Radio

Talk about working without a safety net: No pictures, no paper, no excuses. With radio advertising, all you have are your words and maybe some music or sound effects. In your spot, you have to attract interest, identify your business, give people a reason to buy, and tell them how to buy — all within 60 seconds.

Radio advertising isn't easy, but the rewards can be great. In many markets, radio is a cost-effective alternative (or supplement) to print advertising. And for certain target markets that don't turn to the paper for their primary source of information — such as drive-time commuters or teen audiences — radio may be the your best opportunity to build recognition for your business.

Just as with print advertising, consider the reach and nature of the audiences available on radio before you commit hard cash to any particular slot on a specific station. In addition to giving you a *fee schedule* (your cost for broadcasting your ad), radio stations give you important data about their audience: number of listeners, plus demographic information about age, sex, income, interests, and more. You want to make your broadcast purchases within slots that reach your potential customer base.

Choosing a production method for your radio spot

When you want to produce a radio spot, you have two major options:

✔ **Run with an agency:** A professional ad agency with radio experience can apply its creative and material resources to producing your ad. Agencies aren't cheap, but when they complete the job, you can place the finished radio spot at any station you choose. For the extra money involved, you get a more sophisticated final product and the power to use your ad where you wish.

✔ **Let the station produce the spot:** Stations want your business; many will produce your spot (including writing, voice talent, sound, and music effects) at no additional charge in return for your commitment to run the spot at their station a contracted number of times. In exchange for the free production, however, you lock into that one station and can't bring the finished spot anywhere else. But if you're confident that the station is a good fit with your potential customer base, the station-produced spot can be an excellent deal.

If you let the station produce the spot, you can hand over a set of *copy points* (issues the copy should cover) and let the station write the spot, or you can write it yourself. If you write the spot, I recommend a simple approach: a single-voice, straight-read spot with or without music (MX) or sound effects (SFX). You may be tempted to write comedy or a dialog spot, but unless you have a gift for dramatic writing, you're asking for trouble — without considerable skill, the dialog spot often sounds forced and phony. Go with the single-voice spot, a proven seller with simplicity that encourages clarity and straight talk, two virtues that play in your favor.

Composing your radio spot's copy

In your radio spot, you want to accomplish three things, in roughly this order:

1. **Identify yourself.**

   You want to get your name heard fast and often. Identify your business within the first ten seconds of the ad and repeat it at least two more times.

   In Figure 11-2, I introduce the name of the business, Belleville Auto Glass, in the second sentence and then repeat it three more times during the spot.

2. **Make a promise.**

   Give listeners a *reason* to pay attention and shop with you. Make an offer, state a benefit, or promise a unique quality, virtue, or feature that only your business can provide.

   In Figure 11-2, Belleville Auto Glass offers to fix any glass on any vehicle at any time, night or day.

3. **Complete the connection.**

   Plant your phone number, location, or Web site address firmly in the listeners' minds. You have only 60 seconds, so keep things simple — consider stating either the phone number or the Web site address, but not both. And when you do give your location, use local landmarks as a reference: "Off Exit 12 on Route 92, across from Donut Land."

   Because Belleville Auto Glass brings the repair to the customer, its physical location is irrelevant. Instead, the spot in Figure 11-2 repeats the toll-free number three times: at the beginning, middle, and end of the spot.

Note that the type in Figure 11-2 is in all caps. Even though it may be difficult to read, using all caps in radio copy is typical.

Writing radio ads is easier when you keep these points in mind:

- ✔ **Use short words and short sentences:** Simplicity is key, and sentence fragments are perfectly acceptable if your meaning is clear. Use informal language in a conversational tone.

- ✔ **Read your work aloud:** Sometimes copy that looks great on paper can fail out loud, either by being difficult to read or difficult to discern clearly by ear. For example, the phrase *difficult to discern clearly by ear* would never make it for radio — the alliterative D sounds and the clanging *clearly* and *ear* make the phrase aurally unpleasant. Reading your work out loud is the easiest way to intercept weak radio copy.

- ✔ **Time yourself:** Get a stopwatch and time your reading. You want to be sure you come in under 60 seconds — including time for the sound effects and music cues, if necessary.

Client: Belleville Auto Glass
Spot Title: "Bringing the Fix to You."

MX: Ominous music
SFX: Crackling sounds, then breaking glass

DON'T LET A DING BECOME A DISASTER. BELLEVILLE AUTO GLASS WILL REPAIR OR REPLACE YOUR WINDSHIELD IN MINUTES. JUST CALL 1-800-FIXWIND AND BELLEVILLE AUTO GLASS WILL BRING THE REPAIR TO YOU. OUR TRUCKS ARE ON STAND-BY TWENTY-FOUR HOURS A DAY, SEVEN DAYS A WEEK. AND WE'RE STOCKED FOR ALL COMMON VEHICLE MAKES AND MODELS, AMERICAN AND FOREIGN.

MX: Sweet, soothing violins

Figure 11-2:
Copy for a single-voice radio spot with music and sound effects.

CALL 1-800-FIXWIND FOR WINDSHIELDS OR SIDE WINDOWS ON CARS, TRUCKS OR VANS. IF IT'S GLASS AND IT'S ON WHEELS, BELLEVILLE AUTO GLASS IS READY TO REPLACE IT, FAST. AND REMEMBER, BROKEN GLASS WON'T BREAK YOUR BUDGET. AUTO GLASS REPLACEMENT IS COVERED BY MOST CAR INSURANCE POLICIES. CHANCES ARE, YOUR REPAIR WON'T COST YOU ANYTHING.

CALL 1-800-FIXWIND AND LET BELLEVILLE AUTO GLASS BRING THE FIX TO YOU.

Chapter 12

Creating Effective Press Releases and Press Kits

....

In This Chapter

▶ Using the media in your marketing mix

▶ Crafting press releases that capture editors' attention

▶ Putting together press kits that promote your company and expertise

....

*W*hen you read your newspaper, you may notice an article in the real estate section about a new office complex, or in the business pages, you may find a profile of a hot mutual funds manager. These articles may catch your attention because they're subjects that interest you. That's certainly the editor's intention. But if an article features your competitors, it may prompt a pang of envy — how did they get this special attention? Why did the editor shine a light on *them* and not *you*?

It's nothing personal. Chances are, the editor (or editors) didn't actively seek out these stories or the people in them. Their reporters probably didn't uncover these stories through vast and untiring investigative efforts. Instead, people like you feed these stories to the media every day. People send story ideas to the press because they're looking for favorable attention and free publicity, or they hope to garner the authoritative glow that comes with being quoted by the media.

This information is sent to the media through a process called *public relations (PR)*, a cluster of promotional activities intended to shape public attitudes and opinions, and generate goodwill toward your organization, its mission, and/or its products and services. Although some public relations activities don't directly involve the press, such as corporate sponsorship of charities or community events, a great deal of PR is centered on that vast and mighty communications bullhorn, the media. To use the media to your advantage, you frequently turn to the press release and press kit, the primary tools for feeding story ideas to the hungry media. In this chapter, you can discover why the press can help you generate new business, and you can see just how easy it is to write press releases and put together press kits. And perhaps you can turn a little of the media spotlight your way.

Leveraging the Media to Your Advantage

Like marketing, public relations involves getting your message to the public. But public relations has two key characteristics that distinguish it from marketing techniques such as advertising or direct response:

- ✔ Instead of selling products or services, public relations usually sells attitudes or opinions that reflect favorably on organization and its activities: a company's expertise, a hospital's caring and commitment, a local business's contribution to the community.

- ✔ When you market, you pay an explicit fee to get advertising space, mail your brochure, or broadcast your commercial. In public relations, you try to get the media to serve as the conduit for your message for free. (Well, sort of. Though you don't pay for media exposure, public relations isn't necessarily cheaper than other forms of marketing: Remember to consider the costs of preparing materials for the media, developing relationships with editors, training personnel to speak to the media, and so on.) When it works well, the legitimacy of the publication or broadcaster adds a luster of credibility to your message. The trade-off? You surrender final control of the message about you or your business to the media.

Take a look at these examples for a better idea of public relations in action:

- ✔ **Exploiting topical events:** Sometimes the news itself provides an opportunity for your organization to shine. Suppose that your software company employs many experts in computer security. During one widely publicized e-mail virus outbreak, a major newspaper interviews one of your experts, which gives your company instant, national exposure.

- ✔ **Building goodwill:** Your organization doesn't exist in a vacuum: You're always conducting business within the context of laws, taxes, zoning regulations, employee relations, and other variables that directly involve the public interest. The more goodwill you have, the more likely you are to align the public interest with your own. When a hospital rents a booth at the local "Town Day," offering free blood pressure checks and distributing free medical literature, it not only serves an immediate health interest but also helps build a foundation of goodwill that makes it easier for the hospital to work within its community.

- ✔ **Deflecting bad news:** Stuff happens. You can use public relations techniques to present your case and mitigate the impact of unfavorable news. If, for example, your dry-cleaning business has been the target of complaints regarding an increase of traffic — and possibly pollutants — in your neighborhood, you may write a column for the local paper that discusses the value and virtues that local businesses bring to the community.

Whatever your objective, you can deploy public relations tactics, such as the press release, to your advantage. To succeed, you need to understand a few things about the media and how they work. To begin, however, you have to understand your own organization's nature and needs.

Knowing when to use public relations

Public relations isn't just for politicians, Hollywood stars, and international corporations. If your organization faces specific challenges, public relations efforts can work for you, too.

You may want to consider adding public relations to your marketing plan in the following situations:

- **Your business is complex.** Suppose that you develop statistical analysis software or conduct research in agricultural bioengineering. Your product or service is complicated, abstract, and difficult to summarize without confusion. As a rule of thumb, the more abstract your business, the greater the need for public relations as part of your marketing mix. An article about your financial planning analysis system, for example, may do a much better job than a half-page print advertisement to explain what you do and why your company is necessary.

- **You need to establish authority in your given field.** This is especially true of people who make their living selling their expertise and experience, such as technology consultants or financial planners. The independent and disinterested voice of the media can lend an aura of credibility that you can't get from buying an advertisement.

- **You want a strong relationship with your neighbors.** Your work or your organization plays a significant role in the community. (Think hospitals, banks, or very large employers.) The consequences of your organization's activities go beyond its own walls to affect issues such as taxes, employment rates, and local property development. It's in your interest to open and sustain an open line of communication between your company and your community to encourage trust and support.

- **Customer education is an important part of your business.** Suppose that your product is in a new and unfamiliar category and requires explanation before it can occupy a clear place in the public consciousness. In the late 19th century, Thomas Edison invested considerable time in public relations efforts when he introduced electric light to a world familiar only with gas illumination. In the 21st century, Dean Kamen captured international attention for an entirely new form of transportation, a sophisticated scooter for adults called the Segway. Whatever you say about the device's genuine worth, Kamen's public relations campaign successfully turned an obscure idea into a media sensation.

Public relations, however, isn't for dabblers. A successful campaign requires considerable thought. In many instances, investing your time or money in public relations isn't worth the bother, or it can actually create more problems than it solves. Consider the following situations:

- ✔ **Your business is local, small, and well understood.** An auto parts store, for example, requires little explanation. Although you may use a press release to announce the opening of your store, unless your business operates within an unusual niche (such as components for drag racers), you may not have enough news potential to make large-scale media relations worth your trouble.

- ✔ **You want to maintain a low profile.** Yes, you may have legitimate reasons for doing this. A children's book author, for example, may not want to attract the kind of local publicity that can have his phone ringing off the hook with neighbors who have "great ideas" for the next book he needs to write. Corporations that manufacture legal, yet controversial, products often prefer to be ignored. Likewise, many universities that conduct animal research take great pains to maintain a virtual invisibility.

- ✔ **You don't have the capacity (time, people, money) to respond to widespread attention from either the media or the public.** A restoration carpenter may like publicity to draw in business inquiries. But too much attention can also attract time-absorbing requests for free advice or answers to "just a couple of quick questions" that a lone carpenter can't take the time to answer.

Understanding what the media want

Okay, suppose that your business can benefit from public relations. Then you need to form a working relationship between you and the media. It's not enough to want attention. The media have to want to give that attention to you.

The secret to successful media relations is to serve your interests by serving the media's interests. The more you can match your story to their needs, the more likely they are to publish or broadcast something about you.

Fortunately, they're hungry for material. (You would be too if you had to publish every day, week, and month.) You need to think about what they want:

- ✔ **They want news.** They need to keep current with the latest and greatest news in their geographic area, in their subject area, and in respect to topics of vital interest to their readers.

- ✔ **They want reader relevance.** Apply the fundamental acid test: Is your story of interest to the publication's readers? Don't pitch an announcement about your new tennis rackets to a golf magazine.

> ✔ **They want fresh insights.** Sometimes an issue is so important that even when it's no longer fresh news, it still remains newsworthy. Perhaps you can offer a fresh perspective on home gardening, mutual funds, or raising children. Some things just don't grow old — as long as you have something new and interesting to say about them.

Attracting media attention

Amazing as it may seem, many of the most extraordinary public relations success stories begin with a humble document, usually just one-page long, called the *press release.*

The press release is a short fact-filled document that tells editors the *who, what, where, when, how,* and sometimes *why* of your story. (For more information on these key points, see the section "Preparing yourself before you write," later in this chapter.) Within its handful of paragraphs, the press release makes a compelling case for newsworthiness, reader relevance, and the credibility of the person or organization making the pitch.

You write a press release to attract further inquiry (perhaps a phone call from a reporter) and to generate publicity around your new product or service. Your goal: to get the media to spread your news for you.

The properly organized and well-written press release can accomplish the following:

> ✔ **Attract interest in new products or services:** Your company builds a better mousetrap, and now you're using the press release to get the information out there.

> ✔ **Inspire print announcements (especially in trade or business-related publications) of your change in management or company direction:** If you run a business or nonprofit organization large enough to create economic, political, or social ripples within a sizable cultural pond, then the changes you make within your company are newsworthy.

> ✔ **Lead to interviews of — or articles about — key executives or experts in your company or organization.** If your employees have new insights or fresh perspectives on matters of reader interest, then there's a good chance you can find an editor or reporter who wants to talk to them.

> ✔ **Draw attention to special events you're hosting or significant activities you're participating in:** When you're hosting a blood pressure screening, sponsoring a charity dinner, or offering an informational seminar, you can get the word out quickly with a press release.

✔ **Help sustain relationships with editors, writers, and publishers:** Having a positive relationship with key media personnel may be so important that you want to keep them in the loop even when your latest news may not be especially earthshaking. When editors know and trust you, they're more likely to provide space for your stories. And if anything happens that may put your business in a bad light, you stand a greater chance of getting equal time (or newspaper or magazine column inches) to publish your side of the story.

However, press releases do have their limitations. Press releases *cannot* do the following:

✔ **Create relationships with either the public or the press:** To create lasting relationships, you need sustained, multifaceted efforts, of which the press release may play only a small part. Sound involved? It can be — that's why people hire public relations agencies.

✔ **Solve all public relations problems:** If a skeleton has turned up in your corporate closet, you can't expect a simple press release to settle the matter. You're in the realm of *crisis communications,* a subset of public relations designed to redress bad news (such as corporate embezzlement or sexual harassment charges) that involves lots of face time with crucial opinion leaders: respected citizens, role models, or authority figures who can influence community attitudes and behaviors.

✔ **Shower your organization with leads:** Sorry, the press release rarely solves your sales problems. An announcement in the media can be *part* of a successful marketing campaign, but it won't do all the heavy lifting for you.

Placing your story where it counts

When you're opening a new bank branch or offering a free home plumbing consultation, you can anticipate having a client base that lives or works within a few miles of your business. That means you can be best served by contacting media with a similar base, such as the local paper your customers are most likely to read. But suppose that you don't have a general interest story, like one that can be written about your bank opening or your offer for free plumbing consultations. If you need to reach a special segment of the population, like investment bankers or plumbing supply manufacturers, your local editor won't be interested, and even if she were, her paper can't possibly reach enough of the people you really want to reach. You need special-interest periodicals that aren't limited by geography and are read by bankers or plumbing suppliers nationwide (and even worldwide).

Match your story to the right publication. You need to find the media that speak to the same people you're trying to reach.

If you already have certain media in mind, terrific. If not, use these two easy ways to find it:

✔ You can go to the reference desk in your local library and ask for *Bacon's Magazine Directory.* In *Bacon's,* you can find an inventory of magazines and newsletters categorized by interest, from advertising to woodworking. *Bacon's* gives you just about everything you need to know to target the right editors: circulation statistics, a readership profile, and all the necessary editorial contact info, including addresses and phone numbers, to get your press release into the right hands. If you plan to make public relations an integral part of your ongoing marketing efforts, you may want to subscribe to *Bacon's* online subscription service.

✔ The other idea has a fun, semi-cloak-and-dagger feel to it: Ask your customers what they read! And if you have the privilege of visiting your prospects in their own homes or offices, keep your eyes open and make a mental note of what they're reading.

If you have a particularly strong story to pitch — one so unique or so important that you think it merits an interview by a reporter — you may want to call the newspaper or magazine to open communications. If you're not sure how important or newsworthy your story is, however, stick with just sending a press release, which is considered the appropriate introduction for plenty of reasons. Here are a few situations that merit a press release:

✔ You open a retail or consumer service business in town, and your customer base will be almost entirely local. Announce your opening in the local paper.

✔ You have a new product or service that may be newsworthy in the appropriate trade or industry publication.

✔ You hire executives or other key employees. Depending on the size of your company and the responsibilities of the new hires, their employment may merit notice in local, regional, or national business publications.

✔ In certain industries, such as advertising, attracting a new client may be newsworthy. Again, target the appropriate industry publication — find an industry publication that matches your new client's industry, as well as your own.

✔ In the nonprofit sector, new initiatives may be newsworthy for a number of stakeholders and, depending on the nature of the development (new research discovery, new community service, expanded reach of operations), may be of interest to a variety of media in certain industries and in specific geographic areas that will be affected by the change.

Writing a Press Release That Reels Them In

After you consider all the functions of a press release and the careful decision making involved in using one, you may be amazed to find that when it comes to the writing itself, the press release is refreshingly simple. Just follow three basic steps:

1. **Get a grip on the content.**

   Be sure you have a clear understanding of your story and all the facts that support it, before you sit down to write. (I discuss this in detail in the upcoming section, "Preparing yourself before you write.")

2. **Follow the standard format of the press release.**

   Remember, editors are busy people; the press release format has evolved into a fast, easily skimmed document for their convenience. When you stick to the standard format, you gain a better chance of gaining editor eyes and ears. (See the "Constructing the elements, piece by piece" section, later in this chapter.)

3. **Turn your content into compelling news.**

   Your latest product release isn't news — until you explain *why it's important* to the editor's readers. Think of it as the "so what?" rule: For every announcement you wish to make in a press release, answer "So what?" by explaining its significance: what it does; how it makes the world a better place; what impact it has on people, families, communities; and so on.

And with a little luck, the media takes your story and runs with it.

Preparing yourself before you write

If you want to capture the attention of a journalist, think like a journalist: Ask pertinent questions that go to the heart of a story. The best way to prepare yourself for writing a press release is to collect the answers to these three questions:

✔ **Who is your product or service useful for (or meaningful to)?** Be sure they're explicitly targeted in the release, as in this example:

The Little Smokey is designed for apartment dwellers who would like to bring the excitement of outdoor barbecuing to their window ledges.

✔ *How* **and** *why* **is this product or service used, deployed, or valued?** If it's a new tool, how does it work and where would you use it? If it's a new work of art, why is it important? Here's an example:

By simply clipping the Little Smokey hibachi to any convenient window ledge, today's cook can enjoy the "thrill of the grill" any time.

✔ *How* **or** *where* **can the product/service be obtained?** If you're announcing a new product for sale, don't neglect to mention how and where it can be purchased:

Retailers interested in carrying the Little Smokey may call our City Grilling distribution center at 1-800-123-4567.

Taking notes

In addition to asking the big questions that capture the main idea of your press release, you have to take notes on the little stuff that, added together, fill in the rest of the story. (After you get your information down on paper, I show you how to use it in the section "Constructing the elements, piece by piece," later in this chapter.) These particulars include the following:

✔ **Who:** Who's involved? The "who" includes both the readers or audience for whom your story is relevant and the people involved in the announcement you're making, be it the company president, an honored employee, or a newly hired neurosurgeon.

✔ **What:** The bulk of your press release — the "what" — covers all the specifics of your announcement, whether they're product names and features, organization accomplishments, or the results of a recent survey.

✔ **How:** "How" may include both the way your product or service is used or deployed, and how it can be acquired or ordered. It may also mean how something works or how someone does something.

✔ **Why:** The key question is "Why is this important?" Explain the significance of your announcement to the editor's readers.

✔ **Where and when:** If you're announcing an event, include the location and time. Otherwise, the "where" is simply the location of your business, and the "when" is the time when the information you're relaying takes effect.

Collecting quotes

One of the easiest ways to liven up a release and give it added credibility is to include a direct quote from a person connected to the story, preferably someone who is *not* a member of your organization. It can be a customer who talks about the delicious meals he prepared on your new grill. It may be a homeless person who found a clean bed at your shelter, or it may be a physician who looks forward to prescribing the new medication you're announcing.

If your only recourse is to quote someone *inside* the organization, at least turn to a person close to the story who can say why she thinks this new thing is important. In many instances, you'll be asked to make up a quote for that oh-so-busy executive in your company. If you do, be sure to get that person's explicit approval — in writing — for the quote you've created *before* the release is sent to the media.

Not all quotes are equal — some are much better than others, and some are so poor they can actually weaken your story. Here's the difference between them:

- ✔ **Bad quotes** use vague generalities and lack convincing specifics. Sometimes they're so obviously biased (or promotional) that they defy belief. Don't use quotes that look like these:

  "PharmaDerm works real well. I liked it."

  "My life lacked love, hope, and meaning until I discovered PharmaDerm and found true love!"

- ✔ **Good quotes** use specific language, are rich in particulars, and don't make overreaching claims. For example:

  "In just thirty days, most of my patients reported a noticeable reduction in both the severity and number of acne episodes."

  "Thanks to PharmaDerm, I not only have clearer skin — I've gained more confidence. And I'm beginning to have a real social life."

Designating a contact

When you're self-employed or run a small business, you take the calls from the press, of course. In larger organizations, someone must be assigned this responsibility. That someone doesn't have to be a public relations professional, but must be an informed, polite, cool-tempered person capable of working with the media in a fashion that reflects favorably on the organization.

Your designated contact person is usually *not* the expert featured in the release — you're looking for someone with excellent people and communication skills who serves as the liaison between the organization and the outside world. If the media need to speak to the expert, the designated contact arranges it.

Thinking like an editor (and a reporter and a reader)

I'm sure you think you have a wonderful story, but what really matters is what the editor thinks. When the editor is holding your release in his hands, he always asks himself the same question: "Why is this newsworthy to my readers?" His job is to satisfy the reader's bottomless pit of desire for relevant news and information.

REMEMBER

Your job is to make the editor's job easier. Write your press release so that it clearly meets the hungers of the publication's audience — and thereby meets the needs of the publication's editors and reporters. If you remember nothing else from this chapter, remember this: *Think from the point of view of the reader, the reporter, and the editor.*

Constructing the elements, piece by piece

With your notes and quotes in hand, you're ready to write. Your final product is a mix of standard elements, such as the release date at the top and the sequence of pound signs at the bottom, along with the fresh content you're creating from scratch. See Figure 12-1 for a sample of a press release.

For clarity's sake, I describe the elements of the press release from top to bottom — as they appear on the page. In real life, however, the ideas for the middle of the release — what I call the *body* — may come to you before you can think of a strong headline. If so, great! Create the headline later if you like. The important thing is to do what works for you.

Formatting the top of the release

The press release begins with the standard stuff, like the release date and the contact information.

✔ **Release date:** At the very top, typically at the left just under the letterhead, you indicate the release date (usually in all capital letters). You have two options:

- **Announce this now:** "FOR IMMEDIATE RELEASE" indicates that the announcement may be made immediately, in the next issue of the publication or in the first appropriate broadcast slot.

- **Embargo:** To meet publication deadlines, you may have to notify the press about information — say, the winners of an upcoming awards presentation — *before* the information is made available to the public. When you write "EMBARGO UNTIL [DATE]," the editor *will* respect your need for discretion and withhold the announcement until the relevant date.

Below the release line, type "Date:" and then tab over a notch for the sake of neatness and write the date on which the release has been prepared.

✔ **Contact information:** Underneath the date, add the contact information — *not* the contact information for the publication's reader or broadcaster's viewer or listener, but the information of the designated contact in your company so the editor or writer can contact her.

EMPTY NEST REALTY GROUP
123 MAIN STREET · MELROSE, MA 02176

FOR IMMEDIATE RELEASE
Date: March 12, 2004
Contact: Jane Mouthpiece
              (781) 123-4567, ext. 89

Headline —

Empty Nest Realty Group Sponsors Free Home Sales Seminar for Seniors
March 22 event covers legal, financial, and tax issues for sellers over 60

Melrose, MA—March 12—On March 22, Empty Nest Realty Group will sponsor a free home sales seminar for seniors at the Willow Recreational Center, 9:30 – 11:30 a.m. Titled "Selling After 60," the seminar helps participants understand the unique legal, financial, and tax issues seniors face when selling their homes.

"Recent changes in the Massachusetts tax code have left many seniors confused," says Empty Nest president Lauren Eagle. "Our 'Selling After 60' seminar is designed to give seniors the information they need to make confident real estate choices for a comfortable retirement."

Subhead —

Seminar includes food, workbook, and personal attention

The "Selling After 60" seminar will begin with a continental breakfast and a brief video presentation on the tax impact of home sales for Massachusetts residents. After the video, participants will get a "Retirement Management Real Estate Workbook" that addresses crucial issues such as capital gains, asset transfer law, real estate trusts, reinvestment options, and estate planning. Eagle and her associates will personally guide participants step by step through the home sales process. By the end of the seminar, each participant will have a "blueprint" of real estate and retirement options they can explore on their own or with additional assistance from Empty Nest Realty Group.

Melrose resident Melinda Bailey attended the "Selling After 60" seminar last year. According to Bailey, "The Empty Nest people were fantastic. Before the seminar, just the thought of selling my house overwhelmed me. But Lauren helped me understand my options, in plain English. With her help, I was able to buy a place in a terrific retirement community and still have money left over for income. I recommend the seminar to all my friends."

Subhead —

Register by calling Empty Nest Realty Group before March 20

The "Selling After 60" seminar is free, but attendees must register in advance by calling Jane Mouthpiece at (781) 123-4567, extension 89, before March 20.

Boilerplate —

Empty Nest Realty Group is a real estate brokerage and consulting service specializing in the unique needs of seniors and their families. Since 1993, they have served the residents of Massachusetts from their offices in Melrose.

##############

Figure 12-1:
This basic press release illustrates the principles of news-worthiness and reader relevance.

Creating catchy headlines for releases

In some ways, press release headlines are like any other headlines: They have to communicate the essence of your story right away. (See Chapter 2 for more on headlines.) Unlike other headlines, such as those in letters or leading print advertisements, the press release headline is not a place to make an offer, nor is it an opportunity for flashy creativity. Instead, the headline must get right to the point and get there fast.

Think about it. Editors may receive hundreds of releases each week. You can't waste their time. Your headline must summarize the essence of the release, providing the editor with enough information to assure that this announcement is both newsworthy and appropriate for readers.

How do you write a good headline? Try this: Write about the news plus the benefit the news provides. Think of the news as the actual announcement, and the benefit as the reason why the announcement is important to your target audience.

Consider this example: "Ivymount College Appoints Dr. Richard Smith as Meade Professor of Anthropology: Smith represents Ivymount's ongoing commitment to suburban anthropology and its impact on the social sciences." Notice that creating a long headline or even a headline with more than one line is acceptable. In many cases, such as this example, the news fits in the first line, the benefit in the second line following the colon.

In the press release shown in Figure 12-1, "Empty Nest Realty Group Sponsors Free Home Sales Seminar for Seniors" announces the news. I then use an additional line for the benefit, in italics, to reinforce the announcement's importance: "March 22 event covers legal, financial, and tax issues for sellers over 60."

Leading the body with fundamentals

The press release starts out with the fundamental elements of your story: What's up? Where and when is it happening? Who is involved? Why is this important? And how does this affect the reader?

- **Dateline:** Begin the first paragraph with the location (city, state, or country) and date, in bold. Separate these elements from each other and from the opening of the paragraph with *em dashes* (a form of punctuation that looks like two hyphens placed side by side).

- **Opening paragraph:** Now roll up your sleeves and get to work. Three things belong in the first — and most important — paragraph:

  - **Just the facts, ma'am:** Establish the fundamental facts of your story: the *who, what, when, where, why,* and *how.*

In the release in Figure 12-1, the facts are summarized in the first sentence: "On March 22, Empty Nest Realty Group will sponsor a free home sales seminar for seniors at the Willow Recreational Center, 9:30 – 11:30 a.m."

- **The reason why this announcement is newsworthy:** Articulate why this news is important to the publication's readers.

  In the Empty Nest release (Figure 12-1), the second sentence provides the reason the event is of value: "Titled 'Selling After 60,' the seminar helps participants understand the unique legal, financial, and tax issues seniors face when selling their homes."

- **Proof points:** The claims you make about the newsworthiness of this information must be supported with proof points — evidence that validates your claims.

  I use a brief second paragraph, introducing the company's president, to explain why the seminar is especially newsworthy: "Recent changes in the Massachusetts tax code have left many seniors confused," says Empty Nest president Lauren Eagle. "Our 'Selling After 60' seminar is designed to give seniors the information they need to make confident real estate choices for a comfortable retirement."

Building a healthy body: The middle of the release

Before you race to the conclusion, you have room to elaborate. This is your chance to really back up your promises with just enough detail to create a watertight, rock-solid case for the value and meaning of your story. Some ways to do this include using the following:

- ✔ **Subhead(s):** To help smooth the transition into another element of your story or to highlight another key benefit or newsworthy item, consider using a subhead (or two, depending on the length of the release).

  In Figure 12-1, I use two subheads to break up the text (and prevent monotony). The first draws attention to additional benefits: "Seminar includes food, workbook, and personal attention." The second tells people exactly what to do to get the benefits: "Register by calling Empty Nest Realty Group before March 20."

- ✔ **Quotes:** You didn't gather your quotes for nothing! Now put them to use. Be sure to identify the speaker as precisely as possible (full name, title, and company) and make every effort to weave the quote into the story in as seamless and natural a manner as possible.

  In the Empty Nest example (Figure 12-1), I use a quote from the president to reinforce the news value of the seminar. In the middle, I turn to a customer — who represents a kind of stand-in for the publication's readers — to personally testify to the seminar's wholesome goodness: "According to Bailey, 'The Empty Nest people were fantastic. Before the seminar, just the thought of selling my house overwhelmed me. . . .' "

✔ **More proof points:** Support your case with evidence that doesn't belong in the first paragraph but remains too important to neglect.

The third paragraph of the sample release, for example, describes a cornucopia of goodies for participants, including a continental breakfast; a video presentation; a workbook "that addresses crucial issues such as capital gains, asset transfer law, real estate trusts, reinvestment options, and estate planning"; and personal step-by-step guidance through the homes sales process.

✔ **Special features:** Provide enough information to create a clear, unambiguous idea of what you're announcing, especially if it's unique to you, your product, or your event. When you're writing about products or services, the special features are simply that — things your stuff has that other, competing stuff doesn't.

In my example, I'm describing an event, so its special feature is the promise of what you walk away with after the event concludes: "By the end of the seminar, each participant will have a 'blueprint' of real estate and retirement options they can explore on their own or with additional assistance from Empty Nest Realty Group."

✔ **Access!** Don't forget to provide a means of contact for the reader. When announcing a product or service, tell people how they can order it. Provide your name, phone number, and, if appropriate, Web address, mailing address, and e-mail address. For events, tell people how to register or attend. For every other kind of release, consider adding a means for people to get further information.

The Empty Nest release puts it simply: "The 'Selling After 60' seminar is free, but attendees must register in advance by calling Jane Mouthpiece at (781) 123-4567, extension 89, before March 20."

Coming to the close: The end of the release

Rejoice! The end is near! You're now at the easiest part to write, because the purpose of the closing is to tell the editor that this is the end of the press release. You do that in two ways:

✔ **Add a boilerplate.** A *boilerplate* is a brief paragraph, written in standard language, with no more than two or three sentences, about the company or organization represented in the release. This information remains the same in every press release your organization produces, regardless of its contents, and it simply states who you are and what you do. If you have to write this yourself, keep it short and simple and get approval from all the key players in your organization.

In the sample press release, the boilerplate begins with "Empty Nest Realty Group is a real estate brokerage and consulting service . . ." and includes information about its history, mission, and location.

✔ **Place a special symbol made up of pound signs at the bottom of the page.** If the press release runs more than a page, include "MORE" at the bottom of the page, centered between the margins. At the very end of the release on the last page, center a cluster of pound signs — ###### — to indicate the conclusion.

Considering a few points on style

Many of the writing forms addressed in this book — such as print ads or direct response letters — allow you to take a few liberties with the English language. A sentence fragment here and there or an occasional colloquialism ("Yeah, right!") is perfectly acceptable. After all, these forms are designed to sell; the overriding concerns are persuasiveness and clarity. You're not making a formal petition to the Queen of England — you're making a sales proposition to ordinary people in ordinary language.

The press release is a different story. You're writing to an editor, a professional whose responsibilities require a rigorous attention to accepted language conventions. Indeed, part of the editor's job is to screen out releases that seem overly promotional or laden with marketing hype. To earn the editor's respect and to give your story a fighting chance, obey these conventions:

✔ **Use the third person.** I know that I encourage you in previous chapters to use *I*, *we*, and *you*. Now I'm telling you to be more formal and stick to the third person: *he*, *she*, *they*, *them*, *it*, and so on. Refer to your business by name (not as *we* or *us*) and don't address the editor directly as *you*.

✔ **Follow the rules of grammar.** I'm afraid I must pick up my yardstick and direct your attention to the blackboard: Use complete sentences; apply correct punctuation; avoid slang; and for Pete's sake, get a decent book on grammar, such as *English Grammar For Dummies*, by Geraldine Woods (published by Wiley), and use it.

✔ **Be factual, not flamboyant.** The little rhetorical tricks that can make or break marketing copy — provocative headlines, catchy phrases, direct appeals to emotion — simply break your press release. Build your release on a foundation of facts. Seek to inform, and trust that your information does the selling for you.

✔ **Keep it short.** I've seen press releases that were three pages long, but I've never seen a release that *needed* to be three pages long. Respect the editor's time and intelligence and keep your release to one page.

Presenting Your Business in Press Kits

The press kit is an alternative approach to the media that's almost the opposite of the press release in look and format. Although the release follows relatively strict rules, the press kit can take many forms; although most releases are short and simple, press kits can be a complex compilation of many elements, from biographies to article reprints. In fact, the flexibility of the press kit is its primary advantage: Just as the word *kit* implies, it can be seen as a set of communications tools that helps the media understand your organization and relay that understanding to its audience. These tools may include company profiles, case studies, testimonials, product descriptions, photographs, or even press releases themselves.

Many companies create press kits for their organizations to provide background information about who they are and what they do. In the nonprofit world, many organizations prepare press kits centered on important issues such as "adolescents and tobacco" or "trends in low-income housing."

To get the most impact for your efforts, however, I encourage you to consider writing press kits that present specific people: executives, consultants, technicians, and other in-house authorities who can contribute expertise that readers, and therefore editors, want and need. Remember, when editors need insights, fast, they don't call companies in general (or wade through stacks of information on issues). Instead, they call specific people they trust as credible resources. You want your people at the top of the to-call lists.

Using press kits to promote your business and its experts

You use press releases to sell specific stories to the media. Other times you may want to promote the people working for your organization — along with their talent, expertise, and experience that you believe merit media exposure.

Why would the media surrender precious space (or broadcast time) to you or anyone else? Because expertise is a precious commodity. When a story breaks about a new cure for cancer, a shift in bond rates, or a new trend in pop music, the media depend on outside experts to explain the issue for their viewers or readers. Typically, these people are helpful in the following ways:

- ✔ **For direct interviews** on TV or radio or in print, in which the expert is engaged one-on-one to provide insight and information

- ✔ **As one part of an article or broadcast spot,** in which the expert is one among several who is quoted or referenced

- ✔ **As contributing authors** who write periodical articles of in-depth explorations of important issues and ideas

If your business sells knowledge, know-how, or expertise, this kind of media attention may have you salivating. Every day, universities, healthcare organizations, business consulting groups, and other brain-heavy enterprises spend vast amounts of time and money introducing their best talent to the media. The payoff? They get widespread recognition as a credible authority in their business arenas.

The name of the game is *connection:* You want to connect your talent (you or the person or company you're writing for) with the media's need for expertise.

Constructing a press kit

A press kit is a collection of written materials that is designed to introduce an expert or a company to the media. Often these materials are contained in an attractive folder and accompanied by a cover letter. Your goal is threefold:

- ✔ **Highlight the issues** your expert can address, or that your company is involved in, be it chemical processing in South America or new techniques for bungalow construction.

- ✔ **Establish your expert's or organization's authority** by demonstrating the depth of your company's experience, or explaining *why* the expert is especially qualified — by virtue of experience, education, or abilities — to speak authoritatively on the highlighted issues.

- ✔ **Show how to use the organization's experts** by providing contact information and clarifying exactly what your person is available for, such as giving direct interviews, providing supporting information for articles, or contributing as a writer to an article.

Many of the elements you need may have already been written for other purposes — you just have to compile them. Here's what you need:

- ✔ **A cover letter:** This element introduces the person or the company and the kit, and includes the following information:

    - **Who** the person or organization is — including name and title for a person, or a brief description of the organization. When writing for an individual, summarize the person's unique qualifications as an expert. For instance:

        Linda Terres, Ph.D., president of Brown Fields Associates, is a former Stanford University faculty research scientist specializing in environmental restoration, and has twenty-three years of experience in toxic waste removal.

    - **What** issues the organization or expert can address and why they're qualified to speak about them. For example:

        A noted authority on petroleum waste products, Dr. Terres is recognized for her expertise on toxicity, the impact of petrochemicals on soil composition, and on the most practical methods for removing toxins and transforming polluted sites into environmentally healthy habitats.

    - **How** your experts or organization representatives can be contacted by phone or e-mail:

        To contact or interview Dr. Terres, call Lionel Taylor at (123) 456-7890.

✔ **A brief bio of the expert:** For press kits written for individuals, summarize the person's background information, including relevant education and experience. For the fictional Dr. Terres, I suggest including a list of the clean-up sites she has worked on.

✔ **A brief description of your organization's purpose:** For company press kits, explain what your company does, why it exists, and what its goals are.

✔ **A list of subjects or issues** your expert can address. It can look like this:

Dr. Terres is often asked to speak on the following topics:

Identifying toxic waste sites

Developing action plans for clean-up

Working with government regulatory agencies

Understanding the science of soil restoration

✔ **Brochures and other collateral:** For company press kits or kits written about specific issues, you may include brochures, pamphlets, fact sheets, and other collateral about relevant products, services, or issues.

✔ **A list of suggested questions for your expert:** The beauty of this element is that it not only further articulates your expert's authority but also places the interview in the editor's imagination and helps her see your expert's potential. Consider this example:

Popular questions for Dr. Terres:

How can property buyers find out about potential environmental issues on the sites they're considering for purchase?

How much time and money does it take to perform a clean-up?

Is government assistance available for environmental restoration?

✔ **A list of publications and speaking appearances:** If your expert has published articles under her name or has been quoted in other articles, list the titles, publication names, and dates. You can also add dates, titles, and locations for speaking appearances at seminars, conferences, and events.

✔ **Lists of clients, projects, or accomplishments:** Companies can include annotated lists of current and/or previous work that demonstrate their experience.

✔ **Case studies and testimonials:** Endorsements from customers (testimonials) or brief stories about how your organization or expert helped a client (case studies) reinforce your credibility and provide the media with story ideas.

✔ **Samples of your expert's work:** Include articles your expert has written or case studies of projects involving your expert.

✔ **A photograph of your expert or your organization in action:** This item may be a good idea if you're trying to get television exposure.

Chapter 13

Gaining Credibility with Outstanding Articles

*N*ews flash: A whole, wide world of print and online media — papers, journals, and magazines — is hungry for fresh content from businesses like yours. This hunger is your opportunity: a chance to write articles for the media that give your business greater exposure and greater credibility — two pathways that, in turn, build sales.

So where are these gaping jaws eager for your material? You may have to look beyond your local newsstand. As you suspect, professional journalists or freelance writers craft most, if not all, of the articles people read for news or entertainment. But when you look beyond the famous mass-market publications, you find a smorgasbord of periodicals designed for specialty audiences. Some of these are peer-reviewed journals for scholars and researchers. But many others are periodicals for business categories — such as insurance, manufacturing, or transportation — that aren't only open to contributed material but also depend on it.

The root word of "authority" is "author," and few things give you or your organization as much credibility as being the author of books or articles in your business area. Writing books may demand a commitment of time and energy beyond your current reach. But if you have a pen, paper, and a story to tell, you're probably capable of writing articles — either under your name or written by you for someone else (ghostwriting).

In this chapter, I tell you why articles may fit your needs, how to write them, and how to organize your own newsletters for employees or customers. So grab your trench coat and fedora and read all about it!

Understanding When Writing Articles Can Be Right for You

Not that long ago, you probably wouldn't have thought of setting aside a portion of your time or your marketing budget to writing and publishing material destined for newspapers, magazines, journals, and other media in an effort to bring exposure to your business or product. After all, articles in these publications existed to serve the publications' needs and their readers' needs, not your business's needs. As a result, the articles couldn't be as directly promotional as you may have wished. And when articles did seem worthwhile, the public relations department usually wrote them.

These days, consumers are bombarded with ads wherever they go. TV and radio ads fill the airwaves, Web pages are clogged with banner and pop-up ads, and many magazines display a full-page ad on every other page. In self-defense, consumers have learned to greet these messages with a firewall of skepticism. Your challenge is to find ways to expose your company to consumers without creating just another marketing gimmick consumers can easily ignore. One of the best alternatives to this morass is to create content for magazines, journals, newspapers, and other media. Article writing may be right for you or your business in the following situations:

- ✔ **You're in an industry from which people expect leadership.** Some industries have the honor (or responsibility) of demonstrating public or social commitments that go beyond the drive for profits, including healthcare, education, insurance, pension services, and even manufacturers whose products exert enormous influence on the rest of the economy. When people turn to your business for guidance, articles can be one way you assert leadership.

- ✔ **You want to assert authority.** Many businesses sell ideas rather than products — think business consulting groups, marketing researchers, executive development coaches, and the like. Articles can establish your credibility as an authority in your field.

- ✔ **You want to educate prospects.** In our service economy, you may be obligated to sell items or services that can be fairly complex. It's not easy explaining, much less selling, things like genetic screening, tax-deferred mutual funds, or supply chain management software in a 30 second radio spot or a six-inch print ad. Articles give you lots of breathing room for telling complex stories.

- ✔ **You sell expertise.** It's one thing to ask people to shell out money for a car they can see, touch, and smell. But expertise, whether it's in chemical engineering or flower arranging, remains intangible and therefore more difficult to establish in your prospects' imaginations. Articles give you the space to establish the meaning and value of your expertise.

✔ **Your business has an impact beyond its own walls.** As an employer, property owner, or user of environmental resources, your business may have an effect on your surrounding community that isn't limited to the bottom line in your ledgers. You can use articles to build support, or assuage dissatisfaction, within your region of influence.

Making Plans for Publication

The best way to write an article is to stop. That is, you shouldn't write a word until you've come up with some good ideas, identified a few places that might be right for your writing, and (most importantly) contacted editors with your ideas *before* you commit yourself to writing the article.

Generating bright ideas

Almost all bad ideas for business articles are rooted in one flawed intention: to tell the world just how great your business or organization really, really is. Call it blue smoke, chest beating, or horn blowing, but unless you enjoy ridicule, don't call flagrant self-promotion an idea for an article.

Yes, your ultimate purpose is to create something that reflects favorably on your organization. But your immediate purpose is to write something of value to an editor: an article full of good ideas that are relevant to a publication's readers. This means two things:

✔ First, draw upon your experience (or that of your organization) to identify the problems and challenges your business expertise solves for your customers or to identify the new opportunities your products, services, and business intelligence brings to them.

✔ Second, identify periodicals that speak to readers with similar problems, challenges, or opportunities, so that your information is relevant to them. (For more information on identifying periodicals, see the next section.)

To identify knowledge that's valuable (material that can be the subject of an article an editor may be interested in), start with this technique: Make a list of the things you can talk about, and then sort out the topics by the level of your expertise and their value to prospects/readers. Those areas of knowledge that rank high in both categories — the depth of your knowledge and their capacity to hold the interest of readers — are the ideas worth working on.

Say that you're a physical therapist interested in writing for the local business paper. You obviously know a number of things of value to you yet worthless to your customers or newspaper readers, such as how to purchase and adjust an adequate massage table. On the other hand, you may not know enough to write an article on topics that many people may find interesting, such as proper nutrition or stress reduction.

Your goal is to come up with article ideas that connect your knowledge to reader self-interest. A physical therapist, for example, would concentrate on the topics he's qualified to talk about and that provide valuable information of interest to readers. These may include:

- Finding and selecting ergonomic office and computer furniture
- Providing the instructions for five quick and easy exercises that readers can perform in their cubicles to reduce muscle strain
- Detecting the early warning signs of carpal tunnel syndrome

Figuring out where to publish your article

With the exception of the travel pages, your local (or metro-area) paper has little room for unsolicited material. And unless you're a nationally recognized business figure, big-time magazines probably won't take a look at your work.

But don't overlook three especially fertile grounds for your message: the local business journal, industry-specific periodicals, and newsletters.

Targeting local business journals

Almost every sizable metropolitan area in the United States has a paper, usually printed every week, often in a tabloid format, dedicated to business issues. These papers typically produce two kinds of content: breaking news, such as recent bankruptcies, expansions, or major real estate purchases; and special topic material that's of interest to readers but isn't tied to recent events, on issues such as human resource management or legal services. If your market is largely confined within an identifiable geographic area, it makes sense to get exposure in media with a geographic reach that overlaps your own. You can see which local journals are available at a well-stocked newsstand in your area, and then supplement your in-person investigation with a quick search on the Web.

Breaking news is reserved for articles written by the journal's staff. But the special-interest content is wide open to you! In fact, many journals schedule an editorial calendar — assigning topics to each week's issue — to attract advertisers to the issues of greatest interest to them: for example, accounting firms to the accounting issues, banks to the financial services issues, hotels to the travel issues, and so on. (Get this calendar by first checking out the paper's masthead — the sidebar of publishers, editors, and contributors — or visiting its Web site. Call or write the editor if you still don't find it.) The appeal to the advertiser is obvious, but to attract readers, these special issues need good, relevant content, which is where you come in.

Read all about it: Common business topics

Weekly business journals or papers frequently publish special editions on a variety of business topics relevant to the regions they cover. The following list covers some of the most popular topics. Your business probably has something meaningful to say about at least one, if not more, of these subjects:

- Accounting
- Advertising/communications
- Architects/architecture
- Banking
- Benefits management
- Board governance
- Construction
- Education/higher education/ continuing education
- Employment
- Energy
- Engineering
- Entertainment
- Environmental services
- Facilities management
- Financial services
- Healthcare
- High technology
- Hospitality/hotels
- Human resources
- Intelligence technology/software
- Investments/investment management
- Legal services
- Life sciences
- Management
- Manufacturing
- Marketing
- Nonprofit organizations
- Office equipment or technology
- Pharmaceuticals
- Public relations
- Real estate
- Restaurants
- Retail
- Security/security firms
- Telecommunications
- Transportation
- Venture capital

Focusing on industry-specific publications

Did you know that there's a monthly magazine dedicated exclusively to pharmaceutical clinical trials? A couple of journals with the inside scoop on Angus beef? A few monthly periodicals addressing the sticky topic of adhesives?

No, industry-specific publications probably aren't the first that come to mind when you're asked to name five magazines off the top of your head. Yet they fulfill important roles for their niche audiences, helping their readers stay current and their advertisers find markets. And when you want to reach a niche market yourself, whether it's croquet enthusiasts or nursing home administrators, these are the places where you may be able to tell your story.

By nature, industry-specific publications can be rather obscure; the easiest way to identify them is through *Bacon's Magazine Directory*, available at the reference desk of your local library or online at www.bacons.com. (For more about *Bacon's*, see Chapter 12.) *Bacon's* is conveniently organized by market classifications and even includes an alphabetical cross-index that helps you target publications in any subject area from AAA Motor Club Magazines to Youth Magazines (with intriguing detours to Butane-Propane, Infants Wear, and Nuts & Fruits).

Contributing to newsletters

In addition to the industry-specific magazines, a number of newsletters — many now published electronically — welcome unsolicited content. (*Unsolicited* means the editor doesn't seek you; you initiate contact with the editor.) You may look for these on the Web, but look carefully. Newsletters that are published by organizations as marketing tools have no interest in hearing from potential competitors. (See "Publishing Successful Newsletters," later in this chapter, for more on putting out a newsletter yourself.) But those that make money as publishers may appreciate your interest.

May I ask a question? Querying the editor

When you have an article and a publication in mind, it's time to contact the editor, by phone or e-mail.

Some editors are content to hear your idea before giving you a green light to write the article — withholding, of course, any promise of publication until *after* they've read your finished piece.

Many other editors want to read a query letter first. A *query* is a short (usually one-page) letter that tells editors three things:

- ✔ **Who** you are, including your title and the name of the business or organization you represent. For example:

    I'm a commercial property broker with Hightower Properties, a Cincinnati real estate firm specializing in office space.

- ✔ **What** you want to write about, including not just the subject at hand but also the special angle, slant, or fresh insight you bring to the subject. You might write something like this:

    As interest rates rise and vacancies decline, Cincinnati property owners should reassess their leasing strategies. In my article, I'll address rent trends, projected construction figures for the next twelve months, and negotiation strategies for securing the most attractive leasing arrangements.

✔ **Why** you're especially qualified to write the article you suggest, such as your number of years in business, your academic degrees, your awards and honors (if applicable), your areas of expertise, and so on. For example:

After nineteen years in real estate management — with the last seven in brokerage — I've identified a few simple rules that can help property owners find and exploit the highest value of their properties, even in rapidly changing market environments.

By phone or in the query letter, be sure you request the publication's writing guidelines. The guidelines give you the following information:

✔ **The kind of content the publication is looking for:** Publications may want case studies, trend analyses, personal success stories, or even raw opinion. Newsletter articles (as opposed to articles in journals and industry-specific publications) tend to be less formal in tone and more focused on topical issues and how-to advice. (For more on different article styles, see "Selecting the form," later in this chapter.)

✔ **How you should submit your article:** Some publications ask you to send a complete piece for their consideration; others ask you to submit a query letter first. In the days of yore, you submitted your article by mail. Today, it's common practice to send it as a Microsoft Word file attached to an e-mail.

✔ **The style conventions you should follow:** Should you write in first person or third person? Should you include subheads to break up the story? Should you send a photo of yourself (or the person you're ghost-writing for) to the publication? The guidelines tell you.

✔ **The length of your article:** Most submissions fall into standard word counts of 800, 1,200, or 1,500 words. Occasionally, an editor asks for something as brief as 500 words or as long as 2,000 (rarely more). Newsletter articles (as opposed to articles in journals and industry-specific publications) are typically about 500 words long. No, you don't have to be exact in your count, but your submission should be within range of the requested target — say, 750 to 850 words for an 800-word article.

When an editor says he wants a 1,200-word piece, you may wonder how many pages of writing that amounts to. You can (and will) use the word count feature in your word processor to keep track of length. But there's also an easy way to estimate the page count in advance. Use the accepted standards for your submissions: Set your word processor for 1-inch margins all around; use a Times New Roman font set for 12-point type; format your paragraphs for double spacing; indent the first line of your paragraph by one tab set to five spaces in depth; and don't insert an additional line of space between paragraphs. When you use the standard settings, you get approximately 250 words per page, meaning a 1,200-word article comes to about 5 pages of text.

Writing a Winning Article

I don't care if you haven't written three successive words since high school or college. You still *can* write an article worthy of publication. Keep this in mind: Editors are hungry for content, not style. If you can provide the meat — relevant facts, new insights, fresh advice, a great case study, or some terrific inside tips — the editor can add the sauce.

There are exceptions, but editors at most business publications usually help you polish the article into an acceptable piece for publication, as long as you meet your side of the bargain and deliver juicy content.

Concentrate on the substance of the article and work it into a reasonable shape. It doesn't necessarily have to be flashy, but it should communicate your ideas with unambiguous clarity. Now that you have your article idea firmly in mind and approved by an editor, you need to organize your material and select the form for presenting your idea, whether it's news, human interest, case study, or how-to.

Organizing your material

Everything creative is messy, whether it's gardening or oil painting. Writing is no different. As I write, my desk is cluttered with papers, my computer monitor is encircled with adhesive notes, my notepad is covered with scrawl in two different ink colors, and frankly, I don't look (or smell) too good either.

Aside from the aroma, a certain amount of mess is necessary for organization. I want you free to capture ideas as they come to you, without regard just yet for how and where they'll fit. That's why I *don't* want you to make an outline. It won't work for you now for the same reason an outline didn't work for you in grade school (despite the protests of your nearly apoplectic English teachers). You can't possibly know *how* to order your material until you know *what* your material is.

Please borrow (or steal) my messy, mud-pie approach to writing. It has three basic steps, which I outline in the subsequent steps. If, while following these steps, you find yourself immersed in handwritten notes or scraps of paper or alternating between outbursts of despair and exultation, don't worry — it means you're on the right track.

1. **Focus on one big idea.**

   A good article may have many facts, but they're all centered on just one big idea. I'm sure you know lots of things of value, but limit yourself to one thing per article.

If you've done your homework and identified a few possible article topics (see "Generating bright ideas," earlier in this chapter), you now have to choose one. If they're all equally good, your choice may be a matter of taste (or of going with an idea that has attracted an editor's interest). Otherwise, you may choose the idea that seems to tie most strongly to recent developments in the news or that focuses on an issue that seems to be of the greatest concern to your current customers. In "Generating bright ideas," my make-believe physical therapist came up with three good ideas. For his first article, he's going to concentrate on the one that's been on the minds of many of her patients: detecting the early warning signs of carpal tunnel syndrome.

2. **Identify your subordinate ideas.**

   Although your focus is on one big idea, it will inevitably accompany a group of subordinate ideas that help you make your point. Make believe your article is a book: If your big idea is the title of the book, the subordinate ideas are subjects of your chapters; they're important, but only to the degree that they serve your big idea. The carpal tunnel article, for example, can rely on a number of subordinate ideas to reinforce its message:

   - *Carpal tunnel can be more effectively treated if identified early.*

   - *A number of conditions can exacerbate carpal tunnel.*

   - *Carpal tunnel usually appears with the same warning signs.*

3. **Cluster your facts in groups of related ideas.**

   Without supporting evidence, your article may become little more than a statement of opinion. Apply statistics, quotes from authorities, principles of logic and reason, historical examples, anecdotes, and plain raw facts to support your ideas. As you brainstorm, your subordinate ideas and their supporting evidence or facts may be scattered across many pieces of paper. Before you write, you want to cluster the facts with their ideas, either figuratively in your head or literally on paper. If you use the physical therapy example, here's what the information may look like:

   - *Carpal tunnel can be more effectively treated if identified early.*

     Only 1 percent of cases lead to permanent disability.

     Can be treated by immobilization, anti-inflammatory drugs, or surgery.

   - *There are a number of conditions that can exacerbate carpal tunnel.*

     Diabetes, pregnancy, and obesity can lead to or expose the symptoms of carpal tunnel.

     Work-related competitive motion injuries are one of the most common causes of the disease.

   - *Carpal tunnel usually appears with the same warning signs.*

     Tingling or numbness at night.

     Decreased feeling in thumb and first two fingers.

Selecting the form

After you put your ideas into some kind of order, the next step is selecting the appropriate *form* that will dictate the shape of your material, the tone of your writing, and the style of its presentation. Your choice depends on the nature of the idea or material you have (some ideas lend themselves to stories, some to how-to explanations, for example) and on the editorial policies of the periodicals that interest you.

In business publications, most of the articles contributed by people like you are one or a combination of the following forms:

- ✔ News, also called the inverted pyramid style
- ✔ Human interest or narrative
- ✔ Case study
- ✔ How-to/top tips

Spreading the news

The news or inverted pyramid form begins with the most important information and then progresses through details of descending significance. This format is the one most commonly used in the daily paper. Stories in this form are written in a neutral, matter-of-fact tone and always begin with a paragraph that includes the famous who, what, where, when, and sometimes the how and why of your story. In the physical therapy example, the article might begin something like this:

> *According to a recent study by the National Association of Hand Surgeons, carpal tunnel syndrome — a pinching of the median nerve that causes pain or numbing in the wrist or fingers — has become a workplace epidemic. More than five and a half million Americans are affected by the disease, and approximately 750,000 new diagnoses are made each year. Fortunately, the disease rarely causes permanent disability — if the syndrome is identified early and the patient complies with a few simple treatment strategies.*

Note that all the key elements are identified immediately:

- ✔ **Who:** Millions of Americans
- ✔ **What:** Carpal tunnel syndrome
- ✔ **Where:** Across the country
- ✔ **When:** Now and continuing into the future

By the paragraph's end, the reader arrives at the central premise of the article: the importance of identifying the disease early.

The body of the article is made of the subordinated ideas and their supporting facts, evidence, and/or reasoning. Because the news format moves from the most to the least important (the information readers most need to know in order to understand the point of the article), an order suggests itself, as in the carpal tunnel example:

1. After the therapist has established the premise and its significance, he can go right to the meat of the matter: identifying the warning signs.

2. After the warning signs, the next logical step is to talk about the exacerbating conditions.

3. Finally, he should address the advantages of early treatment. One of the most effective ways to conclude a news format article is to leave the reader with a suggestion for future action. The treatment options fulfill this obligation and finish the article on a hopeful note.

Leading with human interest

The same facts often can be packaged in different forms. In the physical therapy example, the writer can present the same content used in the inverted pyramid form (see the preceding section) as a human interest story, a narrative drama with the following qualities:

- ✔ **It's personal.** The human interest story directs the spotlight away from ideas and facts toward a person or persons.

- ✔ **It's emotional.** Your goal is to create an empathetic response in readers that connects them with your hero or heroine.

- ✔ **It's intimate.** Instead of merely stating the facts, you allow the principal players to tell much of the story themselves through direct quotations.

- ✔ **It's dramatic.** Your article may be rooted in truth (I don't encourage you to do otherwise), but it follows the logic of dramatic fiction. Here's the order of events:

  - **Desire:** The article begins with somebody wanting something, either a goal to be obtained or a pain to be overcome. The physical therapist's article, for example, should begin with a patient who has mysterious and troublesome pains.

  - **Insight:** Instead of a magic ring or mighty sword, the business article introduces insight. And lo! It's delivered by the author of the story or from the author's business! In the carpal tunnel article, the insight comes from the recognition of the disease and the therapist's recommendations for treatment.

  - **Resolution:** Your article achieves a happy ending when the principal character applies the insights to achieve the goal or conquer the pain. The carpal tunnel article ends with the patient's reflections on how much better she feels now that she has a diagnosis and has begun effective treatment.

Like the news format opening, the human interest story does offer the who, what, when, and where, but instead of giving the reader dry facts, the article introduces a real person who speaks for herself and gives us her experience of the disease. Here's how the carpal tunnel article may begin in the human interest format:

> *On a winter night last year, Ellen Lynn, a thirty-four year-old administrative assistant from Lake Cheeki, Florida, awoke with stinging pain in her wrist. At first, she thought her hand had fallen asleep — perhaps she had rested her head on it. But according to Ellen, "The pain wouldn't stop. I took ibuprofen. I even put ice on my wrist. After a couple of hours, I finally got back to sleep." The next morning, the pain was still there. "I knew it was time to get some help," Ellen says.*

Making the case study

Many business magazines love stories, but they don't want stories that are personal and emotional. For their needs, you can write a case study. Like the human interest story, the case study takes root in real-life experience. But instead of presenting feelings and personalities, the case study presents your experience as a model others can follow. It says, in effect, "If you've had this kind of experience, here's what you can go do to solve it (if the experience is a problem) or exploit it (if it's an opportunity)." To write the case study, you can draw on your memory (or the memory of a colleague you interview to collect information) and support it with facts you can find in your organization's files. Or, if you have testimonials from your customers available, you may be able to rework the content of the customer story, with their permission, into a case study. (See Chapter 3 for information about testimonials). Irrespective of source, the case study almost invariably follows a three-step format:

1. **State the challenge.**

   The case study begins with your customer or client's problem — the reason you (or your business) were hired or sought in the first place. (Many marketers take fright at the alleged negativity of the word "problem" and insist that writers use the euphemism "challenge." This word choice fools no one, but in deference to the tender sensibilities of the people who sign my checks, I too say "challenge." Sigh.) The "challenge" portion provides all the background information necessary to articulate the problem and reveal why it's significant. In many cases, for example, problems cost customers a substantial amount of money or time or opportunity. For the physical therapist's story, the challenge may look like this:

   Gonyff Billing Services is a benefits management company with headquarters in Lake Cheeki, Florida, and revenue of more than $23 million a year. Though business was strong, its productivity was compromised by workmen's compensation claims — month after month, at least a dozen of their 150-plus customer service team lost time due to carpal tunnel issues. They hired physical therapist Dayton Armstrong to help them detect the early warning signs of the disease and to design and implement a strategy for reducing its occurrence.

2. Provide the solution.

The middle section is often the longest, as it describes the measures you or your company took to solve the problem. In many instances, the solution is a multistep process that may include investigation, research, technology, management training, project planning, and implementation or execution. Whatever's involved, spell it out clearly in a logical, step-by-step order. Dayton Armstrong's solution section may include this information:

Armstrong began his investigation by going on-site to review the working conditions within Gonyff's office. Within a few hours, it became clear that few customer service employees had appropriate chairs with armrests; that in many cubicles the monitors were situated at awkward angles to the desk; and that the processing forms required an excessive amount of redundant typing. After preparing a summary analysis of the situation, Armstrong recommended a three-part action plan that included. . . .

3. Show the results.

The happy ending! The last section of the case study reveals the effectiveness of your solution and the resulting benefits the client enjoyed. The physical therapist may write something like this:

After purchasing ergonomic furniture, streamlining the software, and encouraging stretches every 45 minutes, Gonyff experienced a dramatic decline in the number of claims for workmen's compensation. Within just three months, the number of workers who requested time off due to wrist pain declined from twelve a month to just two, and those two cases were much less severe, requiring absences of three days or fewer. According to Gonyff CFO Jason Moorebucks, "We're saving at least $1.5 million a year through increased productivity and reduced compensation costs."

Telling people how to perform a task

One of the most popular formats, especially for newsletters, is the how-to article, often presented as a number of tips or hints for doing something better, faster, more efficiently, or more profitably. Of the formats I cover, the how-to is the most forgiving: Your ideas don't necessarily have to appear in any particular order (though often the last tip is to "take action now"), and you're not obligated to tell a story.

The how-to has two parts:

✔ **The introductory set-up:** In the opening paragraphs, you set up the article by introducing *what* the issue is and *why* it's important, followed by a transition line that says something along the lines of, "Here's how you can take control" or "You can master this challenge by taking ten easy steps." The therapist, for example, may begin by saying something like this:

Carpal tunnel syndrome isn't just a pain in the wrist — it's a potentially debilitating disease that affects more than five-and-a-half million Americans. In fact, recent reports from the federal government's Office of Economic

Statistics suggest that as much as $3.2 billion is lost each year in workmen's compensation expenses and reduced productivity related to the syndrome. Fortunately, the disease can be controlled. The following ten points will help you understand, identify, and prevent carpal tunnel syndrome.

✔ **The list itself:** Simply march, step by step, through the points you want to make. There are many correct ways to do this; I recommend beginning each point with a bolded sentence that starts with an active verb and then supporting that sentence with an explanatory paragraph. Here's what one such point may look like for Dayton Armstrong, the physical therapist:

Adjust your office furniture. Many businesses have perfectly adequate chairs, desks, and keyboards, but haven't taken the extra step to see that employees have adjusted the furniture for their individual needs. Armrests, for example, should be set so that the employee's forearm remains parallel with the floor at all times.

Ghostwriting articles

In the end, most business articles are written for the glory of the byline, the brief phrase that identifies the author, as in "By Joe Blow." Many people find that glory so attractive (for reasons identified earlier in this chapter in the section "Understanding When Writing Articles Can Be Right for You") that they hire someone else do the writing for them, a practice known as *ghostwriting*. The person who writes the check gets the byline; the writer gets the money.

If you're assigned to be the ghostwriter, all the previously suggested article techniques still apply, with one new twist: You actually have to gather the information. That may mean research, but in my experience, that research is almost entirely confined to interviewing a knowledgeable person (or persons) within your client organization, most often the person who will ultimately be credited with the byline.

Here are a few tips for conducting a productive interview when you have to ghostwrite an article:

✔ **Get background information.** If possible, see whether you can get and read background information *before* the scheduled interview. Doing so will help you understand the material, prepare better questions, and make more effective use of your mutual time.

✔ **Make the interview subject comfortable.** Some interview subjects are old pros, and many others are babes in the woods. For those new to the process, be prepared to build confidence. Tell them they don't have to worry about phrasing everything in a neat and elegant way; that's your problem. They just have to dig into the vast storehouse of wisdom you're sure they have to pull up the gold you're certain is there. You'll do all the shaping and polishing that makes the article shine.

✔ **Clarify your mutual purpose.** At the very beginning of the interview, be sure that you and your subject share a common vision for the article. This vision determines your content, which in turn guides your questions. Otherwise, you waste a lot of time asking pointless questions and getting worthless answers. You want to concentrate on two things:

- **Why the article is being written:** The purpose of the article may be to establish the company's expertise in a particular area or to alert prospects to a particular problem or issue your company can solve. You're never just communicating general information. Instead, you always want an angle, a particular opinion you want to express on the issue at hand.

- **What you want readers to take away from the article:** Do you want them to be more informed about a new development or a recent trend? Do you want to contradict some element of conventional wisdom? Whatever it is, you and your subject should be in agreement.

✔ **Focus on specifics.** Many interview subjects respond to questions with vague, generalized answers such as, "Market trends look favorable this year" or "Blitz software offers the most power." Dig deeper into the issue by drilling into specifics. Ask, "Which trends look favorable and what's favorable about them?" or "What kind of powers do you mean? What can it do and how can it be measured?"

✔ **Ask for examples.** For any given point that comes up for discussion, ask for examples or anecdotes that reinforce the point. If your subject says, "We're seeing a lot of growth in life sciences," ask for an example. Which life science? Where? Who's growing? By how much? If you can get a good anecdote — a mini-drama with a beginning, middle, and end — fantastic. Few things illustrate a point as strongly as a good story.

✔ **Be attentive to the subject's use of language.** When you ghostwrite, the article belongs to the person you're interviewing, not to you. Keep an ear open to the images, phrases, and metaphors that your subject uses, and see whether you can incorporate them into the article.

After you've written the piece, be sure the "author" credited with the ghost-written article (the person you interviewed) has a chance to review your work and make corrections, additions, and other changes before it's sent to an editor for publication.

Publishing Successful Newsletters

The next step up from writing articles is to create your own medium for them: the newsletter. In exchange for your commitment of time, money, and talent, the newsletter gives you complete editorial control of messaging, content, and distribution. It's your bullhorn to use as you wish. If your business can build a stronger bond with customers by sharing information, especially information that may ultimately lead to renewed or expanded sales, you may want to consider producing a newsletter.

You have two production choices:

- ✔ **Electronic publishing:** E-newsletters, discussed in detail in Chapter 9, give you the advantage of speed and economy — you don't have to pay for paper or postage.

- ✔ **Print publishing:** This newsletter format costs more than the electronic version, but you do have a tangible item that people can read anywhere (what I think of as the, ahem, restroom reach) and that can be shared easily among audiences that may not be technology savvy.

Almost every business has important facts, advice, or statistics that may be helpful to customers and prospects with whom you've already established some kind of relationship. Liquor stores can create newsletters on wine. Computer security consultants can publish newsletters focused on virus updates. Banking consulting groups can keep clients up to date on trends in regulations and financial markets. Although each business is very different, they do share one important thing: Current, up-to-date information is an important part of what they offer to their clients.

Don't use the newsletter as a prospecting tool to reach people who don't already know you. Without a previous relationship in place, your newsletter is more likely to be perceived as a burden than welcomed as a resource. If, however, you wish to maintain communications with a prospect you've already met, the newsletter can help you nurse the relationship toward an eventual sale.

Think of a good newsletter as a companion to someone's coffee break: a short, light read that can be easily absorbed in one sitting — usually, two to four pages will suffice. Feature articles should be about 500 words long; news, announcements, and regular features can be even shorter, as brief as two or three hundred words.

For content, I recommend brief, informative how-to articles, case studies, and analyses of relevant trends, new technology, or emerging market developments. (For more content suggestions, see the info on e-newsletters in Chapter 9.) To truly engage your readers, however, please consider the following suggestions:

- ✔ **Make your customers heroes.** Consider writing case studies or customer profiles of clients who are using your products and services to their advantage. These stories not only demonstrate the quality of your offerings but also illustrate your commitment to your clients.

✔ **Offer real value to your readers.** Sure, you believe in your business and want to talk about how great it is, so I hate to break it to you, but no one cares about your business. Speak, instead, to your customer's hopes, dreams, desires, fears, and challenges and offer information they can really use. When you provide content that satisfies a genuine customer need, you get people to actually read your newsletter and think much more favorably about your business.

Newsletters may be produced by professionals specializing in graphic design, or assembled by employees with appropriate desktop publishing skills and access to adequate computers, software, and printers. (As an alternative to going to a print shop or printing in-house, you can bring your digital files to copy shops that can generate print copies from your electronic data.) Good news: People expect newsletters to look modest, so there's no need to spend extra money on beautiful stock (paper) or on acquiring exquisite graphics, such as illustrations or photographs.

What about distribution? If you have a store or showroom, you can simply leave a stack near the register (or other visible location) with a sign encouraging customers to take one. If you want to mail your newsletter to your customers, you need a list of names and addresses. (See Chapter 4 for more on lists.) You can encourage customers to sign up for your newsletter when they make a purchase at your store (or make orders by phone), or you can include subscription forms on your Web site or in your mail to customers.

Part IV

Managing the Sales Support System

The 5th Wave   By Rich Tennant

"Just how accurately should my Web site reflect my place of business?"

In this part . . .

In marketing, copy doesn't always play the lead. Sometimes, copy fulfills a supporting role, kind of like Art Carney in Jackie Gleason's *The Honeymooners;* Art never got top billing, but the show wouldn't have worked without him.

In this part, you find out how copy works as a supporting player within larger marketing tactics. I give you the insights you need to buttress Web sites, reinforce sales calls with collateral, and improve lead-generation programs in the business-to-business world. When you play your part well, you strengthen the entire show. (And sometimes, when you play it brilliantly, you can steal a scene or two.)

Chapter 14

Creating Web Sites That Attract and Hold Customers

In This Chapter

▶ Making plans for a destination that fulfills expectations

▶ Applying Web-friendly writing tips

▶ Checking out different kinds of online content

*T*hough the Web has lost some of its novelty attraction, it definitely now plays an important role within the larger spectrum of communications mediums. Whether your Web site is the heart of your business or merely one of its appendages, it requires your careful consideration. On the Web, your site isn't merely about you — it *is* you and serves as your virtual representative. You want it to reflect favorably on your organization.

Writing is just one of the elements, including design and software, that contribute to a site's success. It's not as complicated as you may think. Though I believe that writing for the Web requires attentiveness to the Web's unique characteristics, I don't believe that it demands an entirely new way of writing. It's a new medium, yes, but you're reaching the same people. Most of the ideas and suggestions in the rest of this book still apply. The objective is to apply them in ways appropriate to a medium that offers a few new twists.

My crawl through the Web takes you through basic steps: determining what kind of site you have (or want), finding out about a few writing techniques specific to the Web, and applying those techniques to the types of content most frequently found on the Internet.

Planning a Must-See Destination

The Web has a come-hither quality, unlike most of the mediums discussed in Parts II and III. Letters, e-mails, and ads are imposed upon the readers. When they're well targeted and written to address prospect needs, readers may forgive your impertinence and even pay attention to what you have to say. But the Web doesn't impose; it beckons. You don't go out to readers; they come in to you. Your Web sites aren't messages that you drop into prospects' laps — they're destinations at which people arrive.

The fact that visitors *freely choose* to visit your sites is the Web's single, most significant characteristic, more important by far than interactivity or its ability to present flashy graphics or audio files. When you write for other mediums, you have to give the readers a reason to pay attention; but when prospects arrive at your Web sites, they already have a purpose in mind. Your job is to fulfill their expectations, whether it's by offering the information they seek or completing the purchase they wish to make.

Thinking strategically for customer action

If you're writing additional material for a site that already exists, you have to conform to the architecture that's already in place. But if you're part of a team that's creating a site from scratch, you have an opportunity to build a site that's a meaningful destination. Your overall strategy for the Web site should be guided by the answers to two crucial questions:

- **What do you want people to *do* at your site?** When it comes to content, too many organizations think of their sites in terms of the messaging they want to communicate. But as destinations, Web sites are primarily places where visitors do things, such as make purchases, compare prices, gather information, and so on. So yes, messaging is a significant yet subordinate issue. First choose the kinds of actions people can take at your site; those actions dictate the messaging and content you need.

- **What role does the site play in your business?** Both the quantity and the nature of your copy depend on the purpose your site serves within your organization. For some companies, such as Amazon.com, the Web site *is* the business — all sales, marketing, and customer service functions are performed via the Internet. For others, the Web site is little more than an online brochure with contact info. Between these extremes lie various purposes (described in greater detail in the next section), such as customer relationship management and community building. Your site's role, together with the activities you expect customers and prospects to perform at the site, guide your copy and design.

Inventing specific places for specific purposes

People once looked upon the Web as a kind of technological messiah that could do just about anything. But now, after the blue smoke from the tech bubble has drifted away, commercial Web sites — created with a business purpose in mind — have tended to fall within a range of functions. Your Web site will probably serve one of, or a combination of, these purposes:

✓ **Selling products:** Someone types "widget" on a search engine, follows a link to your site, and then gets all the information he needs to select, order, and pay for the widget, directly from the Web. In structure, your site needs processing capabilities for inventory management, shipping, and credit card processing. To help you with the copy, you may want to read "Describing products," later in this chapter, as well as information on writing about products in Chapter 6 and catalog copy in Chapter 8.

✓ **Selling services:** Simpler services, such as grocery shopping or carpet cleaning, can be treated like products — the customer can use your site to schedule and pay for it. But for more expensive and complicated services, such as investment planning or environmental engineering, the site is but one link in a marketing chain that helps move the prospect closer to the final sale. You find help for writing copy in "Detailing services" and "Showing off your work," later in this chapter. (You can also flip to Chapter 6, where you find information on writing about services, and Chapter 16 on business-to-business marketing.)

✓ **Educating your prospects:** Some topics, such as law or health, naturally depend on a considerable amount of explanation. And when you're marketing big-ticket products or services, especially those that require approval from multiple decision makers (such as wireless networking for a corporate campus), your site can serve as a resource of valuable information and expertise. Find help in the section "Showing off your work," later in this chapter, plus Chapter 9 (featuring info on e-newsletters) and Chapter 13 (all about articles).

✓ **Designing a "front office":** My customers don't need to know that I work in a straw-lined cage where I compete with rodents for scraps of cheese and moldy bread. For a sole proprietor, the Web site serves as the virtual equivalent of an impressive front office or reception area; its purpose is to project professionalism and stimulate confidence. In such a site, graphics plays the same role as quality interior design — its goal is to make the business look good. The copy addresses the who-I-am and what-I-do functions. Try the sections "Introducing your team," "Showing off your work," and "Separating your organization from the pack," later in this chapter. You can also see Chapter 15 for info on big brochures.

✓ **Managing customer service:** You can even provide customer service online, through e-mail connections, live chat, open forums, a virtual library of helpful information, and a Frequently Asked Questions section. Some of these capabilities, such as the live chat and the forum, depend on software and support that you must integrate into the site. For the written material, turn to "Supporting your customers," later in this chapter. You can also try Chapter 13, where I talk about writing how-to articles for customers.

✔ **Sponsoring a community of shared interests:** For nonprofit organizations or for businesses that attract active enthusiasts, you can sustain goodwill through a Web site that includes a bulletin board or forum in which visitors can participate. Because these functions are entirely dependent on the software that makes them possible, you don't have to write much, other than a few explanatory rules; after the software is in place, your visitors create the content for you. (You will, of course, need to assign a moderator to these forums to screen out inappropriate language and other rule-breaking behavior.)

Yes, there's software out there that allows ordinary mortals to build their own Web sites, but I suggest that you get help from a professional designer with a specialty in Web site design. The money spent is more than justified by the results. Unless you're simply creating a personal page featuring pictures of the family dog, you can't afford a site that looks amateurish. To find a good designer, investigate the sites of other businesses in your area. Often the designer is credited (with contact info) on the site itself. If not, contact the business for the name.

Writing in Bits and Bytes

Although it seems as if the Web is old news by now, it's still a relatively new medium for communicating. Or to put it in another, less polite way: Although some research has been done, no one really knows, with any certainty, what the rules are. Opinions abound, but much of it is contradictory. For example, you may read advice that tells you to apply a lot of white space and then come across contradictory advice that tells you *not* to use a lot of white space. Or you may see a tip that tells you to break up long sections of copy into multiple pages and then read a tip elsewhere that tells you to consolidate related information on the same page.

Sure, I've written loads of material for the Web, but without solid research to back me up, my opinions remain just that: opinions. Although I can't honestly give you certainty, I can expose the assumptions behind my thinking so that you can make an intelligent assessment of my advice:

✔ **Web users are actively looking for something.** In the early, incense-and-peppermint days of the Internet, the techno-pundits said that hyperlinks would create the most fundamental change in communications since Guttenberg's printing press. Instead of reading linearly, from beginning to end, people would leap from link to link, making bold, brilliant connections among previously disparate ideas and information. In reality, few people have the time or inclination to idly surf from one thing to the next. Instead, they repeatedly return to the sites that interest them, and when they want something new, they pursue that information with the focus and intensity of a hunter, not the wanderlust of a grazer. The guest who arrives at your Web site is looking for something and wants to know immediately whether you have it or not.

✔ **People will read material that interests them.** If you have the information people are looking for, they'll read it, even if it means — gasp — scrolling for it. The real issue isn't copy length; it's copy relevance.

✔ **Clarity is king.** When you create a Web site, you have to consider, among many things, copy, navigation, graphic design, and software integration for your more interactive elements (such as order forms). Putting it all together isn't easy, but you're on the right track when you focus on clarity. For every design and copy decision, ask yourself, "Will this be crystal clear to my visitors?" Will they understand how to find what they're looking for on your site? Do the headlines tell people what they can expect within the subsequent copy? Is the ordering process simple and unambiguous?" If your answers are affirmative, you've built a successful foundation for your online presence.

Good, clear Web writing means paying special attention to your online entrances, the length of your copy, the ease of scanning your copy, and the descriptive quality of your hyperlinks.

Making each page a doorway

Many sites are built with architecture as their prevailing design metaphor. You start with a home page that serves as the main entrance and then direct visitors to other "rooms" — other pages on your sites — that they should see. But Web sites aren't homes with one front entrance; they're more like open campuses that visitors can enter from just about any point along its borders.

Most search engines work by using *spiders*, automated search-and-retrieve programs, to collect information from all your pages. When Web users conduct a search with their chosen keywords, the engines generate results that direct them to the pages that have those words, regardless of their location within your Web site. Your home page may be ignored entirely — and in effect, every page serves as an entrance to your site. That means you may want to consider a few points as you write:

✔ **Allow navigation from every page.** Whether you use buttons, toolbars, or what have you, visitors should be able to navigate your site from every page within it, not just your home page. As the copywriter, you may not be responsible for creating the navigation tools, but if you're building a site for your own purposes, make sure they're in place.

✔ **Identify yourself everywhere.** You never know where visitors will show up, so put your logo (or other identifier) and your primary contact information on every page.

✔ **Identify the page itself.** Clicking on a search engine listing can be a hit-or-miss affair; many times, I feel as if I've beamed down to an unfamiliar planet, with little idea of where I've landed. So make sure that in addition to identifying *who* you are, you identify each particular page as well. Tell visitors whether they're on the order form, within a product listing, or inside the About Us section. Providing this info in headlines or within banners at the top of the page lets visitors get their bearings.

All simple, basic stuff, right? But it's amazing how many pages and sites fail to provide these three fundamental courtesies. Don't let yours be among them.

Sizing up your copy

Many people would love to have a rule of thumb for the amount of copy that should go on a Web page. (Me, too! If you find one that *works*, let me know.) I know of one popular rule that doesn't work: the one that says you should keep all the important information above the fold. The idea, lifted from newspaper publishing (hence, "the fold"), is that all the significant stuff should appear within one screen shot, without scrolling. But given the variety of browsers, with different settings, on different operating systems, viewed on different monitors, where's the fold? How do you know what constitutes a screen shot, one person to the next?

You can't. So don't worry about the fold. Instead, copy length should be dictated by need — the viewers' needs. Again, your visitors are looking for something; give them as much (or as little) as they need to satisfy their quest without having to make unnecessary (and time-consuming) leaps between pages. Scrolling down isn't a big deal — if you have info that visitors want.

As a general rule, the more familiar your products or services are, such as dog food or elastic bandages, the less copy your readers need to arrive at a purchasing decision. As your products become less familiar or as they increase in price and complexity (for example, a new dietary supplement for reducing arthritis symptoms or a companywide safety training system), the more copy you need to make your case. When in doubt, ask yourself, "Is there enough information here to drive my prospect to the next step?" That step may be an actual sale or a request to speak with a representative.

Scanning is believing

According to the research that *is* available, your visitors scan before they read. Your real challenge isn't about limiting the length of copy per se, but about making your copy easy to scan. Like hunters in the woods, your visitors scan the whole page for clues to relevance: "Do you have what I'm looking for?" Make scanning easier for your visitors by applying the following tips.

Writing you-are-here headlines

Headlines in Web sites serve a vastly different purpose than those in ads and brochures. Instead of introducing a story, their first function is to assure visitors that they're in the right place. As a writer, your job is to get the right people — customers or potential customers — to stick around. Your headlines can be objective and straightforward, or they can add a bit of sell.

The plain-Jane headline is completely objective and states as matter-of-factly as possible what's available on the page. The headlines aren't particularly intriguing, but they're helpful because they tell visitors where they are and what they can expect. Here are some examples of plain-Jane headlines:

- *About Calypso Partners*
- *Digital Cameras*
- *Party Services*

To add "sell" to the headline, you take the statement of fact — the plain description of the page's contents — and add the meaning or significance of the content. The meaning is usually a benefit (what the content does for the reader) or an important feature (something that distinguishes your content from your competitors). If you're looking for a way to spice up your headline but feel stuck, ask yourself this question: "Why is this content important to my readers?" The answer is almost certainly part of the sell. Here's what these headlines can look like:

- *The Calypso Partners Story: More Than One Hundred Years of Travel Planning Experience*
- *How to Select the Right Digital Camera For You*
- *Bring Puppets, Magic, and Merriment to Your Next Party!*

Inserting subheads into copy

Subheads, short phrases distinguished in bold or some other type treatment, are used to introduce blocks of text. They're helpful in three ways: They break up long, intimidating stretches of copy; they help scanners quickly find the content they're looking for; and (in themselves) they tell your story in fast, efficient manner. A good subhead is like a super-short, short story: It immediately communicates a complete message in a handful of words. Like the location-plus-sell headlines, subheads introduce significant (yet subordinate) benefits, features, and even news. Take a look at these sample subhead sets (say that three times fast!) for the following Web pages:

- **About Calypso Partners**

  Experts in the Caribbean

  We plan everything from the tickets to the taxis

  Bulk purchasing power passes the savings to you

✔ **How to Select the Right Digital Camera for You**

Pixels and data storage options

Choosing power versus simplicity

Features: What they mean

✔ **Party Services**

Let one of New York's top magicians cast a spell over your guests!

We have clowns, puppeteers, and storytellers, too

We'll even bring the food and decorations

Highlighting keywords

Within the paragraphs themselves, you can highlight important words in bold to attract scanners. Think from the point of view of your visitors; the keywords you highlight should be facts or features that would interest them — things, in fact, that they would hunt for. Don't overdo the highlighting; if you emphasize too much copy, you defeat the highlight's purpose — to identify genuinely important or special information. Look at these examples:

✔ *Calypso Partners: In fact, our* **Barbados** *tours give you access to exclusive hotel discounts unavailable anywhere else.*

✔ *Digital Cameras: Most digital cameras in the $350 - $550 category come with* **optical zoom** *features that allow you to . . .*

✔ *Party Services: According to the Daily Grind, Captain Bluebeard is one of the* **top ten children's acts** *in Manhattan.*

Using bulleted lists

When you can, turn some of your content into bulleted lists that visitors read at a glance. Lists are typically made of words or short phrases of features that merit notice but that aren't important enough to highlight within headlines or subheads. Here's a tip: When you find yourself composing a long paragraph that looks like a freight train of facts, one following the other, you can probably turn that paragraph into a bulleted easy-to-scan, easy-to-read list. I'm sure you can anticipate lists for the three hypothetical Web sites I've created:

✔ **Calypso Partners:** Lists of key people and their expertise, destinations, and special amenities within each package tour

✔ **Digital Cameras:** Lists of features, actual cameras, and top sellers

✔ **Party Services:** Lists of services, performing acts, and endorsements in the media

Making your own hot hyperlinks

Maybe I have a warped sense of fun, but here's a little to-do activity that I think you'll find entertaining. For the following content I describe, I want you to transform my weak, lame-o, vague hyperlinks into hot, specific, unambiguous hyperlinks that tell readers exactly what they can expect when they click. I describe the content and write a poor link, and then you grab a piece of paper and write a better link. Here goes:

✔ A site that sells valves to hydraulic engineers has a chart of performance characteristics (including temperatures, pressures, and volumes) for valves of different sizes. My lame-o link: Click here for chart.

✔ A site that describes a daycare service for kids ages 3 to 12 includes a page of games and activities parents can play with their kids. My lame-o link: Play with your kids.

✔ A site for a major insurer provides a glossary that describes insurance terms in ordinary language. My lame-o link: Terminology explanations.

✔ Extra credit! Go online and pick a site — perhaps even your own — and target three weak links you can improve. Unfortunately, you probably won't have trouble finding some. But I know you'll do a better job!

Crafting descriptive captions

Be sure that the graphic elements you use, including photos, charts, and illustrations, are accompanied by clear, informative captions that tie the meaning of the graphic to the page's purpose or function. You include graphic elements because they illustrate something; the caption explains exactly what the graphic illustrates. If a chart explains your product's superiority to its competitors, say so. If you include a photo of a customer using your services, describe what the person is doing (or enjoying). In general, captions should be brief, unambiguous, and to the point. Consider these examples:

✔ **Calypso Partners:** For a photo of a tour guide in action:

Linda Chambers leads a Calypso group through Antigua's secret grottoes.

✔ **Digital Cameras:** For a camera comparison chart:

A checklist of key features for our ten most popular cameras.

✔ **Party Services:** For a photo of a puppet act:

Master puppeteer Hugh Wyres brings Snow White to life with music and humor!

Writing descriptive links

Hyperlinks, those buttons or underlined pieces of copy that take us from one page to another, are one of the defining characteristics of the Web. In the right hands, they can be the most efficient way of guiding visitors to the content that interests them most. Applied carelessly, they can drag unwary visitors into dark alleys where they abandon our sites in frustration.

The easiest way to prevent frustration is to use hyperlinks judiciously. Don't break up copy just for the sake of distributing it across various Web pages. Instead, cluster relevant information together. Why make customers go to three different pages for a product description when you can put all the info on one page? And if the material is too long, such as a feature article, make the breaks at logical points, as if the separate sections were chapters.

The other way you can help readers is to make your links descriptive: In the link copy itself, make it perfectly clear what readers get when they click on your links. A poor link is vague — when you read it, you're not certain it will connect you to what you need. A good link builds anticipation for the content that readers will get by following it, and it helps other readers avoid content (and wasted time) they don't need. Here are some examples (the underlined text indicates an example of a hyperlink, just as it does on a site):

- **Not a helpful link:** <u>For more information, click here</u>. What information? Prices? Services? A how-to? This hyperlink doesn't tell me. This kind of obscure link can lose good customers by failing to give them info they need or can frustrate potential prospects by leading them to dead ends.

- **A much better link:** <u>Get our complete list of discounted travel packages</u>. Bam! I know exactly what I'm getting. If I'm looking not just for destinations, but for complete travel packages — and packages at a good price — I now know exactly where to go.

Here are a few links for my hypothetical Web sites that describe exactly what visitors will get when they click on the links:

- **Calypso Partners:** *We cover the entire Caribbean. See our <u>interactive map of island destinations</u>.*

- **Digital Cameras:** *Not all zoom options are alike. <u>Compare digital zoom to optical zoom</u> and see what's right for you.*

- **Party Services:** *See our <u>video of Captain Bluebeard</u> in action!*

Developing Different Types of Online Content

Content rules! Back in the Internet's youth (that is, just a few years ago), interactivity, flashy graphics, and noisy audio clips were all the rage. The experts felt sure that the Web's bells and whistles would be its primary attraction. It turns out that many customers regard those things as annoying distractions. Sure, when you can apply Java Scripts and other tools to truly enhance the online experience, the fancy extras can be great. But they should always be subordinate to the substance — in-depth content about, or related to, your products and services.

Fortunately, you have at your disposal many intelligent options for organizing your content. Depending on the nature of your organization, these are the content categories that are most likely to apply to your commercial site.

Describing products

The most basic kind of Web copy is the kind that goes to the roots of commerce: selling products. Writing about them on the Web is the online equivalent of shouting your wares in a crowded marketplace. Although many of the same rules apply here as they do for ads (Chapter 11), direct response letters and brochures (Chapters 5 and 6), and catalog copy (Chapter 8), the Web adds a few twists of its own you need to consider:

- **Focus on distinctive qualities.** The Internet allows customers to make almost simultaneous comparisons of similar products. On the Web, it is especially important to trumpet the distinctions of your products as opposed to comparable items carried by competitors.

- **Be as complete in your description as possible.** If your Web site is also the point of purchase (people can order directly from your site), be sure to include everything customers need to know before they buy, including

    - **Options:** List sizes, colors, special features, and so on.

    - **Dimensions:** Tell the number of pages in the book, the size of the shirt, the height of the bicycle, and so on.

    - **Shipping information:** Explain how things will be delivered and how much those options cost.

- **Create links to important subordinate information.** Many products sold to manufacturers, especially those that require approval from engineers, must be accompanied by information about tolerances, performance specifications, installation requirements, and so on. Technical demands can be very specific; if you don't have the precise information, you may lose the sale. Fortunately, you can convert a lot of your driest, most technical information into charts or graphs with their own dedicated pages. Be sure, however, that your product descriptions include clear links to the relevant information. (See "Writing descriptive links," earlier in this chapter, for more information.)

Detailing services

By nature, services are less tangible than products and more challenging to describe. Make your job easier by considering visitor psychology: When someone's surfing the Web in search of a service, chances are, he has a problem to solve (from clogged gutters to a lawsuit) and needs help, fast.

To communicate services quickly (because Web readers are scanners), focus on the what, why, and how:

- ✔ **What:** First, tell visitors what your service does for them. (Yup, the benefit, once again.) Get right to the meat of the matter: Tell readers what problems you solve, what processes you improve, what challenges you meet, and what new qualities you add to their lives or businesses. Your tone should match the nature of your product (be it fun and frivolous, or serious and matter-of-fact) and the expectations of your audience: Feel free to speak colloquially to consumers looking for toys, but be sure to respect the sensitivities of visitors looking for information about prostate cancer. Here's a direct, state-the-benefit approach in an example that may appear on an interior organizer's site:

  From planning through execution, Optimal Space Planners will turn your cluttered cubicles into safer, more productive workspaces.

- ✔ **Why:** Explain why your business is especially qualified to perform the service. It could be the experience of your employees, the quality of your technology, your unusual expertise, or a combination of those three, plus other factors. Whatever they are, use them to build a case for employing your company's services as opposed to your competitors. Here's an example of one such explanation:

  The Optimal team includes experts in ergonomics, time management, and occupational kinetics who have more than 25 years of experience helping organizations use their space more efficiently and more productively.

- ✔ **How:** Within your service description, briefly describe how your organization provides or conducts the service. The idea is to create a kind of movie in your prospects' minds that allows them to picture your service at work for them. This step lends credibility to your claims (by demonstrating your ability to deliver on your promises) and leads the prospects closer to the sale by drawing it into their imaginations. You don't have to go into a great deal of detail — think of it more as a sketch than as a finished oil painting. Check out this brief "how" description:

First, we arrive on site to assess your working environment — the physical space, how it's used, and the activities your employees are engaged in. Then we create an action plan based on the site report that includes detailed recommendations for modifying spaces, tools, and behaviors. Finally, our experts, including occupational trainers and physical therapists, arrive on site to implement our recommendations.

Introducing your team

Some purchasing decisions can be made without much regard for the expertise of the seller. When you go online to order flowers or buy a book, all you expect from the staff is the ability to package your item appropriately. But when you're looking for help with complex or intellectually demanding issues that require real knowledge and experience, such as back pain, home sales, or computer network management, evaluating the available talent or expertise is a crucial part of your purchasing decision. You want to know about the qualifications of the persons providing the service.

That's the best reason to post biographies of your key people online: Potential customers want to know whether your company's employees are qualified to help them, whatever their need. Satisfying investor curiosity is another good reason to include biographies; investors want to know who's on the bridge before they back your ship. Satisfying corporate egos is not a good reason for putting executives before the public, but sadly, it's often a requirement. (You're not really surprised, are you?)

Any biography contains two kinds of information:

- ✔ **Professional matters:** This information includes current areas of expertise, current job functions and responsibilities, previous (related) career experience, education, involvements in professional associations and/or societies, professional recognitions (awards and honors), and media recognition in books, articles, television appearances, and so on.

- ✔ **Personal matters:** I hope you're skeptical about this information, because you should be; most personal information doesn't belong in a business biography. However, some personal information may indeed be significant when personality plays an important part of a professional role, as it does in certain types of jobs:

    - • **Creative types:** Creativity is important for artists, writers, ad agency personnel, architects, designers, and so on, so you may want to include details about hobbies or interests to round out a profile. Suppose that you want to encourage readers to think of your boss as an innovative talent; you may want to include her interests in Zen flower arranging and landscape painting.

- **Compassionate types:** When compassion, social commitment, or family values (very broadly defined) is important, you may want to bring on the family, volunteering commitments, involvements in causes, and so on. If you're preparing the bio of the hospital president or the chairman of a nonprofit organization, you may want to mention the person's status as a board member in a cancer fundraising group or her role as a mentor in a local school.

Showing off your work

One of the most attractive aspects of the Web is that it gives a company an opportunity to go beyond talking about what they to do to *showing* what they do. Following are some ways to do that:

- ✔ **Show samples:** If your business involves writing or visual work — such as an advertising agency, architectural firm, research group, and so on — you can literally post samples of your work online. In that case, you may not need to do much additional writing to explain your work. The larger issues involve getting the work itself posted online and determining the point of access to the work. For example, you may create a list of clients (assuming you have their permission) with hyperlinks to samples of the work you've done for each client. Or you may create a list of industries you serve, by category, with each category title leading to representative samples in that area.

- ✔ **Show people how you do what you do.** When you offer a service, you may want to go into considerable detail about your work process (as opposed to the mere summary I discuss earlier in the section "Detailing services"). Given the enormous range of possible services, there's no one right way to talk about how your company does its work. But I do recommend the following:

  - **Break it into small pieces.** Avoid a long-winded narrative. Instead, break out the process into steps, each with its own short, independent paragraph.

  - **Use graphics to help you.** Charts, graphs, and photos of people in action can bring your work process to life.

  - **Use visual and/or active language.** I know, I know, many important processes can be pretty abstract. Anyone have a rip-roaring due diligence story to tell? But even if you don't divert rivers or move mountains, you can conscientiously use verbs such as *review, analyze, prepare, integrate, manage, process,* and so on to help readers see or imagine what you do.

✔ **Post your articles on the Web.** Perhaps you (or others in the organization) have published articles or columns. If so, put them on your Web site! (But be sure to get permission from the publisher first.) They strengthen the value of your site to information seekers, and they attract search engine spiders that will create additional links to your site.

Supporting your customers

As many companies have discovered, much to their consternation, customer support can become one of the most expensive costs of doing business. Every service issue that can be resolved online, as opposed to a phone call to a live person, represents a considerable savings; that's why your phone company so eagerly touts the customer service portion of its Web site.

Many of the service features, such as online chat with, or e-mail queries to, a technical support person, are beyond your responsibilities as the writer. But you may be involved in two helpful things:

✔ **Frequently asked questions (FAQ):** An FAQ list provides help in a question-and-answer format that anticipates the user's most likely queries. Here are a few pointers for writing a handy FAQ:

- **Find the right questions.** You'll probably tap the technical experts for answers, but to know which questions to include in your FAQ, ask the customer service or support people, the people who answer the phones. It's essential to identify as many of the commonly asked questions as you can for your FAQ to be genuinely useful.

- **Write from the point of view of the user.** Chances are, if someone can't resolve a problem himself, he's not going to know the correct technical language for it. So although you'll rely on technical or customer support staff for the content of the questions and answers, you're probably going to do some translating. Help your customers or prospects by writing your questions and answers in the language they're likely to use. For example, "Is a misadjusted tappet clearance audibly detectable?" is much too technical for most people. But a question such as "What's that rat-a-tat-tat sound under my hood?" is wording that most people can understand.

- **Solve the problem.** In your answers, you don't need a lot of background history or science. Just give readers enough information to solve the problem, and present that information as simply as possible. Resist the temptation to go too deep: Readers are looking for fast answers, not lengthy lectures.

✔ **Support library:** The next step beyond the FAQ is a body of articles addressing important technical or service issues. These articles may already have been written (by you or others in your organization); if so, your job is to create a "home" (a dedicated page) with article titles and brief, one-paragraph summaries that help visitors identify the material they want. But if articles aren't available, you may want to collaborate with the relevant parties in your organization (perhaps the technical advisors or marketing managers) to select topics that merit development into articles. (For more info on articles, see Chapter 13.)

Separating your organization from the pack

Call me twisted, but I want to end this chapter by talking about the first thing many people are asked to write for a Web site: a vision, mission, or philosophy statement. Written to distinguish an organization from its competitors by highlighting its unique values or beliefs, these statements almost inevitably use the same language: commitment to excellence, highest standards of quality, dedication to customer service, and so on. (If you absolutely must write a mission statement, see Chapter 10.)

Be honest now: When you visit other company's Web sites, do you read this stuff? And if you do, do you really believe it? Does any rational person actually think, "Wow! These guys are committed to excellence! I'm sold. Send me the contract, now!"

It's perfectly legitimate to want to distinguish your organization by drawing attention to the special ways you do business. But cramming that desire into a philosophy statement is a weak execution of that intention. The following are much more credible and sophisticated ways of reaching your goal:

- ✔ **Imbed your values into the *way* you manage your Web site.** Instead of telling people you're committed to customer service, *show* them by making your site easy to read and navigate and by packing the site with genuinely helpful content.

- ✔ **Provide concrete examples, not vague claims.** Instead of saying, "we pursue innovation," show a few of your company's innovations. Tell Web site visitors what they are and what's innovative about them. Leadership? Show your executives in print or in the media. Excellence? Why not offer visitors a case study or two so they can read about your business *in action.* (See Chapter 13 for more on case studies.)

- ✔ **Let your customers speak for you.** They're more credible than you are. If you've gathered endorsements or testimonials from customers who've given you permission to use them, put them on your site. (For more on testimonials, see Chapter 3.)

Chapter 15

Crafting Collateral: Using Supporting Materials

· ·

In This Chapter:

▶ Checking out collateral's purpose

▶ Building the corporate capabilities brochure

▶ Producing successful sales sheets and pamphlets

▶ Constructing flyers and white papers

· ·

*Y*esterday, I went to my local barber to get a much-needed haircut. While I waited for a chair, a salesman walked in and began pitching a special casino vacation package to the three barbers. They were surprisingly patient with him (the salesman seemed tentative and inexperienced), but after a few minutes, when it became clear that no one was going to sign up and that the salesman had exhausted his limited powers of persuasion, their patience ran thin. After an awkward silence, one of the barbers asked for a brochure; the salesman didn't have any, and he moved on to his next prospect without leaving anything behind.

I tell this anecdote (a true one) because it illustrates both the limits and possibilities of *collateral,* printed material created for sales support. Collateral is limited, because, as you can see from this example, it can't compensate for poor salesmanship. (In fact, the barber may have asked for the brochure to accelerate the salesman's departure.) But collateral can have the power of sustaining a message long after it's been initially delivered — when the salesman, or the advertisement, is no longer present before the prospect. In the shop, the barber may have been too embarrassed to express his interest in front of his colleagues; the brochure may have been a way for him to pursue the matter beyond their eyes. Without the collateral, however, a potential customer was, and is, lost.

In this chapter, I help you select and write the most appropriate collateral for your needs, including corporate capabilities brochures, sales sheets, pamphlets, flyers, and special reports called white papers.

Examining the Role of Collateral

On the surface, collateral seems to be the simplest and most straightforward of our communications tools. After all, it's primarily about information: facts and figures regarding your products, your services, and your business.

Yet dangers lurk beneath the placid surface. For one thing, collateral isn't cheap. Paper, printing, and production cost good money, and many collateral pieces involve multiple pages on expensive stock. Given what your marketing budgets probably are, you have only so much to spend on printed matter that, in itself, can't make or close a sale.

With its inherent design flexibility and its capacity to communicate a large variety and volume of information, however, one or more collateral types may prove useful to you. Businesses of all types and sizes use collateral to educate, market, support sales, provide product information, and more. When you're confident that collateral deserves a role in your marketing plan, these are among the most important issues you should consider:

- ✔ **Format:** You can choose from numerous formats, ranging from simple, one-sided sales sheets to long, multipage pamphlets.

- ✔ **Needs of your intended audiences:** These needs can range from an engineer's desire for complex technical data to a hospital patient's need for compassionate communications on life-and-death issues.

- ✔ **Role within the sales process:** In your interactions with potential customers, is there a point when providing additional information — as a leave-behind or take-away — can help you support the sale? If a sale is like a drama, consider the role collateral plays in your show.

Sound complex? It needn't be — if you begin by establishing the *purpose* of your collateral. After your mission is clear, you can weigh your format options and choose the tone and voice appropriate for your audience.

Reduced to their most basic functions, most collateral fulfills one of two (and sometimes both) functions: to provide more-complete information or to maintain your presence in front of your prospects.

Providing more-complete information

A bag of carrots is a bag of carrots, and unless you're being asked to fork over considerably more money for super-deluxe, organic, hand-tended, mega-carrots, you don't need any information to make your purchase. But plenty of products and services do need the support of information that can't be entirely included in an ad, a direct response piece, or a sales call. Here are two common situations that demand deeper communications:

✔ **You offer lots of options.** Your car comes in five colors and two different engine sizes and has a set of add-on features from power windows to anti-lock disc brakes. Or you have a number of insurance packages whose benefits vary by premium and/or by deductible. In these and many other similar instances, you need collateral to articulate the available options or features. Pamphlets, sales sheets, and brochures can present these details in a clear, well-organized way.

✔ **You want to minimize confusion.** A bank checking account is a bank checking account, but banks are legally obligated to provide explanations for rules, rates, and regulations. Medical facilities that perform MRI (magnetic resonance imaging) scans need to explain the procedure to patients, manage their expectations, and tell patients what to do before, during, and after the procedure. In these cases, collateral can anticipate customers' and patients' needs and minimize confusion and/or misunderstanding. To carry this kind of in-depth information, look toward the longer collateral formats, such as brochures and pamphlets, as opposed to the briefer sales sheets or flyers.

Maintaining your presence with prospects

A prospect has come into your furniture store and looked at some dining sets. Or you've met a potential customer at your trade show booth. Or you made a sales call or talked to someone on the phone. The deal hasn't closed, but the possibility of a sale remains open. In the interim, you want to fill that gap in time and space. In order to keep the sale alive, you want something that maintains your presence. Following are common concerns:

✔ **You need something tangible.** The need for physical representation usually increases with the expense, or luxury quality, of your product or service. A man walks into your auto showroom with a gleam in his eye, but his scruples (that is, the threat of an angered spouse) keep him from making an immediate purchase. To keep his desire burning, you give him a glossy brochure of his dream car; the pictures in his hands remind him again and again that his dream *could* become a reality — if he buys.

✔ **You're making a long and complex sale.** In business-to-business sales especially, the sales cycle — the time between making the first contact and getting the check — can be as long as six months to a year. Why so long? Usually because of one or more of the following reasons:

  • **The product or service is expensive.** The purchase must be carefully considered against competing products or other options.

  • **Many decision makers are involved.** The purchase requires the approval of several executives or even department teams.

  • **The technical requirements are complex.** Several experts have to establish the technical requirements, often specific to their unique needs, before the purchase can be made.

For these reasons, you know that your sales process requires multiple steps that may include meetings, proposals, reviews, counterproposals, and contract negotiations. In the long sales cycle, the right collateral can address specific concerns and move prospects from one step in the cycle to the next. (For more on business-to-business marketing issues, see Chapter 16.) Depending on the number and nature of the steps in your sales process, you may deploy a wide variety of collateral types from simple sales sheets to complex white papers.

✔ **Your sales team insists on collateral.** Sometimes salespeople request collateral for the reasons previously listed. But unfortunately, requests sometimes have more to do with politics than with sound sales and marketing judgment. Although sales and marketing should be integrated functions working toward common goals, they're often very different departments, reporting to different executives, who resent the power and influence the other department has. In these circumstances, the sales team may ask for collateral — as opposed to ads, direct response materials, and so on — because they see collateral distribution as something they can directly control. If you're caught in the crossfire of a political request, I'm afraid I can't do much to comfort you, except to say that you're not alone and you need not take the matter personally.

Tackling the Corporate Capabilities Brochure

In the collateral community, the corporate capabilities brochure is the big kid on the block: It's often 8.5 inches x 11 inches in size, loaded with multiple pages, and printed on heavy, glossy stock. The corporate capabilities brochure doesn't represent any one particular product or service but instead is intended to represent the business or organization as a whole, be it Thirty-Second National Bank or Humongous Steel. This brochure is meant to impress and, given its size and expense, is usually produced by large organizations or smaller organizations that want to make a big impression (and a have a large budget to burn). Once printed, they may be distributed by salespeople, packed in press kits (see Chapter 12), or simply stacked on coffee tables in the corporate headquarters' reception area. Most capabilities pieces include

✔ **A message from the president, CEO, or chairman of the board:** These words are intended to add a personal touch to the brochure, usually written in the first person ("I" and "we") with liberal use of the second person ("you"). Sometimes the person to whom the message is attributed actually writes this so-called personal touch, but most of the time, you're the one preparing it, after an interview with the person whose signature actually appears on the message.

✔ **A mission or vision statement:** This piece articulates the organization's philosophy. If one is already prepared, you can simply drop it into place. If you have to create one from scratch, you have to interview the people who pride themselves on their big-picture visions — the high-level executives. (See Chapter 10 for more on mission statements.)

✔ **A brief company history:** You must, of course, present this information in the most flattering light possible. You may have to dig around to find a person who knows this history or archival material that can help you.

✔ **Sections dedicated to various departments, product groups, or functions:** This information is the meat of the book, and each section demands a new set of interviews with the responsible representatives of the individual functions.

Please don't confuse the brochures discussed here with the brochures described in Chapter 6, which are direct response materials crafted for specific mailing campaigns. The latter must contribute to the persuasive case explored in the other mail elements, including the envelope teaser and the letter. The former are less persuasive and more informative, and they're not tied to any one campaign; they have less sales power but greater flexibility.

When you consider the volume of material you need to master, the capabilities brochure is as much an exercise in organization as it is in writing. I suggest you create a chart that includes columns for subject areas, appropriate interview subjects for those areas, their contact information (phone numbers and e-mail addresses), and space for recording interview appointments. The most time-consuming part of your job, by far, is tracking people down to commit them to interview times. When you plan your timetable for this project, make sure you give yourself ample time to contact and interview your subjects. (For more on interviewing, see Chapter 13.)

Although a graphic designer is responsible for the brochure's overall look (see Chapter 6 for more on design), you're accountable for the written content. Your best bet for success is to anticipate the politics ahead and to prepare your content with an eye to your prospect or customer's interests.

Preparing for politics

In addition to being one of the longest pieces you may be asked to write, the capabilities brochure is also the most dangerous. Because it's intended to be representative of the organization, it becomes a mask for the corporate ego. The capabilities brochure can also be a battleground for all the subordinate egos in management and the executive suite who want to champion their significance and who are quick to find offense in the advancement of anyone else. With so many parties involved, writers in this situation are almost sure to displease or offend someone.

On the brink of despair? Take heart. You can do a few things to make your life easier (and the brochure better):

✔ **Limit the number of chefs.** To play nicely with everyone, the marketing person responsible for the brochure may want to include as many people as possible. You've heard the reasons for doing so: to get everyone's buy-in and to make all participants feel that they're part of the process. But too many chefs spoil the brochure. Ideally, one or two people should determine the main direction of the piece, and a handful of others should contribute the info. If you can't prevail on this point through logic, try winning your way with fear: Tell your boss that if too many people are involved, the interview and revision processes will make it impossible to meet the established deadline (which is true, if manipulative).

✔ **Get a sign-off on the overall message first.** Before you write the actual copy, create a list of crucial messages, culled from your interviews with the highest-level executives, and submit that list back to them for their approval. Be sure the list includes key points about vision, values, major product lines, important competitive distinctions, and/or noteworthy functions or services. After this document is approved, you have a baseline against which all incoming information is measured. When an interviewee resists contributing information you need, or insists that you include material that's off-message, you can support your arguments with the approved messaging document.

✔ **Assign the feedback to one person.** If you can, see whether all the subsequent feedback to your first draft can be assigned to one person, preferably with more power than you, to reconcile contradictory comments and edits. That way, instead of getting a dozen versions of your draft, each marked by a different person, you get one version with all the edits in one place — and all the contradictory comments resolved in favor of one direction or another.

Generating a customer-centric document

Certain types of problems can make a brochure miserable to read. These are the three most common weaknesses of corporate capabilities brochures:

✔ **Narcissism:** When you write about specific products and services, you're obligated to talk about benefits and features. But a brochure about your company in general is a chance for a company to talk about itself, which is a dangerous temptation to puffery, boasting, and self-flattery.

✔ **Compromised vision:** A large company's internal politics almost always lead to compromise. Although negotiations among conflicting parties is a good thing, lack of firm resolutions can lead to strange compromises in the corporate brochure. Ultimately, decisions must be made: Your company can't be both the established industry leader *and* the usurping innovator, the "hip" provider of countercultural accessories *and* the familiar purveyor of Grandpa's duck-hunting boots. Yet some companies still try to be all things to all people, leading to contradictory statements and positions that result in a compromised, confusing vision.

✔ **Vague messaging:** Because the corporate capabilities brochure can be so expensive, it should have as long a shelf-life (the period of time it remains relevant before a new one has to be produced) as possible. Too often that means making broad promises that are sketchy on specifics, on the theory that the specifics change more often and are therefore most likely to date the brochure. But general statements without specific support — from facts, figures, and descriptive processes — undermine credibility. The final brochure may be vague and unconvincing.

Is there an alternative to this bleak picture I've painted? Oh, indeed, but it may seem counterintuitive: Instead of using the corporate capabilities brochure to talk about yourself (your organization), use it to talk about the customer. Instead of focusing on you, reflect customer concerns, desires, and fears. In this way, you accomplish two things:

✔ You position yourself as an organization that truly understands the customer.

✔ You create a rapport that puts you and your prospect on the same side — the best place to begin future negotiations and sales attempts.

The secret to making a customer-centric document? Take all the elements — from the "about us" to the discussions of product lines or functions — and write about them from the point of view of the customer.

Turning "about us" into "about you"

Most capabilities brochures begin with a statement about who the company is and what it does. Instead, you can talk about the customers' needs — and *then* show them how you meet them. This usually involves the following elements:

✔ **Description of "climate":** You can replace your corporate history with a brief summation of the challenges or conditions your customers face now. In doing so, you reveal your understanding of the customers' world and your empathy with their needs.

✔ **Description of solutions:** Instead of a static description of what the company does, you can provide a more dynamic description of how you solve problems or meet challenges. In substance, "what you do" and "how you solve problems" may be the same thing, but the latter angle takes on the customer's point of view and is more immediately engaging.

In addition to making your content more customer-focused, make your rhetoric (the *way* you say what you say) more customer-friendly. Write as you would speak to an intelligent adult you just met in a conference room. Feel free to use the second person, "you," and keep your vocabulary, tone, and sentences clean and simple: Avoid bombast or bloat that would make your organization seem self-important. Take a look at how these principles are applied in this sample transformation:

> **About us:** *In 1862, when Jeremiah Dedwold opened his first office in Hartford, Connecticut, the Shield Indemnity Corporation offered local merchants the security they needed to underwrite bold passages to Europe, India, and China. Since then, Shield Indemnity has grown into an international property and liability insurer, offering numerous products and coverage plans for large and mid-sized businesses across the globe.*

> **About you:** *As your business extends its reach, it may also be exposed to greater risk. Shipping hazards, contradictory regulations, and shifting legal standards can interrupt the profitable expansion of international enterprises. That's why the Shield Indemnity Corporation, an international property and liability insurer, provides a comprehensive suite of flexible liability products and risk management consulting services. Working together, our team helps businesses like yours control risk — and find greater opportunities in the global marketplace.*

Shifting product information onto separate sales sheets

For fear of dating their brochures, many companies won't commit themselves to specifics in their copy. But from the customer's point of view, the details are everything; without them, you risk losing impact and credibility. To meet your need for economy and their desire for precise information, try changing your format: Make the big brochure an attractive folder that can hold sales sheets within its pocket (or pockets). The vision message, which remains relatively constant, can occupy the interior pages stapled in the middle, like a conventional brochure. Then write individual sales sheet for each of the product or service lines. (For more information on sales sheets, see "Writing Sales Sheets and Pamphlets," later in this chapter.) These sheets can go into the pocket. In one stroke, you extend the shelf life of the core material, you give your sales team greater flexibility (they can tailor their selection of sheets to the needs of individual prospects), and you have a convenient way to add timely elements such as press releases or article reprints.

Using endorsements

A personal message from someone inside your organization is okay, but an endorsement or testimonial from a customer is much stronger. Readers are more likely to empathize with your customers than with you. (For more on testimonials, see Chapter 3.)

Writing Sales Sheets and Pamphlets

Unlike the corporate capabilities brochure, sales sheets and pamphlets focus on specific products and services. And unlike much of the marketing material in the rest of this book, these pieces tend to be straightforward representations of facts and figures for people who need hard-core information before they make their purchases.

In format, the sales sheet is just that, a sheet. It's usually an 8.5-x-11-inch document with words and graphic images printed on both sides. The pamphlet has similar elements but comes in a booklet form with multiple folded pages stapled at the spine, and its dimensions can vary.

Sales sheets are simple, inexpensive, and commonly used by

- ✔ **Wholesalers** who want to give product descriptions to retailers who may, in turn, buy the products for their shelves.
- ✔ **Retailers,** such as appliance stores, who want to give consumers info that can help them select the products with the features they want.
- ✔ **Trade show exhibitors** who want to provide lightweight collateral that visitors can take from their booths.

Pamphlets are longer and more expensive to produce, but the additional expense may be justified when you want to

- ✔ **Help distributors** understand the range of product or service options available for resale to their customers.
- ✔ **Help consumers** understand or use the product or service they have bought or are about to buy.

Shaping the message

Sales sheets and pamphlets contain three basic elements: a headline that identifies the product or service; body copy that uses words and images to articulate features and uses; and concluding directions for buying the product, gathering more information, or finding more help.

Writing the headline

Lead with a headline, either on top of the sales sheet or on the cover of the pamphlet, that combines the name of the product with its distinguishing benefit or feature — the thing it does or the problem it solves that makes it different from similar products.

Remember this formula: Name plus the most important feature/benefit/distinguishing characteristic equals a sales sheet or pamphlet headline. Here are some examples:

✔ *RoastMaster 1000: The restaurant-sized oven for serious bakers*

✔ *Hillendale Climbers: Inexpensive mountain bikes for the casual cyclist*

✔ *Laser Therapy at Winslow Associates: The drug-free alternative for treating chronic acne*

Developing the body

For the body, you need to consider two things: the content you want to include and the options you have for communicating that content.

Selecting content

The best way to determine what should go on the sales sheet or in the pamphlet is to anticipate the customers' questions. Think: What are the questions they are most likely to ask before buying your product or service? The answers become your content.

For example, I think the prospects for the following products and services would ask these questions:

✔ **RoastMaster 1000:** This expensive oven is made for consumers who want restaurant performance and interior-design good looks.

- How many BTUs does it create? What are the oven's interior dimensions? Could I fit two whole turkeys at one time?

- What are its exterior dimensions? (Will it fit in my kitchen?) What do I need to know for installation?

- What are the color options? Do I have the choice of enamel or stainless steel?

- How many burners does it have? Does it deliver convectional heat? Does it include a broiler?

✔ **Hillendale Climbers:** Retail bike shop owners want to know how this line of mountain bikes would fit among their other product lines.

- What's the price point for these bikes? How do the Climbers compare to other Hillendale bicycles?

- What are the key selling points and key features?

- Who are the target customers? How are these bikes especially designed for them? What options (seats, colors, and pedals, for example) are available to my customers?

- How will these bicycles be marketed or advertised?

✔ **Laser Therapy at Winslow Associates:** The staff needs to make patients comfortable by helping them understand the therapy, telling them what to expect, and telling them what they may need to do before and after the procedure.

- What are the advantages of laser therapy for acne? How does it work?

- Who is this therapy for? How do I know if it's right for me?

- Is it safe? Does it hurt? How many sessions does it take?

- How do I prepare for the therapy? What do I need to do afterward?

Structuring content in the right format

The answers to the questions you anticipate supply the content for your sales sheets and pamphlets. The next step is to give your content form. Your options include the following:

✔ **Paragraphs with subheads:** The most important information deserves its own subhead to articulate the substance of the idea, followed by a brief paragraph to support it. You can think of the subhead as the essence or summary of your point, and the paragraph as the way to back your point with facts. For the laser therapy sales sheet, for example, you might write the following:

Lasting relief that targets the root causes of acne.

Winslow Associates is trained to use the Laseraser X5, a precision laser device that disables the sebaceous glands, the root cause of acne. Through the targeted application of gentle heat, the laser . . .

✔ **Charts or graphic illustrations with subheads:** As a copywriter, it pains me to say it, but yes, sometimes a picture is worth a thousand words. But you're still required to write a caption that explains the significance of the illustration — what it is and what it means — and ties it to the rest of your message. (For more on captions, see Chapter 2.) A good caption under a bar graph comparing the RoastMaster 1000's BTUs to its competitors may look like this:

The RoastMaster 1000 provides more BTUs to its oven than any competing model available today.

✔ **Subhead followed by a list of bullet points:** For information that's important to include, yet not significant enough to merit paragraphs or illustrations (such as subordinate features and additional options), you can create a bulleted list led by an introductory subhead that identifies and/or explains the list. Examples of subheads include "Available colors" and "Exterior dimensions by model." Because lists are intended for speed and concision, you're not obligated to write complete sentences; brief phrases or even single words may do, as the situation demands. The Hillendale Climbers sheet may have a list like this one:

> *Features include:*
>
> - *15 speeds*
> - *Gel-cushioned seat*
> - *Cantilevered breaks*
> - *Quick-release front wheel*
> - *Quick-release adjustable seat column*

Giving concluding information

The last thing your piece needs is contact information for ordering or purchasing the product or for obtaining further information. The concluding information may go at the bottom of the sales sheet or on the back of the pamphlet: The important point is that it be easy to find. The bare minimum is a phone number; most of the time you also should include a Web site address, the mailing address, and an e-mail address. Most contact information begins with lead-in sentences that start out "For further information," "To order the . . ." or "For a list of local retailers who carry the . . . ." Then you simply provide the relevant information.

Writing to special audiences

For most consumers and businesspeople, you can't go wrong by writing your sales sheets and pamphlets simply and to the point. A few audiences or industries, however, demand extra consideration on your part, including patients of healthcare services, engineers and other technology-minded customers, and customers or prospects for financial or insurance services.

When the customer is a patient

You may know what it's like to be a patient. You're vulnerable, and you may be afraid and in pain. You may not understand what's happening to you or what's ahead, and when you're in a hospital or other medical setting, you often feel as if you're the least-informed person there. For those reasons, you can see that if there's ever a time for thoughtful, sensitive writing, this is it. These are my suggestions for writing health-related pamphlets:

- ✔ **Explain as simply as possible.** The language that physicians speak is not the one the rest of us understand. Use layman's language when possible; when you must use unfamiliar terms, explain them. When you're done, however, be sure to get a physician's approval of your copy, especially of its medical content or advice, before your work is committed to print.

- ✔ **Tell patients what they can expect.** Uncertainty breeds anxiety. Although you can't provide a crystal ball that prophesies the future, you can walk patients, step by step, through the standard procedures for the subject at hand, whether it's a treatment, a medication, a diagnosis, or some form of medical service. By giving patients solid information, you're giving them a renewed sense of control.

✔ **Be honest but give genuine hope.** If patients are likely to experience pain, say so. But don't stop there. Tell them what services are available to help them. I've worked with healthcare providers for years, and I've never met one who wouldn't go the extra mile to help a patient. Telling the truth also means offering the options and possibilities for relief and hope.

✔ **Ask yourself, "How would I feel if I read this?"** Many times after completing a piece for patients (thinking I had done a good job), I've forced myself to reread the work as if I were the patient — and found some glaring problems in tone or organization. Before you submit your copy, try and read it from the point of view of a patient. Chances are, you'll find areas where you've been too abrupt, too vague, or perhaps a little confusing.

When the customer is an engineer or another tech-savvy person

Engineers and other technology-minded people revel in the arcane details and specifications that may mystify the rest of us. Remember, they actually *need* precise, in-depth information to fulfill their responsibilities. Their professional lives depend on knowing the tensile strength of bridge cable or the temperature sensitivity of high-speed microprocessors.

The issue of respect and whether these technology types give it to you is something else to consider. As a matter of pride, engineers often reject material that comes packaged in marketing talk and give credence only to content that speaks in their technical language.

If you're not an engineer yourself, you may not be fully prepared for this audience. Get help. Talk to people who understand the technology and the people who use it, usually the engineering or technical staff employed or hired by your organization. When you're ready to write, go easy on benefits talk (which arouses suspicion in this audience) and give detailed information about features, specifications, applications, and options.

When the subject is banking, insurance, or financial services

Here, the challenge isn't so much the audience as the subject matter, specifically the issue of disclosure. By law and the rules of various regulatory authorities, much of the collateral for banks, insurance companies, and financial service providers must be accompanied with precise legal disclaimers and disclosures.

You won't be asked to write the legally required portion of the collateral; it's entirely the responsibility of the company's legal department. But you have to anticipate its presence and plan accordingly when you and the designer organize the collateral — the "what goes where." As a purely practical matter, you need to leave room for the obligatory legalese.

Producing Other Types of Sales Literature

I'll admit I'm stumped: A number of miscellaneous collateral materials just don't fit neatly into any category I can think of, and they don't have much in common with each other, either. For these materials, I've come up with the following, brilliant category: other. Almost all of these have something in common with materials described in other chapters, and in fact, some have already been discussed elsewhere, including these:

- ✔ **Case studies:** These give real-life examples of your product or service in action (see Chapter 13).
- ✔ **Frequently asked questions (FAQs):** This info helps customers and prospects find answers to their most common concerns (see Chapter 14).

The remaining collateral types — flyers and white papers — are at the very opposite ends of the collateral spectrum. The former material is short and offer-centric, while the latter is long and informative.

Fashioning offer-specific flyers

The offer-specific flyer comes in many disguises — as handouts, circulars, invoice stuffers, and so on — that share the same essentials. Like the sales sheet discussed earlier in this chapter, they're typically printed on both sides of one sheet of paper. Unlike the sales sheet, however, they're focused on an offer: usually a special price or deal available for a limited time only. Their simplicity and relative low cost of production make them ideal for announcing sales or other special events. As circulars, they're often distributed within newspapers, as handouts, as "take-ones" at sales counters, or by people literally handing them out on busy street corners. As the name suggests, invoice stuffers arrive with the bills that come in the mail.

 Instead of giving detailed information about the product or service, you focus on the offer itself. Your job is to trumpet a great price, a terrific discount, or the availability of something new or seasonal, such as decorative wreaths for the winter holidays.

Composing the offer-centric headline

The copy formula is simplicity itself: The headline is the offer, and the body copy gives the reader more information about how to get the offer. In the headline, state the offer, plus where it can be obtained (who's making the offer) and/or when the offer is available. For example:

  ✔ *Buy one pair of sandals get the second at half price — this week only at Twinkle Toes Shoes!*

  ✔ *Beat the heat with the latest CoolDeluxe energy-saving air conditioners at Bob and Neal's Appliance Hut!*

  ✔ *At Porky's Market now through Sunday, April 4 — prime rib at $2.99 a pound.*

Putting together the offer-centric body copy

Take a coffee break or walk the dog. You won't have much work to do here because graphics — in the form of a photo (or photos) of the thing being offered — occupy most of the flyer. For the little body copy that's required, you need to complete the who, what, when, where, and how of the offer. Be sure the body (usually just a brief paragraph of text) includes the following:

  ✔ **Who is making the offer:** Name the store, company, or organization behind the flyer.

  ✔ **What the offer is:** If the offer isn't completely explicit in the headline, complete the details in the body copy.

  ✔ **Where the offer is available:** Give store locations or Web site addresses.

  ✔ **How the customer gets the offer:** Is it simply a discount? Or does it involve a rebate or purchase of a certain quantity to get the reduced price?

Body copy could look like this:

> *Summer's here and the time is right for sandals. Come in to Twinkle Toes Shoes between June 15 and June 21 and get an additional pair of sandals at half price when you buy a pair at our already exceptional prices. Cutie-Culs, Sand Snipers, Smack Flats — all your favorites are at Twinkle Toes Shoes. Get 'em while it's hot! At the Foggy Bottom Mall, Exit 10 off Rt. 9.*

Showing expertise with the white paper

A common tool in business-to-business communications (see Chapter 16), the *white paper* is a multisectional report that provides an in-depth analysis of a complex business topic, including emerging technologies, new business processes, and market trends in any number of industries or regions. Businesses produce a white paper for two reasons:

  ✔ To establish expertise and demonstrate to prospects their credibility and/or authority in their area of business

  ✔ To educate prospects on complex issues, particularly when the sales process is long, requires a considerable amount of thought and research, and involves cooperation among many decision makers

White papers are frequently used as offers in direct response or ad campaigns: By calling a number or completing a registration form on a Web site, prospects can get access to a white paper on an important subject of interest, such as protecting network security or managing just-in-time inventories.

Writing a white paper is much like writing a news-oriented article: you get the key messages from the high-level managers or executives in your organization and then gather the specific information from the knowledgeable employees who work for them. (See Chapter 13 for guidelines.) But because the white paper is longer, typically 10 to 25 or more pages, you want to break up the material into subsections, much like chapters in a book. Each subsection should cluster relevant information on a common theme. For example, a white paper on network security may have subsections on firewalls, viruses and worms, and Web-based transactions.

The most important section, by far, is the executive summary. Like an intro-duction, the *executive summary* is the first part of the piece, and as its name implies, it summarizes the rest of the paper. Not only do almost all of your readers start with the executive summary, but many of them read nothing else (despite all your hard work). That's why it requires your greatest care and attention. A good executive summary should do three things:

✔ **Define the topic:** At the very beginning, you want to explicitly state exactly what the subject matter is — and perhaps what it isn't. The net-work security paper, for example, may begin by defining its subject as client-server networks with 50 to 250 users, but not mainframe-based networks for thousands of employees.

✔ **Declare your position:** White papers aren't mere statements of fact; they're advocates of a particular approach to, or understanding of, an issue or challenge. Be sure the executive summary articulates your orga-nization's position. For the network security paper, the summary may say that the authors believe in a five-step approach to identifying secu-rity lapses and developing programs for correcting them.

✔ **Submit your conclusions:** The last part of the executive summary pre-sents your (or your organization's) conclusions: recommendations of things to be done or the best way to understand the issue at hand. The network security summary may conclude that, given the trade-offs in cost and returns, most organizations should concentrate their resources on internal controls and submit variable security issues, such as viruses, to outside vendors.

Chapter 16

Writing to Sell to a Business, Not a Consumer

In This Chapter

▶ Understanding business-to-business marketing

▶ Targeting the emotions and concerns of business customers

▶ Writing to promote various business events

A salesman walks into a cubicle within an anonymous glass-and-steel office tower, opens his case, and launches into his spiel: "Sir, allow me to interest you in the latest titanium-lined batch-processing modules — complete with auto-reset valve diagnostics and multiphase pressure adapters — for pharmaceutical manufacturers who want the very best. It can be yours for just four easy payments of $750,000 each. And if you act now, I can throw in a three-year maintenance plan for only $50,000 a year. But you must act now."

What's wrong with this picture? Heck, is anything right about it? Forget about the details for a moment. Intuitively, you may guess that you just can't sell a $3,000,000 manufacturing system to a businessperson the same way you sell a hairbrush to a homemaker. And you would be right.

Yes, business folk are people, too (really!), but their needs and circumstances differ from those of consumers, so to market to them, you need to change your approach to copy as well. This chapter is about that difference. In the following pages, I lead you on a tour through the world of business-to-business (B2B) copywriting, an environment that shares many of the same landmarks as consumer sales (benefits, offers, and emotional appeals) yet has enough of its own unique twists and turns to justify its own special expedition.

Managing a Different Kind of Sales Process

Your B2B copy differs from consumer copy because B2B marketing is different — and the marketing is different because the underlying sales process is different. How so?

For starters, much more money is usually at stake; therefore, the decision-making process is much more complicated, involving, as you see in the following sections, multiple decision makers, many incremental steps over time, and cooperation with a team of salespeople.

Writing to various titles and levels

Although consumer purchases are almost always an individual or a family decision, B2B purchases almost always involve a team effort. For B2B marketers, instead of creating one pitch to one person, you make multiple pitches (or create various marketing materials) to address the issues of different team members.

In B2B marketing, one size *does not* fit all. Even within the same organization, the needs and concerns of the chief financial officer (CFO) may be very different from those of the senior systems technician. To make the sale, however, you may need approval from both. To get it, you have to shape your communications to their individual concerns: You may create different marketing materials for each, or you may need to write variations — targeting their concerns — to a common piece. That means understanding, and writing to, their special issues. Fortunately, most of your B2B prospects can be roughly divided into two categories: influencers and decision makers.

Focusing on the best formats for influencers

Influencers are the people who have the technical knowledge to evaluate the product or service at hand. If you're selling workers' compensation insurance, for example, a risk manager, a benefits manager, a human resources executive, and a corporate attorney may review your offer. Likewise, a major software purchase needs approval from various IT professionals with expertise in network compatibility and security (among other issues) and from people with authority in whatever areas the software addresses, such as accounting or inventory management. Although influencers, by definition, don't have the authority to buy, they make recommendations to those who do, so you need their approval before you can close the sale.

To meet their needs, your copy should answer the following customer questions:

- ✔ How will this purchase help me fulfill my responsibilities?

- ✔ How would this purchase solve my problems/issues/challenges?

- ✔ Is this product compatible with other tools/systems/resources I have?

- ✔ Will the people who report to me need special training to use this product?

In other chapters of this book, I ask you to put benefits ahead of features and to replace technical talk with less formal language appropriate for your audience. But for B2B influencers, you can't really discuss too many features or too many technical details. What may be boring (or incomprehensible) technical talk for others is absolutely crucial to this audience: They need precise information to do their jobs. Do yours by giving it to them.

Some of the more effective formats for communicating to influencers include

- ✔ **Technical white papers:** Influencers appreciate quality information that can help them with their work. By offering white papers (in-depth informative reports — see Chapter 15 for more) on subjects relevant to their responsibilities, you give them something they can actually use while reinforcing your credibility in your area of expertise.

- ✔ **Newsletters or e-newsletters:** Like white papers, newsletters (whether printed or electronic) deliver information your audience values. But where the white paper is a one-shot delivery of lots of material, the newsletter provides more easily digestible material in smaller chunks over time; it's a sustained communication. Newsletters are an excellent option when trends or late-breaking developments play an important role in your industry or in your service. (See Chapter 13 for the scoop.)

- ✔ **Articles in relevant periodicals:** Share your expertise in publications read by your target audience. You may not be able to explicitly talk about your product, but you can use the media to establish your authority or communicate your expertise on a relevant industry issue (that might just get you in the door with prospects). Turn to Chapter 13 for more.

- ✔ **Sales sheets and FAQs (frequently asked questions):** These materials, usually limited to two sides of a single 8½-x-11-inch sheet of paper, summarize the most important technical information that influencers need to know before they can approve the purchase of your product. They also serve as appropriate leave-behinds at convention exhibitions or on sales calls. (See how to write FAQs in Chapter 14 and sales sheets in Chapter 15.)

Checking out the best formats for decision makers

Decision makers are the businesspeople who do indeed have the authority to buy. They tend to live higher up in the corporate food chain, and they have executive titles such as chief executive officer (CEO), chief operations officer (COO), chief financial officer (CFO), and so on. Or they may be a step down on the totem pole and have titles with "vice president" in them.

Irrespective of title, decision makers often have less hands-on technical knowledge than their influencer subordinates, and they're more concerned with strategies and/or value. For them, your copy should answer these questions:

✔ How does this purchase fulfill my company's goals or objectives?

✔ Does this purchase fit within our overall strategy or strategic direction?

✔ What return can I expect from this investment?

✔ How will this purchase be perceived by this organization's stakeholders (employees, shareholders, board members, local community, and so on)?

Like influencers, decision makers may need a bit of education on certain topics before they can commit. In fact, the formats for communicating to them are similar:

✔ **Strategy-oriented white papers:** In-depth reports can work with this audience, but instead of focusing on technical topics, white papers for decision makers should concentrate on industry trends, strategic directions, or obtaining value for their money.

✔ **Articles in relevant publications:** Chances are, the business periodicals read by various titles within the same organization aren't the same. Find the right media and speak to the issues of trends, strategy, and value.

What about sales sheets and newsletters? The former tend to be too technical for decision makers. Newsletters are a possibility, but given the enormous amount of written material directed at this audience, each issue has to be extraordinarily relevant to their needs in order to get read — a challenging task for a document you must re-create repeatedly.

Involving many incremental steps in your sale

Given the amount of money at stake and the number of stakeholders responsible for that money, most B2B sales require a long courtship before you and your prospect reach the altar. As a copywriter, you're less like a smooth-talking Casanova and more like a persistent, patient suitor.

Many B2B marketers make the mistake of concentrating their efforts (and budget) on the two extremes of the sale: the initial lead generation effort to collect prospects for sales calls, and the in-person "close" of the sale itself. This presents two problems: A lot of time can elapse between the lead and the call — without provisions for further communications, prospect and pitchman lose contact, jeopardizing the sale. Yet, if the sales calls are made immediately after the lead comes in, you make an all-or-nothing roll of the dice — with an adequate communications plan, you may have been able to nurse along, over time, those prospects who reject you immediately.

REMEMBER

The alternative approach is a plan for multiple contacts over the long term, anywhere from six months to a year or more. Think of the strategy as a funnel: At the widest point (the mouth of the funnel) is your universe of prospects. With each communications tactic you deploy, your *quantity* of contacts get smaller, but as the funnel tapers, the *quality* of these contacts (that is, the likelihood of purchase) becomes greater. As you move toward the close, you work with a well-defined group of highly qualified prospects — the kinds of prospect most worth the time and efforts of your sales team.

The key to the funnel strategy is an escalating series of offers; with each communication, the offer becomes more valuable and more expensive — and, in turn, the prospect's commitment is commensurably greater. Keep in mind that while the cost of each individual offer may increase, the overall expense remains relatively constant because the number of prospects who'll accept the offer gets progressively smaller.

Here's an example of the funnel in action:

1. **Making the first contact through lead generation:**

   The first step, at the mouth of the funnel, is to target potential prospects with a direct response device (see Chapter 4) that helps you identify qualified contacts. Those who respond to your initial offer, be it a white paper, newsletter, or what have you, show at least some interest in your area of business and merit subsequent follow-up. Suppose that you sell business insurance. You open with an attractive direct mail package to influencers in your target industry, offering a white paper on controlling workers' compensation costs to responders. On the reply card, you request information that gives you an idea of how likely the responder's organization will reconsider its workers' comp insurance in the next six months to a year.

2. **Following up with qualified decision makers:**

   If your first step successfully attracted a body of interested prospects, you now have a narrower — and more qualified — pool of potential targets. Now you can escalate your marketing with a more attractive package to higher-level decision makers. In the business insurance example, you should now have a list of companies that are likely to buy insurance soon; your package should go to the decision makers in those organizations, such as the chief financial officer, the chief operations officer, and/or the vice president for human resources. After sending the white papers to all the responders, you develop a dimensional mailing (a package with an appealing item inside) for the decision makers in those organizations that are renewing their workers' comp contracts in the next six months. The package includes a beautiful scarf; the offer is a genuine luxury wool blanket (your theme is coverage) for those executives who participate in a *Webinar* (an online seminar) on controlling workers' compensation costs.

High-level executives are the belles of the ball — they have scads of suitors (salespeople) who want them on their dance cards. Most decision makers are flooded with mail; many rely on secretaries or other designated "gate-keepers" to screen out unwanted solicitations. Frankly, reaching decision makers isn't easy. Nor is it cheap. Despite their per-piece expense, dimensional mail may prove to be the most cost-effective way to reach true decision makers. Few underlings dare to throw away packages, and few people can resist opening a box that looks like it may contain a present. To hold costs down, narrow your universe of prospects down to real contenders by doing some prescreening first. That's why my hypothetical "funnel" process begins with a mailing to influencers — to help the marketer identify a smaller subset of prospect organizations more conducive to buying. (For more on dimensionals, see Chapter 7.)

3. **Continuing to push the sales process ahead:**

   Even as you're moving up the organization, don't neglect the influencers who initially responded to your lead-generation campaign. Keep them in the loop (and your company at the top of their minds) by sustaining contact. For example, you could register your business insurance contacts (with their permission) for an e-newsletter you've developed on insurance issues. At the same time, you move forward with your decision makers. For those who attended your insurance Webinar (snuggled warmly in their blankets), you make your pitch to set up a meeting: You'll give them a custom analysis of their workers' compensation costs (based on the strategic principles you discussed in your Webinar) when they accept an in-person visit from your representatives.

4. **Going for the close to complete the sale:**

   Chances are, the first in-person sales call won't, in itself, close the sale; the contract negotiations alone will absorb a lot of time. But the sales team can identify the important players, once and for all, and develop the strategy for future contact, whether it be regularly scheduled phone calls or a sustained series of communications, including printed matter, invitations to seminars and events, and further in-person calls.

Working closely with the sales team

Long before they invested in marketing, most B2B industries (such as commercial real estate or commercial banking) had, and continue to have, well-established sales teams responsible for generating revenue. In fact, many organizations remain sales-driven — and skeptical about marketing. Because copywriting is associated with marketing, you may be painted with the same skeptical brush. But in order to write effectively (create copy that meets real sales and marketing goals), you need cooperation from the sales team. You can begin to overcome their doubts by understanding their perspective and showing that understanding in your discussions with them.

They work for the same organization, and they share the same goals, so you may think that sales and marketing teams would play happily together. Sadly, that thinking is naïve. Like farmers and ranchers, they glare at each other over fences (often barbed) that set them apart. What's the beef? Many salespeople look at marketing with scorn; they see themselves as having to perform to set quotas — do or die — while marketing people collect salaries without (so they think) any relation to measurable standards. They see revenue as a direct result of sales efforts, not marketing, and they resent allocations to marketing budgets they believe should be added to their own department coffers.

On the other side of the fence, marketers resent the same lack of quantification: When sales are made, it's difficult to trace the contribution made by marketing efforts, such as advertising, lead-generation direct response, and public relations; as a result, the contribution of the marketing team remains uncredited.

Despite this hostility, or perhaps because of it, you need to coordinate major marketing efforts with the sales team. As detailed in Chapter 3, salespeople can be one of your best sources of information about customer behavior and (naturally) the sales process itself. But even more importantly, the most successful programs — as demonstrated in the previous multistep process — *require* close collaboration between sales and marketing; the left hand needs to know what the right hand is doing to coordinate overall strategy and time your tactics, which include the creation and release of materials you write.

Talking the Talk: Connecting to Businesspeople

Take a look at the advertising in business journals, and you frequently witness a sad truth: The same copywriters who know how to connect to consumers with wit and passion get tongue-tied when talking to businesspeople. Too often, the copy reads more like a schoolchild's five-paragraph theme than a sharp, memorable call to action.

What's gone wrong? It could be a number of things, but I think the biggest underlying cause is a failure to understand businesspeople themselves — specifically, the emotions that drive their behaviors and the stakes (the consequences of business decisions) that occupy their minds.

Appealing to a different set of emotions

One of the most pervasive (and incorrect) myths about B2B copywriting is that, as opposed to consumer copy, it should appeal to the intellect, not the emotions. Now let me appeal to *your* intellect and ask you: Is that a reasonable assumption? After all, consumers and businesspeople are often the *same* people, but in different roles. They may have changed their hats, but they haven't changed their hearts.

Yes, it's true that you wouldn't make the same emotional appeals — such as to look younger or be sexier — that you would make to consumers. But the trick isn't to abandon emotions; it's to identify the right ones. Here are some of the most powerful desires and fears that beat in the B2B heart:

✔ **Desire for recognition:** Certainly businesspeople want to make money and want to be successful; you can't go wrong with either appeal. But I believe you can dive deeper and tap the secret desire for heroism — or at least for praise and adulation — that beats in the hearts of millions of cubicle Walter Mittys. All people like to be recognized for their contributions, and within the confines of the corporate environment, where we may spend more time than with our own families, the desire for recognition is one of the few that can be satisfied without breaking significant social taboos. In your copy, you may want to try an approach that has a touch of the daydream about it, an appeal to your audiences' career fantasies. It may look something like this:

Acoustic tiles: *Build your next office with NoiseBlock ceiling tiles, and all you'll hear is the applause.*

✔ **Fear of failure:** Despite the rhetoric trumpeting America's entrepreneurial spirit, many offices are ruled with a political economy in which the punishments for failure far outweigh the rewards for success. In these environments, employees shun risk, and many workers live by the CYA motto, Cover Your Assets (ahem). The flip side of the desire for recognition is fear of failure. I've found that the best voice for a "fear" message is one that's almost brutally frank, even a bit clipped and terse, like this:

IT security: *If you're not using Detecta-Mail, you may share the same fate as spam. As in canned.*

✔ **Desire for stress relief:** A combination of long hours, high expectations, and fickle management eager to slash jobs to cut costs has made many workplaces quite stressful. In B2B marketing, the stress-relief appeal is the equivalent of the "simple and easy" message often found in consumer marketing. Because the appeal is to relief, the copy can be a little less serious and more empathetic and even carry an element of humor. Here's an example:

Inventory management: *With ShelfAgent, aggravation is the only thing in short supply.*

✔ **Fear of exposure:** Many people in the business world suffer from a nagging anxiety that they're not who they say they are, that perhaps they're just faking it. There's nothing wrong with faking it (no one is *born* to be a surgeon or a marketing director, after all), and there's no shame in making it up as you go along: That's real life. But the anxiety exists, nonetheless, and as a consequence, many people suffer a fear of exposure — of being shown up for who they really are, which may not, in their minds, be congruent with the business roles they occupy. In B2B marketing, a message of authenticity, particularly in regard to social status, often appeals as an antidote to people's social anxieties. As a writer, you want to embrace a tone that implies class, status, and exclusivity; you want to make the readers feel that they're part of the "in crowd" you've identified. Here's one way of expressing this message:

Corporate jet services: *C-Suite Air — Tell the world you've arrived.*

Understanding the stakes

The other gigantically incorrect myth about B2B marketing is that its set of products and services is inherently boring and therefore impossible to write about in an interesting way. What could possibly be interesting about industrial salts for rubber formulizations? Who gives a hoot about deductible levels for business liability policies?

The failure here is one of perspective. If you begin with the assumption that things that aren't interesting to you aren't interesting to anyone else, you're doomed. Your job is to discover what's interesting *to your prospects* and to direct your copy to those interests. To the quality control officer on the factory floor, the consistent elasticity of every batch of rubber is a matter of grave concern. His job is at stake, and if you have something to say about salt that affects his living, he wants to know about it. Likewise, if you're the insurance broker pulling together a product liability package for your client, you want to know everything you can about controlling premium costs and managing risks, including deductibles. To write successfully to your B2B audiences, you have to adopt their perspectives.

The most direct way to uncover what's interesting about the product you need to write about, and to find the correct perspective, is to ask one simple question: What's at stake? For every product you're selling, consider the consequences of buying (which is usually a positive thing, such as a reduction in cost or savings of time) and of not buying (which is usually a negative thing, such as lost opportunity or a failure to stay competitive).

For example, the stakes for a rubber manufacturer include control of the processing variables that are affected by salt (which include elasticity, tensile strength, and bin life) and, in turn, all the business issues affected by those variables, which may include manufacturing expenses, brand reputation, and customer satisfaction. Buying the right salt may improve quality control and all the rewards (such as strong customer relationships) that come with it. Not buying the right salt may put your product and your business at risk. With this knowledge, you can promote the benefit of using your high-quality salt: "Because you want your rubber customers to bounce back to you."

If you're beginning to suspect that this whole issue about what's at stake is just another way of talking about benefits, you're absolutely right. But in B2B marketing, where the products and services you sell can be frustratingly technical and/or esoteric, the stakes question can help you understand benefits that may otherwise remain obscure to you.

Promoting Seminars, Webinars, and Other Events

In B2B marketing, you often spend as much time promoting events — such as seminars, online-based seminars called *Webinars,* and conference exhibitions — as you do traditional products and services. Although live events have a role in some consumer marketing (think financial services or retirement planning), they're much more common in B2B marketing. They can fill the contact gaps between the initial lead generation and the final sale. (See the section "Involving many incremental steps in your sale," earlier in this chapter.)

These events run the gamut from live, multimedia spectaculars at attractive destinations (near golf courses, for example) to humble booths in conference or convention exhibit halls. Regardless of scale, the goal is the same: to make one-on-one contact with hot prospects.

Examining the best promotional options

Assuming that your colleagues have put together a whiz-bang event that prospects can't resist, what are your options for promoting it? Most efforts involve some form of direct response marketing targeted to a select list of likely (or highly desirable) prospects. (See Chapter 4 for an overview of direct response.) Your major options include mail and e-mail.

Getting the news out by mail

By mail, your promotion can be as elaborate as a dimensional mail package (a box with a gift, described in Chapter 7), as ordinary as a classic letter package (see Chapter 4), or as simple as a postcard (see Chapter 8).

For the best ratio of price and performance, consider using a self-mailer (see Chapter 8). The self-mailer gives you plenty of room to tell your story, plus the opportunity to run a splashy graphic on the front that complements the excitement of a live event. In general, producing the self-mailer is less expensive than a letter package (envelope plus letter plus brochure plus reply device), so it may give you a lower total cost per registration.

If you're sponsoring a booth at a trade show or conference, you may want to consider using an inexpensive postcard to draw traffic your way. (Most conference organizers are more than willing to rent you their list of show attendees just for this purpose.) Here's a cheap way to add impact to your card: Create a drawing that attendees may enter by bringing the card to your booth. By doing so, you increase the likelihood that they'll hold on to your card and drop by for a visit at the show.

Spreading the word by e-mail

Although response rates to e-mail are traditionally lower than those for regular mail, e-mail can be especially effective for promoting online Webinars. Why? Because the people with the technical sophistication (and comfort level) to participate in an online event also tend to be the prospects most favorably inclined to communicating by e-mail.

When you go the e-mail route, plan on creating an embedded hyperlink that respondents can use to get to your information page/registration form on your Web site. I don't recommend sending reply forms as Microsoft Word or other attachments with your e-mail; many corporate firewalls block your message as part of their security efforts against viruses, worms, and other Internet nasties. (For more on writing copy for e-mails, head to Chapter 9.)

Crafting your event message

Do not promote your event as an opportunity to "learn about" your product or service — or worse, to learn about your business. No one cares. Instead, the event must offer information or insight of intrinsic value to participants. By doing so, you establish your credibility as an expert who can be trusted. In your copy, you want to "package" the event in a way that encourages otherwise busy people to make time to attend. The most popular reasons to participate in events include the following:

- **Figuring out how to solve a problem:** In business, problems come with every territory, and businesspeople are always looking for new ways to solve them. If your event can provide an antidote to a problem, you can position your event as an opportunity for participants to learn ways to overcome their difficulties. For example, you may tell the prospects for a supply chain management service that you have an event that can teach them how to save money on inventory:

    Learn how to use the IT systems you already have to slash inventory expenses.

- **Gaining insight from case studies:** Business professionals are constantly looking over their shoulders to see what the competition is doing — and to perhaps glean ideas for what they should be doing, too. That's why many of the most credible ideas are drawn from real-world experience. You can leverage this authority by emphasizing case studies that will be explored at your event. An event sponsored by a public relations firm may be described like this:

See how Bigco and El Guapo Technologies turned hostile neighbors into community advocates for their businesses.

See Chapter 13 for more on case studies.

✔ **Acquiring new how-to skills:** There's always the appeal of practical skills that people can apply immediately to their jobs or careers. If your event offers some kind of teaching or instruction, tell potential participants how attendance will give them skills or insights they can apply to their own work. A general contractor sponsoring an event on construction management may want to describe the event's value like this:

Discover the six easy ways you can cut construction costs from your next building project.

Whether you take the problem-solving, case-study, or how-to approach, don't give the answers away. If you do, prospects no longer have a reason to attend. Instead, tantalize and tease. Provide enough information to establish the value of your content, but don't deliver the substance of the content itself. Here's what a good tease might look like:

Learn the three-step approach to product development that saved MegamogulEnterprises $2.3 million in R&D costs.

Note that prospects are told that there's a three-step approach to learn about, and they're given an example of its real-life value, but the three steps remain concealed — until they register and attend.

Part V
Looking at Special Copywriting Situations

The 5th Wave   By Rich Tennant

FRANZ KAFKA-COPYWRITER

"Sheets and pillowcases, Franz, we're selling sheets and pillowcases! This is a little dark for sheets and pillowcases. And what's with the cockroach?"

In this part . . .

Welcome to the Island of Misfit Copywriting Issues! This part is the place to find help when you need to write copy that helps raise money and support noble causes. You also find solace and solutions for the inevitable problems that occasionally arise, such as vague criticism or insufficient product information. Finally, for those who do want to become professional copywriters, I offer helpful hints for turning your talent into a business.

Chapter 17

Raising Money, Getting Votes, and Promoting Health and Education

Some people may say that copywriters are just hustlers out to make a buck. That's not true. Sometimes they're just hustlers out to make a difference in the world. The power of persuasion isn't limited to making money through marketing: It can be a powerful tool for helping charities, supporting political candidates, encouraging better health, and directing people to higher levels of education.

In this chapter, I show you a few of the most common noncommercial applications of the skills discussed elsewhere in this book. I discuss many familiar forms — letters, collateral, articles — each with a few new twists appropriate for their special purposes, whether it's raising money for a health clinic or encouraging adults to participate in a continuing education program.

You'll also find that just as the goals are different, the approach is, too. In other chapters, I encourage you to work hard to find great ideas. Now, I want you to dig deep — and speak from the heart. Sure, ideas still matter. But when you want to make that one-to-one connection (and that's what charity, politics, health, and education all come down to), being genuine means much more than being a genius.

If you're out to accomplish something you know is for the good, you have what it takes to succeed. Now I show you how.

Raising Money with Letters

Lots of organizations need to raise money to survive. Some of the more obvious examples include schools, clinics, charities, religious organizations, political causes, and arts or cultural organizations. Many other needy causes are less common but every bit as needy (and worthy of our support): a children's sports program, a local movie theater restoration, or a drive to preserve open space in the community.

Events, bequests management, and direct personal requests are among the many ways to raise money, but I focus on just one: asking for money by mail.

There are two reasons to raise funds by mail: to raise money and to build support. Now the first reason seems obvious, yet in some cases, the cost of raising money by mail (list management, production, and postage) may exceed the revenue collected by the effort. Does that make it a failure? Not necessarily. Big donors don't come out of nowhere; most of the time they're cultivated from the larger pool of small contributors. The mailing campaign is often the first — and best — chance to introduce your organization or cause and to build a base of support. That's why the second reason you raise money by mail is to expand the base from which you cultivate significant contributors.

Almost all fundraising efforts require a method that's direct, personal, and immediate, and in most instances, that means writing a letter. In Chapter 5, I talk about the general parts of a letter, such as the Johnson Box, the body, the close, and the postscript. But in this section, I give you the details on the language and tone of a great fundraising letter — a letter that's passionate and personal, and that encourages readers to see themselves as active participants in your cause.

Appealing to hearts, not heads

Every nonprofit or not-for-profit organization has a core of true believers, often led or represented by the board of trustees. These people love to talk about their organization's purpose, their organization's policies, or their organization's mission — or just plain talk about their organization.

That's all well and good — but not in a fundraising letter. The fundraising letter's goal is not to talk about issues or missions, no matter how noble these may be. Its goal is to raise money, and that means speaking to the heart, not the head.

Here's how you appeal to the heart:

> ✔ **Be personal.** In commercial letters, the author may seem invisible and serve as more of a conduit of information than a personality. But in a fundraising letter, you must give the reader a strong sense of the author, a real person behind the appeal. A good fundraising letter should come from

(or be credited to) someone close to the organization's activities: a doctor, social worker, museum curator, volunteer, director, and so on. If you need to interview someone from the organization for your material, be sure to listen to feelings as well as facts. You want to capture some of the fire of that person's emotional involvement. Write from your (or the attributed author's) personal experience. And, of course, feel free to use "I" and "you."

- **Not compelling:** *Today, more than ever, children need a resource for expanding their horizons. The Walcott Center is dedicated to . . .*

- **More compelling:** *As a third-grade teacher, I know first-hand how much a good book can mean to a young boy or girl. That wide-eyed look when they turn from page to page — there's nothing like it. It's the face of a child who's learning, growing, right in front of you. That's why I want to tell you about the Walcott Center . . .*

✔ **Be urgent and immediate.** Good fundraising letters communicate urgency; they talk about what the needs are *right now.* If the roof's falling in, by all means so say. If you're running low on rent money, tell readers about it. Use deadlines to your advantage and let readers know that the clock is ticking. Say that without treatment, 34 lives are lost every day, or that your historic theater is scheduled for the wrecking ball in just three months unless concerned citizens act now. People respond to immediate threats or goals, not distant objectives.

- **Not compelling:** *By raising $10,000, we can meet our year-end goals and further our mission to . . .*

- **Compelling:** *Frankly, books aren't cheap. And we have a waiting list of 543 children who are eager to read. They're ready, but we're not — yet. We need $10,000 to . . .*

✔ **Be physical and concrete.** Make it real. Don't say, "We need money to meet our goals." Say, "We need $150,000 to lease a van, order syringes, and buy the medications our homeless patients need to survive on the streets." Use concrete details to paint a vivid picture in your readers' minds. Let them see your organization in action.

- **Not compelling:** *Our mission makes literacy a top priority for educators and families . . .*

- **Compelling:** *Every day our volunteers come to schools with boxes of picture books, novels, legends, folk stories, adventures, science experiments, and more. When they see us coming, the children often press their faces to the window and shout, "The Walcott books are here!" To tell you the truth, it can get a little crazy sometimes, but I promise you this: not one child goes empty handed — every one of them gets a brand new book, a book they choose themselves!*

✔ **Be fearless.** Your enthusiasm is one of your greatest assets, so let it shine. If your grammar isn't perfect or you flub one of the fine points of punctuation, no one will give a fig — it just makes you more human. Concentrate on passion, not perfection.

Telling personal stories

Many nonprofits address important issues. But to raise money, don't talk about issues; talk about people. Why? Because one story about one girl in a homeless shelter beats dozens of statistics about thousands of children. The latter may make us think, but the former makes us *feel* — and people give money when they're emotionally moved.

For every given issue, you can probably find some story or anecdote that can bring passion (or compassion) to the fore. Organizations that explicitly help people, such as charities, health clinics, or social services programs, can easily find human interest stories. But even environmental or preservation groups that don't seem overtly people-centered have stories to tell. The key is to find and use a story that links what the organization does to the impact of its work. Here's what you should look for:

- **Drama:** In the classic formula for drama, desire (what you want) plus danger (a threat to what you want) equals drama — and drama is what holds an audience's interest. Suppose that your organization sponsors a veterinary hospital for wild animals. You could focus on the story of one animal rescue that places the readers' sympathy for an injured animal (the desire) against the threat of death (the danger):

  A rock climber gave us a call. She was sure she had seen an eagle at the base of the cliff, running in short bursts as if trying to fly, but unable to get off the ground. By the time we got there, the situation was worse — the eagle lay on its side, barely breathing. Her left wing was broken, and if we hadn't arrived before dark, she probably would have been devoured by coyotes.

- **Sentimental meaning:** Not every story has to be life-or-death to capture an audience's sympathy. Instead, you can appeal to the reader's sentiments, to the emotional meaning that underpins your organization's activities. For example, restoring an old theater may not be as important as feeding the hungry, but that fact doesn't diminish the value of the work. Here, the challenge is to go beyond the bricks-and-mortar issues to focus on what the theater means to its surrounding community:

  The Montgomery Theater is more than an old movie house — beautiful as it may be. It's where our community sought solace in the Great Depression, where they followed the progress of World War II through black-and-white newsreels, where they delighted in the magic of Ginger Rogers and Fred Astaire, Humphrey Bogart and Lauren Bacall. Here, many couples went on their first dates . . . and later brought their entire families for inexpensive entertainment. The Montgomery has been the center of our downtown for decades, and frankly, its destruction would leave a big hole in our town.

The truly great fundraising letter writers go to the source. They visit the clinics, hike the nature trails, talk to the homeless, and meet with the artists and their supporters. Sure, they could get good information through secondhand sources. But the reason they go out to the field is to find the *stories* that make the cause or organization come alive. Whether it's a baby otter returned to the wild or a neighborhood park restored to its former glory, a good story makes an immediate connection with the reader that transcends mission statements or position papers.

How do you find good stories? Get away from your desk and experience the organization in action. Talk to people; more importantly, listen to them. Take notes and get permissions, but whatever you do, be attentive to the impact of your organization's work and mission. Remember, you're looking not only for what the organization means but what that organization means *to someone.*

If you absolutely can't go out in the field, talk to people who have. Ask whether your organization has a file of thank-you letters or expressions of appreciation from people who have benefited from your organization; these may be a good source of stories.

You helped, too! Building a sense of participation

When your letters are successful, they help your organization create long-term relationships with supporters who are willing to commit money, time, and even political or social support over an extended period of time.

To build desirable, high-value relationships, you have to continually remind your readers of the value of their participation. Your donors should never feel that they're mere afterthoughts, people tapped on the shoulder for money after all the decisions have been made and the work has been done. Instead, your letters should continually and explicitly tell readers what their contributions have done and what their future donations will do. In the body of your letter, you want to constantly remind readers how their contributions affect specific actions and accomplishments. Your job is important but not difficult. Tell people where their money goes (or has gone) and be sure to be as explicitly detailed as possible. Don't say that contributions "fought disease," but that they paid for "25,000 measles vaccinations in sub-Saharan Africa." Consider these examples:

- ✔ *Your generous contributions helped us bring life-saving medical services to more than 3,200 children in Rwanda.*

- ✔ *Thanks to your generosity, we were able to design, create, and install four beautiful new stained-glass windows in our Blessed Mother chapel.*

- ✔ *With your support, we can add five new kennels to our animal shelter and hire an additional full-time veterinarian.*

Tying everything together in your letter

After you assemble all the essential elements of your fundraising letter — heart appeal, personal stories, and participation building — you're ready to put your letter together. Figure 17-1 is an example of a sample letter that incorporates the specific requirements. (Chapter 5 has the in-depth, step-by-step guidelines for creating letters in general.)

My staff and I are in the middle of a vicious flu season emergency. Our waiting room is packed full of sick, feverish patients counting on us for help. Can we count on you, too?

Dear Friend of the Archibald Clinic:

I'm writing this letter between patient calls. Though it's only 10:35 in the morning, I've seen 12 people already. Another 32 are outside my door, waiting for me. They have little choice—as the only free clinic in Springfield's most needy neighborhood, we're the place to go when you have no money, no health insurance, and in many cases, no documentation of citizenship.

It's flu season, and by rights I should be seeing the next patient. But frankly, <u>the Archibald Clinic is overwhelmed and we need your help</u>. Fast.

You may know about the flu from the newspapers or TV news. Here at the Clinic, we're living it first hand: babies with 104 degree fevers...seniors struggling to breathe...mothers, sick themselves, struggling to care for their sick children.

Diagnosis and treatment is just the beginning. For many of our patients, adequate care means finding them food, clean water—and all too often, a warm, safe place to sleep.

   <u>There's no way for me to soften this: we're at the end of our rope!</u> The need for medications, tests, staff overtime—even things as basic as tissue paper and bottled water—has almost completely drained our entire year's budget.

We need an emergency infusion of cash just to get through the flu crisis. Please help us. Your contribution of $100, $50, or even $20 would go a long way to helping us meet the demand for basic medical care. A clean bed. And a hot meal.

Thank you so much for your generosity! You've been a source of strength for the Archibald Clinic, and it's a great comfort to know we have your support.

Sincerely,

Alyssa Watson, MD

Alyssa Watson, MD

PS — The flu crisis has pushed the Archibald Clinic to the breaking point. We need staff, medicines, food and more. Please give what you can to help us help those in desperate need.

Figure 17-1:
A fundraising letter with an urgent appeal.

In my sample, the big strategy is urgency — an emergency need (an overwhelming flu season) that requires an immediate infusion of cash. The sample letter supports this sense of urgency and makes an appeal to the readers' hearts in several ways:

- ✔ **It's short.** In order to tell a compelling story, some great fundraising letters are as many as four pages long. But I deliberately keep this one short to communicate urgency, as if it were a bulletin.

- ✔ **It's written from the point of view of a busy doctor.** In fact, she says she's writing the letter between patient calls! She even tells you the time of day and the number of patients waiting for her.

- ✔ **It articulates the value of the clinic.** Why does the clinic matter? Because "we're the place to go when you have no money."

- ✔ **It's ruthlessly concrete.** The doctor doesn't just tell you that people are sick; she describes "104 degree fevers" and "seniors struggling to breathe."

Instead of telling a story about a patient, the letter in Figure 17-1 tells the doctor's story: an urgent cry from the heart, from a busy, committed professional. The Johnson Box that leads the letter opens with the essence of the story: "My staff and I are in the middle of a vicious flu season emergency." Then the first paragraph in the body of the letter picks up the theme, providing further details about this dire situation.

Lastly but not leastly, the sample immediately makes the reader a participant in this story. The Johnson Box ends, "Can we count on you, too?" The conclusion of the letter reminds the reader, "You've been a source of strength," and in the direct request for money, the reasons are explicit: to "meet the demand for basic medical care. A clean bed. And a hot meal."

Vote for Me! Generating Political Support

I live in a modestly-sized town in Massachusetts that faces the same political issues as most small American towns: education, zoning, and property taxes. These issues don't make the nightly news or the *New York Times,* but they're the meat of most people's local political lives. As elections approach, I can be sure to see letters, flyers, and even brochures addressing these issues, touting candidates, and encouraging people to vote.

These written pieces needn't be complicated. In fact, simplicity is a virtue. Most of the suggestions for letters, brochures, and stand-alone pieces such as flyers (Chapters 5, 6, and 15, respectively) still apply. But politics does have a few unique considerations that you need to be aware of.

Identifying and personalizing hot-button issues

The ancient Greeks believed that the key to a successful democracy was the cultivation of educated, well-rounded men (women weren't allowed to vote). Similarly, Enlightenment thinkers such as Thomas Jefferson imagined a voting populace of thoughtful citizens who would balance self-interest and the public good in their considerations.

Spend a half-hour cycling through any assortment of cable news channels, however, and you can clearly see that political discourse isn't quite on the high level earlier theorists may have wished for. In fact, political activity — making votes or contributing money — is often motivated less by thought and more by passion.

Sadly, carefully thought-out policy based on compromise and good sense rarely produces a winner. Inspiring political action means linking your cause or candidate to hot-button issues — issues, ideas, and values that stimulate passion. Just as in marketing, the two sides of the hot-button coin are fear and desire. What is to be feared or desired depends, of course, on your political perspective, but whether you're left, right, or in the middle, chances are, you're moved by these fundamental passions.

- ✓ **Fear issues:** Examples include rising taxes versus declining public services, the threat of public chaos versus restrictions to free expression, and weakening security versus a strengthening police state.

- ✓ **Desire issues:** Examples include decreasing taxes versus improving public services, stronger social order versus greater individual liberties, and laissez-faire economic policies versus interventional economic policies.

So how do you find the hot-button issues you (or your candidate or organization) can build a platform on? Consider these options:

- ✓ **Read the letters to the editor.** Newspapers cover a variety of political topics that may or may not resonate with their readers. The letters-to-the-editors pages, however, can give you an excellent snapshot of the issues that matter — the subjects that inspire people to write. Sure, you find the occasional lone letter on an obscure topic, but when you see specific issues addressed over multiple editions, you know you've found a hot button. Often, these may not be what you expect. For example, you may think that the high school's graduation rate is an important issue, but instead you find that letters protesting fees for team-sport participation outstrip letters about graduation by three to one.

- ✓ **Hang out with the locals.** Find that place where everyone seems to go, whether it's the local coffee shop, hardware store, or hair salon. Then open up your ears and listen. Chances are, you'll hear some local scuttlebutt loaded with hot-button issues.

Sometimes hot-button issues can be a bit abstract, and abstract ideas usually fail to move people to action. But when you transform the abstract into the personal and give the issue a face, you turn up the heat. Medicare funding is an extraordinarily complex subject. But an elderly couple struggling to pay for medications is something that anyone can understand. That's why political ads regarding Medicare almost always include testimonials from seniors.

You've seen this personalization tactic thousands of times in large-scale political campaigns. But that shouldn't prevent you from trying it with local politics. Your goal is to transform the abstract into the personal by communicating how the issue at hand affects real people. Just as you talk about benefits — what your product *does* for your customers — in marketing copy, your political copy should explain your issue's *impact* on voters. Make these impacts visceral. People respond to concrete threats to their family, health, property, pocket books, and future prosperity. Look at these examples:

✔ **Property taxes:**

Abstract: *Without a larger commercial base in Smallville, residents have to bear a disproportionate amount of the tax burden.*

Personal: *Adding more businesses downtown isn't just about giving us more places to shop. For families like yours, it may mean paying a lot less in taxes.*

✔ **Environmental issues:**

Abstract: *Without new land-use regulations, Beaver Pond will suffer continued environmental degradation.*

Personal: *The swans on Beaver Pond will die — unless we take action now.*

✔ **Public services:**

Abstract: *Littleton needs a new firehouse to maintain state-mandated safety regulations.*

Personal: *Last year, fast action by the brave men and women of our fire department saved the Ryan family. But if your house caught on fire, you may not be so lucky.*

What a great guy (or gal): Communicating the candidate's personality

Like many people, I take the observations of most political pundits with a grain of salt. But I recently heard a political scientist say something that made sense: When voters feel overwhelmed by the complexity of the issues, they put greater emphasis on the character of the candidates. Their reasoning? No one can anticipate all the problems or come up with all the answers, but a person of sound character (that is, someone like yourself) is likely to make the right choices.

I advocate promoting the virtues of your candidate, not denigrating the character of your (or your candidate's) opponent. Although negative advertising may work on a national or state level, I suspect that, on a local level, it would be like playing with fire. And besides, effective or not, it's just plain offensive.

By communicating personality, I mean two specific things:

- **Managing the tone of your writing:** To the degree it's possible, the tone of the written pieces should match the personality or style of the candidate. If the candidate is running as an experienced, fiscally responsible, no-nonsense businessperson who can bring accountability to government, the pieces should talk about facts and figures in a straightforward manner: "Here are the issues, and this is what I'm going to do about them." If the candidate is running on a platform of compassion, compromise, and social responsibility, the pieces should reflect more of a person-to-person tone: "I want to help hard-working families like yours get the education and services you need."

- **Listing the candidate's commitments:** The first question I ask myself when I receive a piece from an unfamiliar candidate is "Who is this person?" The piece should give me an answer. In local politics, you need to list the candidate's local commitments and/or involvements, which may include her local business, place of worship and/or role within it, volunteer commitments, activity of charitable boards, and previous political experience.

Take a spin at the spin machine

Spinning isn't just for Beltway wonks and talking heads — you can do it, too! I give you a plain statement of fact. Then you take that fact and state it two entirely different ways. One way will make the fact seem positive, productive, and beneficial; the other will make it seem negative, destructive, and unwelcome.

Take this example of a plain statement of fact: Linden Lane will become a one-way street. If you put a positive spin on it, you may say, "By making Linden Lane a one-way street, we're making our neighborhood safer for children and families." A negative spin may result in something like, "Turning Linden Lane into a one-way street punishes commuters and will create unnecessary traffic burdens on surrounding streets."

Now apply positive and negative spins to the following pieces of information:

- The middle school will integrate special needs and ordinary classrooms.

- A culvert (covered drain) has been proposed for Elbows Creek at the local park.

- Local liquor stores will have extended weekend hours.

- New parking restrictions are in effect on Main Street.

- The mandatory teacher retirement age has been changed from 65 to 68.

Articulating winning positions

You always want to present your candidate's positions in the most favorable light, or to phrase this in less flattering words, you want to spin the issue to your advantage. You apply spin by the way you describe, frame, or articulate a given issue.

Many political positions may be relatively neutral in value — until that issue is cast in a positive or negative light. Perhaps the ballot includes a referendum regarding a tax surcharge to support the reconstruction of a local elementary school. In itself, the issue is just about money and education. But you can frame the issue within contexts that give it entirely different meanings. On the one hand, the referendum may be a way for the town to invest in the future by improving children's educational opportunities and, by doing so, sustaining local property values. On the other hand, the surcharge may be an exercise in fiscal waste that puts unnecessary burdens on taxpayers, especially those on fixed incomes. The difference between the two is a matter of perspective — the "spin" placed on the issue.

To spin an issue to your favor, you define the issue in the terms favorable to your cause (or candidate). Your spin can be positive or negative and may include any number of details, depending on the nature of the issue at hand and your (or your candidate's) stance on the issue. Here are a few examples:

- ✔ **Standardized testing:** A candidate in favor of standardized testing may define the issue "as a way to hold educators accountable for student progress," while an opponent may say, "Standardized testing enforces arbitrary measurements with little bearing on real learning progress."

- ✔ **Police hiring freeze:** A flyer supporting the freeze may say, "The hiring freeze eliminates patronage and helps balance the budget," while the opposition may send out a mailing that says, "The hiring freeze leaves the town with a dangerously insufficient police force."

- ✔ **Zoning restrictions:** Those in favor would say, "Mandatory minimum lot sizes preserve the historic character of the town and its high quality of living," and those opposed might counter with, "Enforcing minimum lot sizes is an elitist tactic to discourage the growth of affordable housing."

Getting to the Heart of Healthcare

The healthcare industry generates an enormous amount of printed material. Some of it (like most of the communications discussed in this book) is intended to sell or market healthcare products or services. But the greater proportion of printed matter is dedicated to explaining medical issues or promoting specific aspects of care. As copywriters, you have to exchange your roles as salespeople for new ones as educators. That means helping people understand the issues and taking care to select the appropriate mediums for your messages.

Helping people understand the issues

One of the biggest contributors to a feeling of helplessness is ignorance — not knowing what's happening. No matter how alarming the situation may be, having greater knowledge means having greater power and more control. By articulating the issues as clearly as you can for your readers, you help people master difficult situations. Here are a few things you should do to ensure that your writing clearly conveys your message:

- ✔ **Know your audience.** The healthcare audience is divided among three different audiences with very different needs:

  - • **Patients/consumers:** These people use or receive the health products or services. They need clear explanations, in layman's terms, that let them know what to expect and how to proceed. For example, they may need to know when to take medications, how to change bandages, and what symptoms to look for. (For more on writing for patients, see Chapter 15.) Because consumers form the largest healthcare constituency, they're the audience for the vast amount of health-related materials you may be asked to write.

  - • **Medical professionals:** These people include physicians, nurses, technicians, and anyone else who provides care to patients. They need precise, technical information that includes both the underlying science behind the issues and the practical guidelines for addressing them appropriately. Write to them as you would other qualified experts — with great attention to technical precision. (See Chapter 15 for information on writing to technical audiences.)

  - • **Administrators and managers:** These folks are the behind-the-scenes professionals who handle the financial, insurance, and infrastructure issues that make the delivery of modern medical services possible. They need current information on management and managed care issues that are consistent with the latest regulatory guidelines and fiscal best practices. Although healthcare is their field, their skills and areas of interest are more related to business, management, and finances. Write to them as you would other businesspeople. (See Chapter 16.)

- ✔ **Explain your terms.** Healthcare providers and administrators have a good grasp of the terminology relevant to their professions, but patients need definitions of unfamiliar language. Don't exclude the scientific terms — patients may need them to communicate with their caregivers or to look for more information on their own. But do include the layman's language, perhaps in parentheses, with the medical terms. For example:

The most common symptoms of myocardial infarction (heart attack) include . . .

✔ **Anticipate needs.** Patients may have hundreds of questions, but they almost always boil down to three major concerns:

- **What's happening to me?** For a medical condition or diagnosis, describe what it is, what may have caused it, and the most common symptoms. For a procedure, provide a thorough description of the treatment and why it's performed or used.

- **What can I expect?** The physician is responsible for providing a prognosis (an assessment of likely future outcomes), but you can tell the reader what usually happens during an illness or course of treatment.

- **What do I need to do?** Patients need information that tells them what to do to prepare for treatments, surgery, or medication; what to do or not to do during the therapy or while on medication; and finally, what to do after a treatment or surgery. Telling patients which symptoms can be safely ignored and which require the attention of a medical professional is also helpful.

Choosing mediums for messages

Healthcare messages fall into one of two broad categories: those intended for individuals, such as patients and consumers, and messages intended for entire communities or constituencies.

Messages for individuals

Individual messaging usually focuses on specific diagnoses, treatments, or therapies, and it incorporates all the considerations addressed in the preceding section. The most common mediums, or formats, for individuals include

✔ **Single-sheet handouts** that briefly list the key points or items of information a patient must know. This is an excellent choice for describing simple procedures, explaining follow-up treatment, or reminding patients what to do after therapy or during a course of medication.

✔ **Brochures or pamphlets** that offer more in-depth information, often with illustrations, for more complex issues, treatments, or diagnoses.

Although these formats are effective, they're most easily distributed one-to-one in a hospital, clinic, or physician's office. (See Chapter 15 for more details on these formats.) For reaching a large group of people, say a hospital's local community, you want to turn to something with more reach, such as a Web site, newsletter, or article.

Messages for communities

Articles can be an excellent way of providing up-to-date information on specific health topics, such as sports injuries or osteoporosis, or broader public health concerns, such as sexually transmitted diseases or exposure to environmental toxins. (For more information on writing articles, turn to Chapter 13.)

Here are three common ways of distributing articles:

- ✔ **On the provider's Web site:** Hospitals, physicians' groups, and other health organizations can dedicate a portion of their Web site to topical articles. As you produce new articles, you can archive the older ones in an online library that visitors can access.

- ✔ **Through newsletters:** Many hospitals and health maintenance organiza-tion (HMOs) encourage patient loyalty to their services through electronic or print newsletters. In fact, a cottage industry of newsletter publishers has arisen that provides newsletter templates — complete or with room for custom content — for healthcare providers. These newsletters may be vehicles for your health articles.

- ✔ **In local newspapers:** I think the most productive way to spread impor-tant health information is through a collaboration with the editor of a local paper. It's a win-win situation: The paper needs quality content on a regular basis, and you need a medium for your articles. Contact the editor and ask whether she's interested in a series of articles printed on a regular basis on a number of health topics agreed upon by both parties. These articles may be assigned to one writer in the organization, or they can be distributed among many people in the organization.

The idea is to have the articles written by physicians (or comparable pro-fessionals) or written by physicians in collaboration with a ghostwriter. In this way, the articles are reinforced with the authority and expertise of a professional — and it's a great way for a health organization to introduce its caregivers to the community.

Back to School: Communicating to Students and Prospective Students

Marketing publications for higher education — colleges and universities offering undergraduate, graduate, and postgraduate certificate programs — occupy an unusual gray area. On the one hand, recruiting students means selling your school; on the other, you must maintain a standard of integrity that doesn't undermine your institution's reputation (or make the accrediting authorities knock at your door). Always balance your need to sell with a requirement to inform.

I cover the mediums for communicating to students and prospective students elsewhere in this book: letters (Chapter 5), collateral (Chapter 15), Web sites (Chapter 14), and e-mail (Chapter 9). But to balance salesmanship with educational responsibility, you may want to consider a few specific requirements in this area: the delivery of information in anticipation of students' needs, the creation of a vision that distinguishes your school from other similar schools, and the ability to articulate not only your program but also the kind of person your program molds or shapes. This kind of knowledge both informs your writing so that it can be more precisely targeted to the right audience and helps you (and other members of the marketing/recruiting team) generate ideas for content.

Anticipating needs

Think of this section as the nuts-and-bolts department: all the stuff that a prospect has to know when evaluating schools or information that a student needs to know to get through school. On the Web site, in course catalogs, or in recruiting brochures sent to prospective students, you need to include some fundamental information for your audience:

- **Admissions requirements:** What does a person need to be a candidate for your school? This may include diplomas or degrees, life experience, a portfolio review, auditions, letters of recommendation, and admission tests. This is not an opportunity for displaying your exquisite prose style. Just present the facts bluntly, and consider using bullets for information that can be communicated as a list (like course prerequisites).

- **Format/schedule:** How is the education delivered? Although many schools still run with a traditional two-semesters-per-year format, many schools offer other options, such as online coursework via the Web, three-year or five-year programs, independent study, evening and/or weekend classes, and so on. Prospects need to know whether your school requires a full-time or part-time commitment and whether they can hold down a job while attending your school. Again, clarity is king. At this stage, the last thing prospective students need is confusion (they probably already have their fill of it), so take extra pains to articulate the format as simply as possible.

- **Living/lifestyle:** What's campus life like? Students want to know about dormitories versus off-campus housing; a rural versus an urban campus environment; access to sports, arts, and other cultural/social amenities; whether the prevailing culture is progressive/exploratory or traditional/studious; and so on. Here, you *finally* have an opportunity to shine. You're not writing lyric verse, but you do want to embed your descriptions with enthusiasm. You want to communicate the excitement of campus life — some of its vivacity and/or diversity.

- **Student aid options:** How will students pay for their education? Simply state the possibilities. Be sure to explain options for grants, loans, work-study, and other student loan options.

Developing a vision

In the commercial world, establishing an idea for your organization that sets it apart from its competitors is called *positioning*. In education, people prefer to speak of a school's *vision:* a mission, or cluster of important traits, that distinguishes one school from another. Whatever it's called, the vision is frequently written for inclusion in the school's Web site, course catalogs, and recruiting materials (such as brochures or program pamphlets).

Several different factors can help define a school. Too often, a school intones its vision as if it were a modern-day Moses descending Mount Sinai with the Ten Commandments. Yes, some formal dignity may be required, but temper your tone with regard for your audience. Students understand that they have to attend lectures, but otherwise, they don't want to be lectured to. Speak simply, and let the substance of your vision present itself through the facts you describe.

These are a few of the factors most frequently addressed in a school's vision message:

- ✔ **Commitment to research:** Many schools, particularly those with extensive graduate programs, emphasize their research commitments and their ability to attract grants.

- ✔ **Commitment to undergraduate education:** Other schools prefer to emphasize their commitment to undergraduate education, focusing on their low faculty-student ratios and the opportunities for mentorship and close academic guidance. (This is particularly common, for example, with Catholic schools.)

- ✔ **Special constituencies:** Some schools, such as women's colleges or traditionally African-American schools, focus on particular student bodies. They promote the advantages of learning among students who share some fundamental commonality.

- ✔ **Alternative formats:** In some cases, the way education is delivered is in itself a defining characteristic. Things such as internship requirements, mandatory study abroad, or independent research projects can form the core of your school's vision.

- ✔ **Elite status:** Finally, some schools, such as those in the Ivy League, are so highly esteemed that their prestige is their defining quality.

Talking about lives, not subject areas

Of all the things you may buy, consume, or use, education is unique because it makes a special promise: transformation. At the root of any desire to get an education is the expectation that, by the time you graduate, you're somehow changed from the person you are into the person you want to be, whether that's a doctor, businessperson, social worker, teacher, or artist.

Instead of focusing your communications on degrees and the subject areas approached within them, concentrate on lives — the kind of persons your school creates. This isn't merely an issue of occupations; it includes values, ethics, and the sense of personal mission and what people want to accomplish within their lifetimes. In this way, you can reach beyond the practical considerations within the decision-making process to speak to its underlying core: a person's dreams.

Here are a few ways to make your communications more personal:

✔ **Speak to values.** In education communications, two of the most important words you can use are "We believe." Even the most practical diploma-chaser believes in something, even if it's simply the economic value of his degree. Tell students what your school stands for so that they can judge whether or not they share your school's values. After all, in a nation crowded with four-year liberal arts schools, your values may be your greatest distinction. If your education program emphasizes inclusive classrooms and a commitment to diversity, say so. Or maybe your school encourages an entrepreneurial spirit through self-initiated projects or creative approaches to familiar problems. Put your school's or program's values front and center.

✔ **Connect curriculums to ambitions.** Describing courses, projects, or research requirements isn't enough; you want to *show* how they help students reach their goals. Instead of writing mere descriptions, write stories with the prospective student as the potential hero. Tell readers how your field-work assignments prepare them for real-world engineering projects, how your internships form networking opportunities, or how your course work sharpens their writing, critical-thinking, and decision-making skills. In short, show them how your school plays a practical role in the pursuit of their ambitions.

✔ **Try endorsements and case studies.** Selecting a school can be intimidating. An endorsement — in an ad or within collateral (see Chapter 15) — shows how your school welcomes and encourages people like the prospective students themselves. Case studies take the idea one step further by actually describing in some detail the transformation story — how a person from one kind of background acted on her ambition and was able to move forward through your school or program. (For information on how to write a case study, see Chapter 13.)

Chapter 18

Solving Problems When Good Copy Goes Wrong

. . . .

In This Chapter

▶ Preventing problems before they begin

▶ Dealing with criticism tactfully

▶ Finding solutions to specific copy problems

. . . .

*I*t's the age-old story: You raise your copy in a good home, send it to the finest schools, teach it right from wrong, and give it every opportunity money can buy. And what's your reward? There's your copy, hanging outside the local drugstore with a cigarette dangling from its mouth, making vague offers, forming ambiguous messages, completely ignoring benefits. For this you labored over keyboards? Oh, my aching carpal tunnel syndrome!

Despite your best efforts, your copy can go very wrong. And no matter how good you are — or how diligent your efforts — you're going to run into rogue copy now and again. In this chapter, I reveal the most common causes of copy delinquency and show you preventive measures you can take to forestall (or at least minimize) problems.

I recognize, however, that many of you who have turned to this chapter are smack-dab in the middle of a crisis; it's way too late for prevention, and you need answers, now. For you, I present a variety of common crises and some ideas for fixing problems — or at least doing the best you can under trying circumstances. In case of emergency, turn to "Bandaging the Wound: First Aid for Hurting Writers" and "Fixing Your Copy in Special Situations," later in this chapter.

Putting Processes in Place to Prevent Problems

As in health, so in copywriting: Prevention is the best medicine. By putting a few processes in place before the writing begins, you go a long way to either preventing problems from happening or minimizing their impact when they do. Although many little things can be done, most fall within four broad areas: establishing the team, defining the goals, creating the message, and setting a schedule.

Establishing the team

Although writing itself may be a lonesome business, the process that determines your goals and then evaluates your work can involve any number of people — and may make you wish for an isolated booth on an outer planet.

You know the old saying about too many chefs spoiling the broth? Well, the same thing applies to copy, especially when too many of the chefs don't understand the menu, don't know the recipe, and can't distinguish a beef consommé from a lobster bisque. Try your best to limit the team (the people with the power to review your work) to a handful of players who know the overall strategy, understand the tactic at hand and its purpose, and are capable of submitting feedback that's congruent with the organization's previously defined expectations and messaging. If you're the owner/operator of your own business, you need not bother with anyone else.

Without a defined team, anyone from the inventory manager to the doorman may review your copy, sometimes recklessly. Instead of helpful criticism, you may receive ignorant feedback that either delays progress or, even worse, leads you down paths that are far astray from the project's original goals.

Defining the goals

Many marketing campaigns begin with the vague recognition that the organization must do something about getting its message out or increasing sales. Although the clarion call to "do something" is a good beginning, it's a terrible conclusion. To succeed, your vague desire must be transformed into a precise plan that answers three crucial questions: What do you want? How will you achieve what you want? How will you measure success?

Setting great expectations

First things first: What do you want from your marketing (and therefore your copywriting) efforts? Do you want more name recognition? A 15 percent increase in qualified leads? More productive community relations? Fewer delinquent accounts? A 10 percent average increase in sales per order?

You can't proceed without clear answers that define your expectations. After (and only after) you know what you want, you can match your goals to the tactics most likely to fulfill them. Although it may be impossible to establish exact targets (there's no way to guarantee a response rate, for example), it's important that you specify your ambitions as precisely as possible. You can't navigate your copy if you don't have a firm destination in mind.

Selecting the right tactics

When you know what you want, how will you get it? By the application of tactics — more specifically, by the accomplishment of tactics appropriate for your needs. If you want community support for a hospital expansion, for example, you may start by looking at public relations (PR) efforts. Conversely, if you need to generate leads for your company's in-house sales team, you may take a look at targeted direct response techniques.

You can get a better grip on your options by reading Chapter 1, a handy overview of strategies, tactics, and marketing purposes — and a rough directory that can guide you to deeper information throughout this book.

Be a marketing matchmaker, because matchmaking is one of the keys to sound strategic marketing. Remember that all marketing tactics, from humble postcard mailings to elaborate PR events, have their strengths and weaknesses. You can optimize your chances for success (and minimize the potential for disaster) by carefully selecting tactics suitable for your expectations and goals.

Deciding on clear benchmarks

After you've completed a project, how will you know whether it's successful? Or whether it has been worth your time and money? Or whether you can improve it? You won't — unless you establish *benchmarks,* real numbers (or objectives) against which you can compare your actual results.

Benchmarks may be drawn from previous experience, from your insights into your competitors' experiences, or from your understanding of current trends. Regardless of source, they should always be tied to something that matters to your organization. If what really matters is hard sales, then measure sales results, not what an opinion poll reveals about the popularity (or lack thereof) of the company logo's colors. (For more on measuring results, see Chapter 4).

Many marketers fear benchmarks because market conditions tend to be fluid, customers unpredictable, and some results, such as awareness or education, difficult to measure. True enough, and for those reasons, you may have to set your benchmarks within a range of numbers or use "soft" targets (such as favorable press exposure) in order to be fair. Despite these qualifications, however, I still argue for benchmarks; without them, marketing tactics are conducted for their own sake (which is a waste of time, money, and talent) instead of for their meaningful contribution to the organization's goals (which is what you should all want).

Creating the right message

For any given company and any given product, you can probably think of dozens of legitimate (and many more illegitimate) things to say about them regarding benefits, price, value, features, brand identity, positioning, and so on. But to craft an effective piece of copy, you must whittle all those many possibilities down to one key message, with, perhaps, a small cluster of sub-ordinate messages.

The need to focus on one message is yet another reason to control the size and scope of the team. As team membership increases, so too do the number of competing agendas and the messages each agenda demands. Ultimately, your organization must choose one agenda with one message.

Keep in mind that all copy contains two different, yet complementary, layers of messaging:

- ✔ **Overall identity:** Call it branding, positioning, identity, or simply "this is my business and this is what it does," all organizations have a message about themselves that remains the same in all their communications, regardless of format, offer, or tactic. The most obvious expressions of this identity are the logo (the graphic that labels the company) and the tag line (the little strip of copy that often follows the company's name). As a copywriter, you must be sure that your work remains consistent with the overall identity — don't write playful, elbow-in-the-ribs copy for the solemn manufacturer of funeral monuments, for example. (See Chapter 10 for more on branding.)

- ✔ **Project message:** The second layer is the message unique to the project at hand — what your ad, mail, e-mail, brochure, or Web site is all about. This may be, among other things, about your offer, an important benefit, or a new feature you want to tout. Here, your job is to maintain focus. Be sure that one and only one message shines and that other competing messages don't cloud that message. For many businesses without vast investments in brand advertising, the project message dominates. Therefore, collecting appropriate information about the project at hand — the product or service featured in your project — is more important than gathering messaging about brand.

In agencies or in organizations with sizable marketing departments, all these issues about messaging are committed to paper in the form of creative briefs or copy input documents. On the surface, these documents seem to create an extra layer of paperwork; in real life, however, they save time and money. After these documents are approved, they form a foundation that allows you — and every other member of the team — to productively move forward with a common understanding of goals and messages.

If your organization doesn't produce these kinds of documents, consider writing a brief memo that states the key message and lists the subordinate points beneath it. Then ask for approval (or corrections) from the applicable powers that be (boss, manager, owner, creative director, and so on) before you proceed with your work. Believe me, the small amount of time you put in upfront will save you tons of aggravation later. With this document approved, no one can claim that she didn't know what you were doing or why.

Setting a schedule

It may not be sexy, but a schedule sure is desirable. First of all, it gives you a way to control your time and track your progress. Better yet, it provides an objective reality check that encourages cooperation from all the participating parties and helps everyone sing from the same page.

Although the exact contents of a schedule vary from project to project (some, like a Web site, require considerable allowances for design and technical work, while others, such as press releases, are primarily about managing the writing time), they should all account for the following:

- ✔ **Input:** This is the date by which everyone submits everything you need, from product specifications to messaging guidelines, so that you can start writing.

- ✔ **Deadline for the first draft:** Ask not for whom the bell tolls. The deadline is the date you submit your first draft for review and/or approval.

- ✔ **Review deadline:** Funny thing: The very people who stand over your shoulder waiting for you to finish your draft will then sit on your copy for days or weeks unless they're held accountable to a deadline, too. By the review deadline, they should have all their comments back to you.

- ✔ **Final draft:** The number of rounds of revisions varies with the complexity of the project, but at some point (especially when printing or studio time has been scheduled), the final round has to be written, approved, and released on its merry way. This deadline is also known as the *drop-dead date*.

Bandaging the Wound: First Aid for Hurting Writers

Sometimes you're unable to take preventive measures. Or the preventive measures don't work as well as you had hoped. Or malevolent forces in your organization are so great that they overcome both reason and sound, preparatory work. Whatever the cause, something's gone wrong, and now you're feeling the full weight of the consequences: Ouch, that hurts. I want to relieve a few major emotional, social, and political pains in this section.

Taking a breather and buying some time

Under most circumstances, criticism and correction are a natural part of the writing process, especially when you collaborate as part of a team. Your ability to respond appropriately to feedback is an essential part of your professional responsibilities. But criticism sometimes crosses the line from constructive commentary to destructive assault. Sometimes, your copy will be returned to you slathered in hostile red ink — in fact, the marked-up document may have more corrections (and comments to those corrections) than original copy.

You can tell yourself that the criticism is just business and it's nothing personal, but you're still human, and your personality (and the emotions that go with it) doesn't punch out when you punch in.

There's no point in denying your emotions — you're going to feel what you feel, regardless. But whatever you do, *don't act from them!* Hurt puts you on the defensive; anger, on the attack. Neither feeling puts you in a position of strength, which can come only when you're able to think clearly and plan your response.

When you're overcome with emotion, buy some time. Get some coffee, go for a walk, and give yourself a chance to decompress and let your intellect kick in. If you have to, claim a dental appointment or an emergency client meeting to give you the cover you need to get out of the office. Create a breather to let your passions run their course and to give yourself time to think.

Receiving criticism and requesting better feedback

When I say that you have a right to ask for "better feedback," I don't mean asking your critics to upgrade their judgment from "Yuck!" to "Yowzah!" I mean that you have a right, even a professional duty, to insist upon criticism that's actionable. Such feedback gives you a clear understanding of what the critic (client, employer, or colleague) wants and what needs to be done next to bring the work closer to what's desired.

Just as there are differences in the quality of writing, there are important distinctions between good and bad criticism.

Recognizing good criticism

Good criticism gives you specific feedback, consistent with predetermined strategy and goals, that makes your next steps crystal clear. It looks like this:

- ✔ **It's objective.** The focus is neither on you, the writer, nor on the critic's feelings, but on the text at hand:

  - *This "convenience" message is off-brand. Talk about value, instead.*

  - *Change "portal" to "Web site" — that's what our customers call it.*

- ✔ **It's specific.** Good criticism isn't ambiguous; it specifically identifies what the reader wants changed, edited, or modified:

  - *Focus the headline on saving time and make it shorter.*

  - *Customers hate making all these clicks on our Web site. Have them call our 800 number for service.*

- ✔ **It's consistent.** The comments are both consistent among themselves and with previously agreed-upon objectives, goals, and strategies. Note these comments, both in the same paragraph:

  - *Our target demographic tends to be more serious — this is funny, but inappropriate.*

  - *Remember our audience. They might think you're being frivolous.*

Handling bad criticism

Bad criticism expresses its opinions in ways that make it impossible, or very difficult, to improve the copy under consideration. It usually involves one or more of the following characteristics:

- ✔ **It's personal.** Helpful criticism stays focused upon and directs its comments to the text at hand. Personal criticism either assaults the writer personally or expresses the critic's feelings without revealing the underlying causes behind the feelings:

  - *You're way off message here! What were you thinking???*

  - *I'm not comfortable with this sentence. Please change it.*

✔ **It's vague.** Bad criticism is frequently ambiguous, open to many (possibly contradictory) interpretations. Without specificity, you can't possibly make the appropriate changes:

- *Make this headline punchier!* (What does "punchier" mean? Shorter? More aggressive? More benefit focused? More offer focused?)

- *Can we make this more customer-friendly?* (In what way? Easier ordering options? More casual language? Less technical talk?)

✔ **It's self-contradictory.** Perhaps the worst offender is criticism that asks you to go in two opposite directions — at the same time. For example, note these comments, two sentences apart in the same paragraph:

- *Sounds jokey; make this more serious.*

- *Lighten up! You're going to scare our customers.*

You don't want to be defensive or appear defensive when you receive bad criticism. That's why I recommend a three-step approach (in person if possible; by phone or in writing if absolutely necessary) that will help you get better input while making you look like a winner, not a whiner:

1. **Acknowledge their criticism.**

   Don't begin by showing your critics where they're wrong. Instead, open the conversation on an empathetic, collegial note by acknowledging that there's a problem (even if you think — to yourself — that it's not with the copy, but with their understanding of the copy): "I see from your comments that there's a problem with the headline; let's talk about it."

2. **Express your willingness to make changes.**

   Even if you think the copy is excellent as it is, don't say so just yet. First, reassure your critic by saying that you are, indeed, open to criticism and willing to make changes: "I'm looking for your help because I want this to come out right."

3. **Ask for clarification.**

   Now that you've demonstrated your ability to be (as they say in cubicle land) a team player, you're in a position to make requests for clarification: "I see that you think the headline should be punchier. Do you want it to be shorter? Or are you thinking of a different lead benefit? Would you like me to push the offer upfront?"

In most cases, most of the time, this approach gets you what you want: clear direction. Even if you think that your copy is sound as is, this tactic helps you lay a foundation of trust that makes it easier for you to present your case.

Knowing when to push and when to give

Not surprisingly, you're not always going to agree with the criticism you get. When that happens, instead of requesting clarification, you'll really want to stand up for the copy you've written.

If you think you've done good work and you want to stand behind it, I offer two major suggestions: Be prepared to explain why and choose your battles.

Explaining why your work should stand

Here's where all that preparation — in the form of strategies, creative briefs, and other such documents — really pays off. Instead of defending your work on subjective grounds, you can link it to objectives and ideas that have already been approved. You can explain why your copy works by connecting it to one or more of the following:

- ✔ A brand identity that is already in effect

- ✔ A benefit (or benefits) that have been identified as important

- ✔ An understanding of the customer or prospects that your organization has defined

- ✔ An offer you've agreed to promote

- ✔ Other points and issues that have been established as critical to the success of the project

Choosing your battles

Right or wrong, you can't expect to win every point. In fact, if you push back on every comment or suggestion, you lose credibility. Your colleagues will regard you as a prima donna (and, in this case, they may be right). Regardless of your critics' behavior, you should always remain calm and professional. A proper demeanor helps you carry your points and helps prevent any hurt feelings that may cause lasting damage to your relationships with colleagues.

Choose your battles carefully. Stand up for the things you really think are important — the issues (such as offers, benefits, and brand messaging) that have a real impact on the effectiveness of your work. For those things you don't entirely agree with but are less significant, consider them as necessary sacrifices and be willing to let them go. By demonstrating your willingness to bend, you build credibility with your colleagues (or clients or employers) and are more likely to win your points when they really count.

Fixing Your Copy in Special Situations

It's time to roll up your sleeves (or wipe the nervous sweat from your brow) and dig deep into specific problems. If you're in a hurry, simply scan the following headings to find the topic that applies to your problem (and with luck you may find a useful answer underneath it). If you have more time, reading this entire section may give you some ideas for pre-emptive action to prevent problems before they arise.

You don't have enough prospect information

Your understanding of your prospects' fears and desires puts all the facts at your disposal — benefits and features — into a meaningful context. It enables you to tell your audience *why* your product or service is important, and it helps you create an empathetic voice. But if you don't know *who* your prospects are, you won't know *how* to speak to them.

For starters, turn to Chapter 3. There, you find tips for talking to three groups that can give you prospect insights: customers, salespeople, and service representatives.

But suppose that you can't find these people or you haven't the time to track them down? What next? Here are a couple ideas:

- **Look at your competitors' material.** You don't want to lift their copy or concepts, but you can gather clues about your market from your competitors' ads, mail, Web sites, and other communications. Look for

  - **Ad placements:** If your competitors are placing print or broadcasting advertising, *where* are they making the placements? Are they concentrating in certain geographic regions? If they're buying radio time, are they targeting rock 'n' rollers or easy listeners? Are they advertising in upscale magazines or supermarket tabloids? Their placements may give you an idea of the kind of prospects — by region, class, interests, and income — you may want to target.

  - **Appeals:** What kind of appeals are your competitors making? Is it to luxury, discount values, or something in between? The kind of appeals being made can give you an idea of your prospects' social status, values, and interests.

  - **Overall look and feel:** What's the gestalt of your competitors' marketing materials? Do they suggest the top shelf or the bargain basement? Are they fun and frivolous or solemn and serious? Again, these may be clues to your prospects' attitudes and beliefs.

✔ **Create an imaginary customer.** Sometimes you just have to work backward from the product and ask, "Who would buy this?" Then use your answer as the foundation for creating an imaginary, composite customer and coming up with an appropriate copy tone to match. I once had to write a piece about a doll that was — get ready for this — half frog, half angel. Yep, a green toad with wings, a white robe, and a gold halo. Stumped, I had to ask myself, "Who would buy such a thing?" Well, some people do collect frog stuff, and some people do collect angel stuff, so maybe there's an intersection of people who buy both. Their tastes may not be sophisticated (they probably don't have Jim Dine prints on the wall or pre-Columbian pottery on the mantel), but they like things that are cute, cuddly, and a bit whimsical. Based on this profile, I stressed the frog/angel collectible angle in a tone that was a bit humorous (but not condescending) to play up the fun of the item.

You don't have enough product information

It seems like a sci-fi movie from the '50s: "The Pluto Product — It came from the skies and landed in your lap. Now you have to write about it!" Unfortunately, this situation is sometimes too close to real life. Occasionally, you just don't have enough information to write intelligently about the product at hand. Here are a few things you can do:

✔ **Corner a salesperson.** Do an end-run around the product people (or the marketing people), contact a salesperson, and ask, "What is this and how do you sell it?" The second part of the question is important because it forces the salesperson to identify the product qualities (features and benefits) that really matter — and that you should write about.

✔ **Focus on the product benefit.** Maybe you have absolutely no idea how a product works, but you know what it does for the customer. When you don't have a lot of product information, resign yourself to being vague on the details. Instead, play up the benefit, be it convenience, flavor, speed, and so on. If you know, for example, only that the ChickQuick bakes chicken in a flash, talk about all the virtues of delicious baked chicken and how getting it so quickly is great.

✔ **Focus on the customer.** What if you don't know how a product works and haven't even seen a picture of it? In the case of your product, the ChickQuick, you think it may bake chicken in a flash, but you're not even sure of that. So focus on the customers and make them the stars. Create a story that puts the prospect in the center of the action, and feel free to use "you" a lot. For example: "You've worked hard all day, and your family is hungry. Don't worry — get ChickQuick! With ChickQuick, you can prepare a delicious baked chicken in no time at all. Soon, the bird is on the table — and you're the hero of the roost!"

Your product is similar to other products

Uh-oh. All the marketing books tell you that you have to identify your unique selling proposition and find the special position your product (and only your product) can occupy. But gosh darn it, truth be told, your product is pretty much just like your competitors' products. What are you going to do (other than sob quietly by the coffee machine)?

Once again I tip my hat to the late David Ogilvy for this advice: When you can't talk about *difference*, make your talk more *memorable*. In a field of competing products with the same (or very similar) benefits and features, the company that can describe those benefits and features in the most compelling, urgent, and unforgettable way wins. Use the richest, most descriptive language in your arsenal. If your product has a sensual feature, such as a flavor, make it the most delicious, sensual flavor possible. If your product is useful (like a tool), describe it as a handy helper no one should live without.

Your product or service isn't very good

Double uh-oh. Your product is not just similar to its competitors; it's not even as good. What now?

Your job is to sell, not to judge. Just because *you* think the product is weak doesn't mean that many potential customers won't find the product satisfactory or better. Be a pro: Don't lie, exaggerate, or conceal necessary information, but do emphasize whatever favorable qualities the product has to the very best of your abilities. Make your strongest case for the product and then let the prospects be the judge.

You have a weak offer

Despite your efforts at persuasion, your marketing team has decided that the offer will be a non-offer: an opportunity to request further information.

When this happens (and it does), draw attention away from the non-offer and hammer away at — you guessed it — the primary benefit. Make it the hero, trumpet it in the headline, and cast spells about it in the body copy. Describe the benefit in detail to demonstrate its value to the prospect. If the benefit is compelling enough, it will attract interest.

Your deadline is insane

Your deadline is insane, and you're reading this book? Get back to work! (Just kidding.) Here's what you can do:

- ✔ **Concentrate on the headline and subheads.** When time is in short supply, spend it on what's most important: the headlines and subheads most likely to be read. Get these in shape (see Chapter 2) and then do your best to fudge the body copy in whatever time is left.

- ✔ **Steal from yourself.** If you're really, really pressed for time, see whether you can recycle your copy from previous projects (for the same organization, of course). Keep the body copy and then freshen up the piece by tweaking the headlines and subheads.

You're out of ideas

It happens. Your mind goes blank, and before you know it, you've spent 45 minutes counting the little patterns in the ceiling tiles. In the interim, the magic elves haven't arrived to finish (or even start) your copy. Try the following:

- ✔ **Read Chapter 22.** This is where I put ten of my best ideas for getting you unstuck.

- ✔ **Think stupid.** Sometimes, you just may be trying too hard to think of something brilliant. Run with the most obvious "stupid" idea you can think of and then walk away for a little while. When you return, you can judge its merits; chances are, it'll work out fine.

Chapter 19

So You Want to Be a Copywriter

I wrote the other chapters of this book on the assumption that you *don't* want to be a copywriter — you just happen to have responsibilities that require, among other things, that you write copy. This chapter is the exception: For the next few pages, I address copywriting not as a task, but as a career.

Ah, the copywriting career! The trips to Monte Carlo; the endless nights of champagne and laughter; men in crisp, black tuxedoes and women in low-cut, sequined gowns; giddy rides in chauffeured limousines that greet the Manhattan sunrise — these are the fantasies that absorb copywriters when they should be meeting their deadlines.

I'm sure you aren't shocked to learn that the copywriting life isn't very glamorous (though it can be a lot of fun). But you may be surprised that writing itself is just one part, and perhaps even a smaller part, of the overall career. Much of it is about talking (and asking questions). Even more of it is about listening. And all of it is about diplomacy and social grace: Your talent may make you a fine writer, but your people skills, more than anything else, determine the quality of your career.

For those of you who want to make a living as a copywriter or just have a morbid curiosity about the lives of copywriters, read on and get the inside, behind-the-scenes look at the world where words and commerce collide.

Considering Your Career Options

In many ways, the context of your career shapes its content. The options that are open to copywriters offer very different kinds of experiences, each with its own pros and cons — and with different career trajectories. I review the three major paths in the following sections — writing directly for businesses, writing for agencies, and independent freelancing — but keep in mind that their boundaries are porous. You can (and many writers do) move back and forth among them. Read on to see which career option appeals most to you.

Getting employed on the client side

In agency lingo — and agencies set the tone for describing marketing functions — working as an employee of a business or organization (one that may hire an agency at some point) is called working "on the client side." As a copywriter, you work as part of a marketing department that may include a marketing director, a graphic designer, a Web designer/electronic media expert, and, depending on how that company is structured, perhaps a public relations professional as well.

Mapping the career trajectory

Many companies that hire copywriters are betwixt and between: They're not large enough (or don't produce a volume of marketing material) to justify the expense of an agency, yet they're too big to rely on one marketing professional, with the assistance of freelancers, to produce their work.

These organizations typically begin with one marketing person who serves as a jack-of-all-trades, doing all the strategy, media buys, copywriting, and sometimes even rudimentary design by herself. As the business grows, she may work with freelancers to execute various elements she oversees. When the volume becomes overwhelming, the company considers developing a real staff, including copywriters.

In such a business, copywriters are hired at a level (say, junior versus senior) that depends on their experience and the needs of the business. In such a business, a senior writer may supervise a junior writer. Senior writers, in turn, report to marketing directors or marketing communications directors, who may or may not be responsible to a vice president of marketing.

If you choose to build your career on the client side, the highest level you can reach is marketing director, marketing communications director, or vice president of marketing — an excellent choice if you're interested in all aspects of marketing, not just copywriting, and would enjoy the responsibility of making strategic marketing decisions. As an alternative, many marketers use their experience to start their own businesses.

Examining working conditions

As you know, working conditions can (and do) vary dramatically among companies. But in general (please don't flog me if your individual experience markedly differs), the hours, volume of work, and level of stress tend to be less or lower than that found at advertising and other marketing agencies. You'll keep regular hours, and you can expect a wide variety of assignments, from letters (see Chapter 5) and print ads (see Chapter 11) to collateral (see Chapter 15), event invitations, and Web site copy (see Chapter 14).

Client-side copywriters and agency copywriters often develop different kinds of expertise. On the client side, you usually develop exceptionally in-depth knowledge of your particular business and its industry while tackling a hodgepodge of assignment types. Agency copywriters, on the other hand, often work within a wide range of industries but become especially skilled at particular formats, such as print ads or direct mail packages.

In general, client-side projects tend to be more conservative than those promoted by agencies. This type of work includes many more meat-and-potato projects, such as sales sheets and product brochures, and far fewer bold ads or daring mailings than you may create in an agency. You work closely with the marketing director, who establishes the objectives of your individual projects in conformance with the strategy (assuming that there is one — cross your fingers) she's established with her bosses. With her authorization, you'll probably work directly with people in other departments to gather information and collect feedback on your work.

Making money

Okay, you're thinking: Working conditions, blah, blah, blah. What about the money? Client-side entry-level writing positions tend to have higher salaries than comparable positions in agencies. But as you move higher up the ladder, the agencies pay better. Their competitive environment is structured to weed out the poor performers. Those who prove themselves and prosper get the rewards, including good wages.

When you're considering an in-house career, remember that the value of the copywriting position, and hence its compensation, is directly tied to its capacity to generate revenue. The closer copywriting is to the organization's core business — such as producing catalogs or promoting subscriptions — the higher the pay. Why? Because copywriting has a measurable impact on the bottom line. The opposite applies as well: The further writing is from the core mission — as in healthcare or banking — the lower the pay. Copywriting has little measurable impact on the delivery of medical care or the quality of a loan portfolio, so it's less likely to garner either respect or hard cash.

Going to work for an agency

The alternative option for full-time, wage-based employment is the agency, either in advertising or direct marketing. (But usually not public relations agencies; their account executives do the writing — mostly press releases, but sometimes an article — themselves.)

Checking out the career path

Unless you pack a portfolio that demonstrates considerable experience, you start as a junior writer working long hours for little pay. (See "Building your portfolio," later in this chapter, to find out how to show off your work.) Numerous people redline (edit and comment on) your work, and much of it isnever even used at all. As you gain experience, you'll have greater input on *concepts* (ideas for individual projects) and *strategy* (the guiding vision across a campaign or a brand identity).

Junior writers can become senior writers, who can then become assistant creative directors and, finally, creative directors — the creative sages responsible for concepts and for managing the creative team.

If you love guiding new ideas into finished, successful projects, the life of the creative director may be for you. The pressure's enormous, to be sure, but so is the satisfaction of nursing an idea into fruition. The alternative pathway is opening and running your own agency. Copywriters have launched many of the most famous advertising agencies, such as Ogilvy & Mather.

Understanding the agency environment

A personal life? Forget about it. The agency is often all-consuming, devouring your early-morning and late-evening hours. Your work will be hard and long, and you have no guarantee your work will be appreciated.

You'll labor under the guidance of the creative director, who's responsible for the concept, and the account executive assigned to the client, who's responsible for ensuring that the work meets the client's objectives. Because almost all assignments involve visuals, you'll cooperate with a graphic designer to coordinate words and images and to fit your message within the given format.

In an agency, copywriters have to be quick studies, as you're expected to sometimes absorb vast amounts of information about subjects as disparate as construction bonds and dog food. Be prepared to do a lot of reading and ask a lot of questions.

Earning a paycheck

At first the pay is poor. The competition for available entry-level jobs can be fierce, and few agencies want to invest good money on untested talent. But as you prove your worth with an ever-expanding portfolio of successful work, your pay will increase as well. Good copywriters can command up to six-figure salaries (or close to it) in the top agencies; creative directors can make even more.

Establishing your own business

Whether you work for the agency or for the client, you work as an employee collecting a wage. The third option is to break away from the cubicle and work for yourself as a freelancer. Instead of a wage, you collect a fee for every project you complete. You assume all responsibility for taxes, health insurance, overhead, and the like. In exchange for this responsibility, however, comes freedom: You set the terms and conditions for your work.

I'm a freelancer myself, and I have a lot to say about the subject in an upcoming section, "Marketing Yourself as a Freelancer." For now, the question is whether the freelancing life is for you.

Freelancing may be for you *if* the prospect of freedom and self-determination is greater to you than the anxiety that comes with risk and responsibility. If you're an employee, your work is brought to you. As a freelancer, you have to rustle it up yourself — you eat only what you kill. That means applying a disciplined approach to your work, not just in the fulfillment of your projects and the attendant details (such as taxes and overhead), but in marketing your business to land assignments. If you play your cards right, you can make more money and gain greater control of your time by freelancing. But you lose the security (such as it is) of a regular paycheck, and you assume responsibility for all the aspects of a business that wage earners need not fret over. Is this the life for you? Only you know.

Preparing for Your Career

I don't expect that copywriter ranks up there with firefighter or ballerina in the dreamy ambitions of 6-year-olds looking toward their future. (Just think of it — some dewy, gap-toothed little tot declaring, as Mom or Dad tucks her in, "Some day, *I'm* going to write a memorable 30-second spot for a line of citrus-based bathroom cleaners!") No, copywriting comes at the crossroads of creative dreams and hard-nosed reality — a way of turning a literary talent into cold cash. Copywriters, therefore, come from a large variety of backgrounds; there's no one established pathway. That said, you may want to consider a few things regarding education and your portfolio.

Educating yourself

Though a college education isn't, in itself, either a necessary component of the copywriting career or a guarantor of success, most copywriters, like most white-collar workers in general, are college educated. If your college days are already behind you (mine have receded into a distant, Stygian mist), don't worry about the kind of degree you obtained. No one single degree prepares you for copywriting, and no type of degree excludes you, either.

If your college days are ahead (or if you're in the middle of them), however, you may wonder if you should major in communications or business or marketing. My definitive answer? Maybe. Because the truth is, the relationship between "business" as a degree and "business" as a successfully practiced enterprise is tenuous at best. And, funny thing, of all the copywriters I know, not one (repeat, *not one*) majored in a business-related degree. Instead, they studied literature, visual art, music, dance, engineering, chemistry, social work, and so on.

The dean of copywriters, David Ogilvy, was a passionate advocate of the "well-furnished mind." He believed in reading deeply and widely and appreciated the quality of critical and creative thinking — absolutely crucial to successful writing and marketing — that comes from the serious pursuit of what we think of as the traditional liberal-arts curriculum: arts, sciences, and humanities.

Though it may seem counterintuitive, I suggest that if you're seriously considering copywriting as a career, you should major in a subject that's dear to your heart and challenging to your mind (whether that be physics or philosophy). Then, whether you're in college or out, you can supplement your education with the following options as you pursue a career in copywriting.

Take business and marketing courses

Most of what you'll need to know about business and marketing you'll learn by working in a business and by engaging in marketing. But by taking a few courses (in college, night classes, or a continuing education program), you can survey the landscape and learn the basic vocabulary. That way, when you're ready to work, you'll be able to talk the talk when you're interviewed, and you'll have a grip on a few fundamental ideas that can help put your subsequent experience into perspective; that is, you'll have a rough sense of what's going on and why.

Participate in internships

Each year, an increasing number of colleges and universities require students to participate in some real-life activity outside their ivy-covered walls. By all means, get involved and take advantage of this opportunity! (If you're still in the application stage, take the extra effort to find out about the internship programs, including their reach and quality, as part of your selection criteria.)

Yeah, I know that most internships aren't glamorous; you're going to spend a lot of time at the copying machine. But if you keep your eyes and ears open, you'll get a firsthand look at how marketing decisions are made in the real-world context of limited budgets, office politics, and widely varying levels of talent and expertise. And if you get lucky, you may even land your first writing assignment or two and get precious (if painful) feedback on your work. These assignments, in turn, can give you a head start on building a portfolio of sample work (see "Building your portfolio," later in this chapter).

Seek out professional associations

Guilds aren't around any more, but their heritage lives on in the form of thousands of associations dedicated to sharing information and encouraging individual professional development in hundreds of industries. For copywriters and would-be marketers, these include The Ad Club (www.bostonideagroup.org), the American Marketing Association (www.marketingpower.com), the Business Marketing Association (www.marketing.org), the Direct Marketing Association (www.the-dma.org), and many, many others.

These organizations exist to encourage networking (so people can get or swap business leads), to provide insight into current trends and best practices, and to elevate the standards of their respective professions. Although the marketing associations cover the entire spectrum of relevant issues, they often offer seminars and workshops dedicated exclusively to copywriting — and sometimes they're even free. If you've already completed college and want an easy way to get a basic education in marketing, look at these organization-sponsored seminars. In addition to convenience, these sessions have another big advantage over college-based courses: They're usually led by (and attended by) professionals who bring street-level, school-of-hard-knocks experience to these lessons. Pay attention to the questions your colleagues ask: They usually arise from real-life problems you may encounter yourself.

If you're a young person still in school, you may be intimidated by these groups. Don't be. They not only welcome students but also hungrily seek them. On one level, it's in their interest to train and encourage the next generation of up-and-coming marketers. But I think a powerful personal motivation exists as well. Frankly, members of these groups are flattered. Work can be a grind, especially in the difficult, temperamental, and often underappreciated world of marketing. So when a bright-eyed, bushy-tailed student full of promise seeks wisdom and guidance from a member, it just might make their day. Chances are, you'll be greeted with enthusiasm.

In addition to getting a warm welcome, you'll meet people who can help you find internships and, after graduation, real jobs. And because their careers depend on it, association members insist upon, and get, the most current information and insights on emerging trends — the kind of stuff that won't appear in college syllabuses for years to come.

Not sold yet? But wait, there's more! I'm talking money here. Many of these groups offer scholarships and/or award monies to either defray the costs of attending college marketing courses or seminars and workshops that they offer themselves. Too few students apply, so your chances of winning are excellent.

Read, read, and read some more

In addition to reading the many, many fine books on marketing in general, and copywriting in particular, I encourage you — nay, I beg you — to read quality literature constantly. Writers, like musicians, must develop an ear for tone and voice; the best way to begin is by absorbing the work of the best.

You don't have to be Robert Frost to write effective copy, but reading Frost (among others) opens you to the extraordinary powers and possibilities of language. If you limit your reading to business books, you'll never be able to do more than regurgitate prevailing conventional wisdom. Reading quality writing — be it novels, poems, or essays — cultivates the faculties you need for breakthrough thinking and brilliant execution.

Building your portfolio

In the most literal use of the word, the portfolio is the leather case you lug around from interview to interview, packed with examples of your work. Figuratively, *portfolio* refers to your experience and accomplishments. It's the body of work that demonstrates your talent and expertise. Ideally (meaning to the best that you're able), you should create a large body of samples that reflect many types of work (from direct mail to Web site copy to print ads to radio spots and so on) in various industries or areas. As you meet potential employers or clients, you can then literally pack your portfolio case with the samples most likely to be relevant to their specific needs.

For beginning writers, the portfolio represents something of a Catch-22: Without a portfolio, you can't get assignments; without assignments, you can't build a portfolio. Don't panic. I have some ideas that can help you.

Writing pro bono

I don't believe in writing for free. There are, indeed, sharks in the water who exploit young writers by offering them assignments in return for exposure. Ignore them. Either the work is illegitimate, such as writing papers for college students, or it won't lend you credibility, even if the work is legit.

You don't gradually become a professional. You begin your career as a professional by conducting yourself with self-respect. From day one, portfolio or not, you hold yourself to the highest standards and insist on a reasonable amount of respect in turn. If you act like a bottom feeder, you'll be treated like a bottom feeder.

The only exception I make to the no-freebie rule is pro bono (free of charge) work for charities, social or political causes, and other related nonprofit enterprises. For experienced writers, pro bono assignments are an opportunity to do good; for beginners, they're a chance to build your portfolio as well.

To get these assignments, you have to ask for them, which means doing a little research, via the Web and perhaps a phone directory, to identify groups that can use your services. If you're already a volunteer or contributor, you have a leg up; someone at the organization knows you and may be able to introduce you to the appropriate authority, usually someone in charge of public relations or development (raising money). If you don't know anyone at the organization, a quick call in which you explain your objective will almost always lead you to the right person, who may be the director or the person responsible for development or public relations. (In many small organizations, one person may hold all three responsibilities.)

Be sure that your expectations are reasonable. The large, famous organizations, such as the Republican Party or the Sierra Club, retain powerful, prestigious agencies to handle their work. You'll have more success by thinking small and local, not big and national. Some fertile ground may include the following:

- **Public libraries:** Your local library does much more than shelve books, and it's almost always underfunded. Among other things, libraries need flyers for events they sponsor (such as children's puppet shows or adult book groups) and may appreciate help writing guides (as in pamphlets or Web site copy) that help patrons use various library services.

- **Local social-service organizations:** Whether they assist the handicapped or help tenants with landlord disputes, many social-service organizations produce (or need to produce) many written materials to help them fulfill their missions. In fact, one of my earliest pro bono assignments was researching and writing newsletter articles for a group that provides free services to the blind and visually impaired.

- **Local political candidates or causes:** They need it all: ads, press releases, letters, e-mails, Web copy, brochures, and flyers. Ask for the candidate, campaign manager, or director.

- **Local arts groups:** Their big needs are press releases to announce their events and articles for their Web site. If they have an organized list of donors or patrons, you may be able to try your hand at a fundraising letter as well. (See Chapter 17 for more on fundraising.)

- **Local preservation groups or historical societies:** Both groups need considerable amounts of public relations material (press releases and articles), and the groups interested in saving old buildings, such as movie houses and historic homes, need help with fundraising material, too.

✔ **Small, underfunded museums:** When you think of museums, you probably tend to the think of the giants: the Met, the Louvre, the Getty, and so on. But for every one of these world-class wonders, dozens, if not hundreds, of tiny museums operate in their shadows. Most aren't dedicated to art per se, but to local history, geology, Native American artifacts, and almost random collections of whatnot from eccentric benefactors. They can use your help with public relations, fundraising, and advertising.

As a general rule, be forthright about your motivations. Candidly explain to the contacts you've made that, in addition to your desire to support their organizations, you want to further your career by developing a portfolio that can help you land paying work. This admission in no way diminishes your contribution and, in fact, encourages a level of mutual understanding that will increase their confidence in you.

Creating speculative pieces

You can also create *speculative pieces,* creative work for businesses that don't exist, or fictional assignments for businesses that do. (In either case, you must clearly and unambiguously identify these pieces as speculative when you present your portfolio to potential employers or clients.) You can simply write bare copy decks (plain copy that isn't placed within its finished graphic format), or you can collaborate with graphic designers who share your need for spec pieces to create finished work.

If you choose to go this route, first write a brief assessment of the business and its challenges so that you have a context for your work. For example, if you want to tackle a speculative print ad for an independent appliance store, begin by creating an imaginary budget, a target audience, a picture of the competitive landscape, and a quick list of the pros and cons of the store and its offers in terms of the quality of its prices, service, benefits, and features.

By establishing a make-believe business environment first, you accomplish two things:

✔ **You create a spur to your imagination.** Instead of working out of thin air, you can begin by developing a strategy that resolves key issues. Should you emphasize special benefits? Is your client weak on price? Is a certain feature or set of features especially important to your market? By answering these questions for yourself, you create a foundation of insight on which to build your copy.

✔ **You demonstrate your understanding of real-world business.** When the time comes to present your speculative work, you can talk about how your creative decisions were made in response to problems or challenges commonly found in the real world. By doing so, you demonstrate your grasp of broad marketing issues and your willingness to apply your talent to resolve them.

Marketing Yourself as a Freelancer

The alternative to seeking employment as a wage earner is to work as an independent or freelance writer prepared to take on projects from any number of clients. By doing so, you gain control of your time, work, and income.

The key to success, however, is not so much your skill as a writer but your determination and commitment as a businessperson. As soon as you become a freelancer, you suddenly assume two jobs: You're a writer, *and* you're a business owner responsible for marketing and managing your enterprise. In the previous chapters, I do my best to help you write; in the rest of this chapter, I share some insights into what it takes to make writing work as a business. (If you're interested in even more freelancing-related information, such as handling money and managing client relationships, check out *Freelancing For Dummies* by Susan M. Drake, published by Wiley.)

I've seen many freelancers fail, and in every instance the story was the same: initial success followed by deterioration and then downright failure. In each case, this failure was *not* due to lack of talent, but to lack of consistent marketing. Typically these writers (or artists) had achieved success in an agency (or agencies), where they developed a reputation for quality work and a number of close relationships with the agency's clients. After making a few queries to see whether these clients would be interested in working with them directly, they made the leap into independence. At first, things went well. These freelancers didn't do any marketing because they already had more business than they could handle. But by the second year, the cracks appeared — a few major clients went bankrupt, changed business direction, or simply sought fresh talent. Suddenly, the freelancers' revenues dried up. And because these freelancers hadn't done any real marketing, they had no pool of potential clients or projects to draw from. Inevitably, these freelancers return to agency life where they tell the other creative talent that freelancing doesn't work. Moral of the story: Don't run from full-time employment unless you're prepared to run a business, which means assertively marketing your talents.

Marketing includes all the things you do and choices you make — including your selection of services, pricing, distribution, and promotion — to connect to your customers' wallets. Market yourself in the ways best suited to your temperament and ambition.

In most discussions of marketing, much emphasis is placed on excellence, which I think is a shame: The great can be the enemy of the good. All too often, the pursuit of excellence is merely an excuse for procrastination or a rationalization for an unwillingness to be decisive. The truth is, even mediocre marketing, executed diligently, works; brilliant marketing, when achieved, performs even better. But the one sure-fire way to fail at marketing is to suspend activity in the perpetual pursuit of an illusory standard of excellence.

Selecting your services

Sure, you're a copywriter. But what kind of things do you write? Brand ads? Direct response packages? Web copy? Ghostwritten articles? And in what industries? Will you focus on consumer sales, such as retail apparel or entertainment catalogs? Or do you see yourself as more of a business-to-business writer selling high-tech software or financial services?

For many writers, like me, these decisions are made by opportunity: One healthcare assignment leads to another; after you get a few solid direct mail packages under your belt, finding other assignments gets easier. Eventually, however, you'll come to a crossroads: You have only so many resources (time and money), and you need to focus your efforts to promote yourself successfully. If you see yourself as a direct marketing writer, for example, target direct marketing agencies and/or clients, such as publishers and non-profits, that produce a lot of direct mail. Writers often fear, however, that if they define themselves too narrowly, they may drive away good business.

I call this the generalist-versus-specialist dilemma. Declaring yourself a generalist, capable of many kinds of assignments in many industries, leaves you open to a broad range of assignments, but doing so can dilute your marketing efforts and undermine your credibility with prospects seeking specific expertise. Identifying yourself as a specialist gives you focus and allows you to promote your expertise, but at the risk of limiting your options. What's a copywriter to do?

I recommend a hybrid approach: To extend your reach *and* leverage your particular areas of expertise, specialize in several areas. When you approach prospects in each specialty, tailor your messaging for them. Your healthcare clients needn't hear about your work in music sales, and your public relations clients needn't concern themselves with your direct response skills. There's absolutely nothing unethical about this approach as long as you're genuinely skilled, knowledgeable, and experienced in each of the areas in which you claim expertise.

Pricing your services

If you're looking for hard numbers, I'm afraid I'm going to disappoint you. The amount of money you can command varies with what you do, who you do it for, and where you do it (you can demand higher fees in the major metropolitan areas than in the outlying areas). I do, however, make two important suggestions about pricing.

Compete on value, not price

Whatever you do, don't position yourself as the low-cost copywriter in order to generate more volume. You not only undercut your profits by committing yourself to projects at fees far less than they're worth, but you also attract the wrong kind of clients: bottom feeders. This fact may seem contrary to common sense, but cheap clients are the ones who prove most difficult to please. They're the ones who demand endless rounds of revisions and then reward your efforts by bad-mouthing you to their peers and colleagues.

I don't know exactly why this is so, but here's my stab at the underlying psychology: The clients who believe that price is the most important criteria for selecting a copywriter have little or no regard for copywriting. They don't understand the relationship between quality copy and profits (or problem-solving), and they generally perceive marketing as a necessary evil they must grudgingly pay for. That means your relationship begins with distrust: They see you as either a fool or a white-collar pickpocket or both, and they have no respect for your advice or input on the project.

Now look at the flip side: Clients who pay good money for your services have high expectations, to be sure, but they also bring a positive attitude to the table. They value copy, respect its powers, and genuinely *want* your input — after all, it's what they've paid for. They made an investment in you and are eager to see you succeed.

Some writer, somewhere, somehow, stands ready to undercut you on price. If a prospect challenges you with a quote from such a writer, hold your ground and talk about value — the talent, experience, and expertise you bring to a project as demonstrated by your samples, your references, and your record of success. Bottom line: It's poor economy to save a few hundred dollars on a writing project if it costs the client many thousands of dollars in lost sales, lost leads, or lost reputation.

Bill by the project, not by the hour

One of the first issues that arise in client negotiations is your fee: How much do you charge per hour? If you're smart, you tell prospects that you don't charge by the hour; you charge by the project. Here's why:

✔ **You want to focus attention on value.** The basis for your compensation should be the value of your contribution — what your work does for your client — not an arbitrary rate based on your time. Suppose, for example, that you create a direct response package with a reasonable expectation of generating a 1.5 percent response rate for revenues in the area of $250,000. The *value* of your contribution is directly tied to the revenue you help generate, so no one will think it unreasonable to pay $2,500 (just 1 percent of total sales) for a $250,000 return.

✔ **You don't want to be penalized for working efficiently.** As you hone your skills through experience, you accomplish more (and better) work in less time. It just doesn't make sense to accept less pay for submitting excellent work in 5 hours rather than 10, especially when the faster turn-around benefits the client.

✔ **You want to give the client a fixed fee.** Billable hours can extend beyond expectations, driving up costs. But when you offer a project quote that includes the initial work, the revisions, and any time spent in meetings and/or interviews, you give the client the benefit, and confidence, of a fixed price. What they see is what they get.

Selecting your channels

In marketing lingo, a *channel* is a kind of sales site or a route between the producer and the consumer. Channels include retail stores, catalogs, and third-party resellers.

For your purposes, the channels are the three major classifications of potential customers, irrespective of industry. These channels and the pros and cons of working through them include the following.

Businesses/organizations

These are the clients themselves, the businesses or organizations that actually use (or "consume") your copy.

✔ **Pros:** You work directly with the clients, giving you opportunities to develop deep relationships that generate a wide variety of work. Without any intermediaries in the way, you can collaborate with the client on strategy and concepts.

✔ **Cons:** The pool of potential customers is enormous, even when you narrow your targets to specific industries in specific regions, forcing you to cast a wide net with your marketing efforts. It can also be difficult for lone wolves (freelancers) to identify and reach the alpha males and females (the actual decision makers) within their respective organizations. Finally, the levels of marketing sophistication vary widely; you may find yourself educating many of your clients (about marketing in general, or about the specifics regarding the projects at hand). Although the teaching role may help you establish your authority and value, it can also devour a lot of your time.

Advertising/marketing agencies

In every major metropolitan area, numerous advertising, direct response, and public relations agencies, plus marketing consulting groups, are trolling the waters for the big fish: clients with deep pockets. Many have industry specializations that may overlap your target markets. One way or another, you end up either working with them or around them, but you can't ignore them.

- ✔ **Pros:** By working as a subcontractor with an agency, you get to ride on its marketing coat tails — a considerable advantage, given the greater resources an agency can apply to marketing and sales. Agencies can introduce you to clients and projects much larger than you can ordinarily get on your own, and their professional conduct and expertise usually streamline the working process, from concept to finished project, significantly.

- ✔ **Cons:** When you work through an agency, it runs the show. The client and the project belong to the agency, and it gets to set the strategy and the concepts (although the agency often asks for your input and advice). You sit in the back seat, and part of your job is to play nicely with all the other passengers: the account executives, the database managers, the artists, and so on.

Never, never, ever succumb to the temptation to cut a side deal with — or outright steal — a client you meet through an agency. First of all, doing so is unethical: The agency has invested (and continues to invest) a considerable amount of time and money to attract and hold this client. Openly competing for any client is perfectly acceptable, but drawing away business from a client that the agency has introduced to you, as a matter of trust, is thievery, plain and simple. Secondly, doing so is professional suicide. Word of your conduct *will* get out, and when it does, you're done. No agency will want to work with you. Sometimes clients themselves may make a "pass" at you, suggesting they have a little project they don't want to involve the agency in (or pay them for). Don't take the bait. Simply respond politely by suggesting that they run their request for your services through your mutual contact person at the agency. In most cases, the client will get the hint and drop the matter at once.

Job placement agencies

The third category includes human resource agencies that place the appropriate talent into full- or part-time positions or freelance assignments. If you're interested in working with these agencies, look for those that specialize in marketing and/or creative talent.

- ✔ **Pros:** They bring you the assignments on a platter. You just sit back and do the work. And instead of submitting invoices and waiting 30 days (or more) to get paid, the placement agencies cut you a check every week you're on assignment. (They even handle taxes, just as if you're an employee.) Some agencies also offer health plans and insurance programs you can participate in.

✔ **Cons:** For any given assignment, you'll always make much less than had you fulfilled the project directly with the client or as a third-party contractor working with an ad agency. Although the job placement agency may claim to be the virtual marketing department that generates business for you, it'll never promote you with the same fire and perseverance you'd promote yourself with.

Job placement agencies are more successful placing talent with lengthy client lists than with beginners, so their value is somewhat contradictory. Although their services are most attractive to new freelancers who haven't found their marketing legs yet, they're not likely to generate much work for them. And for the experienced writers, these agencies can rarely pull in the fees that the writers can attract on their own. Personally, I find job placement agencies most helpful as a way to get into new industries and as a source of quick money that can patch the gaps in my cash flow.

Promoting your services

The last marketing challenge I address is usually the first one people think about: promotion, which for my fast and loose purposes includes advertising and public relations.

I put promotion last for a reason: You'll make better, more-informed, and more cost-efficient decisions about promoting your services when you resolve issues of service selection, target markets, price, and channels *first*.

Deploying effective methods

Chances are, you won't deploy just one method of promotion. Instead, you'll probably arrive at a balanced mix of techniques that reflect your budget, ambitions, and personal experiences of success or failure with each effort. Although each method places different demands on your time and purse, they all share one important factor: To succeed, you must pursue them *persistently*; don't expect powerful results from one-shot promotions. Your options include

✔ **Networking:** *Networking* is simply business-speak for socializing with potential prospects, partners, and colleagues to swap leads, ideas, and business. One of the easiest ways to begin is with professional associations formed primarily for this purpose. An online search with the words "marketing," "professional association," and the name of the nearest city of consequence will generate a list of options for your area. In addition to associations that address marketing in general, look for groups that address the needs of specific industries you may be interested in, such as high-tech, banking, or catalogs.

✔ **Sending direct mail/e-mail:** See Chapter 7 to see how you can use direct response techniques for getting mail out quickly to your advantage. In my experience, the two fastest and cheapest sources of names, titles, and addresses of potential clients (to build your mail or e-mail lists) are online Internet searches of your target industries and the directories you can get when you join professional associations. I've had a lot of success sending mail with lists of clients and representative projects. These illustrate my experience and give prospects an opportunity to request specific samples relevant to their needs.

✔ **Writing articles:** Several publications, including local business journals and regional or national trade publications, welcome articles on marketing issues. Consider building your reputation by getting your name in print. (See Chapter 13 for further information.) And don't neglect newsletters or online e-newsletters as possible places to publish.

✔ **Promoting your Web site:** Having a Web site with information about your experience and expertise (including samples, if possible) is a fine start, but unless you promote it aggressively, it's like setting up a lemonade stand in a cornfield — don't expect many visitors. Do some research on search engine optimization and consider my suggestions about advertising on the Web in Chapter 11. You also may want to check out *Search Engine Optimization For Dummies,* by Peter Kent (Wiley).

✔ **Using active word of mouth:** The key word is *active;* people won't spread the good word about you without any effort on your part. Ask for referrals and take the time to develop real, honest-to-goodness relationships with the movers and shakers in your target markets and regions.

Avoiding my mistakes

Mistakes are inevitable, so you shouldn't be unduly discouraged when you make them. Instead, try to understand what went wrong and *why;* the insights you gain will help ease the sting and make you a stronger copywriter.

A survey of my mistakes could be a book in itself (I sure hope this isn't it!), but to spare you my pain, I limit myself to a couple points.

✔ **Placing print ads:** To be effective, print ads require a real commitment to buying quality space and buying it often. Most freelancers don't have this kind of cash (and even if they do, they could more effectively spend it elsewhere), so they place little text ads under the "professional classifieds" in the advertising trade magazines. If you plan to sit by the phone and wait for the calls to come in, bring a stack of sandwiches and a jug of water because you'll be there awhile. I've never met a creative director or marketing director who's hired a copywriter on the strength of a little ad. Instead, they go by referrals (which you can facilitate with active word of mouth and networking) and by reviewing samples and or information about writers (help them along by marketing yourself to them through direct mail/e-mail, the Web, and articles).

✔ **Responding to classified ads:** Early in the game, I had the bright idea of responding to classified ads seeking full-time writers. I reasoned that I could persuade these would-be employers to use my services as a stop-gap measure or as a substitute for a full-timer entirely. I sent hundreds of letters — and received not one response. This approach failed for several reasons, but I suspect the biggest one is related to the hiring process: These ads aren't managed by creative or marketing people but by human resource (HR) people. Given their broad responsibilities to the entire organization, human resource people usually don't have a deep understanding of the underlying hiring needs of their organization's specific departments. As a consequence, they're unlikely to consider any candidate who doesn't precisely match their initial job description, even if that candidate could better serve their colleagues' interests. When they receive a response that's not exactly what they've set themselves to look for — zing! — away it goes into the circular file.

Don't target people in human resources. If you want to make any progress in a company, agency, or other organization, you want to talk to professionals in marketing, communications, or public relations. When these professionals are sold on you, they'll make the necessary contact with human relations to address hiring negotiations or freelance contracting arrangements.

Part VI
The Part of Tens

The 5th Wave   By Rich Tennant

"Well, for months I'd been on my postal route
delivering those catalogues that use stories of
far away places to sell their travel clothes..."

In this part . . .

*I*t happens from time to time — you lose steam, insight, or inspiration. And often the closer the deadline, the more dramatic your loss of ideas.

Do not panic. Instead, look in this part for sparks to light your creative fire. In three fast chapters of ten suggestions each, you find a whopping total of thirty ideas that can help you get back on your feet — er, I mean, in your chair — and writing again. Turn to this part for prewriting suggestions, cures for common writing ailments, and inspiring hints.

Chapter 20

Ten Things You Should Always Do Before Writing

. . . .

In This Chapter

▶ Deciding on your team, purpose, benchmarks, and format

▶ Collecting the basic facts

▶ Crafting copy points (including benefits and features)

▶ Making sure you talk to the customer

▶ Anticipating challenges

▶ Choosing the best tone for your copy

. . . .

*M*ore often than not, the success of your copy is determined by the decisions you make before you write (or type) the first word. In fact, the real difference between great copywriters and mediocre ones is usually not talent, but the way they gather information, interpret it, and develop a strategy for delivering their messages.

The best way to start a writing project is to stop, take a break, and think through the core issues behind your assignment. When you do the following ten things, the writing itself is easier, and the end results are more effective.

Creating the Team

Unless you work for yourself, you'll probably be part of a team charged with creating marketing materials. In many organizations, the team can be rather loosely defined and may change from project to project. What you'll almost always find, however, is that although many people want input on a project and many more are willing to share the credit if it succeeds, few people want to accept responsibility for it.

You and your organization need a clearly defined core team of professionals who have both authority and accountability — the power to make decisions and the responsibility of living with the consequences. These may include marketing executives, marketing managers, product line managers, brand managers, merchandisers, the boss's second cousin — it all depends on how your organization is structured. Whatever its components, the important thing is that such a team exists. Without this core group, marketing efforts tend to devolve into chaos. (For more on establishing a project team, check out Chapter 18.)

Together the team takes the following steps:

1. **Defines purposes and benchmarks:** The team defines the purpose of a given project — be it sales, leads, awareness, or another objective — and the terms by which it will be measured. (See the following sections.)

2. **Gathers input:** The core team collects all the necessary input on product, price, position, messages, offers, and so on from the broader organization and consolidates it for the next step. (See "Gathering the Facts," later in this chapter.)

3. **Assigns individual tasks:** Each member is assigned various portions of the project to be completed according to the team's standards and within a set budget and timeline.

4. **Reviews the finished work:** Finally, the team reviews all its work twice: first, *before* the work is released (printed, mailed, published, posted online, and so on) to see that it conforms to the purposes it has previously defined, and then *after* the work has been released to see how it has performed against the team's benchmarks and to make plans for improvements.

Clarifying the Purpose

I can't tell you the number of input meetings that have ground to a silent, awkward halt by one simple question: "Why are we doing this?" Although it may seem absurd that people would pursue a project without a clear understanding of its ultimate purpose, it happens all the time. Habit, ignorance, confusion, and the strange ways of office politics can all conspire to set otherwise intelligent people to work on assignments with no clear goals. Without an objective in mind, forming a strategy is impossible; without a strategy, you can't make sound writing decisions: All your choices become arbitrary, and your final written piece becomes doomed to irrelevance.

So first things first. Are you writing to make sales, generate leads, boost brand awareness, or fulfill some more ancillary objective, such as driving customers to your Web site? Think of your writing as an arrow: Where's your target? What's your aim? After you have a firm grip on your purpose, then you can make intelligent decisions about format, messages, offers, tone, word choice, and more.

Setting the Benchmarks

Benchmark simply means a point of comparison, some means by which you can measure the relative success or failure of your work. These marks vary according to the purpose of your project (see the preceding section) and may include "hard" targets that can be measured in numbers, such as response rates or the number of visits to your Web site, or "soft" targets, such as press exposure or focus group responses to your work. These numbers may be pulled from your previous results with other initiatives, or from industry averages you've uncovered through research.

Though benchmarks may seem intimidating (no one savors the prospect of being weighed in the balance and perhaps found wanting), they're an essential tool for improving your writing and marketing efforts. Without some idea of whether you're succeeding, your work staggers forward in the dark. When you have a benchmark to compare your results to, you have an objective standard that guides your subsequent improvements. It also makes collaboration much easier: When someone asks why you chose one way of phrasing an offer over another, pointing out a difference of, say, 2.3 percent in response rate — or 542 units in raw sales — greatly simplifies the discussion.

Gathering the Facts

Whether alone or with a team, you need to collect all the nitty-gritty information that serves as the raw clay for your creation. (See Chapter 3 for more on collecting the basics.) Among the things you want to gather are the following:

- **Products and services:** Find out what's for sale and then learn what you can do about it: What does it do? Who's it for? How does it compare to competitors' comparable products and services? What are its key benefits and features? What are its dimensions? Does it come with options (colors, sizes, add-ons, and so on)?

- **Price and pathway:** In addition to price, you want to know how the customer can make the order or complete the purchase. You want phone numbers, addresses, Web site addresses, and/or e-mail addresses. Find out whether there are any restrictions (by age or by state, for example) or special requirements for shipping, installation, or use.

✓ **Previous marketing materials:** You'll want to take a look at previous efforts for a number of reasons. For starters, your work may have to maintain a consistent look or feel with earlier work. You may also pick up themes and ideas you can rework or extend in your work. Finally, you want to get an idea of what worked and what didn't so that you can incorporate the most effective elements in your writing. But be careful: If you're writing about new products or embarking on a new strategy for an old product, old materials might drag you down into old and irrelevant messages.

Resolving the Format

There's no way to write a generic message that works in any medium, from print ad to brochure, a letter to a radio broadcast. To be effective, your writing must take advantages of the strengths of a particular medium and work within the limitations of that format.

Fortunately, you usually determine the format at the very start of a project, so you know from the outset whether you're writing for a self-mailer or a Web site. But as a practical matter, you want to get an idea of the copy's length and its "geography" — where it's intended to fit. With multi-page print projects that include art, it's especially important to work with the artist or designer to determine what goes where and to indicate in the copy your intentions (where you think your copy should go). Through a careful consideration of placement, you improve the flow of the piece, making it easier to read and less likely to create confusion (which can reduce responses and sales).

Establishing the Copy Points

When you take all the raw information you've gathered and then sift them through the purpose you and/or your team has clarified, you arrive at a set of *copy points*: information that you must include in the final written piece. These points usually include the following elements:

✓ **Offer:** This is what you're selling at what terms (price, discounts, shipping charges, and so on).

✓ **Main benefit:** This is the most attractive or valuable thing the product or service does for the customer.

✓ **Subordinate benefits:** These are additional benefits that help encourage prospect action.

✔ **Key features:** Although your product or service may have many features or qualities, the ones that are important (and deserve to be written about) are those that help substantiate or fulfill the benefits you've promised.

✔ **Brand identity:** From piece to piece, your business or organization may have consistent messages regarding its positioning or identity that you must incorporate in your work. (For more on positioning and branding, see Chapter 10.)

✔ **Call to action:** The concluding element should lead to action — what you want the prospect to do to take advantage of the offer, whether it's to go to a retail location or Web site, call a phone number, or return a reply card.

See Chapter 2 for more on the building blocks of copy.

Turning Features into Benefits

Features are qualities a product or service has; *benefits* are what your products or services do for the customer. They are not equals — benefits have much greater value. Benefits are centered on the customer's self-interest, and they make important promises (of health, youth, beauty, success, power, and so on) that often have a powerful emotional hold on us.

Unfortunately, many organizations understand the features of the work they produce much more deeply than the benefits of those products for the customer. One of your biggest challenges, therefore, is to turn features into benefits: to unlock the value of a given feature for the prospect. (For more on features and benefits, see Chapter 2.)

Profiling the Customer

One of the most powerful ways that copy can strengthen any marketing project is by creating a sense of empathy — a suggestion of a common bond between the seller and the prospect. Whatever the specifics of your particular message, you always want to imply that you understand prospects' needs and that you're on their side.

That means that your understanding of your customers will determine the manner in which you present your message (drawn from your copy points — see "Establishing the Copy Points," earlier in this chapter). In other words, you need to know your customers' needs, desires, fears, and things such as the way they like to shop and the language they speak. Before you write, imagine the customer as a flesh-and-blood person. Hear her speak; "listen" to what she wants and how she wants it. Then write your copy as if you're having a one-to-one conversation with that customer. (See Chapter 3 for more insights on understanding your customers.)

Identifying the Marketing Challenges

Most people want to conceal their weaknesses and hide their vulnerabilities — that's just human nature. It's no different in business. You don't like admitting that your prices may be high, your quality control a little weak, or your reputation for customer services perhaps a bit short of what it should be. But if you operate your own business, you should be honest with yourself; if you're writing within or for a larger organization, you should encourage people to openly and honestly discuss potential problems. After all, your weaknesses won't remain secret; your prospects will see them soon enough and ignore you — unless you take measures to anticipate their concerns up front.

When you know where the trouble spots are, you can work around them by either attempting to alter a current perception or by stressing other strengths. If your widget is more expensive that its competitors, you may want to emphasize its superior quality rather than its price. If quality is an issue, perhaps you can talk up convenience. And if customer service has been a problem, you may want to add a paragraph about a new calling center or online troubleshooting forum. The focus of your copy will vary with each situation, but to arrive at them, you first have to anticipate the potential problems.

Setting the Tone

After you throw the copy points, the challenges, and the customer profile into the hopper (your brain), you can consider the overall tone of the piece: casual or formal; sober or humorous; short and snappy or richly detailed.

The tone you choose, based on the nature of your offer and the kind of customer you're targeting, becomes the "voice" of your organization, so choose carefully. Be prepared to meet your prospects on their turf (the conventions of the language they use), and remember that you're shaping the personality of your business.

Chapter 21

Ten Cures for Common Copywriting Problems

I'd like to believe that if you've read the rest of this book, you wouldn't need to read this chapter. But I'd also like to believe in the fat man in red who comes down chimneys and that our legislators spend our tax dollars wisely. Too bad for me.

Problems happen. Fortunately, so do solutions — if you're prepared to take action. In this chapter, you find ten of the most common copywriting problems and the easy-to-apply solutions that put you on the right track, fast.

Establishing Focus When Your Message Is Diffuse

Good copy is like a rifle shot, not a shotgun blast: It's carefully aimed at a precise target for concentrated impact. Yet a lot of copy skitters in too many directions at once, and like a drop of water in a hot frying pan, it simply fizzles out. This can happen when you're overwhelmed by riches — loads of good stuff to write about — or when too many people contribute their input on a piece. Either way, your copy ends up communicating too many ideas that compete for attention and ultimately lose your prospects' interest. Here's what this looks like:

When you open a Second National NOW account, you can collect interest on your checking account balance, month after month. Stop by our branch for details. And if you have a small business, ask about our revolving line of credit — you can apply online at www.secondnat.com. There, you'll also find a free library of answer sheets that can help you get a grip on your finances.

In one short paragraph, I see two different products with two different audiences (NOW accounts for consumers and revolving credit for small businesses), two different calls to action (go to branch and go online), and then a detour to an entirely unrelated premium — answer sheets on finances. No message stands out, and the credibility of the bank is undermined by its scattershot approach.

The cure is focus: concentrating on one audience with one big idea, be it an offer or benefit. For this hypothetical client, look at the extra impact you gain when you target one market (small businesses) with one big message — Second National is your partner — that's supported by a few subordinate points.

Make Second National your partner for business success. We offer a variety of credit options that give you flexibility, including a small business revolving line of credit. Get the complete picture and free answers to dozens of the most common small business finance questions by visiting us online at www.secondnat.com.

For more on creating a clear message for your copy, see Chapter 18.

Getting Specific When Your Writing Is Vague

Fear of commitment not only keeps middle-aged men at home with their mamas; it also keeps organizations from making clear, pointed promises that their prospects can understand (and potentially respond to). That's why you often read vague, noncommittal copy like this:

Turn to Lavender Designs for a fresh approach to office interiors with a distinctive touch.

What's the "fresh approach?" Or the "distinctive touch?" So far, this copy offers only fluff, not facts. To make a sale, this copy needs to deliver some specifics — such as facts, features, and "how we work" descriptions — that make its promises come alive:

Lavender Designs combines a workflow analysis with your branding ambitions into an effective design for your interiors. The end result is more than visually attractive. You get functional spaces that make your employees more productive. And you'll work within a virtual 3D advertisement that becomes your brand's most memorable representative.

For more information on using specific evidence in your copy, check out Chapter 2.

Getting Real When Your Copy Is Jargon Filled

Many business people like big, high-minded words such as "innovative," "commitment," "proactive," and "paradigm." I have no idea what these words mean to them, but I do know what they mean to customers: nothing.

Self-flattering boasts and vague promises of value get you nowhere. Here's an example of an express train to failure:

Fulsome Brothers is reshaping a new paradigm in customer relations: A commitment to proactive service renown for its innovative time resource distributions.

What is Fulsome Brothers trying to say? Your guess is as good as mine. But copy like this finds its way into collateral, Web sites, and advertisements every day. Instead of jargon, speak in plain English and talk about real things your prospects can see, feel, and understand, like so:

Call Fulsome Brothers anytime, 24 hours a day, 7 days a week, for immediate attention. If we can't fix your problem by phone, we'll send one of our associates to you by the next business day.

Speaking the Customer's Language When the Tone Is Wrong

In copy, there's usually only one right way to write: the way your prospects talk. (The exception occurs when your audience has firm expectations about how certain authority figures, such as doctors, lawyers, and politicians, should sound, and you're obligated to write within one of those roles.) To connect with your readers means you'll have to change your style to accommodate the people you want to reach — because there ain't no way they're going to make a special effort to accommodate you. Here, for example, is the wrong way to pitch an oversized pickup truck for muscle-car fans:

> *The Dodds Bull brings a curvaceous profile and oodles of torque to the crowded category of sizable pickup trucks for commercial contractors and casual truck enthusiasts.*

Yeesh. This copy sounds like it comes from a guy in tassel loafers sipping a white wine cooler. Think about your market: who they are, what they value, and how they talk. (See Chapter 3 for more information on understanding your customers.) This product needs a beer-and-baseball-caps kind of approach:

> *Got what it takes to ride the Dodds Bull? 'Cause the only thing meaner than its looks is the beast under the hood — we're talking about a 5.7 liter HEVI V8 packing 345 horses of raw, bone-shaking POWER!*

Talking about the Customer When Your Copy Is Self-Flattering

Hi, let me tell you all about — me! Are you still there? Well, you're a lot more patient than your prospects. Because when you sound off on your years of experience, your awards and honors, and your record levels of sales, you send prospects packing. Don't do this:

> *At HighTower Associates, our twenty-five years of experience as tax consultants sets us apart as the gold standard for tax preparation expertise.*

The alternative? Talk about your customers and what you can do for *them:*

> *Frustrated by the tax code? You're in good company — even the brightest and most responsible money managers get tangled by the code's complex rules and regulations. Fortunately, HighTower Associates can make tax compliance easier and less expensive.*

Using Active Words to Fight the "Flat"

Remember, copy is ultimately about action and getting prospects to do something, such as ordering a product or visiting your store. Frankly, dull, passive copy won't get them there. For example:

There is a place where you can find flavor. It's at Vito's Italian Kitchen. This is where quality home-cooked meals are prepared by our expert chefs. It's where fresh produce becomes fine meals.

Still awake? Good, because you'll need the energy to read Chapter 2 so you can write better copy, loaded with active subjects and active verbs like this:

Savor the flavor at Vito's Italian Kitchen. Vito's European-trained chefs turn farm-fresh produce, just-caught seafood, and prime meats into unforgettable meals ala Italiano.

Being Bold When Your Pitch Is Too Soft

If you don't really believe in your product, no one else will. Your copy just isn't the place to be the shy, retiring type (charming as that may be). Don't apologize for your business with softball pitches like this:

Time for a new look? Then maybe you should try Betsy's Hair Salon. We might have that something special for a new, even more beautiful you.

Maybe? Might? Hey, Betsy, you go girl — and I mean go for something assertive. Cut out the wimpy qualifiers, such as "may" or "might," and reach for language that captures the emotional appeal of your product, like this:

Your old look says . . . old. Revitalize your hair — and your life — with a brand-new look from Betsy's Hair Salon. Make your appointment now, and we'll greet you with a free tint and rinse. Call 1-800-555-5555.

Trimming Text When Your Copy Is Wordy

Watch out for inflated rhetoric, choo-choo trains of excess prepositional phrases, and overloaded modifiers (adjectives and adverbs) that create clutter, not clarity. Long copy can be perfectly acceptable (and is often required — see Chapter 5 for details), but your writing should be stuffed with benefits, features, reasons why, evidence, and other motivational language, not empty puffery. Otherwise, your sales message gets lost in a fog of unnecessary verbiage. For example:

Unleash your potential for achieving ever-greater success in an expanding economy with multiplying career options by pursuing your graduate degree at Blowhole College.

Now, get out the knife and cut out the copy that isn't immediately tied to the core of your message:

Advance your career with an advanced degree. At Blowhole College . . .

Making an Offer When Your Conclusion Is Wilting

You start off strong with a great benefit. You follow up with a terrific, customer-centered story loaded with specifics. But when you race into the final stretch to release that last, irresistible call to action, your copy wilts into a shameless, wimpy disgrace:

For more information about the Musclator Complete Body Makeover Machine, call . . .

"For more information"? Why don't you threaten the prospect with a tedious, overbearing sales call — which is, in effect, just what you did? I know: Sometimes you just don't have a better offer (a gift, free shipping, or a discount) at your disposal. So here's what you do: You turn "more information" into *valuable* knowledge and give the prospect a good reason for wanting to get it, such as:

To learn how to turn excess body flab into fabulous, rock-hard muscle, call . . .

Check out Chapter 2 for more on crafting inspiring calls to action.

Going Back to the Source When You Have Writer's Block

Ninety-nine out of a hundred times, the root cause of so-called writer's block is insufficient immersion in the basic background information: who the prospects are, what the product is, what it does for the customers, how it compares to competing products, and so on. Before you pull your hair out in frustration, go back to the source and read (or re-read) all the available information about the subject of your copy.

If doing those things fails to inspire you, read Chapter 3 on finding inspiration. (Chapters 20 and 22 have quick tips, too.) Then take two aspirin and call me in the morning.

Chapter 22

Ten Fast Ways to Find Copywriting Inspiration

Stuck on a copywriting project? It happens from time to time. Fortunately, you don't need a miracle or even a flash of brilliance (and I encourage you not to waste your time waiting for either of them). Almost invariably, what you really need is a change of perspective, a fresh look at the subject at hand.

That's what the following ten suggestions are all about. They're fast and simple (except the last one, which is a lifetime commitment), and they all work because they help you move out of your rut and into a new groove.

Reviewing Customer Letters or Testimonials

What *you* think the value of a product is and what *customers* think that value is may be two very different things. Of course, their opinion is more important and may be available to you in the form of letters they sent on their own initiative or as testimonials your organization has actively solicited. (For more on collecting customer testimonials, check out Chapter 3.)

Either way, request these letters and testimonials and read carefully. Keep an eye open for the following:

- **Alternative uses:** You sold your product as car wax, but the customer loves the way it makes her lamp bases shine. These alternative uses (or recipes or suggested projects) may open your product to new markets or create new angles for your copy.

- **Service kudos:** If you hear a lot of applause for the quality of your service, consider emphasizing your organization's personal touch, especially if it's uncommon or unexpected in your industry.

- **Real-life benefits:** You knew that your scheduling software makes business easier, but thanks to your customer's letter, you discovered three ways it saves time, too. Benefits are treasures; the ones customers identify are golden.

Always get permission from customers before you use their testimonials in your copy.

Talking to Salespeople

When push comes to shove, rubber meets the road, or nose hits grindstone (pick your cliché), salespeople are the ones who close the sale and therefore have the hard-won insights on clinchers — the things that ultimately turn prospects into buyers. Salespeople have a wealth of insight, yet so many marketers fail to ask them for it. Talk to them to discover the following:

- **Key benefits and features:** Obviously. But as your product may have many of these, the question here is this: Which are most important to customers? The salespeople should know.

- **Path of least resistance:** Of all the different roads that lead to a sale (ad to phone call to meeting to contract as one route, or mail invitation to seminar to personal sales call as another), which is most effective? Which is easiest and most convenient for the customer? Your copy should facilitate the path of least resistance.

- **Unexpected hooks:** Just as customer letters or testimonials can spring surprises, so too can salespeople by alerting you to unexpected connections between customers and features. SUVs, for example, were designed as macho vehicles for men who fantasized about adventure, but they found an unexpected audience among women who liked the extra traction of an all-wheel vehicle that wouldn't leave them stranded and vulnerable. Bingo — a new direction for positioning, messages, and copy. Salespeople can point you there.

See Chapter 3 for more details on talking to salespeople.

Running a Web Search

The Internet puts a vast library of information at your fingertips. Although I don't recommend making life-or-death decisions based on what you find online (the Web has as much misinformation and disinformation as real information), it can be a wonderfully fast and cheap way to gather insights on your product category, competition, and prospects. Here are some things to look for:

- ✔ **Competitive intelligence:** Run a search for your product or service on any search engine and see what comes up. Who appears in the top ten listings? What appeals and offers are they making? How does your product compare in price, features, quality, and overall value? Most importantly, can you identify special claims about *your* product that aren't being made by your competitors?

- ✔ **Customer intelligence:** For just about every interest you can think of, from lace doilies to cold fusion, some Web site forum is dedicated to true believers who swap tips, projects, and opinions. A quick query on any major search engine usually pulls up what you need. You don't have to believe; you just have to show up and "lurk" (read comments without leaving any of your own). Within a matter of minutes, you'll gather more than you ever thought possible about current trends, rumors, interests, brand favorites, and collective pet peeves. Lurk and learn.

Getting Support Beyond Your Desk

You don't win extra points (or earn higher fees) for arriving at ideas all by yourself: Ask for input. Solicit ideas from colleagues, friends, and in-laws. Given that most of them will not be privy to the project's background requirements (brand, positioning, and so on), they may not deliver the Big Idea, but they almost invariably give you fresh perspectives that can jump-start your imagination. Here are a couple of questions that can help you understand what prospects are thinking and how you can reach them with your copy:

- ✔ **What do you think of when you think about this product?** Let them free-associate — without your critical judgment — on your product, its name, or even its image in the marketplace. At the very least, you'll get a set of new words or ideas you can play with, along with new insight on how the public at large may perceive your product.

- ✔ **What do you expect from this product and the company that makes it?** Similar to the preceding question but intended to dig a little deeper, this question helps you tap the emotions your prospects may bring to the sale. Listen carefully for unexpected feelings that may guide the way you think about your product.

Reading the Copywriting Classics

Just steps away from my desk (okay, okay, in a big messy pile on the floor), I keep a short stack of reference books on copywriting and marketing, such as *Tested Advertising Methods* by John Caples (Prentice Hall), *Ogilvy on Advertising* by David Ogilvy (Vintage Books), and *Successful Direct Marketing Methods* by Bob Stone (NTC Business Books). When I'm at a loss, I pick one up and skim.

Though I've read these books before (perhaps many times over), I'm often struck by something that I'd failed to remember earlier. These reminders — about perspective, value, word choice, and more — are frequently just what I need to reinvigorate my writing.

These books can work for you, too. Get them, read them, and then keep them by your side. You never know when they'll come to your rescue.

Experiencing the Product or Service

Take it for a spin; play with it; wear it on your back. Sometimes the only way to appreciate the value of something is to experience it yourself. When you do, ask yourself a few questions that can lead to valuable copy angles:

- **How is this useful?** If the item is a means to an end, such as a tool or a service, think about what it did for you. Did it make your life easier? More convenient? Did it allow you to do things you couldn't do before? Or in a better way?

- **How did it appeal to your senses?** For those things, like food or collectible plates, that are to be enjoyed in and of themselves, examine the sensual appeal: flavors, touch, look, craftsmanship, and so on. Can you play up these sensual appeals in your copy?

- **How did it make you feel?** When people buy products from Victoria's Secret or Harley-Davidson, they buy more than underwear and noisy motorcycles; they buy a magic mirror that reflects what they want to see. Does the product make you feel sexy, powerful, or youthful? Look "under the hood" for the special identities your product might confer on a customer.

Pretending You're the Prospect

Give yourself a few minutes to close your eyes and become your prospect. Of course, you want to dig into hopes and fears — the emotional core at the heart of the purchase. But to make your insights relevant to your particular copy project, remember these questions:

✔ **How would I buy this?** After you understand how a prospect may buy (whether it be an impulse purchase at a cash register or a decision discussed among close friends), you may be able to adjust your copy to address anxieties (guarantees, "millions sold" claims) and create a path of least resistance (buying or ordering options suitable for your customers).

✔ **What might stop me from buying this?** Try to anticipate all the obstacles to the sale: price, lack of familiarity, or fear of ridicule or failure. You may not be able to address all of them, but you can tackle the most important ones. If the issue is price, emphasize value; familiarity, use endorsements; fear, counter with facts and information.

Travel to Chapter 3 to find out more about walking in your customers' shoes.

Playing a Free-Association Game

Media personality Barbara Walters will always be remembered for two things: her lisp and her infamous question, "If you were a tree, what kind of tree would you be?" The stuff of late-night-comedy cheap shots? Yes — but a clue for writers, too. When you're stuck, play free-association games that help you gain deeper insights into your product's character. You can begin by asking some questions:

✔ **If your product were a car, what kind of car would it be?** This is a question about category to help you understand your market position. Is your product a value option like a Hyundai, a luxury item like a BMW, or a novelty statement like a Mini Cooper? You may be able to exploit your product's position — the place it occupies in your prospects' minds — to give your copy focus and credibility.

✔ **What can you compare owning this product to?** Having a reliable friend? A helpful road map? A get-out-of-jail-free card? Thinking of this analogy helps you find the most attractive product benefit.

Immersing Yourself — Then Taking a Break

Go over all the input material you have. Reread the product descriptions, creative briefs (marketing input documents), customer endorsements, and whatever else you have. Then walk away. Don't think about your product. Don't mull over any ideas. Just get away from your desk, cubicle, or office, and get some fresh air.

My preference is to simply walk. Others may choose to go for a drive or buy a cup of coffee. Do whatever floats your boat — as long as it puts time and distance between you and your project.

When you've felt some tension dissolve, return to the task. I don't know why this advice works, but it does. Sometimes the ideas come flying fast and furiously. And even when they don't, your little breather helps you continue your search for ideas in a more relaxed (and usually more productive) way.

Opening Your Mind

Finally, a parting thought for lasting inspiration: Indulge your appetite for art, literature, music, and any other form of culture that excites you. No, reading Tolstoy or listening to Charlie Parker doesn't instantly transform your writing. But over time, the good stuff you digest subtly reasserts itself when you need it most. It prompts the apt metaphor that suddenly pops into your head, or it beats the steady rhythm that carries readers from the beginning of your copy to its end. With a nod to Lewis Carroll's dormouse and Jefferson Airplane's Grace Slick: Feed your head.

Index

● C ●

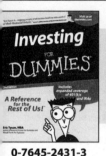

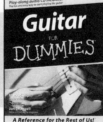

FOR DUMMIES®

A world of resources to help you grow

TRAVEL

Italy FOR DUMMIES 2nd Edition
A Travel Guide for the Rest of Us!
0-7645-5453-0

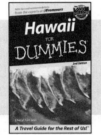

Hawaii FOR DUMMIES 2nd Edition
A Travel Guide for the Rest of Us!
0-7645-5438-7

Walt Disney World & Orlando FOR DUMMIES 2003
A Travel Guide for the Rest of Us!
0-7645-5444-1

Also available:

America's National Parks For Dummies
(0-7645-6204-5)

Caribbean For Dummies
(0-7645-5445-X)

Cruise Vacations For Dummies 2003
(0-7645-5459-X)

Europe For Dummies
(0-7645-5456-5)

Ireland For Dummies
(0-7645-6199-5)

France For Dummies
(0-7645-6292-4)

Las Vegas For Dummies
(0-7645-5448-4)

London For Dummies
(0-7645-5416-6)

Mexico's Beach Resorts For Dummies
(0-7645-6262-2)

Paris For Dummies
(0-7645-5494-8)

RV Vacations For Dummies
(0-7645-5443-3)

EDUCATION & TEST PREPARATION

Speak Spanish — the fun and easy way!
Spanish FOR DUMMIES
A Reference for the Rest of Us!
0-7645-5194-9

Algebra FOR DUMMIES
A Reference for the Rest of Us!
0-7645-5325-9

U.S. History FOR DUMMIES
A Reference for the Rest of Us!
0-7645-5249-X

Also available:

The ACT For Dummies
(0-7645-5210-4)

Chemistry For Dummies
(0-7645-5430-1)

English Grammar For Dummies
(0-7645-5322-4)

French For Dummies
(0-7645-5193-0)

GMAT For Dummies
(0-7645-5251-1)

Inglés Para Dummies
(0-7645-5427-1)

Italian For Dummies
(0-7645-5196-5)

Research Papers For Dummi
(0-7645-5426-3)

SAT I For Dummies
(0-7645-5472-7)

U.S. History For Dummies
(0-7645-5249-X)

World History For Dummies
(0-7645-5242-2)

HEALTH, SELF-HELP & SPIRITUALITY

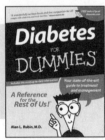

Diabetes FOR DUMMIES
A Reference for the Rest of Us!
Alan L. Rubin, M.D.
0-7645-5154-X

Sex FOR DUMMIES 2nd Edition
Dr. Ruth K. Westheimer
A Reference for the Rest of Us!
0-7645-5302-X

Parenting FOR DUMMIES 2nd Edition
Sandra Hardin Gookin Dan Gookin
A Reference for the Rest of Us!
0-7645-5418-2

Also available:

The Bible For Dummies
(0-7645-5296-1)

Controlling Cholesterol For Dummies
(0-7645-5440-9)

Dating For Dummies
(0-7645-5072-1)

Dieting For Dummies
(0-7645-5126-4)

High Blood Pressure For Dummies
(0-7645-5424-7)

Judaism For Dummies
(0-7645-5299-6)

Menopause For Dummies
(0-7645-5458-1)

Nutrition For Dummies
(0-7645-5180-9)

Potty Training For Dummies
(0-7645-5417-4)

Pregnancy For Dummies
(0-7645-5074-8)

Rekindling Romance For Dummies
(0-7645-5303-8)

Religion For Dummies
(0-7645-5264-3)

Available wherever books are sold. Go to www.dummies.com or call 1-877-762-2974 to order direct

FOR DUMMIES®

Helping you expand your horizons and realize your potential

GRAPHICS & WEB SITE DEVELOPMENT

Photoshop 7 For Dummies
0-7645-1651-5

Creating Web Pages For Dummies
0-7645-1643-4

Macromedia Flash MX For Dummies
0-7645-0895-4

PROGRAMMING & DATABASES

C++ For Dummies
0-7645-0746-X

Visual Studio .NET All-in-One Desk Reference For Dummies
0-7645-1626-4

XML For Dummies
0-7645-1657-4

LINUX, NETWORKING & CERTIFICATION

Red Hat Linux 7.3 For Dummies
0-7645-1545-4

TCP/IP For Dummies
0-7645-1760-0

Networking For Dummies
0-7645-0772-9

Available wherever books are sold.
Go to www.dummies.com or call 1-877-762-2974 to order direct

WILEY